3DS MAX® 7
FUNDAMENTALS

Ted Boardman

New Riders

Berkeley, California

3ds max® 7 Fundamentals

Ted Boardman

New Riders
1249 Eighth Street
Berkeley, CA 94710
510/524-2178
800/283-9444
510/524-2221 (fax)

Find us on the World Wide Web at: www.peachpit.com
To report errors, please send a note to errata@peachpit.com
New Riders is an imprint of Peachpit, a division of Pearson Education

Copyright © 2005 by New Riders

Editor
Jill Marts Lodwig

Production Editor
Alan Reade

Compositor
Owen Wolfson

Proofer
Glen Torbert

Indexer
James Minkin

Cover Design
Aren Howell

Book Designers
Louisa Klucznik
Owen Wolfson

ISBN: 0-321-32138-3

9 8 7 6 5 4 3 2 1

Printed in the United States of America

Dedication

I'd like to dedicate this book to my brother Jeff Boardman, just for being my brother.

About the Author

Ted Boardman is a traveling Discreet 3ds max and Autodesk 3D Studio VIZ training consultant. He is one of a handful of Discreet Authorized Master Trainers. His training sessions are custom classes designed to increase 3D modeling and animation productivity for a wide range of clients, from architects to aerospace engineers, to television and computer-gaming professionals.

An integral part of Ted's training process includes the books he authors and co-authors about the production issues people encounter when using 3ds max. These books include *3ds max Fundamentals* and several books from the *Inside 3D Studio Max* series and the *Inside 3D Studio VIZ 3* series, all from New Riders. Ted has also contributed to several other books about 3ds max and to Discreet Advanced Modules. He writes a monthly column covering topics related to 3ds max at *www.cgarchitect.com*. He is also an award-winning speaker at the annual Autodesk University symposium covering CAD and visualization topics.

Outside the 3D world, Ted has traveled, lived, and worked in Europe for many years. He ran a small architectural design/build firm that specialized in hand-cut post and beam structures for nearly 18 years. Long-distance bicycle travel and 28,000 miles of blue-water yacht deliveries served as a diversion from work for many years. Photography, painting, and opera are other interests.

Ted lives in Portsmouth, New Hampshire.

About the Technical Reviewer

 **Tim Wilbers** has been teaching at the University of Dayton in Ohio since 1983. He started working with digital imaging in 1986 and 3D computer modeling and animation on a professional level in 1988. He began teaching digital imaging/photography in 1988 and offering courses in 3D for computer graphic artists in 1992. His courses are central to the Computer Imaging concentration in the BFA Visual Communication Design program. Tim is a Forum Assistant on Discreet's 3ds max user-discussion Web board and is committed to making 3D computer modeling and animation accessible to students and professionals. He lives south of Dayton with his wife and son, and has a reputation for overfeeding the native wildlife in his front yard, including a small herd of white-tailed deer.

Acknowledgments

I can't stress enough how important good editing is in making the reader's experience a pleasant one. I would like to acknowledge the hard work and dedication of my editor, Jill Marts Lodwig, in polishing my rambling verbal training style into a more understandable grammatical form that allows you, the reader, to focus on the lessons and not the reading. Thanks also to Tim Wilbers, my technical reviewer, for making sure the exercises in the chapters function correctly and to convey to you the important concepts that will help you become productive with 3ds max 7. And thanks also to Alan Reade, Owen Wolfson, and the production staff at Peachpit for crafting a collection of text and images into a high-quality publication.

Contents at a Glance

Contents

Part II: Modeling

Part III: Lighting and Cameras

Part V: Animation

Part VI: Special Effects

Introduction

Learning 3ds max 7 is similar to learning to speak a foreign language. On the first day of class, everything is confusing, and you may leave feeling a bit frustrated. You might even feel that you know less than when you came in. Then you spend the next few classes learning about the fundamental building blocks—nouns, verbs, and adjectives—and before long you find you're able to assemble these elements into sentences and paragraphs that can be understood by others. Learning 3ds max 7 is very similar—you may struggle a bit at first, but if you invest some time in learning the fundamentals, the rest easily falls into place.

The content and tutorials in this book assume you're already familiar with the basic 3ds max 7 interface and that you have spent enough time reading and studying the manuals, tutorials, and online reference tools that ship with the program to be able to concentrate on the lessons. As the book title implies, you'll learn some fundamental workflows of 3ds max 7. These are not basic topics designed for first-time users. Instead, they are techniques that anyone can use to build a solid working knowledge base. Both new and experienced users will find techniques in this book that can help speed their day-to-day workflow.

The Concepts

Chapter 1, *Workflow*, explains the fundamental workflow of 3ds max 7 and provides planning steps to help you get started, while Chapter 2, *Fundamental Concepts*, introduces basic concepts that are fundamental to the way 3ds max 7 is designed. These concepts will help you understand why the approaches to modeling, materials, and lighting presented in later chapters can help you get the most from the software.

If you're like most 3ds max users, you're eager to dive into the new features introduced in 3ds max 7 and start producing stunning results as soon a possible. However, if you take the time to get a good grounding in the fundamentals, the fancy footwork will come much more naturally to you as you dig deeper into the software.

A good strategy for tackling each chapter is to read through it first to see where it leads, and then return to perform the exercises, keeping in mind the intended goals. Finally, skim through the text again to make sure you have a solid understanding of the important concepts covered before moving on to the next chapter.

The CD-ROM that accompanies this book contains project files for the beginning and end of each exercise so that you can jump into the book at any point and begin learning. However, I recommend you start at the beginning of the book and work through the chapters and exercises sequentially.

The Techniques

Beginning with Chapter 3, *2D Shapes: Starting with the Foundation*, the exercises in the book walk you through the techniques and workflow that are essential to an understanding of how 3ds max 7 functions, and the discussions show you how you might apply this fundamental knowledge to your projects. You'll learn about

- The reference coordinate systems that let you manipulate objects in 3D space efficiently.
- Working in 2D and applying modifiers to create complex 3D scenes that can be edited quickly and easily.
- Lofting techniques for building objects in scenes. Because lofting is a powerful but underutilized modeling strategy for creating complex geometry, I cover lofting techniques extensively.
- Reducing scene overhead to get the most out of the hardware you have available—this is one of the most important lessons presented in this book.

- Making efficient materials that simulate complex geometry using Bump and Opacity maps for increased rendering speed and for unique scenes.

- Applying cost-effective and convincing lighting effects to scenes using 3ds max 7's Radiosity and Global Illumination features.

- Basic animation methods you can use as a starting point for building your own techniques and styles. The animation exercises walk you through fundamental aspects of keyframe animation and animation controllers and constraints.

The Exercises

A simple country airport serves as the basis for both exterior daylight scenes and interior scenes presented in this book. The intent is to introduce you to the fundamentals of a variety of scenarios for modeling, materials, lighting, and animation.

The exercises walk you step by step through a process similar to what you might encounter modeling a real-life project. The processes and methods are designed to help you form work habits that will be relevant whether you are a gamer, background artist, stage or set designer, or engineer.

While performing the exercises, try to project how you might apply the methods and techniques covered in your own line of work. When I'm showing you how to create a building, for instance, you might be planning to use the same process to create the rough form of an automobile.

Use the lessons you learn from each exercise to produce scenes of your own that incorporate the techniques and methods presented until you understand the process. Start with simple scenes that let you focus on understanding the concepts, and the fundamentals will quickly become part of your daily routine.

Hopefully, when you work on your own projects you will not be thinking, "I learned this from Ted Boardman." Instead, the lessons learned here should become an automatic reaction to challenges that you face every day in your own production schedules.

The Project Files

The CD-ROM that accompanies this book includes all the files you need for the exercises, as well as more complete versions of the basic exercise files that you can disassemble to see how some of the techniques in the book might be applied in other projects.

You can use these files to analyze how the objects were modeled, how the lights were placed, and how the materials and animation were created. Better yet, you can use the files to play with each scene until you produce your own approaches to improving them. The image files on the CD-ROM are color figures, as opposed to the black-and-white versions in the book, so they should be much more helpful, particularly with the materials and lighting chapters.

The exercises and work methods in this book are derived from situations that develop in my max classes and during my consulting work. I try to make the exercises as real as possible while staying true to my teaching strategy of helping you build a base of fundamental information.

Wherever 3ds max 7 may take you, good luck and have fun!

PART I

The Basics

CHAPTER 1

Workflow

In This Chapter

Creating 3D scenes is often a complex task, but it can be accomplished much more efficiently with a little foresight and planning.

In this chapter, you'll learn what to be aware of before beginning and while executing a 3D project.

Some of the topics covered in this section include:

- **The chain of command.** Clearly defining the responsibilities of team members.
- **Needs assessment.** Determining the scope of the project and the needs of the audience.
- **Storyboarding.** Creating a visual outline of the project.
- **Choosing a team.** Selecting the right talent and capabilities for a specific project.
- **Setting up a productive working environment.** Both equipment and training are critical to productivity.
- **Knowing when to stop.** Avoiding the temptation to "tweak" the project into financial loss.
- **Developing office standards.** Written procedures and standards speed work.
- **Working in layers.** Layers, in this case, are compositing tools.
- **Cinematic animation techniques.** Watching film and TV for successful camera and editing methods.
- **Output capabilities.** Planning production to include a variety of output-type possibilities.

Key Term

- **Storyboard.** A storyboard is a graphical outline that informs the team of the scope of the project.

Preparation and Planning

Good planning is essential to the success of any project. Everyone knows this instinctively, but putting it into practice is often more effort than most people realize. Typically, a team will discuss a project until close to the deadline, and then suffer through long hours of high-pressure work, only to generate a mediocre presentation. It's better to learn to channel that discussion time into a clear "battle plan" so that everyone knows the expectations and obligations of the project.

Even the smallest projects with only one or two members of the staff will benefit from a solid plan going into production. And when the project involves more than a few collaborators, developing a solid script that each team member can refer to as the work progresses is paramount to ensure everyone is working toward a common goal in an organized manner.

Once you've developed a good plan of attack, it's unrealistic to think it will never change. 3D projects often seem to be in a constant state of flux for a variety of reasons—the client's expectations, technical problems, or budget constraints. However, the changes will be much less disruptive to the overall goals if those goals are spelled out in the beginning for everyone involved.

Skipping the planning step in the creation process won't save you time; it will simply be an exercise in false economy.

The Chain of Command

Critical communication paths between those who order the work, create the content, and present to the client must be established, with each team member having an understanding of the available talent and resources.

Communication between the client and production staff will constantly evolve and become more refined as the visualization process matures. However, educating the client about the general process involved in creating the visualizations can smooth these communications. The client doesn't need to know specifically how scenes are created, but should know what types of requests will take time and which can be done quickly.

Letting the in-house management sit in on a half-day, hands-on training session with the 3D software can be very helpful in helping them gain more insight into some of the difficulties the production staff faces—eventually they will understand that there is no magic "make art" button on the computer.

Regular short meetings between the production staff and the in-house clients can keep each team up-to-date on processes that either increase or hinder productivity on either side.

Needs Assessment

An important step in productivity is determining the scope and quality of work required to satisfy the client's expectations within the confines of time and budget.

Not every job that goes out the door requires photorealistic-quality images to communicate the important messages. Feature films certainly need all the cutting-edge refinements technology has to offer, but public service announcements that will be shown on regional television might not have the same budget considerations. So you'll need to determine where you can trim production costs with the least effect on quality.

Flexible stages of production can help you avoid costly changes that require you to start from scratch. If complex modeling and high details are developed too early in the design development, or if complete materials with high-resolution maps are applied to models, for example, it may focus unnecessary attention on decisions that are better left for later.

A better approach might be to rough out models much the same way a stone sculptor would and then go back and add details as they become necessary.

You could use highly compressed stand-in maps while developing the scenes to allow for faster test rendering, for instance, and then replace those with the quality maps near the end of the project.

Storyboarding

Storyboarding is the process of creating a graphic outline that illustrates the story and the workflow and provides insight into potential production issues before any actual production begins.

Storyboards can range from simple sketches to airbrushed or hand-painted panels, some of which could be classified as works of art in their own right.

For rendered still images, as an architectural visualization artist might require, the storyboard panels could contain the camera angles and direction and notes describing specific colors or materials. Lighting scenarios and notes about the quality of lighting might prove to be helpful in storyboards too.

Animation storyboards could contain the same information, plus notes and sketches referring to action in the scene. One storyboard panel per major action change in the animation motion is a good place to start.

You may even include additional information pertaining to timing codes and dialogue or sound effects in the margins of the panels.

FIGURE 1.1 *High-quality storyboard panels by Andrew Paquette.*

A storyboard for a small project can be created on a few sheets of paper with several panels or sketches on each sheet. For more complex projects, however, a large cork-board with individual panel sheets pinned in place gives a quick overview and is easy to change. Avoid the temptation to use sticky notepads, because you may come back from lunch to find that a change in temperature or a breeze has scattered your story-board across the room, like so many fallen leaves in an autumn storm.

The importance is not so much on the quality of the artwork of storyboards, but on how clearly they explain the scope and scheduling of the project.

Execution

Another crucial component of high productivity is planning the use of available talent and tools. Meet with team members and management to discuss some of the following topics before getting into actual production.

Choose a Team with Both Desire and Talent

Familiarize a broad range of personnel with the creation process and cultivate a pool of artists with a strong desire to apply the extra effort required to become proficient.

Forcing staff to become directly involved in processes they are not comfortable with, whether it's modeling, lighting, materials, or animation, leads to bad office politics and pulls good talent from areas where they could probably be more productive.

Set Up a Productive Working Environment

Provide and maintain current and powerful computer systems. Hardware is a fixed-cost item that can be passed through the office, first as rendering stations and then as clerical machines for years to come. Do not, however, buy new hardware as the sole method of increasing productivity until you have mastered the art of scene optimization, such as reducing the amount of geometry or tweaking shadow parameters. Using new hardware as a fix for poor production practices is a waste of resources and time.

In a production office, pay particular attention to seating, lighting, and input devices. For example, a mouse and a tablet at each workstation can minimize stress and injury during long work sessions. A clean, stable network system for network rendering can increase production (while requiring very little cost and maintenance).

Make sure that team members have an understanding of all the tools available to them before deciding on a production process. With a little practice, choosing the right tool for the right job becomes second nature, and you'll avoid many of the pitfalls that come with forcing a tool to do a job for which it is not appropriate.

Know When to Stop

Focus on the elements of 3D production that will impact the output the most, and leave the rest by the wayside. For example, radiosity rendering may not add enough to your story line to justify the extra time involved in setting up or rendering.

Do not use the technology for the sake of the technology alone.

Upon reaching a certain level of quality or communication value, it is important to be able to stop and move on to the next task. Perfection is an unobtainable goal—always worth striving for, but only up to the point where it becomes a burden on production.

FIGURE 1.2 *The image on the left, by the author, is low quality and was made from scratch in about 4 hours. The image on the right, by Tangram3ds, is very high quality and required about 21 hours to create the scene and match it to the photo.*

Integration and Output

You may be called upon to simultaneously create content for multiple uses. For instance, you might be creating a computer game, but you will need higher quality scenes for the marketing trailers, and you may need even higher quality still images.

Don't forget that more than one software package can be used to generate content. Just make sure you use the appropriate converters and workflow methods so that the output is cross-compatible.

Develop Office Standards

Object-naming conventions, material and map libraries, and 3D object libraries are some of the areas in which establishing and maintaining standards can go a long way in enhancing productivity.

Standards for object naming cannot be stressed enough. Good naming control can provide an enormous return in productivity for a very minor cost.

Material-naming standards and material-library organization can also help avoid duplication of effort. Develop central depositories for maps and basic materials that are organized by category so that all users have easy access to a fundamental starting point to create custom materials for projects.

Rendering standards that everyone has ready access to ensures the renderings from one team member will match the renderings of others on the team. Nothing is more frustrating than having occasional frames in an animation or perhaps a whole scene that are rendered using a different anti-aliasing setting or shadow parameter that no one else uses.

Work in Layers

Layers in this sense are elements such as background walls, mid-ground furniture, or foreground details that are based on the distance from the camera or viewer. Layers let you omit detail for faster rendering but include as much detail as necessary for communicating information to the client. For example, you can simulate geometry that will not change with pre-rendered images for the background objects while modeling and manipulating the foreground objects.

Investigate compositing, the combining of 2D information in layers, using programs such as Discreet Combustion or Adobe After Effects or even Adobe Photoshop for still images. Compositing may prove especially important in offices that use multiple software packages to generate content.

Layers also enable you to work discretely. For instance, using layers, you can manipulate special image elements to modify shadows, reflections, or object color without having to re-render the entire 3D scene.

Learn Cinematic Animation Techniques

Learn traditional film and television movement techniques so that you can develop short-duration animations that you can edit into a cohesive presentation. These movement techniques will enable you to develop much smaller scenes with minimal camera movement—scenes that are easy to manage and that clients will find exciting and informative. Everyone wins!

Determine Output Capabilities in Advance

Predetermine file types and image resolutions that will enable you to reuse content in a wide array of output types (for instance, videotape and DVD, streaming media and Web sites, and large printed still images). Render all scenes to individual still image sequences and convert to compressed animation files as necessary.

Summary

You no doubt can think of more processes that can be streamlined in a typical office to speed up content creation. However, if you can make use of just several of the suggestions in this chapter, it will be a good beginning and you can adapt your office practices to fit your needs.

Start with an office-wide naming scheme and materials organization, and then focus on scene optimization (only modeling what you will see and making that as efficient as possible). All the while, focus on integrating a new spirit of communication between those who order the work and those who do the work to minimize the necessity of changes later.

Finally, consider the benefits that compositing and layering of scene elements provides to speed the workflow. It is not uncommon in film and video work to combine 30 or more layers that come from a variety of production sources into a single output image or animation. These methods will work equally well for architecture, computer gaming, film and television, and engineering fields.

CHAPTER 2

Fundamental Concepts

In This Chapter

In this chapter, you'll learn some basic concepts that will help you more fully understand 3ds max 7's tools and processes.

A good strategy for tackling this chapter is to read through it quickly to get an overview of the processes, and then read through it more slowly, experimenting with your own simple scenes to test the concepts in their basic form. After a little practice, and by incorporating these concepts into your daily work routine, you will find that your productivity has been enhanced, without your having to think about what you're doing.

This chapter covers the following topics:

- **Coordinate systems.** The various ways to describe the three axes (*X*, *Y*, and *Z*) in 3D space.
- **Layers.** A method of organizing objects into common groups and assigning properties to those objects.
- **Setup and startup files.** Files that store parameters you want to have active when creating new files.
- **Lofting.** A powerful modeling technique that requires a knowledge of basic concepts for an understanding of how to work efficiently.

Key Terms

- **Coordinate system.** Coordinate systems in 3ds max 7 define the directions of the *X*, *Y*, and *Z* axes as they relate to the 3D workspace.
- **Layers.** Layers are organizational entities used to select or set properties of sets of objects on the active layer.
- **Lofting.** Lofting is the modeling technique that creates 3D objects by extruding one or more 2D cross-section shapes along a 2D path.

Coordinate Systems in 3ds max 7

Users can easily identify the World reference coordinate system in 3ds max 7 because the default grid planes that display in the viewports when you start 3ds max define it. Keep in mind though, that while you may get more face time with the World reference coordinate system, it is really only the starting point for all the possibilities for maneuvering and manipulating objects in 3D space.

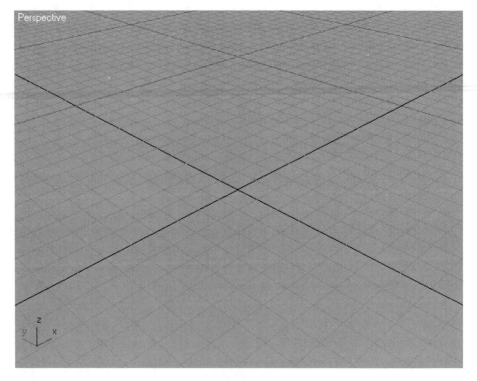

FIGURE 2.1 *The Perspective viewport with the grid defining the World reference coordinate system.*

I emphasize coordinate systems because one issue in 3ds max that I see as a fundamental hindrance to production for many users, both new and experienced, is a lack of understanding of the complete coordinate system.

To use several important commands (the Align and Transform Type-In commands being the most notable), 3ds max 7 users must understand the various coordinate systems in the software. In both Align and Transform Type-In, you are asked to enter numeric data to align or array objects along the X, Y, or Z axis. However, the direction of X, Y, or Z depends on the active coordinate system and the active viewport.

tip

The axes of the World reference coordinate in 3ds max 7 follow common mathematical practice. If you were graphing on paper, X would be the horizontal axis and Y the vertical axis of the paper. 3D space is defined by the Z axis, which projects off the paper toward you.

The Reference Coordinate System

On the main toolbar menu, to the right of the transform buttons, is a View field with View displayed as the default. This is the reference coordinate system that is currently active. Click the View field and you will see a pop-up menu of the different reference coordinate systems available (**Figure 2.2**).

caution

There is also a View Render window to the far right of the main toolbar that you do not want to change.

Figure 2.2 *The menu that displays the available reference coordinate systems for 3ds max 7.*

Next, we'll do a simple walkthrough of the various reference coordinate systems to illustrate some of their differences. You can either try the exercises on your computer or, better yet, just read along to get the idea, and then go to the computer and do the exercises afterward. In any case, at some point you should sit down and just play with very simple objects to get a feel for how the system works. At the end of this section, you can read a summary of the attributes of each system.

As with many 3ds max 7 tools, don't try to learn this during a deadline crunch on a large project. With a little practice, the reference coordinate systems will become second nature, and your productivity will increase accordingly.

Getting the Lay of the Land

Start with a new session of 3ds max 7. The display should be set to four viewports: Top, Front, Left, and Perspective. In the Top viewport, create a cylinder in the middle of the display (**Figure 2.3**) and click the Zoom Extents All button, which is the upper-right button on the lower-right corner of the display (**Figure 2.4**).

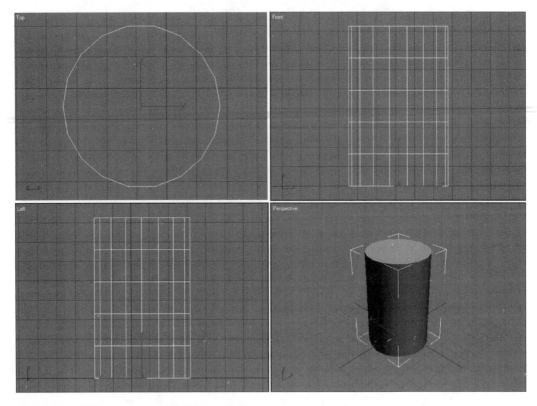

FIGURE 2.3 *All four viewports fill with a cylinder.*

FIGURE 2.4 *Click the Zoom Extents All button.*

The following subsections provide descriptions and some exercises that highlight the individual reference coordinate systems that appear in Figure 2.2.

The View Reference Coordinate System

In the Top viewport, notice the following:

- The red and gray axis tripod at the bottom center of the cylinder shows positive X to the right, positive Y up, and positive Z out toward the viewer.

- The current active reference coordinate system is set to View in the main toolbar (**Figure 2.5**).

FIGURE 2.5 *The View reference coordinate system is the default setting found on the main toolbar to the right of the three transform buttons.*

Right-click on the Front viewport to activate it without deselecting the cylinder. Notice that the axis tripod adjusts so that the positive axis is pointing in the same relative direction it was pointing when the Top viewport was active. Right-click on the Left viewport to see a similar change. When using the View reference coordinate system, the axis tripod adapts itself to the orthographic viewports so that positive X is always to the right, positive Y is always up, and positive Z is always out toward the viewer.

Next, right-click on the Perspective viewport. Notice that the axis tripod corresponds to the World reference coordinate system by aligning with the Home grid. You can check it against the small tricolor tripod in the lower-left corner of each viewport, which always indicates the World reference coordinate system. When the View reference coordinate is active, the World reference coordinate is the default system for all nonorthographic viewports—Perspective, User, Camera, and Light. (The orthographic viewports are viewed from the top, bottom, left, right, back, or front.)

The Screen Reference Coordinate System

Right-click on the Top viewport to activate it, and then click View on the main toolbar and choose the Screen reference coordinate system from the list. Right-click in the other viewports and notice that the axis tripod behaves the same as it did in View mode.

The Screen reference coordinate system is exactly the same as the View reference coordinate system for orthographic viewports—the positive X axis is always pointing to the right, the Y axis is pointing up, and the Z axis is pointing out. However, for nonorthographic viewports, the positive Z axis points out of the screen toward the viewer. Use the Arc Rotate button, located on the lower-right corner of the display in the Perspective viewport, and watch the axis tripod move in the other viewports.

The Screen reference coordinate system lets you move objects in space based on your line of sight in nonorthographic viewports and is useful for doing things like moving flying logos across the scene.

The World Reference Coordinate System

Right-click on the Top viewport and switch to the World reference coordinate system. Right-click in the other viewports and you will see that the World reference coordinate system is always active for all viewport types.

The Parent Reference Coordinate System

The next reference coordinate system in the list is Parent, which requires an object to be hierarchically linked to another object in the parent/child relationship. In the Parent reference coordinate system, the child always uses the parents' Local coordinate system (discussed in the next section).

> **note**
>
> Hierarchical linking is beyond the scope of this fundamental exercise, but the option will be obvious to you when you use linking in Chapter 17, *Hierarchical Linking: Ease Meets Complexity.*

The Local Reference Coordinate System

Right-click on the Top viewport and choose Local in the reference coordinate system list. Right-click on the other viewports, and you'll find the axis tripod performs the same as it did when using the World reference coordinate system. This is a coincidence because you created the cylinder in the Top viewport, which has the same axis directions as the World reference coordinate system. To see that the Local reference coordinate system stays local to the object, you can right-click on the Perspective viewport, click the Select and Rotate transform button on the main toolbar, and rotate the cylinder roughly 45 degrees in both the X and Y axes by clicking and dragging on the red or green circle of the Rotate gizmo in the viewport (**Figure 2.6**).

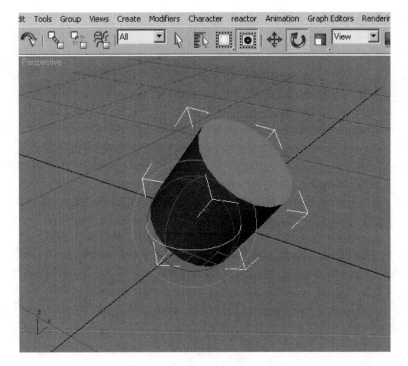

FIGURE 2.6 *Click the Select and Rotate button on the main toolbar and rotate the cylinder about 45 degrees in the X and Y axes.*

Notice that even though you had the reference coordinate system set to Local while in Select mode, it switched automatically to View when you clicked the Select and Rotate button. This is because the active reference coordinate system works independently for each transform, such as Move, Rotate, and Scale. The transform will use the reference coordinate system you set in the current session until you change it again. The axis tripod also changes the red and gray gizmo to the Transform gizmo when the transform buttons are clicked.

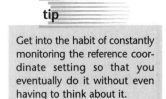

Get into the habit of constantly monitoring the reference coordinate setting so that you eventually do it without even having to think about it.

Right-click on the Top viewport, click the Select and Move transform button in the main toolbar, and set the reference coordinate system to Local. Right-click on the other viewports, and you'll see that the Move Transform gizmo orients itself with the object as it was created (see **Figure 2.7** on the next page). Familiarize yourself with the Local reference coordinate system. It's an especially powerful production tool because it is most closely related to the object itself, regardless of the object's rotation.

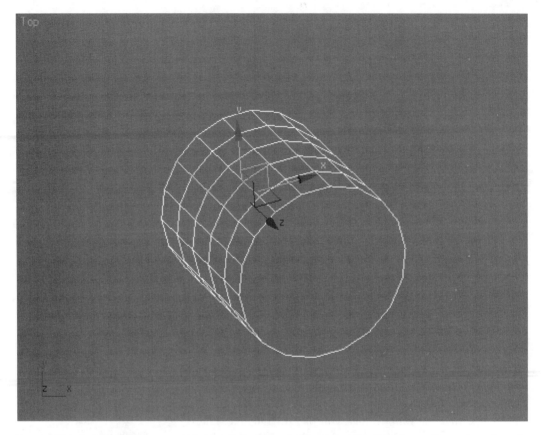

FIGURE 2.7 *In Local reference coordinate mode, the axis tripod and the Transform gizmo stay aligned with the object's creation axes.*

The Grid Reference Coordinate System

The Grid reference coordinate system requires you to create a new grid "helper" object as the active work plane. Right-click on the Top viewport to activate it.

On the Create panel, expand the Geometry rollout, click the Box button, and activate the AutoGrid feature by selecting the AutoGrid option. As you move your cursor over the cylinder, notice that a tricolor cursor tracks the face normal of the face under the cursor. Press and hold the Alt key, and pick and drag a box primitive on the end cap of the cylinder. Click the Select Object button on the main toolbar and select the new Grid object at the top of the cylinder (**Figure 2.8**).

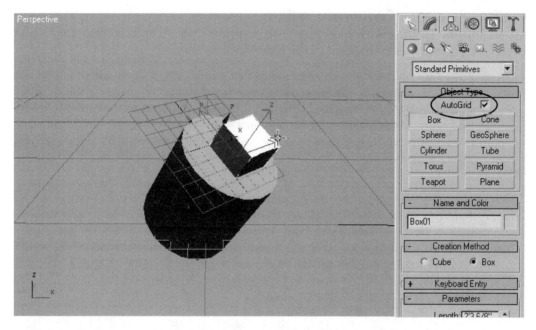

FIGURE 2.8 *You can create objects directly on any surface using the AutoGrid feature. Pressing and holding the Alt key during the process creates a permanent grid object on that plane.*

Holding the Alt key while creating an object in AutoGrid mode concurrently produces a new, active grid in the scene.

Click the Select and Move button and switch to the Grid reference coordinate system. The X, Y, and Z axes of the grid will be used for the current transform.

With the new Grid object selected on the active viewport, right-click the grid and, in the pop-up menu, choose Activate HomeGrid to return to the default grid system. You can have as many of these grid helper objects as you want, but only one can be active at any time. You can reactivate the new grid at any time.

note

Face normals in 3ds max are invisible vectors that point perpendicular from any face. They are used as alignment tool aids and for such things as face visibility, for example.

The Pick Reference Coordinate System

In the Pick reference coordinate system, you can assign the coordinate system of another object in the scene as the active system.

Right-click on the Top viewport to activate it, and create a small sphere to one side of the cylinder. Click the Select and Rotate transform button, change the reference coordinate system to Pick, and click on the cylinder on the Top viewport. The Sphere is now using the cylinder's Local reference coordinate system axes directions, and Cylinder01's coordinate system will be added to the list of available reference coordinate systems.

Pivot Point Options

Another aid to production that goes hand in hand with the reference coordinate systems is the active Pivot Point type, which lets you switch to different types of pivot locations when rotating objects. Just to the right of the reference coordinate system window is a flyout menu with three choices of pivot point types. Choosing the bottom option, called Use Transform Coordinate Center, changes the rotation center to be at the base of the cylinder (**Figure 2.9**).

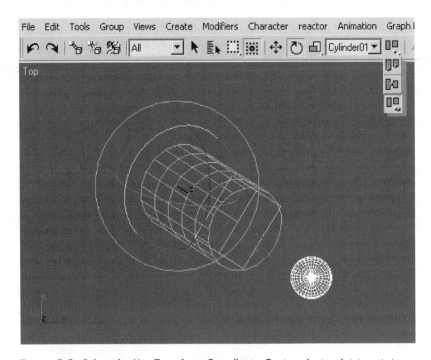

FIGURE 2.9 *Select the Use Transform Coordinate Center pivot point to rotate the sphere around the cylinder's Local Axis pivot point.*

Use Pivot Point Center

On the Top viewport, select all the objects in the scene. Choose the Use Pivot Point Center pivot-point option. Notice that as you rotate the selection set, each object is transformed based on its current active reference coordinate system around its own individual pivot point rather than the center of the selection set. This is particularly useful when you are in Rotate mode and you need to rotate many objects at once on their own individual pivot points.

Use Selection Center

Choose the Use Selection Center pivot point, and you'll discover that the entire selection set of objects uses a single pivot point in the geometric center of the bounding box of the selected objects. This keeps the objects in the same relative positions to each other. Like Use Pivot Point Center, the Use Selection Center pivot point is most useful when rotating.

Use Transform Coordinate Center

The Transform Coordinate Center pivot point uses the Absolute World coordinate point (coordinate location 0,0,0), unless the Pick reference coordinate system is active. If it is active, the selected object then uses the pick object's pivot point as its own.

Coordinate Systems Summary

The following list summarizes the attributes of the various reference coordinate systems:

- **View.** The axis tripod adapts itself to each orthographic viewport so that the positive X axis is pointing to the right, the positive Y axis is pointing up, and positive Z axis is pointing perpendicularly out of the display. Nonorthographic viewports resort to using the World reference coordinate system.

- **Screen.** Same as View in orthographic viewports. In nonorthographic viewports, the positive Z axis always points at the viewer.

- **World.** The coordinate system always corresponds to the Absolute World coordinates, as measured from the 0,0,0 point in World space.

- **Parent.** The child object uses the parent's Local coordinate system in a hierarchically linked parent/child relationship.

- **Local.** The coordinates always remain with the object as it was created, regardless of the rotation angle of the object.

- **Grid.** Uses the active grid system's coordinate system.

- **Pick.** Uses the Local coordinate system of another object that is picked in the scene.

For the Align, Array, and Mirror commands in 3ds max, always check the active reference coordinate system to see which *X*, *Y*, and *Z* axis is being used by the command. The mode is noted in the Align Selection or Array dialog box (**Figure 2.10**).

note

The View reference coordinate system is never listed in Array, Align, or Mirror commands. You will always see Screen, which is the same for all orthographic viewports.

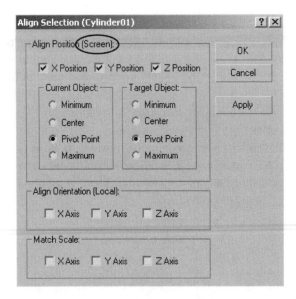

FIGURE 2.10 *The active reference coordinate system is shown in parentheses on the title bar of the Align Selection dialog box.*

Layers

Knowing how to work in layers using 3ds max 7 is an important skill in a production environment. Although layers have been available in previous versions of 3ds max, version 7 provides improvements in workflow that make layers more user friendly and functional.

Layers are organizational elements containing objects you've placed on the layers. You can use layers as selection tools to quickly select specific objects so that you can transform them or to change the visibility of the layer's objects in the viewports or the renderer. You also can use layers to set object properties, such as setting the radiosity lighting properties for all objects currently on a layer.

I don't want to rewrite here all the layer information contained in the 3ds max 7 user reference manual, but I do want to make sure you're aware of the concepts behind this production tool. I also want to point out that two 3ds max 7 elements affect how layers are managed: the Layers Manager and the Object Properties dialog box.

The Layers Manager

Figure 2.11 shows the Layer Manager. In this example, the scene contains four layers—three with teapots and the default layer, with nothing on it.

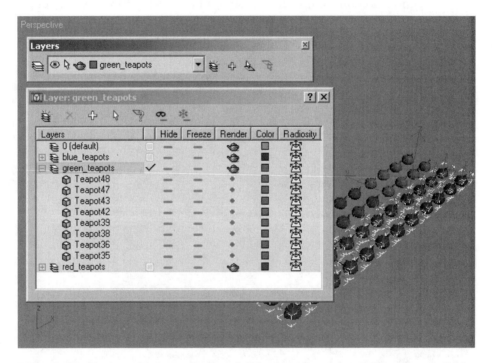

FIGURE 2.11 *The Layer Manager menu and dialog box show some of the options available for creating and manipulating layers.*

The Layer Manager menu and dialog box enable you to create and manipulate layers and toggle on and off Layer object properties, such as renderability, visibility, and radiosity settings.

To further investigate layers and their functionality, use the 3ds max 7 Help files. Work with a simple file similar to this teapot example so that you learn the fundamentals of how the concept can be applied to your production workflow.

The Object Properties Dialog

When you first begin using the layers in 3ds max 7, it's easy to be confused by the fact that, by default, the objects you create in max have their properties determined by the object settings, not by any layer settings. This means that no amount of layer manipulation will have any bearing on the properties of the objects on that layer until you enable the By Layer option for the object's properties.

Figure 2.12 shows the Object Properties dialog box with the General tab and Advanced Lighting tab selected. On the General tab, the Display Properties and Rendering Control sections of the selected objects have been set to By Layer control, whereas the Motion Blur section on the General tab and the Geometric Object Properties section on the Advanced Lighting tab are still set to the default By Object control.

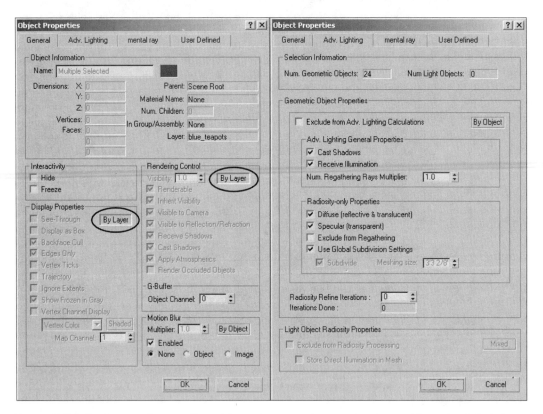

FIGURE 2.12 *For layer settings to affect objects, the properties must be changed from the default By Object to By Layer.*

Again, search the 3ds max 7 Help files for "using layers to organize a scene" to get a more complete overview and more details on layers.

Settings and Startup Configuration

You can use several files in 3ds max 7 to enhance productivity, such as 3dsmax.ini, maxstart.max, plugin.ini, and MaxStartUI.cui. These files can store such settings as how units are expressed (metric or U.S. standard units, for example) and which menu and viewport layouts will be available when you open a new scene or reset the current one.

Of these files, maxstart.max is the most important timesaving tool. The maxstart.max file lets you save the state of the workspace so that it displays using the same settings each time you start a new file or reset the scene. Unlike the other setup files that have preset default values, however, it does not exist until you create it.

Although it would be possible to save a maxstart.max file that contains objects or lighting to load with each new file or reset action, you usually only want to change the viewport configurations to your preferences, as each new scene typically would have different objects and lighting.

The maxstart.max file will be saved by default in the /3dsmax7/scenes subdirectory (at least it should be), but you can save it anywhere on your hard drive and use the Configure Paths dialog box to point to the location.

In Chapter 3, *2D Shapes: Starting with the Foundation*, you'll create and save a maxstart.max file that you'll use for many of the exercises throughout this book.

Basic Lofting Concepts

In my view, lofting is the most powerful modeling tool in 3ds max, but one that is underutilized because it often exhibits "strange" behavior when you're using it. In reality, the behavior is not strange. Rather, because lofting is unlike any creation method you use in other software, it requires that you understand a few simple concepts before it will make sense to you.

The term *lofting* comes from old shipbuilding practices in which the patterns for ribs of a ship were all laid out in the upstairs loft of the shipbuilders shop. Long, thin metal bands, or splines, were set on edge and bent to the curvature of the hull at given points along the keel. To hold the splines in place so that the lines could be traced on the patterns, the ship designer placed heavy steel or lead "ducks" at the tangency points. To create the hull, the ribs (loft shapes) were then attached along the keel (loft path) and the planking was attached to form the hull (mesh object).

But I Don't Speak the Language!

To fully understand 3ds max lofting, you need to know the following terms:

- **Shape.** A 2D object in 3ds max. It may occupy 3D space as a helix shape does, but it does not have any surface information. A shape has a name and a color, and it must contain at least one sub-object-level spline. If it has more than one spline, it is a compound shape. For example, the donut primitive is a compound shape made of two splines (that is, concentric circles).

- **Spline.** A sub-object-level component of a shape.

- **Loft path.** The shape that defines the extrusion length of the loft object.

- **Loft shape.** The shape that defines the cross sections of the loft object. A loft object can have only one closed or open spline as a path, but it can have an unlimited number of open or closed shapes as cross sections. Each shape or path can have an unlimited number of vertices, and different shapes can have different numbers of vertices. However, each shape on a path must have the same number of splines. For example, you cannot loft a circle and a donut primitive on the same loft path.

- **Local reference coordinate system.** 3ds max 7 has several different reference coordinate systems, as you learned earlier in this chapter; however, the Local system is the most important one in lofting. The Local system is the coordinate system of the shape as it is created. When you create a shape in any given viewport, the rule is that the local positive X axis is pointing to the right, the local positive Y axis is pointing up, and the local positive Z axis is pointing out toward the viewer. This Local reference coordinate system stays relative to the shape as the shape is rotated.

- **Pivot point.** The pivot point of a shape is usually positioned at the geometric center of the bounding box of the shape. It can be repositioned through the Hierarchy panel. The pivot point defines the apex of the X, Y, and Z axes of a shape.

- **First vertex.** Each spline has a first vertex indicated by a white box when in Vertex sub-object mode (**Figure 2.13**). Open splines can have either end vertex as a first vertex, and closed splines can have any vertex as a first vertex.

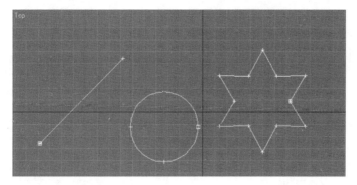

FIGURE 2.13 *Viewport showing a white box, indicating the first vertex of various shapes, and the red X and Y axes tripod at the pivot point of the circle.*

The pivot point and first vertex are very important in the lofting process, and a lack of understanding of them is probably the prime reason for frustration while lofting.

The pivot point of the shape attaches to the first vertex of the path.

The orientation of the shape on the path is a bit more complex. I'll talk you through it and show an example here, and then discuss it in more detail in Chapter 5, *Lofting: Control Is Everything.* The local Z axis of the shape aligns itself "down" the path; the local Y axis of the shape aligns with the local Z axis of the path (**Figure 2.14**).

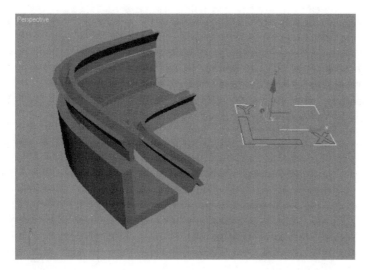

FIGURE 2.14 *The curved path and L shape have been created in the Top viewport. The loft object shows the orientation of the shape on the path. You also can see the local axis directions of the 2D shapes, indicated by the Move Transform gizmo arrows.*

Lofting Options

The lofting process itself is simple enough, but a couple of options are worth mentioning. You can access lofting from the Compound Objects pull-down menu (Create panel > Geometry > Compound Objects). You must have a valid 2D shape selected or the Loft button will be grayed out in the Object Type rollout.

In the Creation Method rollout are two buttons: Get Path and Get Shape (**Figure 2.15**). The usual workflow is to have the path selected and to use the Get Shape button. However, you could select the shape and use Get Path. The determining factor is that whichever object is selected remains in place and the other shape or path reorients and moves to the selected shape. Generally, I prefer to select the path and use Get Shape.

Underneath the Get Path and Get Shape buttons are some other options: Move, Copy, and Instance. The Instance radio button is selected by default. This means that a clone of the shape jumps to the path, not the original shape itself. The advantage of this option is that you can modify the original 2D shape, and the lofted 3D mesh will change accordingly.

The Move option actually moves the original shape to the path, and Copy places a clone of the shape with no connection to the original (making either choice much less editable). I have never found the need to use either Move or Copy.

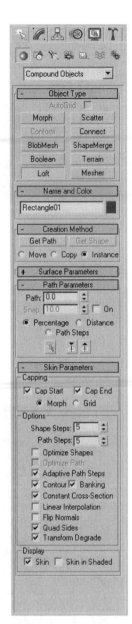

Figure 2.15

The Loft panel with Name and Color, Creation Method, Path Parameters, and Skin Parameters rollouts expanded.

In **Figure 2.16**, most of the petals, stems, pistil, and vase are lofted from 2D shapes, allowing for quick and easy editing.

As mentioned earlier, the fundamental process is simple enough, but you must understand more options to make an efficient lofting modeling choice.

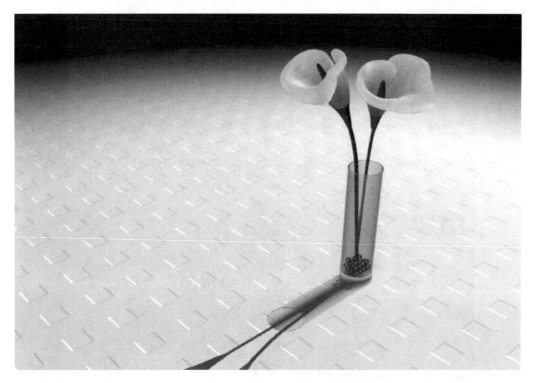

FIGURE 2.16 *This simple lily scene was created primarily with lofting. Lofting allows for quick editing at the 2D shape level to make major changes to 3D objects.*

The Importance of the First Vertex in Lofting

3ds max 7 builds the lofted mesh objects by first connecting the first vertex on each shape along the path and then building a mesh surface using the shape steps and path steps. Therefore, the relative position of the shape's first vertex determines the twisting of the object along the path.

To remove (or apply more) twisting, you must modify the loft object itself at the sub-object level to rotate either of the shapes on the loft path—not the original shapes, mind you, but the instance clone of the shape that has attached itself to the loft path. **Figure 2.17** shows a circle and a rectangle lofted along a straight-line path, illustrating the twisting that can occur.

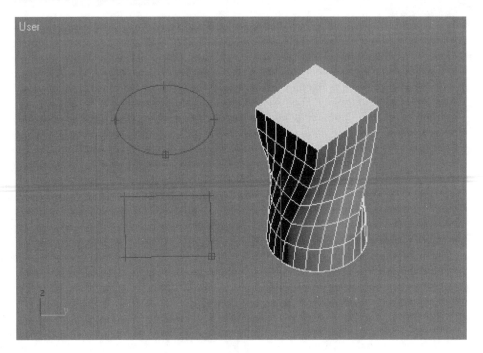

FIGURE 2.17 *Circle and rectangle shapes lofted along a straight line produce a twisted object because of the relative positions of the first vertex of each shape.*

Modifying the lofted object at the Shape sub-object level and rotating the circle on the loft path by 45 degrees (in this case, around its local axis) removes the twisting (**Figure 2.18**).

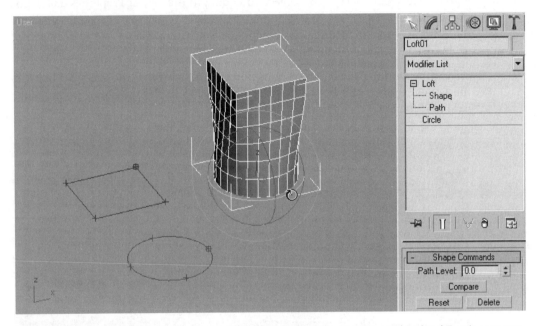

FIGURE 2.18 *By rotating the circle shape at the base of the loft object around its local Z axis, you can easily remove or enhance the twist.*

Lofting Efficiency

If you want 3ds max 7 to be a cost-effective tool in your office, you *must* keep models as simple as possible. (Modeling overhead is the primary hindrance to production that I encounter in my training sessions.) Each vertex and face in a model uses valuable computer overhead, and you can very quickly overwhelm even the most powerful systems and render them ineffective in a production scenario.

Lofting offers controls for adjusting the mesh density of models while retaining the necessary details. First you have two new terms to learn:

- **Shape steps.** Intermediate points between vertices of the shape that define curvature in the connecting shape segment.
- **Path steps.** Intermediate points between vertices of the path that define curvature in the connecting shape segment.

When a shape is lofted along a path, segments are created in the loft mesh for each vertex and path step or shape step. These segments can clearly be seen in the preceding loft example, which has the Edged Faces option enabled in the viewport. Right-clicking the selected Loft object and going to the Object Properties dialog box shows that the object has 332 faces. On the Modify panel, Skin Parameters rollout, there are two numeric fields: Shape Steps and Path Steps. Each is set to 5 by default in 3ds max 7.

Setting the path steps to 0 reduces the information that shows the curvature between the path's vertices. The object shows less definition in the transition from circular base to rectangular top (**Figure 2.19**).

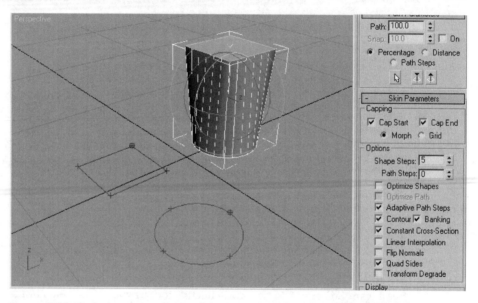

FIGURE 2.19 *Reducing the path steps from 5 to 0 reduces the definition of the transition from circular to rectangular along the length of the object. It also reduces the number of faces from 332 to 92, with a corresponding loss of visual detail.*

Increasing the path steps to 3 might give an acceptable level of detail, depending on the distance from the camera or the background, and increases the overall face count to a moderate 236. You must be the judge of how much detail is enough, but you have the option to change it at any time to optimize the object for any occasion.

Reducing the shape steps of this loft object to *0* ruins the integrity of the object because the base is changed to a rectangular shape. A circle has four vertices, so removing any intermediate steps that define the curvature makes it rectangular (**Figure 2.20**).

Increasing the shape steps to *3* might result in an acceptable mesh object with a total face count of 156, less than half the original 332 faces.

The important fact is that you can easily adjust the density of your lofted objects at any time to achieve an optimum balance between the detail of the object and the efficiency of the object, which is so critical to production.

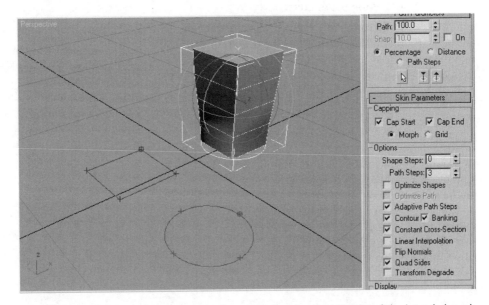

FIGURE 2.20 *Setting the shape steps to 0 completely ruins the integrity of the intended mesh by removing all curvature from the circular shape.*

Summary

This chapter presented several important concepts:

- **The reference coordinate systems in 3ds max 7.** These include View, Screen, and Local. Without a fundamental understanding of the them, particularly of Local, you'll have a difficult time navigating through 3D space, transforming objects in scenes, and taking full advantage of the alignment tools available in the program.

- **Layers.** A management tool that lets you manipulate objects as a group to transform them as one entity, or to change properties such as object visibility or radiosity rendering parameters.

- **Lofting.** A relatively straightforward modeling technique that requires a fundamental understanding of underlying concepts before you can use it efficiently. These concepts include the orientation of shapes and paths, the first vertex, and path and shape steps. While you hopefully had a chance to experiment with lofting in this chapter, the information presented here serves to set the stage for the indepth lofting practice you'll do in Chapter 5, *Lofting: Control Is Everything*.

PART II

Modeling

CHAPTER 3

2D Shapes: Starting with the Foundation

In This Chapter

In this chapter, you'll learn about creating and editing 2D primitive shapes in 3ds max 7. You'll also begin to apply some of the concepts you learned in Chapter 2, *Fundamental Concepts*, into a workflow that should become the basis of much of your production.

This chapter covers the following topics:

- **2D primitive shapes.** 3ds max 7 lets you create parametric 2D objects, such as lines, circles, rectangles, or helices, to name a few, which you can use in constructing more complex objects or as animation paths.

- **Object naming.** Assigning logical names to newly created objects is critical to production.

- **Sub-object level.** 2D shapes are built from sub-object-level components, including Vertex, Segment, and Spline, which let you edit and manipulate the shapes.

- **Vertex tangency.** An important feature in editing 2D shapes is control of the tangency of the curve coming into and going out from each vertex.

- **Modifiers.** An important part of the workflow process in 3ds max 7, modifiers let you stack discrete operations on objects to create a history that you can maneuver within to adjust the parameters that edit objects.

Key Terms

- **Shape.** Shapes in 3ds max 7 are 2D objects that, by default, do not show in the rendered images, but are used as a basis for construction of 3D objects or as animation paths, for example. Shapes have names and a specific color in the viewport.

- **Spline.** Splines are subsets of shapes. Think of a spline as one continuous, unbroken line. A simple shape contains only one spline. Splines may be open, such as a helix, or closed, as in a circle or rectangle.

- **Compound shape.** All shapes must contain one sub-object-level component called a *spline*. However, compound shapes made of multiple splines are useful for creating complex 3D objects.

- **Parametric primitives.** Shapes have parameters, such as the length and width of a rectangle, that may be adjusted when creating or editing the shape.

- **Editable spline.** An editable spline lets you access sub-object-level components, such as Vertex, Segment, or Spline, for flexible editing.

- **Bezier curve.** Curved shapes in 3ds max 7 are not arcs but parametric polynomial curves with varying radii between vertices. (Bezier was a French mathematician of the twentieth century.)

- **Renderable spline.** This attribute makes shapes visible in rendered images or in the viewports.

- **Transform.** Move, Rotate, and Scale make up the three transform actions available when editing objects in 3ds max 7.

2D Basics

2D shapes in 3ds max 7 will most likely form the basis of much of your modeling workflow. As such, you can edit them easily, which can profoundly affect your 3D objects in the scene.

Each shape has numeric creation parameters that can be adjusted during creation or while editing to allow flexible changes.

Shapes can also be converted from parametric objects to editable splines or can have an Edit Spline modifier applied to give you access to the building blocks of shapes: vertex, segments, and splines. This provides another level of editing control that lets

> **note**
>
> You should already be familiar with the location of the basic panels and commonly used buttons you learned while performing the tutorials in the manuals and online reference tutorials that ship with 3ds max 7.
>
> If you need a refresher, pause the cursor over a button to see a tooltip displaying the name of the button.

you change such elements as the curvature of the shape, the number of vertices in the shape, and the position of vertices.

2D line work exported from other programs, such as most CAD software or Adobe Illustrator, can also be imported as shapes into 3ds max 7.

In this chapter, you'll learn to create and modify 2D shapes that will be used as the basis for constructing other objects (Chapter 5, *Lofting: Control Is Everything*) and importing objects (Chapter 8, *More Modifiers: Orderly Progression*).

note

The terms *shape* and *spline* are used interchangeably throughout the 3ds max menus and documentation. Technically speaking, a spline is a sub-object-level component of a shape. A shape has a name and a color associated with it, whereas a spline does not.

To access the 2D shape creation area, open the Create panel and click the Shapes Category button to access the Object Type rollout (**Figure 3.1**).

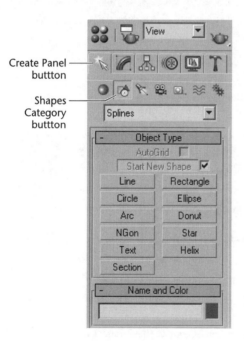

Create Panel buttton

Shapes Category buttton

FIGURE 3.1 *To create Shape primitives, choose the Create panel, and click on the Shapes Category button to display the Object Types rollout, which contains the buttons for line, circle, and other primitive shapes.*

Parametric shapes are created in the viewports using a sequence of click-and-drag operations with the left mouse button. The exact sequence depends on the type of shape you're creating. For example, a circle requires a click and drag to define the radius of the circle, while a helix requires a click, a drag to define the bottom radius, a release of the left mouse button and move to describe the height, a click and move to define the top radius, and a click to finalize the top radius.

While it is sometimes desirable to modify shapes in 3D space, it's much too easy to accidentally move vertices out of the original creation plane, causing the resulting 3D object to become distorted. **Figure 3.2** shows an example of shape editing in the 2D plane and a similar edit in 3D space with the resulting 3D extruded objects.

2D shape edited in creation plane

2d shape edited in 3D space

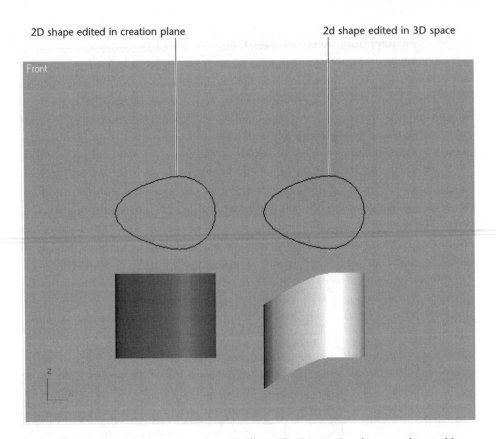

FIGURE 3.2 *While the two shapes appear similar in the Perspective viewport, the resulting extruded objects demonstrate that editing in the third dimension can have unexpected results. For this reason, editing 2D shapes in orthographic viewports is advised.*

Try creating each of the different 2D Shape primitives so that you get comfortable creating each type of primitive. Then on the Modify panel, select each of the shapes you created, and adjust their parameters. If you create a line shape, you'll notice the Modify panel has no parameters, and the panel has a completely different set of tools than it would if another shape were selected (**Figure 3.3**).

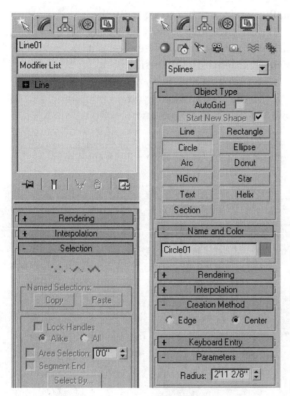

FIGURE 3.3 *The Modify panel for a line primitive on the left has no parameters, but it does let you directly access sub-object-level editing, as you can see by the Selection rollout and sub-object-level buttons on the panel. The Modify panel for a circle primitive on the right lets you adjust the Radius parameter.*

Creating and Modifying Lines

A line shape is perhaps the simplest of the 2D shapes, but for new users it is often one of the most difficult to create, requiring some practice to gain control.

By activating the Line button in the Object Type roll-out (Create panel > Shapes category) and picking points in a viewport, you'll create a series of straight-line segments. However, if you click and drag, you begin to describe the tangency for the vertex where you clicked. This causes the segments on either side of that vertex to curve, based on the distance and direction of the cursor from the point where you clicked. **Figure 3.4** shows straight and curved lines.

tip

You can force straight-line segments by setting the Drag Type to Corner in the Creation Method rollout of the Line command.

Clicking to place vertices creates straight segments

Clicking and dragging vertices creates Bezier curve segments

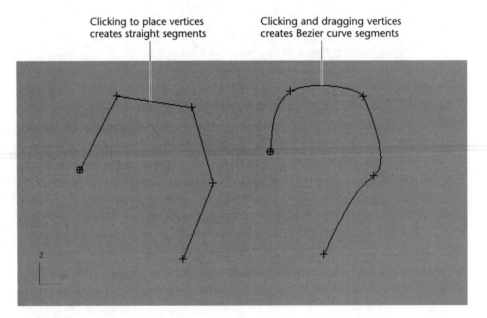

Figure 3.4 *Straight-line segments are created by clicking and releasing the mouse button, while curved segments are created by clicking and dragging to define the tangency at vertices.*

Take some time to practice creating lines with a mix of straight and curved segments to develop a feel for how far and in which direction you need to drag the cursor to define the desired curve.

note

When you have placed the last vertex in your line, you can right-click to end the creation process.

Another important feature that can have a significant effect on shapes, especially on Bezier curve lines, for instance, is the Interpolation setting. This setting determines the *interpolation*, or number of intermediate steps between vertices, thus defining the smoothness of the curve. The higher the setting, the smoother the curve. In **Figure 3.5** are two copies of the same shape. The copy on the left is using the default Interpolation setting of *6*, which results in segmented curves, while the copy on the right has an Interpolation setting of *12*, which adds intermediate points that smooth the curve. The Interpolation setting can be adjusted from the Modify panel.

caution

When a shape is modified to become a 3D object—by extruding, for example—the extra interpolation steps in all curved segments will translate into 3D edges in the 3D object. This can greatly increase the density of the 3D object, which can be very inefficient.

If you want to add a new vertex to smooth a curved segment locally rather than globally using Interpolation steps, you can often use the Refine command at the Vertex or Segment sub-object level.

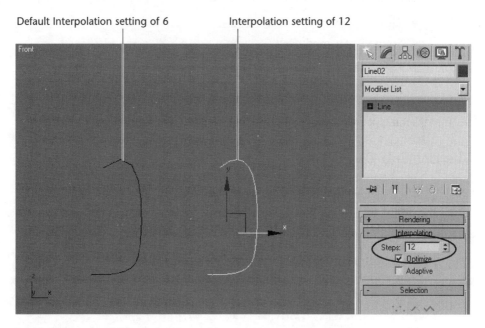

FIGURE 3.5 *Increasing Interpolation adds more intermediate steps between vertices to smooth curves.*

Sub-Object-Level Editing

An important concept in the structure of 3ds max 7 is *sub-object-level editing*. Whether you're editing 2D shapes, 3D meshes or polygons, modifiers, or animation controllers, there are often multiple levels of editing capability in which you can adjust the components that make up the object. As I already mentioned in this chapter's introduction, the sub-objects of shapes are Vertices, Segments, and Splines. 3D mesh objects are composed of Vertex, Edge, Face, Polygon, and Element sub-objects that can be accessed and edited.

To get the most out of the power of 3ds max 7, you must learn to access and adjust the various sub-object level components throughout the program. It is beyond the scope of this book to show you all the options. Instead you must experiment at the various sub-object levels so that you can incorporate the functionality into your daily workflow.

In this section, you'll learn some of the controls available at the sub-object level that enable you to create relatively complex geometry from basic 2D shapes.

There are several methods of accessing the sub-object level of 2D shapes:

- Line sub-object-level control
- Spline Select modifier
- Edit Spline modifier
- Convert to Editable Spline command

All of these methods have their advantages, but some work better than others, as you'll soon discover.

The Line Sub-Object Level

As mentioned earlier, line is the only shape that allows direct access to sub-object-level editing. The easiest way to enter sub-object mode for a line is to expand the Line entry in the Modifier Stack view on the right and choose the sub-object level you want to work with (**Figure 3.6**). The sub-object component you chose becomes highlighted in the stack view, and symbols appear at the right of the stack view to indicate the level chosen.

tip

When creating selection sets in 3ds max 7, you can drag a selection window to select multiple objects, use the Ctrl key to add to a selection, or use the Alt key to subtract from a selection.

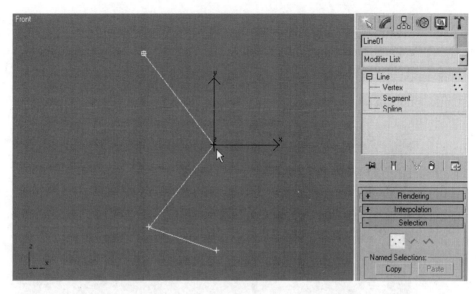

Figure 3.6 *Select a line and, in the Modifier Stack view, click the plus sign to the left of Line to expand the list. Highlight the sub-object level you want to access, in this case Vertex. Then select the vertex you want to edit. It will turn red in the viewport and display the axis tripod.*

When working at the sub-object level, it's very important that you highlight the appropriate sub-object level in Modifier Stack view, and then pick the selection set in a viewport to highlight the selection in red before performing the edit. New users sometimes forget to make the selection set and find that the editing options are grayed out or have no effect.

The Spline Select Modifier

For shapes other than the line shape, you can't directly access Vertex, Segment, or Spline sub-object levels from the Modify panel. Instead, when you have a 2D shape selected in the scene, you can access these sub-object levels using the Spline Select modifier, located in the Modifier List in Modifier Stack view. Keep in mind, though, that while you can access the sub-object levels, you can only create selection sets that will be passed to subsequent modifiers placed higher in the stack.

tip

You'll learn more about the functionality of the Modifier Stack in Chapter 4, *Modifiers: Stack Them High.* The power of this view is that modifiers can be added or deleted at points in the history of your object, allowing for more flexible editing.

For example, say you're creating an animation path that might be a rectangular shape or only one or more segments of the rectangle. In **Figure 3.7**, a rectangle object has a Spline Select modifier added. At the Segment sub-object level, the top horizontal segment is selected and a Delete Spline modifier is added to the stack. This Delete Spline modifier only operates on the selection just below it and deletes only the top horizontal segment.

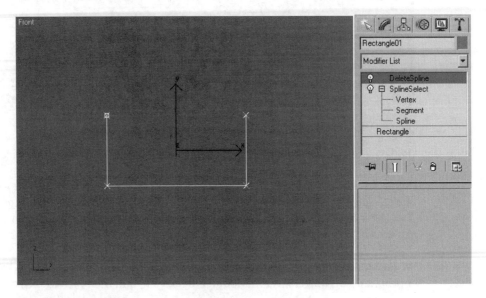

Figure 3.7 *Using the Spline Select modifier, you can make sub-object-level selections that will then be passed up the stack to subsequent modifiers.*

You can quickly change the sub-objects that are deleted by dropping to the Segment sub-object level in the Spline Select modifier and selecting other segments, and then returning to the top of the stack. This workflow is both very flexible and very efficient.

note

There are corresponding Mesh Select, Patch Select, and Poly Select modifiers that provide the same capabilities and advantages as the Spline Select modifier at the 3D object level.

The Edit Spline Modifier

Sub-object editing can be accomplished with the Edit Spline modifier applied to a 2D primitive shape. The resulting options in the Modifier Stack are the same as the default options that are available when you're working with a line shape (**Figure 3.8**).

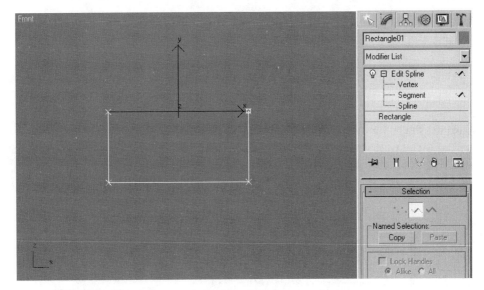

FIGURE 3.8 *Select a line and, in the Modifier List, choose Edit Spline. This gives the same sub-object editing capability as the default line shape.*

The advantage of using the Edit Spline modifier is that you can do all the editing directly in the stack but still drop below in the stack to access and edit the base Rectangle parameters if you need to.

However, the main disadvantage associated with the Edit Spline modifier is that every time you apply an Edit Spline to a shape, the full footprint of the shape is stored in memory, which can increase overhead and reduce productivity because the memory footprint of 2D shapes is surprisingly large. Another disadvantage is that if you make any changes to the topology of the shape at the sub-object level, such as adding or deleting vertices, segments, or splines, you'll get a warning message that you may experience unexpected results when you try to drop down in the Modifier stack (see **Figure 3.9** on the next page).

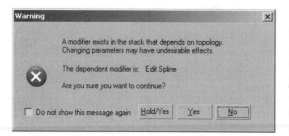

FIGURE 3.9 *Dropping down in the Edit Spline Modifier stack produces a warning that you may have unexpected results if you have added or deleted sub-object topology. Editing at the sub-object level often involves changes to the topology.*

For this reason, the extra overhead of the Edit Spline modifier offers no advantage, because you can't drop lower in the stack for further editing.

The Convert to Editable Spline Command

You can convert a parametric shape to a simple editable spline and still have access to all the sub-object-level editing options by using the Convert to Editable Spline command. Select a shape, right-click in the viewport, and choose Convert To > Convert to Editable Spline in the Quad menu (**Figure 3.10**).

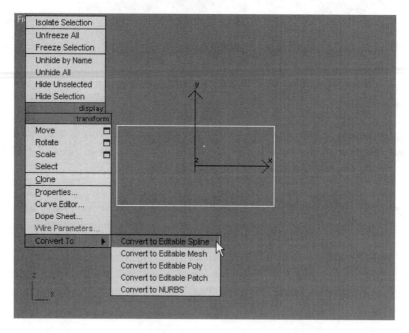

FIGURE 3.10 *Converting a parametric shape to an editable spline gives you access to sub-object-level editing and adds no overhead to the object.*

There is no method of converting back to a parametric shape once you have converted to an editable spline (other than to use the Undo command), but in most cases you'll have changed the topology, so you won't be able to alter the parameters anyway.

Using the Convert to Editable Spline command is an efficient method of gaining access to sub-object-level editing without adding overhead.

Putting Shape Theory into Practice

To apply some of the functions you have learned about 2D shapes into processes that might be found in a real world production office, let's work through some relevant exercises. The exercises are designed to be simple and straightforward so that you can focus on the concepts and workflow that will help you apply the lessons to situations you encounter in your projects.

There are four exercises divided into two parts in this chapter. The first part comprises three exercises:

- You'll create a foundation for an airport hanger that's used again in Chapter 8 to gain some hands-on experience with the Outline tool at the Spline sub-object level. You'll practice extruding the foundation shape into a 3D object and give the object a logical name.

- You'll practice modifying the base shape using the Outline tool, learning about compound shapes.

- You'll edit the compound shape for a door cutout to learn to attach shapes and perform trimming operations for cleanup. Another important topic called *vertex welding* will be introduced in this third exercise.

In the second segment, you'll do one exercise in which you turn a rectangle parametric shape into a cross section of a wing of an airplane. This shape will be used in Chapter 5 when you learn about using lofting to create 3D objects.

Creating a Foundation from a 2D Shape

Beginning with a rectangle 2D primitive, you'll apply an Extrude modifier to turn the parametric shape into a 3D box object. Then you'll take advantage of the Modifier Stack to edit the base rectangle by changing its size.

Exercise 3.1: Creating a Foundation

1. Open **Ch03_maxstart.max** from the CD that accompanies this book. This file is an empty file, but it has settings for the units, grid visibility and layout of the viewports, and grid spacing. Save this as a special file called *maxstart.max* into the \3dsmax 7\Scenes folder on your hard drive. This is a special file that will load automatically each time you start a new scene or perform a File > Reset operation. Next, save the file in your current project folder with the name *Ch03_foundation01.max*.

2. Right-click in the Top viewport to activate it. Always right-click to activate viewports so that you avoid inadvertently transforming objects when you left-click. You'll see a yellow border around the viewport indicating it is active. Open the Create panel, select Shapes, and then click the Rectangle button. Click and drag a large rectangle to nearly fill the Top viewport. For now, the size doesn't matter.

3. On the Modify panel, rename *Rectangle01* to *Foundation*. Always assign objects logical names soon after you create them. In this case, Foundation becomes a 3D background object, so the name begins with a capital letter so that it stands out in object name lists (**Figure 3.11**).

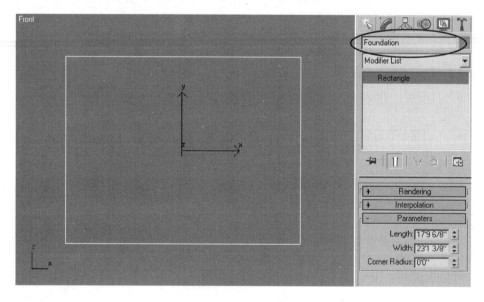

Figure 3.11 *Create a large rectangle in the Top viewport and, on the Modify panel, name it* Foundation.

4. On the Modify panel, select Modifier List, and then choose Extrude from the drop-down list. This option turns the rectangle into a shaded flat plane in the Perspective viewport. In the Parameters rollout, enter *4* in the Amount numeric field and press Enter. The display units are set to Feet w/Fractional Inches, so entering a number with no sign after it is understood as feet. However, you'd need to add a quotation mark to create a 4-inch extrusion. Setting the amount and pressing Enter extrudes the rectangle in the object's Local positive Z axis to make a box. Right-click in the Perspective viewport and use the mouse wheel or Zoom tool to view the entire box. The scene will look similar to **Figure 3.12**.

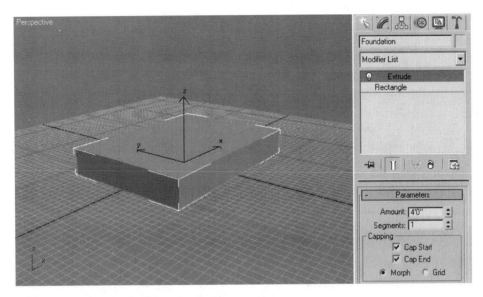

FIGURE 3.12 *Add an Extrude modifier to the Foundation shape and set the Amount field to 4 and press Enter. The 4 will be understood as 4'0".*

5. The foundation should be 40 feet long by 30 feet wide. On the Modify panel in Modifier Stack view, select Rectangle. In the Parameters rollout, enter *30* in the Length field and press Enter. Enter *40* in the Width field and press Enter (see **Figure 3.13** on the next page). This sets the foundation to the desired size. Select Extrude in the Stack view to return to that level.

note

Width, Length, and Height terminology on the Modify panel are relative terms and may not correspond to what you think they should represent in the actual object.

FIGURE 3.13 *On the Modify panel, highlight the Rectangle level in the Stack view. Change the parameters to 30 feet long and 40 feet wide.*

6. Save the file. It should already be called *Ch03_foundation01.max*.

A More Convincing Foundation: Using a Compound Shape

In the next exercise, you'll use the Modifier Stack view again to drop to the Rectangle level and apply an Edit Spline modifier below the Extrude modifier. A modifier is always added above the currently highlighted level in the stack. Edit Spline is not an option when the Extrude modifier is highlighted because the Edit Spline modifier can only operate on 2D shapes.

At the Spline sub-object level within the Edit Spline modifier, you'll use the Outline tool to create a compound shape by offsetting the existing spline. When you return to the Extrude modifier in the stack, you'll see that the 3D object looks quite different.

Exercise 3.2: Sub-Object Editing Using a Compound Shape

1. Open the file from your hard drive or from the CD-ROM called **Ch03_foundation01.max**. Save it to your project folder as *Ch03_foundation02.max*. To save files incrementally, choose File > Save As and then click the plus sign to the left of the Save button in the lower right of the dialog (**Figure 3.14**). This saves a new file and increments the number at the end of the existing file name.

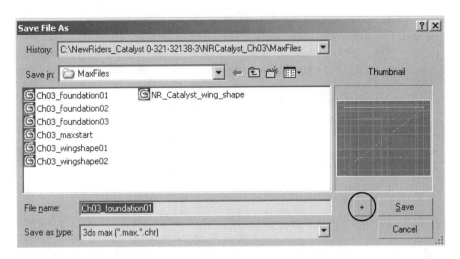

FIGURE 3.14 *To save incremental files, choose File > Save As and then click the plus sign. If the current file name has no number, 3ds max 7 will add* 01 *to the existing name.*

2. Click the Zoom Extents All button to fill the viewports with all objects. Select Foundation in the Top viewport by clicking the Select button on the main tool-bar to make sure it is highlighted and then selecting the visible edge of the box. On the Modify panel in Modifier Stack view, highlight Rectangle to make that level active. Click on the Modifier List to open the drop-down menu, and double-click Edit Spline modifier to add the modifier above the Rectangle level but below the Extrude level. You can toggle the Show End Result button to see either the extruded object (toggle on) or only the active level of the Stack (Edit Spline, toggle off) in the viewport. This is a convenient method of seeing what each modifier does to the model. Make sure you toggle the Show End Result button back on before you continue (**Figure 3.15**).

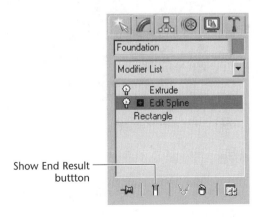

Show End Result
buttton

FIGURE 3.15 *On the Modify panel in Modifier Stack view, highlight the Rectangle level and add an Edit Spline modifier.*

3. In Modifier Stack view, expand the sub-object levels by clicking the plus sign to the left of Edit Spline, and then select Spline. In the Top viewport, select the rectangular spline; it will turn red. This shape has only a single spline, but it still has to be selected before the options will function. To access areas of the Modify panel that are not visible, you must position the cursor in empty space within the panel to show a hand cursor. Click and drag upward to reveal the lower areas of the panel. Near the bottom of the Geometry rollout is an Outline button with a numeric field to the right and a Center checkbox underneath. Enter *1* in the numeric field and press Enter. There are now two rectangular splines in the shape, spaced 1 foot and 0 inches apart. This is a compound shape (**Figure 3.16**).

caution

Do not click the Outline button and enter a value in the numeric field. These are two separate operations. Clicking the button lets you manually click and drag on the spline to visually create the new offset spline in the viewport.

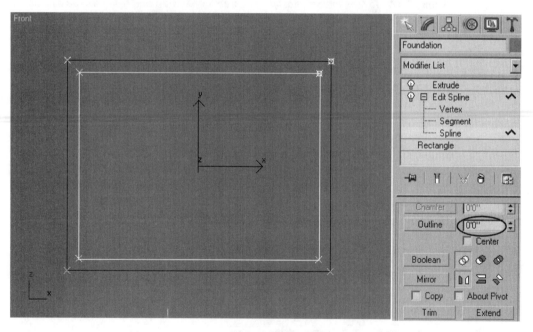

FIGURE 3.16 *On the Modify panel in the Geometry rollout, enter 1 in the Outline numeric field and press Enter to create a compound shape. A shape with two or more splines is a compound shape.*

4. On the Modify panel in Modifier Stack view, click the Edit Spline level to exit sub-object mode, and then click the Extrude Modifier level to return to the top of the stack. The resulting 3D object is now a perimeter foundation (**Figure 3.17**).

Nested compound shapes create 3D objects by creating a 3D surface from the outermost closed spline to the next "island" spline. Within the island spline it becomes a void. This pattern of 3D surface and void repeats as deeply as the splines are nested. See **Figure 3.18** for an example of a more complex compound shape.

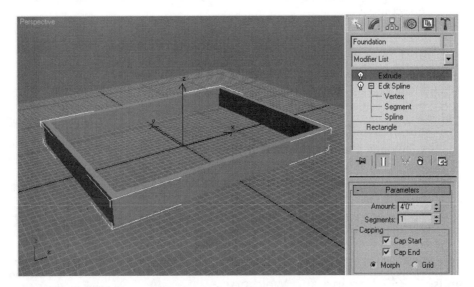

FIGURE 3.17 *When you exit sub-object mode and return to the top of the stack, the foundation displays as a rectangle with a rectangular opening.*

FIGURE 3.18 *A compound shape with multiple levels of nesting creates 3D surfaces or voids, depending on the nesting level of the "island" splines, beginning at the outside edge of the shape and moving in toward the center.*

5. Save the file. It should already be named *Ch03_foundation02.max*. Understanding compound shapes lets you create complex 3D objects from 2D shapes in an efficient, easy-to-edit manner.

Creating compound shapes with Extrude modifiers is an ideal technique for designing walls with window openings, window sashes, flat plates with cutouts, walls from floor plans, and countless other objects. You can make simple or major changes to underlying shapes by editing them at any time at the Vertex, Segment, or Spline sub-object levels.

Compound Shape and Trim Operations

Now let's say you decide the foundation shouldn't be a continuous perimeter and must have a break for 20-foot-wide doors in the center of the front wall.

In this exercise, you'll attach a new rectangle to the compound shape and clean up the edges by selecting the Spline sub-object and then selecting Trim from the Geometry rollout. This will create the correct opening, but it will leave unwelded or open vertices (a common problem) that you need to correct before the foundation will become a solid object again.

note

Unwelded vertices can result from trimming (as in this example) or from selecting one or more vertices and using the Break command, which turns each selected vertex into two vertices to open the shape.

2D shapes imported from other software, especially CAD programs, can also produce unwelded vertices. These are a result of rounding errors that occur when importing shapes from double-precision math programs (the CAD programs) into 3ds max 7, which is a single-precision math program.

Exercise 3.3: Trimming and Welding

1. Open the file from your project folder or the CD-ROM called **Ch03_foundation02.max**. Save it to your project folder as *Ch03_foundation03.max*. Right-click in the Top viewport to activate it. On the Create panel, click the Shapes button, then click the Rectangle button, and drag a rectangle of any size in the Top viewport. On the Modify panel, change the size of the rectangle by entering *8* in the Length field and pressing Enter, and then entering *20* in the Width field and pressing Enter.

2. To align the new rectangle with the center of the bottom wall in the foundation, click the Align button on the main toolbar and select Foundation in the Top viewport to display the Align Selection (Foundation) dialog. Clear the Z Position box and make sure the default Center radio buttons in the Current Object and Target Object sections are selected. This centers the rectangle in the wall in the *X* and *Y* axes of the View Reference Coordinate System to the center of the wall. Click the Apply button to clear the X and Y Position checkboxes. Now select only the Y Position and select the Minimum radio button in the Target Object column to overlap the bottom wall with the rectangle (**Figure 3.19**). Click OK.

note

The Align tool uses the current Screen reference coordinate system in this case to determine the direction of the *X*, *Y*, and *Z* axes. It uses the bounding box of the current and target objects to determine the Minimum, Maximum, and Center locations. Align will never report that it is using the View reference coordinate system, because View behaves like Screen in orthographic viewports and like World in non-orthographic viewports. Review Chapter 2 for more detail on these very important concepts.

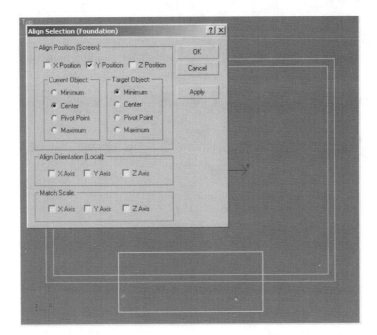

FIGURE 3.19 *Use the Align tool to first align the center of the rectangle with the center of the foundation in the* X *and* Y *axis. Then in the* Y *axes, align the center of the rectangle to the minimum of the foundation. Click OK to finish all of the alignment.*

3. In the Top viewport, select Foundation. On the Modify panel in Stack view, highlight Edit Spline. In the Geometry rollout, click the Attach button. Move the cursor over the new rectangle in the Top viewport until you see the Attach cursor (**Figure 3.20**). Select the rectangle. It attaches to the foundation shape to become a new spline within the compound shape. The rectangle will turn white when it is attached to indicate it is part of the foundation shape. Click the Attach button to exit that mode. Return to Extrude level in Stack view and observe that the new rectangle is a solid shape, not an opening in the wall. Return to Edit Spline level.

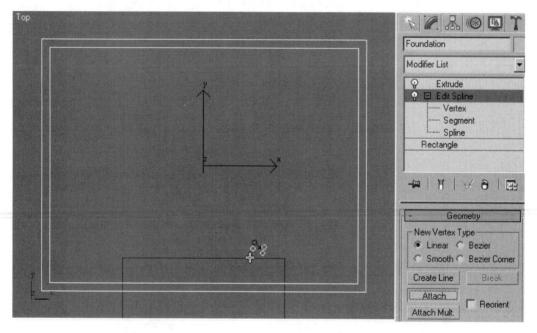

FIGURE 3.20 *Using the Edit Spline modifier in Stack view, click the Attach button to add the new rectangle as a spline to the compound shape.*

4. Using the Edit Spline modifier in Stack view, select the Spline sub-object level. In the Geometry rollout, click the Trim button. Move the cursor over the horizontal line of the wall within the new rectangle and click when you see the Trim cursor. Repeat this process for the other wall line in the rectangle (**Figure 3.21**).

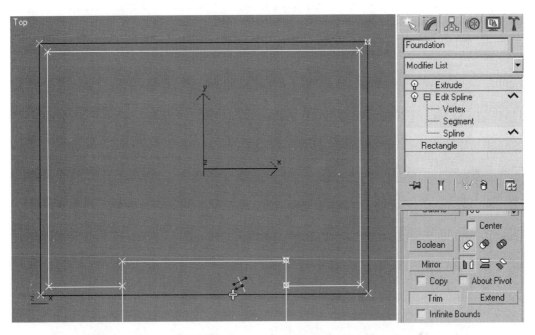

FIGURE 3.21 *In the Edit Spline modifier in Stack view, select the Spline sub-object level and click the Trim button in the Geometry rollout. Then select the horizontal wall lines within the rectangle to remove them.*

5. With the Trim button still highlighted, select the top and bottom horizontal lines of the new rectangle to trim the spline back to the walls. This leaves walls on either side of the new opening that appear to be a closed shape. Exit sub-object mode and return to the top of the stack. The wall appears to have no top or bottom and missing faces at the sides and back of the foundation (**Figure 3.22**). This is because the trimming has left "open" splines with unwelded vertices.

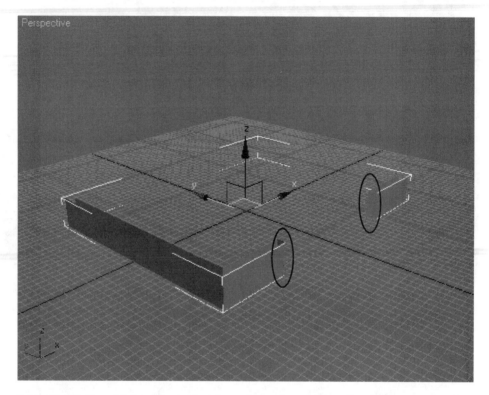

FIGURE 3.22 *Unwelded vertices in the trimmed area leave open splines in the compound shape, resulting in extruded objects with missing faces.*

6. On the Modify panel in Stack view, select the Vertex sub-object level. Drag a window around the eight vertices at the ends of the new stub walls. YOU'll see only four vertices, but remember four more vertices are located directly below as you're viewing from the top. In the Geometry rollout, enter *1"* in the Weld Threshold field (you must use the inch symbol) and press Enter (**Figure 3.23**). Click the Weld button on the left to perform the operation.

note

The Weld Threshold value describes the radius of a sphere around each selected vertex. If the spheres of two or more vertices overlap, the vertices will be welded into a single vertex. If the threshold is set too large, the geometry collapses unexpectedly.

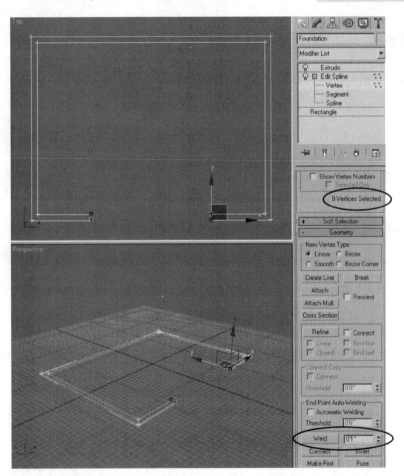

FIGURE 3.23 *Select the eight unwelded vertices at the ends of the new stub walls. Enter 1" as the weld threshold and click the Weld button to weld the eight vertices into four and close the splines.*

7. Exit sub-object mode by selecting Edit Spline in the stack, and then return to the Extrude modifier at the top of the stack. The foundation now has a 20-foot-wide opening for the doors (**Figure 3.24**).

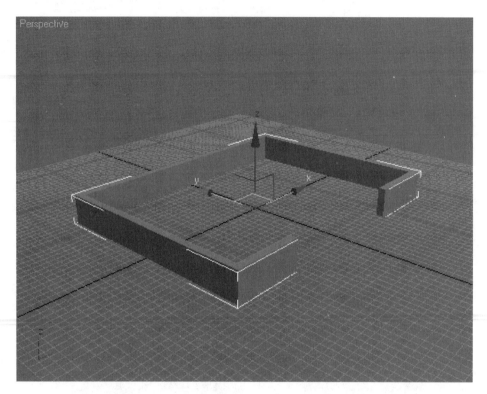

FIGURE 3.24 *Welding the vertices and returning to Extrude in the stack creates a capped foundation with a door opening.*

8. Save the file; it should already be called *Ch03_foundation03.max*.

You now have a foundation wall created from 2D shapes that is easily edited at any sub-object level. While creating a flexible and efficient foundation using sub-object editing and an Extrude modifier is a good method of working, there are other methods of achieving the same end in 3ds max 7, including 3D Boolean operations in which you subtract 3D primitives from 3D primitives. However, the 3D Boolean operations in 3ds max 7 use large amounts of computer

tip

In Exercise 3.3, you used the Attach function to create a compound shape so that you could trim the shapes. If you have two or more shapes that you do not want to attach to a single compound shape but still want to trim splines, first select the shapes and then apply a Trim/Extend modifier to the selection.

resources, are more difficult to edit, and are prone to failure. The point here, and throughout this book, is for you to learn the concepts and tools available to you and apply them in a fashion that works best for your situation.

Bezier Curves and Tangency

In the previous exercises, you worked with rectangular shapes and splines that had no noticeable curvature. However, 2D shapes have tangency information stored in the vertices and segments by default, and it is often very helpful to adjust the tangency to get the curvature you want.

Fundamental curvature types are assigned to both vertices and segments. Vertices can have the following tangency:

- **Corner.** Straight incoming and outgoing tangency with no curvature.
- **Smooth.** Least squares, a mathematical formula for curvature based on the distance and direction to the next vertex. These have no adjustments.
- **Bezier.** Curved tangency with incoming and outgoing adjustment handles opposing each other.
- **Bezier Corner.** Curved tangency with independently adjustable handles for incoming and outgoing tangency.

Segments have these tangencies:

- **Linear.** No curvature at either end vertex.
- **Curve.** Curvature at either end vertex, adjustable at the vertex level.

The tangency type of a vertex or segment can be changed by selecting the appropriate sub-object mode and right-clicking in a viewport to choose a new type from the Quad menu.

The next exercise involves opening a file that contains a flat plane with a material applied that is an image of the cross section of an airplane wing. The scene also has a rectangle that was created to fit the cross section. In this exercise, you'll edit the rectangle at the sub-object level by moving vertices and tangency handles to fit the curvature. This shape will be used in Chapter 5 again when you loft the 3D wing.

In Chapter 7, *The Editable Poly: Box Modeling*, you'll learn to create and apply a material used for tracing that is similar to the method used for this exercise.

Exercise 3.4: Adjusting Vertex Tangency

1. Open a file from the CD-ROM called **Ch03_wingshape01.max.** Save it to your project folder with the name *Ch03_wingshape02.max*. You can do this by choosing File > Save As and then clicking the plus sign in the dialog box. In the shaded Top and Perspective viewports, you'll see a white-wing image on a black background that has been applied to a plane 3D primitive. The Show Map in Viewport option has been enabled in the Material Editor to allow you to see the image in the viewports. A rectangle has been placed to fit the extremes of the wing cross section.

2. Click the Select Object button on the main toolbar and select the rectangle. On the Modify panel, rename *Rectangle01* to *wing_profile*. Right-click in the Top viewport and on the Quad menu choose Convert To > Convert To Editable Spline (**Figure 3.25**).

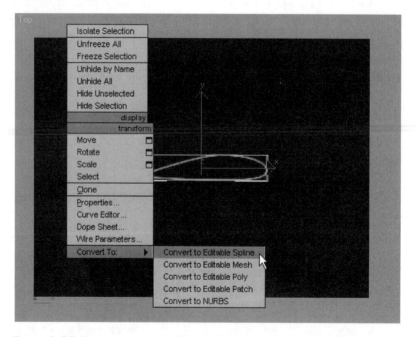

FIGURE 3.25 *You can convert a 2D primitive shape to an editable spline by selecting and right-clicking, and then choosing from the Quad menus. This enables sub-object editing.*

3. On the Modify panel in Stack view, expand Editable Spline by clicking on the
    plus sign to the left. Then select Vertex sub-object mode. Press the keyboard
    shortcut Alt + W to toggle the Maximize viewport option. You can use the
    mouse wheel to zoom in and fill the viewport with the rectangle. Click the
    Select and Move button on the main toolbar and select the upper-right vertex
    of the rectangle. A Transform gizmo appears, which helps restrict the transfor-
    mation in specific axes. Position the cursor near the base of the Transform
    gizmo and click and drag on the edge of the yellow-shaded square that appears.
    This allows you to move in either X or Y axis. Move the red vertex onto the
    white-wing image, similar to **Figure 3.26**.

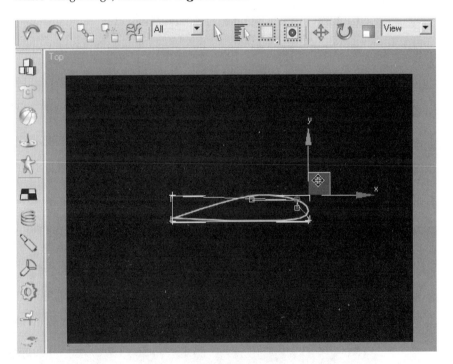

FIGURE 3.26 *Select the upper-right vertex, click the Select and Move transform button
on the main toolbar, and use the Transform gizmo to move the vertex into position on
the white line.*

4. Next use the Select and Move tool to adjust the tangency by moving the green handles to define the curvature at that point in the image (**Figure 3.27**).

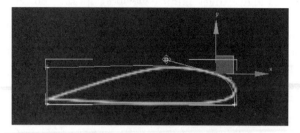

FIGURE 3.27 *Use the Select and Move transform button to adjust the tangency handles to fit the curve.*

5. Press the *X* key to toggle the Transform gizmo off. If you don't do this, it's difficult to freely move a vertex or handle that is directly below the Transform gizmo's restrict arrows for the *X* or *Y* axis. Move the lower-right vertex onto the image and adjust the curvature to fit, similar to **Figure 3.28**. The closer the Bezier handles are to the vertex, the less pronounced the curvature near the vertex will be.

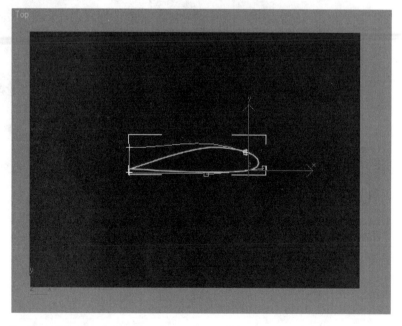

FIGURE 3.28 *Toggle the Transform gizmo off by pressing the X key and adjust the lower-right vertex into place.*

6. Move the upper-left vertex into place and adjust it for proper curvature (**Figure 3.29**). Notice the tangency handles are lying nearly on the curve where the tangency is flat.

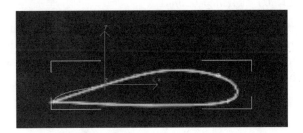

FIGURE 3.29 *Move and adjust the upper-left vertex onto the image. (The wing image appears fuzzy because of the way the graphics cards show maps in viewports.)*

7. Select the lower-left vertex in the Top viewport and move it to the point at the left of the image. Right-click in the viewport and choose the Corner tangency type from the Quad menu (**Figure 3.30**). This removes all incoming and outgoing curvature from that vertex to ensure the shape comes to a sharp point.

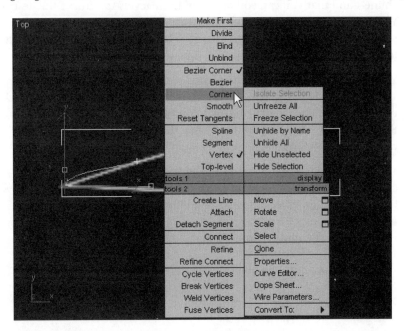

FIGURE 3.30 *Move the lower-left vertex into place, right-click in the Top viewport, and choose Corner from the Quad menu. The shape now comes to a sharp point with no curvature on the left.*

8. Make any final adjustments to the vertices and tangency to make the image appear the way you want. On the Modify panel, Stack view, choose Editable Spline mode in the stack to exit sub-object mode. Save the file; it should already be called *Ch03_wingshape02.max*.

Working at sub-object levels to adjust the tangency at vertices is a common and useful workflow in 3ds max 7. Practice on simple shapes at first until you develop a feel for the relationships of the different types of tangencies, and you'll increase your productivity in your projects.

Summary

This chapter introduced the methods of working with 2D shapes—important fundamental objects in 3ds max 7 that set the stage for creating complex 3D objects. You learned about creating and editing parametric 2D shapes, such as circles and rectangles, and the importance of assigning logical names at the time of creation to avoid confusion later, especially in a collaborative work environment.

You also learned that 2D shapes are composed of sub-objects—Vertex, Segment, and Spline—and that you can edit at any of these levels to achieve the desired end result. You practiced adjusting vertex tangency to change the curvature of the segment coming into or going out of the specific vertex and selecting multiple vertices for manipulation.

You learned about the concept of compound shapes—shapes containing two or more splines—and demonstrated in exercises that closed splines within closed splines can be turned into a 3D objects by applying modifiers that have holes running through them. You also learned that the 2D shapes can still easily be edited to change the 3D object.

You learned how modifiers and the Modifier stack let you move up and down the creation history of an object to make changes at any level without adversely affecting the levels above or below. The ability to navigate within the Modifier stack is undoubtedly one of the most powerful functions in 3ds max 7 and is a technique that you will encounter throughout this book.

CHAPTER 4

Modifiers: Stack Them High

In This Chapter

In the last chapter, you learned about some of the tools available for working with 2D shapes, and you applied some basic modifiers to create 3D mesh objects. In this chapter, you'll learn more about the Modifier stack and other useful modifiers, such as the Lattice modifier, as you create an airport control tower like the one in **Figure 4.1** on the next page. Again, everything will begin as a simple 2D shape, which allows for flexible editing on many levels.

You might think of this chapter as a design exercise in which you experiment with techniques that produce results you may or may not want to retain. You'll learn to use the Hold/Fetch commands to create a "bookmark" so that you can return to a certain state in editing anytime you decide the experiments are not working. The file saved with the Hold command is above and beyond the files that you save with the Save or Save As commands and is one of the safety net features, along with automatic backup files, that help increase productivity.

Chapter 2 presented the concept of using Modifier parameters to clone objects for easier editing. In this chapter, you'll put that concept into practice by working through a simple cloning exercise using modifiers that let you edit all cloned objects by changing the parameters of any one of the clones.

FIGURE 4.1 *You'll create an easily edited airport control tower using just three simple 2D shapes.*

The creation of space-frame structures can be a daunting task to the new user of 3ds max 7. However, the Lattice modifier is designed to simplify the creation of a variety of space-frame-type objects, from radio towers, web beams, and construction staging, to wire baskets and shelving. You'll also learn to manipulate the edges of 3D objects to control the exact layout of the framework created using the Lattice modifier.

3ds max 7 has a new modifier called *Edit Poly*, which provides the functionality of the Editable Poly object type within the Modifier stack for more flexible editing choices.

You will also learn to use the Taper and Bevel Profile modifiers to change or create objects. As with any methods in 3ds max 7, more than one approach can be used to create and modify objects, but your focus should be on the underlying concepts of the exercises more than the end results.

This chapter covers the following topics:

- **Taper modifier.** Applies a taper to objects with controls for amount, taper axis, and center position.

- **Lattice modifier.** Lets you create space-frame or open-webbing structures from the visible edges of 3D objects.

- **Edge sub-object-level editing.** Edges, or the connections between vertices in 3D objects, have parameters such as visibility and direction, which can give you greater control over the surface.

- **Hold/Fetch commands.** Saving a copy of your scene to a file at any given point in time using the Hold command and then retrieving it using a Fetch command lets you experiment safely.

- **Bevel Profile modifier.** With two 2D shapes, a base and a profile, you can create complex 3D objects that are easily edited by adjusting the shapes.

- **Edit Poly modifier.** This new modifier in 3ds max 7 allows all the Editable Poly commands and controls to be placed in the Modifier stack.

Key Terms

- **Instance clone.** A clone method for objects or modifiers that contains a two-way link for modifications. Modify either the original or the clone, and they are both modified.

- **Bounding Box.** Used in this chapter for alignment purposes, the bounding box of an object represents the extremes of the object in space.

Getting Started

The next five exercises walk you through a variety of steps, some of which are directly related to building a control tower, and others that illustrate a concept or technique that produces results you will later discard. You'll use the control tower again in Chapter 11, *Photometric Lights: Bouncing Basics*, and Chapter 14, *Mapping Coordinates: Getting the Right Fit*. It will be placed in your airport scene.

Focus on two major themes as you perform the exercises: efficiency and flexibility. Always strive for models with the lowest polygon count that satisfies your requirements in the scene, but leave the door open so that you can perform flexible editing when the need for design changes arises.

And remember, the biggest drag on production by far in many offices is unnecessary detail in modeling. Objects that are hidden from view should be eliminated, and objects in the distance should contain only a level of detail that makes them convincing to the viewer from that distance.

Experimenting with Modifiers

Sometimes when you're designing a scene, you'll want to perform some steps that could produce results you won't want to keep. You can always save your file before-hand, or use Save As to repeatedly create incrementally numbered copies. The latter is generally good practice at regular intervals. However, there are times when you might want to make a few changes but be able to abandon the process without com-mitting to the saved copies.

3ds max 7 provides two tools for this purpose: Hold and Fetch. Both are found in the Edit pull-down menu. Hold saves the entire scene in a buffer file on your hard drive. The file isn't directly accessible, but you can retrieve it at any time using the Fetch command. The Hold file contains only the most recently held information: Whenever you select Hold, all the information in the buffer file is discarded and replaced with the current scene information. The information saved with Hold is available even after you have exited 3ds max 7 or shut the machine down. You can use the Fetch command as many times as you like without altering the stored infor-mation.

In addition to learning how to create a buffer file of your current scene, the follow-ing exercise will hopefully expand your knowledge of sub-object-level editing by investigating some of the sub-object functionality of modifiers—in this case, the Center sub-object of the Taper modifier.

Exercise 4.1: Editing at the Sub-Object Level and Creating Buffer Files

1. From the CD-ROM, open a file called **Ch04_tower01.max**. Choose File > Save As, point to your project folder, and click the plus sign in the dialog to save the file using the name *Ch04_tower02.max*. The scene contains a 2D shape named *tower_profile* that you will use in Exercise 4.4. Right-click in the Top viewport to activate it.

2. In the Shapes category of the Create panel, click the Rectangle button and drag a rectangle primitive of any size around the 0,0,0 World coordinates, as indicated by the black grid lines in the viewport.

tip

It's possible to change the parameters of an object on the Create panel as you create the object, but to avoid confu-sion I recommend getting into the habit of switching to the Modify panel to make any changes.

3. Click on the Modify panel tab and rename the shape *Tower01*. Then in the Parameters rollout located at the bottom of the panel, enter *36* in both the Length and Width fields, pressing Enter to finalize the process (**Figure 4.2**). Again, you do not need to enter any sign after the number if the value you intend is expressed in feet.

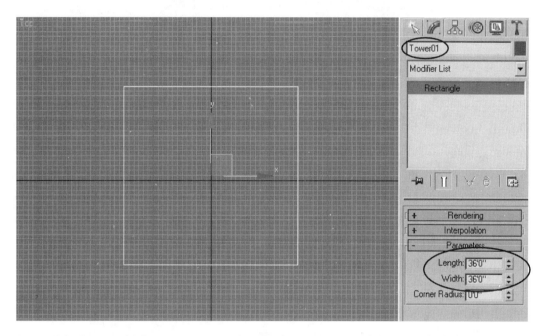

FIGURE 4.2 *Create a 36-foot square rectangle named* Tower01 *around the 0,0,0 World coordinate.*

4. On the Modify panel, choose Extrude from the Modifier List. In the Parameters rollout, enter *60* in the Amount field for a height of 60 feet, and enter *6* in the Segments field and press Enter to add six segments along the height of the box (see **Figure 4.3** on the next page). In the Parameters rollout, clear the Cap Start and Cap End checkboxes, which open the ends of the box so that you can see through to the other side in the shaded Perspective viewport. For our purposes, the ends create unnecessary geometry. You can return to the Extrude level in the Modifier List at any time and enable the caps if you decide you need them. Even minor optimizations like this improve productivity, so get into the habit of reducing geometry as you model, while leaving yourself an easy way out, if possible. Click Zoom Extents All to see all objects in all viewports.

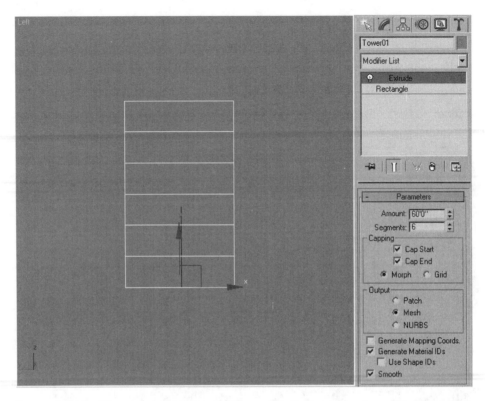

Figure 4.3 *To create a segmented box that represents the tower, apply an Extrude modifier set to 60 feet using six segments.*

5. In the Modifier List, choose Taper. In the Parameters rollout, enter *-0.5* and press Enter. This makes the box 50 percent smaller at the top with straight sides (**Figure 4.4**). At this point, you'll want to experiment with the Taper modifier to see if there is a tower design that you or the client prefer. In the Edit menu on the Main menu at the top left of the display, click Hold. This stores everything in the current scene in a buffer file on your hard drive so that you can retrieve it using the Fetch command later if necessary.

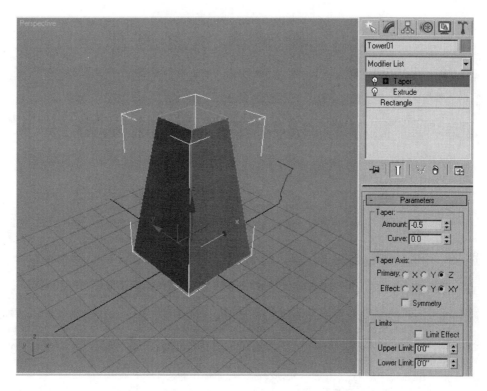

FIGURE 4.4 *Apply a Taper modifier set to -0.5 to make the box half the size at the top.*

6. Enter *-0.5* in the Curve field to curve the tapered sides inward. In Stack view, click the plus sign located at the left of Taper to expose the sub-object levels of the Taper modifier. Highlight Center. The Select and Move tool is activated automatically. In the Front viewport, click the *Y*-axis restrict arrow and move the yellow center tick near the top of the box. This tapers from the top downward. In the Taper Axis section of the Parameters rollout, select the *Y* radio button for the Effect control. The taper is only in the *Y* axis now (see **Figure 4.5** on the next page).

You can highlight text or values in any field and right-click the mouse to cut or copy the text. You can then right-click in another field to paste the information there.

You can right-click on the spinners to the right of any numeric field to reset the value to either *0* or its lowest setting.

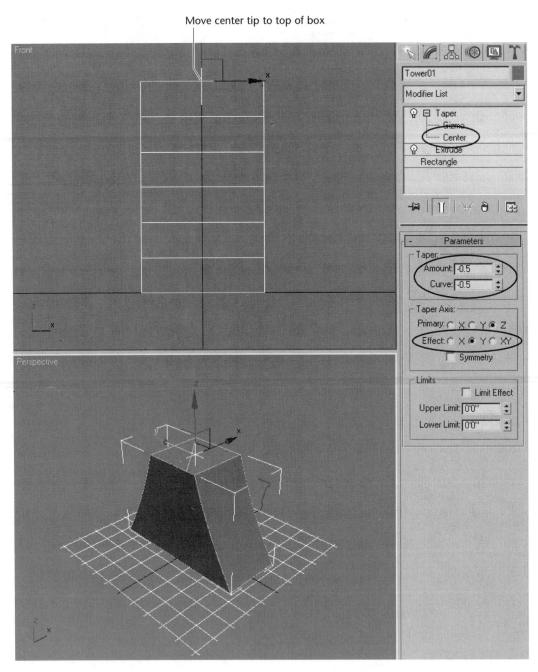

FIGURE 4.5 *Using the Taper modifier, you can change the position of the center in sub-object-level mode, adjust the curvature of the sides, and change the affected axis.*

7. Say you decide at this point that the changes you've made since the Hold operation in Step 5 are not what you want. From the Edit pull-down menu, click Fetch. You will be prompted in a dialog that you are about to Fetch information stored in the buffer file and that you must click Yes to retrieve your scene or click No to continue working. Click Yes. Select the Tower01 object, and you'll see that everything has been returned to the state just before you started to experiment.

8. Save the file; it should already be named *Ch04_tower02.max*.

You have again applied multiple modifiers to a 2D shape and adjusted the modifiers at the sub-object level to easily create complex 3D geometry. You have also learned to use Hold and Fetch commands to save a buffer file and use it as a bookmark for returning to the state of the scene prior to your experimenting.

Exercise 4.2: Using and Cloning the Lattice Modifier

1. Open file **Ch04_tower02.max** from the last exercise or from the CD-ROM. Save it with the name *Ch04_tower03.max*. In the Perspective viewport, select Tower01. The final tower will not be a solid box like the one you see in this file, but will be edited to become a space frame of struts and braces.

tip

There is nothing more disappointing than losing your work after investing hours in creating and editing it. So get into the habit of saving your files often when working at stretches of more than 10 or 15 minutes. The keyboard shortcut that will overwrite the current file on the hard disk with the latest information is Ctrl + S. You might also get into the habit of choosing File > Save As to perform incremental saves periodically.

tip

If you want to be able to create a new incremental file using Ctrl + S, choose Customize > Preferences, and then on the Files tab in the File Handling section, select the Increment on Save option.

There are also adjustments for the Auto Backup feature in the Files Preference Settings dialog that are enabled by default. At 5-minute intervals, a file named *AutoBak1*, *AutoBak2*, or *AutoBak3* is saved in the \3ds max 7\autobak folder. Then the first file is overwritten at 20 minutes, and so on. These files may be renamed and recovered in the event your files are lost or corrupted. Be safe or be sorry.

2. From the Modifier List on the Modify panel, choose Lattice. The Lattice modifier creates struts from the visible edges of a 3D object and joints from the vertices. If you zoom in close to the base of the tower, you can see the four-sided struts and tetra joints of the Tower01 object (**Figure 4.6**).

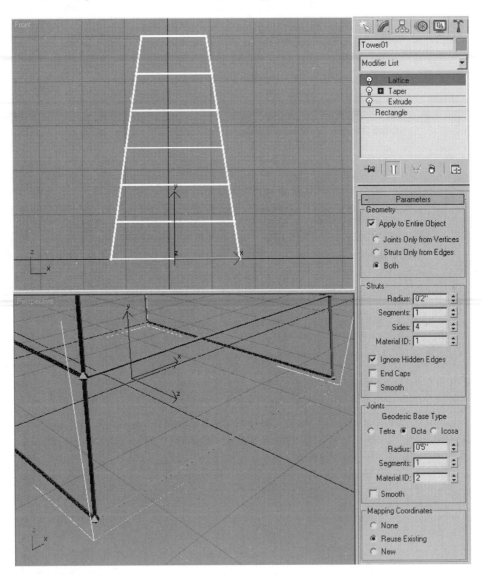

FIGURE 4.6 *The Lattice modifier uses visible edges and vertices of a 3D object to create a space frame.*

3. Zoom back out in the Perspective viewport to see the entire tower and, in Stack view, toggle the Light Bulb icon to the left of the Taper modifier (**Figure 4.7**). This disables the Taper modifier (or any modifier in the stack if you toggle the Light Bulb icon beside it) without affecting its settings, which is handy when you want to accentuate the effects of other modifiers in complex stacks or if you need to reverse-engineer someone else's modeling techniques. Make sure to toggle Taper back on when you are finished.

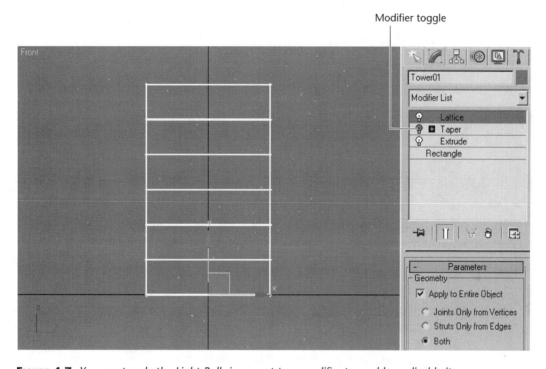

FIGURE 4.7 *You can toggle the Light Bulb icon next to a modifier to enable or disable it.*

4. On the Create panel, Geometry category, click the GeoSphere button. In the Perspective viewport, click and drag near the tower to create a geosphere with a radius of around 20 feet. The position is not important.

5. In the main toolbar, click the Select button. In the Perspective viewport, select Tower01, click on the Modifier panel tab, and in Modifier Stack view, highlight Lattice. Then right-click Lattice and choose Copy from the menu (**Figure 4.8**). This copies the modifier with its settings to a buffer.

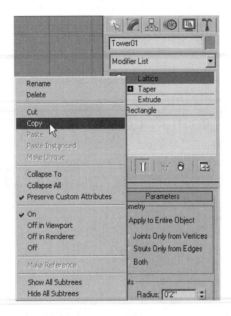

FIGURE 4.8 *You can copy or cut modifiers to a buffer by right-clicking on the highlighted modifier in the stack.*

6. Select the geosphere. In Stack view, right-click on Geosphere and choose Paste Instanced. This applies a Lattice modifier on the sphere with a two-way connection to the original: Change one, and the other will change. Notice that the modifier name (Lattice) in the stack is in italics, indicating it is an Instance clone of at least one other Lattice modifier in the scene. In the Parameters roll-out, select the Struts Only From Edges radio button to discard the joints. Increase the Struts Radius to *6"* (you need to use the inch sign) and the Sides to *6*. Both objects in the scene change (**Figure 4.9**).

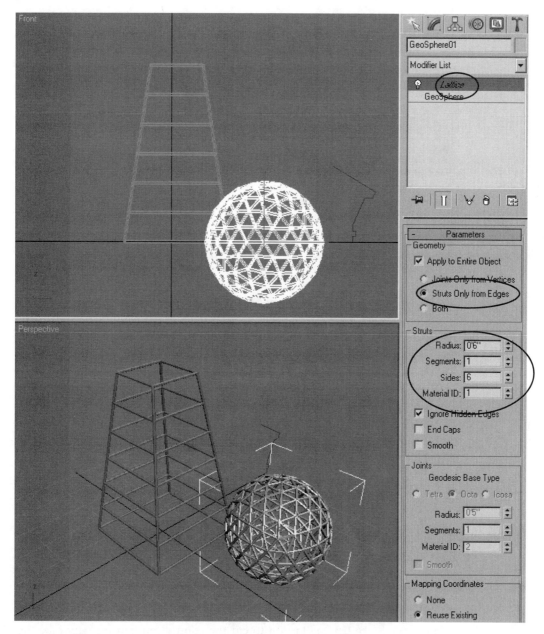

Figure 4.9 *Changing the values for one instanced modifier affects all instances.*

7. With the geosphere selected and the Lattice modifier highlighted in Stack view, click the Make Unique button just below Stack view (**Figure 4.10**). Lattice is no longer in italics in Stack view and any changes you make affect only this Lattice modifier. The connection between this modifier and all other instances has been broken.

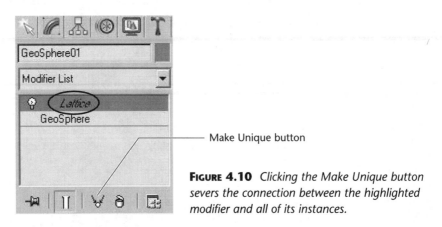

Make Unique button

FIGURE 4.10 *Clicking the Make Unique button severs the connection between the highlighted modifier and all of its instances.*

8. Click the Remove Modifier from the Stack button, located just to the right of the Make Unique button. This discards the highlighted modifier or modifiers.

9. Press the Delete key to delete the geosphere— it was only in the scene as an example of instanced modifiers. Select Tower01. Save the file; it should already be named *Ch04_tower03.max*.

Once you have applied a modifier to an object and changed the settings, subsequent applications of the modifier will have the same settings until you change them again.

Instanced modifiers can simplify the editing of many similar objects, but any modifier can always be made unique if the parameters for that object must be different from the others.

Modifiers may be copied or cut from the stack and then pasted to other locations in the stack or onto other objects in the scene as instanced modifiers or plain copies with no connection. The modifier name becomes italicized in the Stack view when it has an instanced clone associated with it to help keep track of the type of modifier.

You can use the Make Unique button to cut the connection between any modifier and its clones if you need to adjust the modifier independently.

Sub-Object-Level Editing

It would be great to have more control over the Lattice modifier, wouldn't it? Well, you do, but it's not within the Lattice modifier itself. Rather, it's in the way the modifier works—creating struts from visible edges of the 3D object.

At the Edge sub-object level of Editable Mesh objects or using the Edit Mesh modifier, you can edit edges to control what the Lattice modifier is using.

In the next exercise, you will drop below the Lattice modifier in the stack to the Taper modifier and add an Edit Mesh modifier. At the Edge sub-object level, you'll learn to make edges visible or invisible and to turn and divide edges.

Exercise 4.3: Using the Edge Sub-Object Level for Lattice Control

1. Open **Ch04_tower03.max** from your project folder or from the CD-ROM. Save it to your project folder as *Ch04_tower04.max*. It contains the Tower01 space frame object and a 2D shape. Select Tower01. On the Modify panel, Stack view, highlight the Taper modifier. You will insert a new Edit Mesh modifier between Taper and Lattice. In the Modifier List, choose Edit Mesh modifier. The tower turns to a tapered box with no end caps and no lattice. This is because the Show End Result toggle button, located just below Stack view, is turned off (**Figure 4.11**). Toggle it on by clicking it, and you will see the end result of all modifiers, not just to the level you have highlighted. Toggle the Show End Result button back off again.

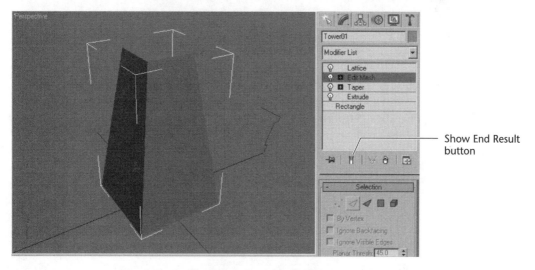

FIGURE 4.11 *Inserting an Edit Mesh modifier underneath the Lattice modifier lets you control the mesh edges and pass that information up the stack to the Lattice modifier.*

2. Next you need to perform two steps to make the edges of Tower01 visible. With the object selected, right-click the Perspective viewport label. Choose Edged Faces to view the visible edges and the shaded object (**Figure 4.12**).

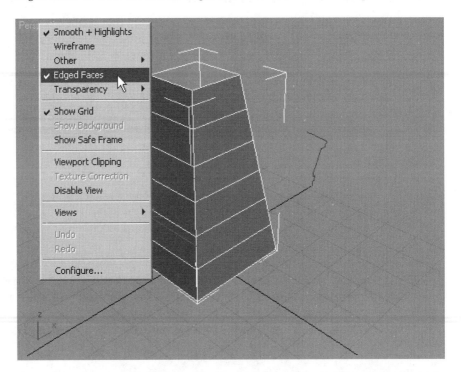

FIGURE 4.12 *Enabling Edged Faces by right-clicking the viewport label lets you see the visible edges and the shaded object in that viewport.*

3. Right-click in the Perspective viewport and choose Properties from the Quad menu. In the Object Properties dialog, Display Properties area, clear the Edges Only checkbox (**Figure 4.13**). Click OK. This lets you see the dotted invisible edges of the mesh so that you can access them for editing.

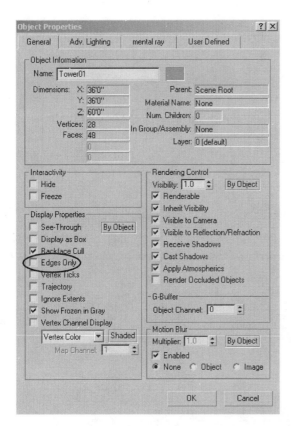

FIGURE 4.13 *Clearing the Edges Only checkbox in the Object Properties dialog lets you see invisible edges as dotted lines in the viewports.*

4. On the Modifier panel in Stack view, expand the Edit Mesh modifier and highlight the Edge sub-object level. Drag a selection window around the entire Tower01 to select all edges. They will turn red. In the Surface Properties rollout at the bottom of the Modify panel, click the Visible button. This makes all edges solid red lines in the viewport. Toggle the Show End Result button and you will see the tower now has diagonal bracing (see **Figure 4.14** on the next page). Toggle Show End Result off. Click on any empty space in the Perspective viewport to deselect all edges. The Visible and Invisible buttons operate on all selected edges.

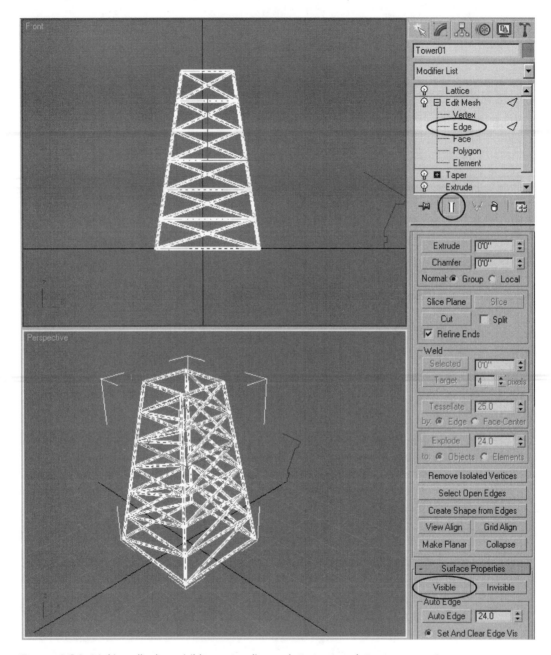

FIGURE 4.14 *Making all edges visible creates diagonal struts at each tower segment.*

5. In the Selection rollout, select Ignore Backfacing. This keeps you from inadvertently picking edges on the back side of the mesh that you cannot see. In the Edit Geometry rollout, click the Turn button. Starting from the top down, click every other diagonal edge to turn it in the polygon for the two sides of the mesh that you can see in the viewport (**Figure 4.15**). The Turn tool only works on the edge you pick after clicking the Turn button.

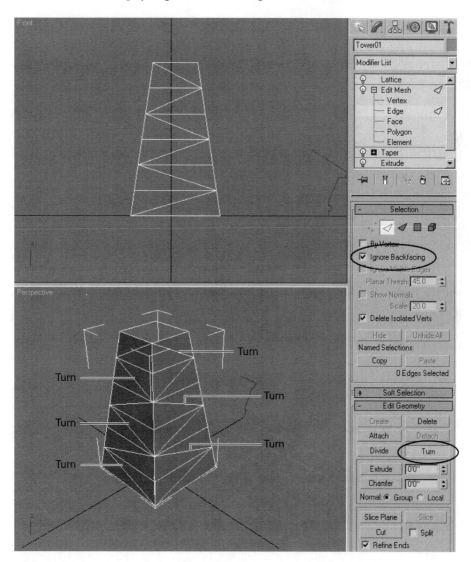

FIGURE 4.15 *By enabling Ignore Backfacing, you can select only the edges you can see to turn them one at a time.*

6. In the Edit Geometry rollout, click the Divide button and, in the third segment up from the bottom on each side that you can see, pick near the midpoint of the diagonals (**Figure 4.16**). This divides the edge at the point you pick and adds new invisible edges. Click the Select button in the main toolbar, hold the Ctrl key and pick each of the four new edges to make a selection set. In the Surface Properties rollout, click Visible to make the edges visible.

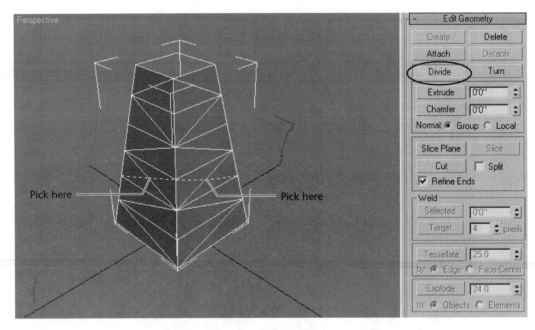

FIGURE 4.16 *The Divide button lets you pick an edge to create two new invisible edges and divide the existing edge in two.*

7. Right-click the Perspective label viewport and disable Edged Faces. On the Modifier panel, Stack view, highlight Edit Mesh to exit the Edge sub-object level, and then highlight Lattice to return to the top of the stack. Your tower now has diagonal bracing on two sides to keep it rigid (**Figure 4.17**).

caution

It is important to exit the sub-object level before returning to the top of the Modifier stack unless you intend for the modifiers to operate only on the sub-object selection set.

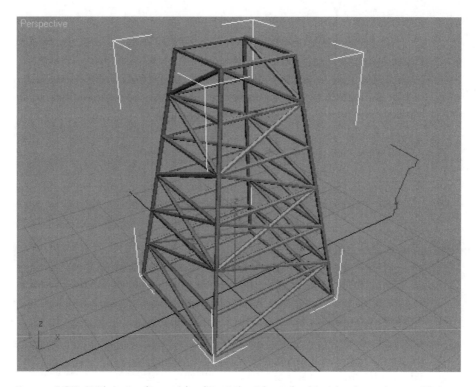

FIGURE 4.17 *With just a few quick edits at the Edge sub-object level, you have added diagonal bracing to your tower.*

8. Save the file; it should already be called *Ch04_tower04.max.*

You have learned that you can control exactly what your Lattice modifier space frame looks like by using Edge sub-object-level editing with the Edit Mesh modifier or with an Editable Mesh object. With an understanding that the Lattice modifier operates on vertices and visible edges of 3D objects, you have great flexibility in creating space frame objects of all types.

A few things to keep in mind:

- The Lattice objects look fine from a moderate distance, but under close scrutiny the intersections of struts and joints do not look as refined.
- Using the Lattice modifier to create joints from object vertices can quickly increase the face count of your object, so this option can be unproductive. Make sure you need the joints when leaving this option on.
- Deselecting Cast Shadows in the Properties dialog for the Lattice object can increase efficiency when shadows are not needed.

Take the time to edit your tower for the strut layout that you find effective. As with all the lessons in this book, practicing a little at a basic level will make it easier to use the same tools and techniques in your daily work.

High-Profile Modeling

You have a tower structure for your airport, but you also need a control room at the top of the tower to complete the model. In the next two exercises, located in this section and the next, you'll learn different skill sets to expand your repertoire of modeling techniques as you create a control room.

The first exercise utilizes a modifier called *Bevel Profile*, which requires two 2D shapes—a base shape you'll create, and a profile shape that is already in the scene.

The Bevel Profile modifier works similarly to the Extrude modifier, but rather than simply extruding straight in the *Z* axis, it uses a 2D shape to define the extrusion.

In the second exercise, you'll apply a modifier that's new to 3ds max 7—the Edit Poly modifier. It is similar to the Edit Mesh modifier in that it gives you access to sub-object-level editing, but it defines the 3D Poly object as being created primarily of quad polygons rather than the triangular faces produced using Edit Mesh. This, in turn, offers a powerful new toolset for modifying the 3D object.

note

As mentioned earlier in this chapter, previous versions of 3ds max have included an Editable Poly object with many of the same controls as the new Edit Poly modifier. The inclusion of the tools in the form of a modifier that may be placed anywhere in the Modifier Stack and may be removed or disabled adds a lot more flexibility to your workflow.

Exercise 4.4: Creating the Exterior of the Control Room

1. Open the file called **Ch04_tower04.max** from your project folder or from the CD-ROM. Save it to your project folder with the name *Ch04_tower05.max*. In the Perspective viewport, select Tower01, right-click and, in the Quad menu, choose Hide Selection to hide the tower (**Figure 4.18**).

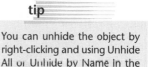

tip

You can unhide the object by right-clicking and using Unhide All or Unhide by Name in the same Quad menu or through the Display panel.

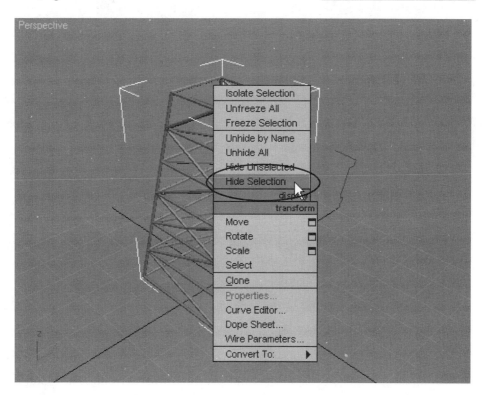

FIGURE 4.18 *You can hide selected objects by right-clicking in the viewport and clicking Hide Selection from the Quad menu.*

2. Right-click in the Top viewport to activate it. In the Shapes category of the Create panel, click the NGon button in the Object Type rollout. In the Top viewport, click and drag an NGon of any size. On the Modify panel, rename the object *Tower_building01*. In the Parameters rollout, enter *16* in the Radius field and press Enter. Select the Circumscribed radio button and enter *8* in the Sides field. The eight-sided polygon is created with the midpoint of each segment being 16 feet from the center of the shape (**Figure 4.19**).

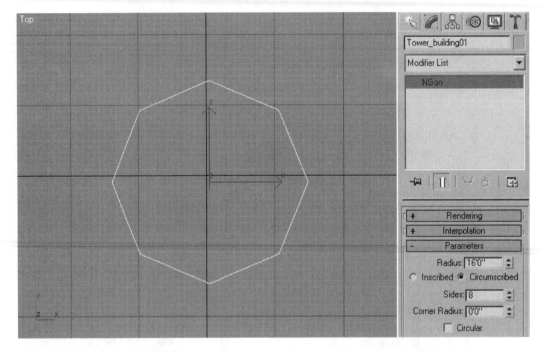

FIGURE 4.19 *Create an eight-sided polygon that is 16 feet from the segment midpoint to the center of the shape.*

3. On the Modify panel, Modifier List, choose Bevel Profile. The NGon will turn into a flat surface with no thickness. In the Parameters rollout, click the Pick Profile button. Press *H* to display the Pick Object dialog (**Figure 4.20**). Double-click tower_profile in the dialog. This extrudes and bevels the NGon in the shape of the profile to create an eight-sided control tower (**Figure 4.21**).

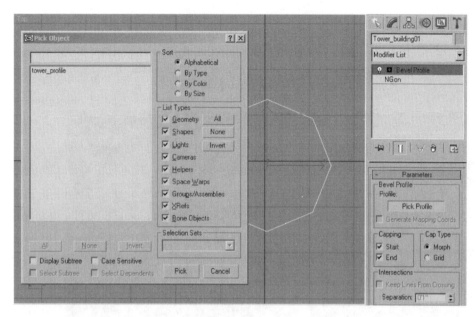

FIGURE 4.20 *When using the Bevel Profile modifier, pressing the H key when you're prompted to pick a profile lets you choose valid shapes from the Pick Objects dialog. This method of choosing shapes can be easier than trying to locate the shape in the viewports, but just how easy it is depends on how consistent your naming conventions are.*

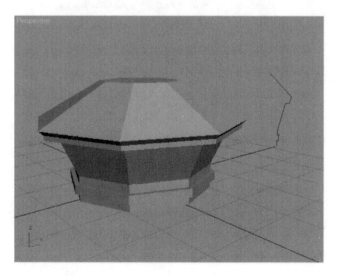

FIGURE 4.21 *A complex 3D object is created from two simple 2D shapes using the Bevel Profile modifier.*

4. Right-click in the Front viewport to activate it and select the tower_profile shape. In Stack view on the Modify panel, highlight the Vertex sub-object level. In the Front viewport, make sure the top-left end vertex of the shape is selected and red. Right-click in the viewport and click the Transform Type-In button next to Move in the Quad menu (**Figure 4.22**).

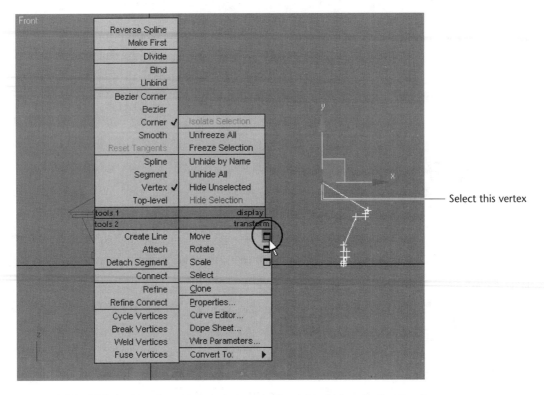

FIGURE 4.22 *Click the Transform Type-In button to the right of Move in the Quad menu.*

5. In the Move Transform Type-In dialog, enter *-2* in the *X* field of the Offset:Screen area and press Enter (**Figure 4.23**). The vertex will move left (negative amount) in the *X* axis of the Screen reference coordinate system, and the number will revert back to *0'0"*. Close the dialog. The 3D object's roof is a lower pitch than it was before, and the flat at the top is 4 feet smaller than it was previously.

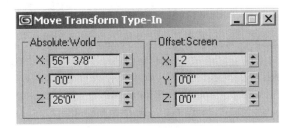

FIGURE 4.23 *By adjusting the 2D shape, you can edit the 3D object that uses the shape to define the profile.*

6. On the Modify panel, Modifier Stack, highlight Line to exit the sub-object level. Again, remembering to exit the sub-object level is a very important step. If you forget to do this, you can end up making unwanted changes to the profile, and it is impossible to select other objects in the scene when you are in any sub-object level.

7. Save the file; it should already be called *Ch04_tower05.max.*

You have created and edited another complex 3D object by modifying simple 2D shapes.

Practice creating objects you find around your desk or in the room you are working in using the Bevel Profile modifier. You'll be surprised by the power and flexibility that Bevel Profile provides.

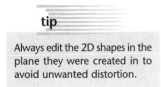

tip

Always edit the 2D shapes in the plane they were created in to avoid unwanted distortion.

The Edit Poly Modifier

Having the functionality of the Editable Poly object from previous versions of 3ds max in the form of a modifier—the Edit Poly modifier in 3ds max 7—can increase your productivity by providing you a more versatile tool.

In the next exercise, you'll first apply an Edit Poly modifier to Tower_building01 to create a parapet on the flat area of the roof. You will then add another Edit Poly modifier to create window frames and windows. Unfortunately, adding two Edit Poly modifiers results in a much larger memory footprint because each Edit Poly modifier must store a copy of the object. However, the advantages of being able to edit the windows independently from the roof may outweigh the potential performance degradation. You will learn through experience based on your workflow whether it makes sense for you to keep the editing separate or not.

The Edit Poly modifier also lets you use the Settings dialogs to try different settings before committing the changes to the model.

Exercise 4.5: Using Edit Poly Modifiers to Refine the Control Room

1. Open the file called **Ch04_tower05.max** from your project folder or from the CD-ROM. Save the file as *Ch04_tower06.max*. Make sure Tower_building01 is selected in the Perspective viewport. On the Modify panel, Modifier List, choose Edit Poly. In Stack view, expand Edit Poly. Notice the sub-object levels are different from the Edit Mesh modifiers. A Border sub-object level is visible in the Edit Poly modifier instead of the triangular Face sub-object level in the Edit Mesh modifier.

2. In Stack view, highlight the Polygon sub-object level. In the Perspective viewport, select the uppermost octagon-shaped polygon at the top of the roof. In the Edit Polygons rollout on the Modify panel, click the Settings button to the right of the Extrude button. In the Extrude Polygons dialog, enter 5 in the Extrusion Height field and press Enter. The octagon polygon is moved 5 feet in the local positive Z axis, and new polygons have been created at the sides (**Figure 4.24**). Once you have the setting the way you want it, click the OK button to finalize the operation.

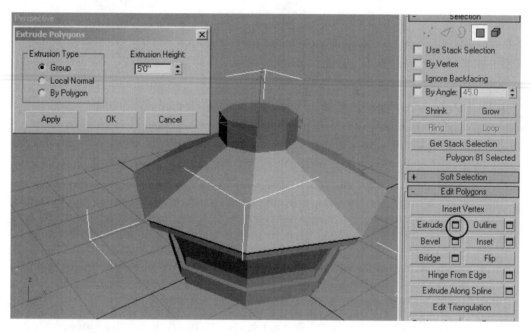

FIGURE 4.24 *The Settings dialog of the Edit Polygon modifier lets you see the result of your edits before committing them to the model.*

3. With the octagon polygon still selected, click the Inset Settings button in the Edit Polygons rollout. In the Inset Polygons dialog, enter *1* in the Inset Amount field and press Enter. This reduces the size of the selected polygon in its own plane and creates new polygons. Click OK. Click the Settings button beside the Extrude button on the Modify panel again. Now enter *-3* in the Extrusion Height field of the Extrude Polygons dialog (**Figure 4.25**). Click OK. You now have a parapet for the octagon roof. Click on Edit Poly in Stack view to exit the sub-object level.

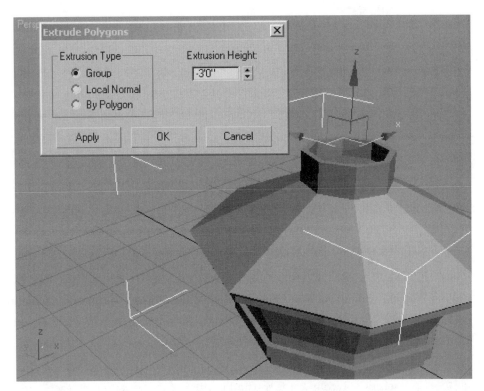

FIGURE 4.25 *Entering a negative amount in the Extrusion Height field extrudes the polygon inward.*

4. Right-click Edit Poly in Stack view and choose Rename in the menu. Click to the right of the Edit Poly name and change it to read *Edit Poly-parapet*. Renaming is a good habit to get into so that you and your coworkers have a better idea what each modifier does in the stack (**Figure 4.26**).

FIGURE 4.26 *You can rename modifiers in Stack view to clarify their function.*

5. On the Modify panel, choose Edit Poly in the Modifier List and rename it *Edit Poly-windows*. Expand the modifier and highlight the Polygon sub-object level. On the main toolbar, click the Select button and make sure the Window/Crossing Selection toggle (located to the left of the Select and Move button) is set to Crossing Selection mode. In the Front viewport, drag a narrow selection box through all the angled window polygons (**Figure 4.27**). When Crossing Selection mode is enabled, all polygons within or touching the selection window are selected.

6. In the Edit Polygons rollout, click the Inset Settings button. In the Inset Polygons dialog, enter *1* in the Inset Amount field and press Enter. This creates two new sets of polygons at the top and bottom of the selection set, each 1 foot wide. Click the By Polygon radio button and each polygon will be inset around its own center, creating a frame around each window (**Figure 4.28**). Click OK to accept the changes.

Team 4 Limited · Unit 10 Arlington Business Park · Whittle Way · Stevenage · Hertfordshire SG1 2BD
t. +44(0) 1438 722444 f. +44(0) 1438 722445 www.team4.co.uk

t4

TEAM 4

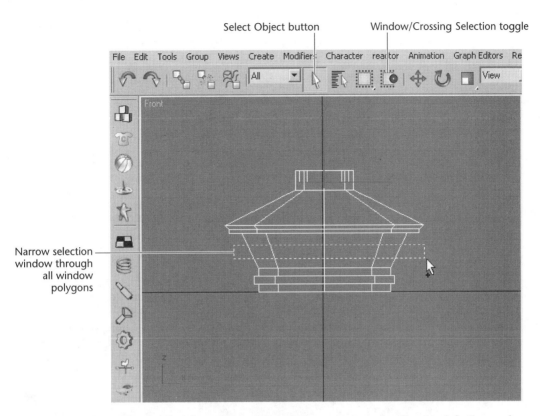

Select Object button   Window/Crossing Selection toggle

Narrow selection window through all window polygons

FIGURE 4.27 *Select all the angled window polygons using Crossing Selection mode.*

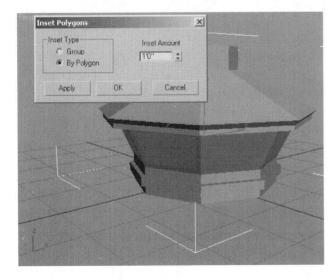

FIGURE 4.28 *Enabling By Polygon mode in the Inset Polygons dialog works on each selected polygon independently.*

7. In the Edit Polygons rollout, click the Settings button to the right of the Bevel button. *Enter -6″* in both the Height and Outline Amount fields in the Bevel Settings dialog (**Figure 4.29**). Make sure you enter inch marks (″) in both fields. Click OK. The windows are now beveled inward. Exit the sub-object level in Stack view. You can now use the Light Bulb icons to the left of each Edit Poly modifier to disable or enable the changes of each.

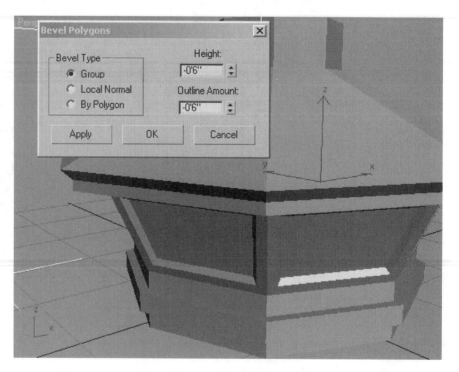

FIGURE 4.29 *Entering -6″ in the Height and Outline Amount fields creates windows in the frames.*

8. Right-click in the Top viewport and choose Unhide All in the Quad menu that appears. With Tower_building01 still selected, click the Align button on the main toolbar (you can find buttons by pausing the cursor over a button to see the tooltip) and pick the Tower01 object. In the Align Selection (Tower01) dialog, select X Position, Y Position, and Z Position. Select Center for Current Object and Target Object. The center of the bounding box of the current object, Tower_building01, will be aligned with the center of the bounding box of Tower01 (**Figure 4.30**).

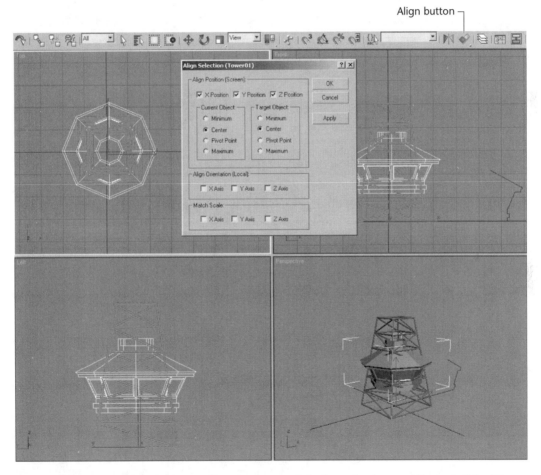

FIGURE 4.30 *Use the Align button to align the centers of the bounding boxes of Tower_building01 to Tower01.*

9. In the Align Selection (Tower01) dialog, click the Apply button. This clears the current settings and leaves the objects in the new alignment. In the dialog, select Z Position. In the Current Object area, select the Minimum radio button; in the Target Object area, select the Maximum radio button. This aligns the bottom of Tower_building01 to the top of Tower01 (**Figure 4.31**). Click OK to accept the alignment and close the dialog.

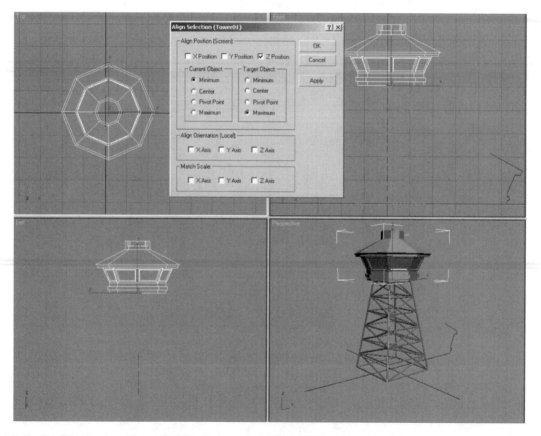

FIGURE 4.31 *To place Tower_building01 on top of Tower01, align the objects in the Z axis of the Top viewport Minimum (the extreme point of the bounding box in the negative axis)with the Maximum (the extreme point of the bounding box in the positive axis).*

10. Save the file. It should already be named *Ch04_tower06.max*. You now have two complex objects that are properly aligned, which you can easily edit at any time. You have named the Edit Poly modifiers in the Stack view to be more meaningful to you or your coworkers at a later date.

Use the lessons learned in this chapter to build some of your own models. Keep in mind that efficiency and flexibility are great advantages in your workflow. These fundamental techniques require a little pre-planning, and each situation will require slightly different planning, but with practice you can integrate these techniques into your daily workflow.

Summary

In this chapter, you learned how to do the following:

- Apply other modifiers to 3D objects or 2D shapes to create complex geometry.

- Change the parameters of simple modifiers, such as the Taper modifier applied to 3D objects, and the Bevel Profile modifier that uses pieces of 2D information to generate complex 3D objects that are easily editable and very efficient.

- Use the sub-object editing capabilities of 3D objects by manipulating both the direction and visibility to affect the result of a Lattice modifier higher in the Modifier stack.

- Use the Hold/Fetch buffer to safely store and retrieve your work, while experimenting with editing.

- Access the editable poly tools within the Modifier stack at various stages using the Edit Poly modifier.

CHAPTER 5

Lofting: Control Is Everything

In This Chapter

This chapter unlocks the secrets of lofting, one of the most powerful modeling tools in max 7. Lofting is frequently underutilized because, for the uninitiated, the tool often seems to behave strangely. Because lofting is unlike any other creation method in 3ds max 7, you must be familiar with a few simple lofting concepts before the tool will make sense.

Take the time to carefully read through the lofting concepts presented here and in Chapter 2, *Fundamental Concepts*, before moving on to the exercises at the end of this chapter. Familiarity with lofting terminology and control features will help you perform complex modeling using simple shapes. For the exercises, you'll apply your knowledge of lofting to create an airplane wing that you'll use in Chapter 7, *The Editable Poly: Box Modeling*.

This chapter covers the following topics:

- **Shape orientation.** You'll learn how to correctly orient shapes on a path by rotating them or repositioning their first vertex. You can use this technique to control the direction of the lofted model and to avoid twisting or distortion.

- **Pivot points in lofting.** You'll learn how to adjust pivot points for placing the shape on the path.

- **Path steps and shape steps.** You'll learn how to use path steps and shape steps to control the density of resulting meshes. Path and shape steps provide a level of detail and efficiency not easily achieved using other modeling methods.

- **Loft deformations.** You'll learn to use loft deformations to scale lofted objects with visual feedback.

- **Material placement.** You'll learn about the special attributes of material application and mapping that are uniquely inherent to lofted objects, which allow patterns to bend and twist automatically as the model changes.
- **Material sizing.** You'll learn techniques to control the application of materials at the 2D-shape level for gaining greater flexibility and to size patterns accurately on lofted objects.

Key Terms

- **First vertex.** A single vertex on a shape that defines the direction of the shape. It is identified by a white square around a visible vertex (**Figure 5.1**).
- **Loft path.** The shape that defines the extrusion length of the loft object.
- **Loft shape.** The shape that defines the cross sections of the loft object.

Lofting Basics

While lofting is a very versatile modeling tool, you need to keep in mind several things as you begin to loft on your own projects:

- A loft object can have only one continuous closed or open 2D spline as a path.
- A loft object can have an unlimited number of open or closed shapes as cross sections, but each shape on a path must have the same number of splines. For example, you cannot loft a circle that has one spline and a donut primitive, which is a compound shape with two splines, on the same loft path.
- Each shape or path can have an unlimited number of vertices, but they should be kept at a minimum for efficient models.
- The pivot point position and the Local reference coordinate system of paths and shapes are important in the alignment of the shapes to the path. (See the lofting section in Chapter 2 for more information on alignment.) **Figure 5.2** shows a lofting example.

tip

You can view the first vertex of a shape in two ways: in Vertex sub-object mode or by selecting the shape(s), right-clicking and choosing Properties, and then selecting Vertex Ticks in the Display Properties area of the By Object menu.

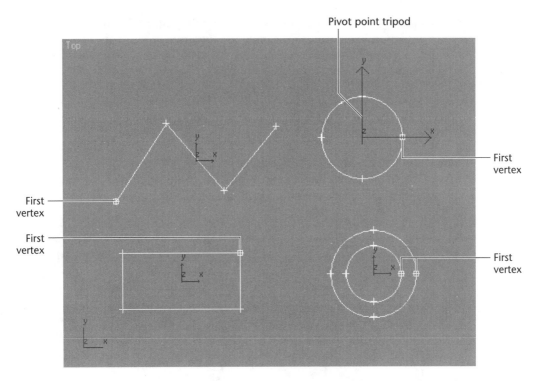

FIGURE 5.1 *A Selection set of shapes. The white box around the vertex indicates the first vertex.*

FIGURE 5.2 *A lofted garden shovel created with four simple 2D shapes. You can view the shovel file by opening **Ch05_shovel_example.max** from the CD-ROM.*

The pivot point and first vertex are particularly important in the lofting process, and not understanding them is probably the prime reason for frustration while lofting.

The pivot point of a shape attaches to the first vertex of the path. Using the pivot point for lofting in 3ds max is comparable to using the insertion base point on a block in AutoCAD.

The orientation of the shape on the path is a bit more complex. I'll talk you through it here and show you an example, and then discuss it in more detail later. The local Z axis of the shape aligns itself "down" the path, and the local Y axis of the shape aligns with the local Z axis of the path (**Figure 5.3**).

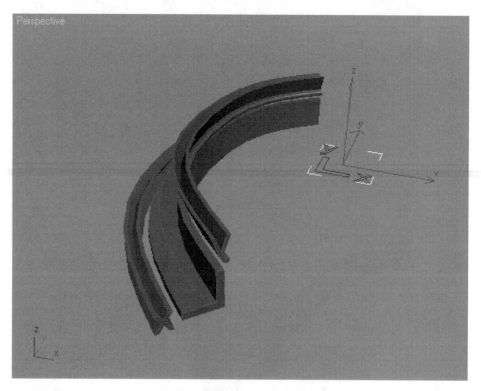

Figure 5.3 *A curved path and* L *shape created in the Top viewport. The lofted object illustrates the orientation of the loft shape when it is on the path. The Local* Z *axes of both 2D shapes point "up," as illustrated in the Perspective viewport.*

The lofting process itself is simple enough, but a couple of features are worth mentioning specifically because they can expand your control of the process. To access the Lofting controls, choose the Create panel, Geometry category. Select Compound Objects from the pull-down menu, and click the Loft button (**Figure 5.4**). You must have a valid 2D shape selected or the Loft button will be grayed out.

In the Creation Method rollout are two options: Get Path and Get Shape. The usual workflow is to have a path selected and then use the Get Shape option. However, you could select a shape instead and use Get Path. The method you use depends on which element you want to remain stationary, with the other element reorienting itself to it. For example, if you select a path and choose Get Shape, the path remains in place and the shape reorients and moves to the path, and vice versa. For all examples in this section, we'll be selecting the path and using Get Shape.

Just below the Get Path and Get Shape options are some other important radio button options: Move, Copy, and Instance. The default option in this section is Instance, which when selected causes a clone of a shape, not the shape itself, to jump to the path. The advantage of this option is that you can modify the original 2D shape, and the lofted 3D mesh changes accordingly. The Move option actually moves the original shape to the path, and Copy places a clone of the shape with no connection to the original. Both of these latter options produce shapes that are much less editable than those produced using Instance.

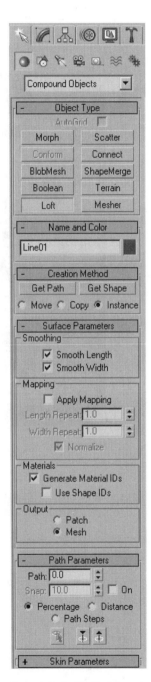

Figure 5.4 The Loft panel, a subset of the Create panel.

In **Figure 5.5**, most of the walls, glazing, and seating are lofted from 2D shapes, which allows for quick and easy editing.

FIGURE 5.5 *Example of a few lofted objects that are very easily changed by editing the 2D shapes.*

As already mentioned, the fundamental process is simple enough, but there are more options that you must understand to make lofting an efficient modeling choice.

Efficiency

If you want 3ds max 7 to be a cost-effective tool in your working environment, you must keep the models as simple as possible. Each vertex and face in a model uses valuable computer overhead, so you can very quickly overwhelm even the most powerful systems and render them useless. Modeling overhead is the main hindrance to production that I encounter in my training sessions. Lofting can be of great help in this respect because it provides controls for adjusting the mesh density of models while retaining the necessary details using shape steps and path steps.

When a shape is lofted along a path, segments are created in the loft mesh for each vertex and path and shape step. **Figure 5.6** shows the previous loft object with Edged Faces turned on in the viewport configuration options. (You can access these options by clicking the viewport label of a shaded viewport.)

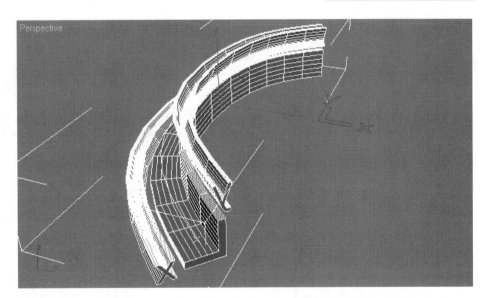

FIGURE 5.6 *An example of lofted objects with segmentation caused by the settings of the path and shape steps and the original shape and path vertex locations.*

If you right-click on the selected mesh object in the example and choose Properties from the Quad menu, you'll see in the Properties dialog that the object has 6,072 faces. If you access the Skin Parameters rollout on the Modify panel, you'll see two numeric fields with spinners for shape steps and path steps. Each is set to 5 by default in 3ds max 7 (**Figure 5.7**).

If you change the Path Steps setting to *0*, there won't be enough information to show the curvature between the vertices. The object may have less detail, but it also won't look right to the viewer (**Figure 5.8**).

Changing the Path Steps to *3* might provide an acceptable level of detail, depending on the distance from the camera or the level of detail in the background that could hide faceted edges. It also would reduce the overall face count to 4,200. You must be the judge of how much detail is enough. But also be aware that you can change these settings at any time if you need to optimize the object further.

FIGURE 5.7 *The default settings for Shape Steps and Path Steps is 5 in 3ds max 7.*

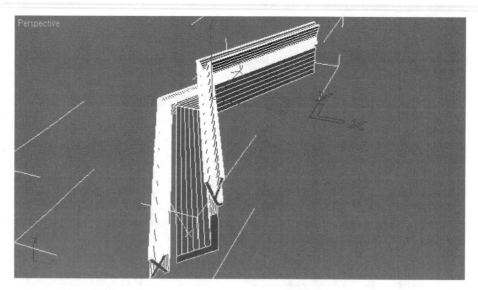

FIGURE 5.8 *Setting Path Steps to 0 results in no curvature between path vertices.*

Notice on the shape for the loft the L-shaped spline has no curves, and the letters x and y contain minimal curves. So setting Shape Steps to *0* in this case has little effect on the visual quality of the mesh object (**Figure 5.9**).

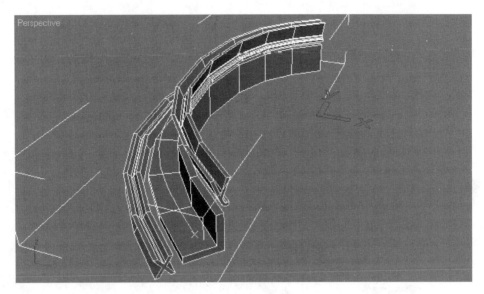

FIGURE 5.9 *Setting Shape Steps to 0 has little effect on the quality of the mesh object because there's minimal curvature between shape vertices.*

Reducing the Shape Steps to *0* of this loft object has no effect on the quality and reduces the face count to 690. This is a huge savings in memory resources if you do it for all your lofted objects in the scene. As a matter of fact, you can now increase the Path Steps back up to *5*, which provides much higher visual quality, and you'd still have only 1,002 faces.

Just below the Path Steps and Shape Steps spinners is a checkbox labeled *Optimize Shapes*. If you had selected this option instead of setting Shape Steps to *0*, the economy would be about the same. The curve at the bottom of the letter *y* is not optimized in this case.

note

The Optimize Shapes option provides an intelligent analysis of the shape, resulting in a reduction of the number of steps in the straight portions of the shape, while at the same time leaving the curved portions set to the number in the Shape Steps field. For most shapes used in lofting, this option provides the best of both worlds.

Remember the definition of shape steps and path steps—intermediate steps *between vertices* that define curvature in the segment. If you don't have an adequate number of steps, then you must use vertices to define the curvature.

Figure 5.10 shows a rectangle lofted along a filleted path. This could be a sidewalk, road, or countertop; in fact, it holds many possibilities if you use a little imagination in applying the tools. If you want to work along with the following description of lofting, open **Ch05_walkway01.max** from the CD-ROM, select walk_shape01, and loft the Rectangle01 shape along it to create the initial walkway.

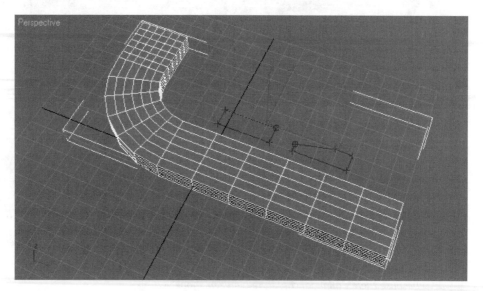

FIGURE 5.10 *A rectangle lofted along a filleted path using the default settings for Shape Steps and Path Steps. The loft object has 908 faces.*

On the Modify panel, Skin Parameters rollout, notice the Optimize Path option is grayed out. To enable it, you must select the Path Steps mode instead of Path Percentage mode in the Path Parameters rollout. If you don't want to change modes, you can adjust the number of vertices to get the same results. However, in this case, while setting Shape Steps to *0* or selecting Optimize Shapes produces 148 faces, reducing the number of path steps quickly destroys the detail in the curve portion of the sidewalk and results in a useless object (**Figure 5.11**).

To correct the lack of curvature at the corner, you would select the original loft path shape, Rectangle01, and select the curved segment of the path from the Segment sub-object level of the Modify panel. The selected segment would not highlight in red because it's "inside" the loft object. The tripod axis indicates its selection.

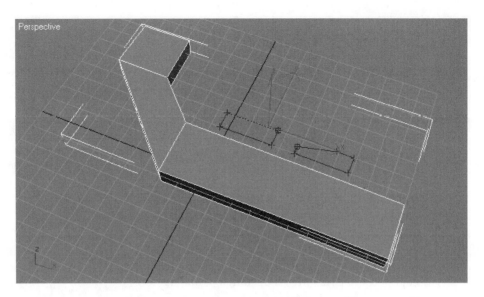

Figure 5.11 *Setting Shape Steps and Path Steps to* 0 *results in no curvature between path vertices and produces an unacceptable object.*

In the Geometry rollout, you would enter *4* in the Divide field, and then click on the Divide button. Four vertices would be added along the segment, and the curvature to that segment would be redefined without adding unnecessary detail along the straight segments. The result would be an object that balances detail and efficiency using only 60 faces in the walk (**Figure 5.12**).

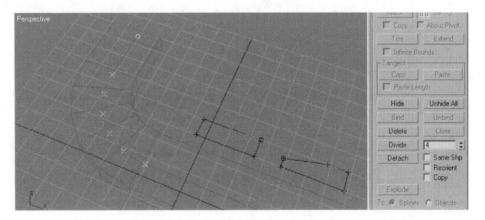

Figure 5.12 *Setting Path Steps to* 0 *and using the Divide function to add vertices to segments provides local control for efficiently lofting objects.*

Methods

In this section, I'll demonstrate how to apply a handicap "curb-cut" to the sidewalk by lofting multiple shapes along the same path. Remember, there is no limitation to the number of shapes on any given path or the number of vertices in each shape. However, each shape must have the same number of splines. For example, you cannot loft a donut shape (two splines) and a circle shape (one spline) on the same path.

Figure 5.13 shows the rectangle used to loft the curved sidewalk, which produces a rectangular cross section along the entire walk. Notice also the copy of the original rectangle, which has been edited by adding a vertex and moving one corner to create a sloped section. The original rectangle shape has four vertices; the copy has five.

note

The example file (**Ch05_walkway01.max**) has an intentional glitch in the first vertex that illustrates a problem quite common in lofting production, one that causes many users to abandon lofting in 3ds max 7. Can you guess the problem by looking at the shapes?

To make sure you can see the shape's vertices in the viewport (I'm dropping a hint here) without being in Vertex sub-object mode, the shapes were selected and Vertex Ticks was enabled in the Object Properties dialog.

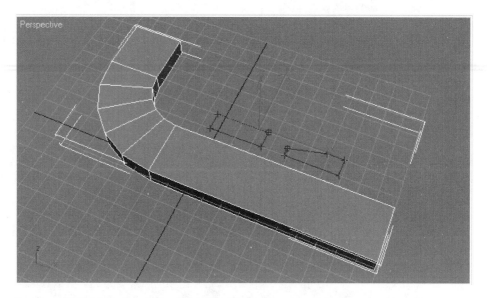

FIGURE 5.13 *This rectangle has been lofted on a curved path to create a sidewalk.*

Contending with Multiple Shapes on a Path

Lofting multiple shapes on a path is straightforward: You simply change the percentage level on the path in the Path Parameters rollout and repeat the Get Shape operation. To do this, the loft object is selected, and changes are made in the Path Parameters rollout on the Modify panel (**Figure 5.14**).

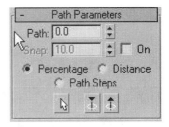

FIGURE 5.14 *The Path Parameters rollout lets you loft multiple shapes on a path.*

The value expressed in the Path field represents the current active level of the loft object. It is measured as a percentage from the first vertex of the loft path. In Figure 5.14, the Path value is set to 0 or at the first vertex.

You can also measure the actual distance along the path from the first vertex by selecting the Distance option at the bottom of the rollout. If you select this option to determine the active level on the path, the numeric display in the Path field will be expressed in feet and inches (or the current unit setting) rather than as a percentage. So if you enter *12'0"* in the Path field, for example, a yellow tick on the path moves 12 feet along the path and becomes the active level (**Figure 5.15**).

tip

To find the length of a shape, select the shape, and from the Utilities panel choose Measure. The Measure function for 3D objects displays the surface area and volume. You can then use the Distance option to place shapes along the path.

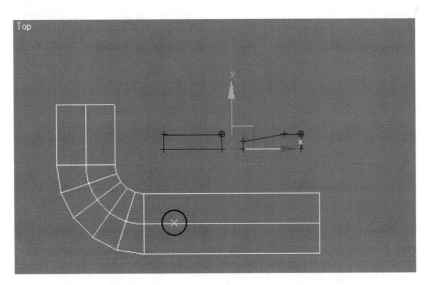

FIGURE 5.15 *A yellow tick on the path indicates the active Get Shape level.*

The last step involves selecting Get Shape on the Modify panel and then selecting the new cross-section shape to set it at a point 12 feet from the first vertex of the path. The result, however, might not be exactly what you expect, let alone what you want (**Figure 5.16**).

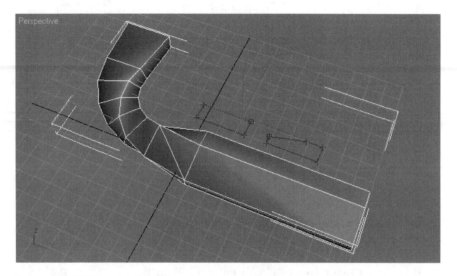

FIGURE 5.16 *Using the Get Shape command to choose the new shape at the 12-foot level creates a nasty twist to the sidewalk.*

The twist is caused by the first-vertex position on the shapes. The first vertex appears as a box on a vertex in the viewport and, as you can see, they are not in the same relative position on each shape. (This is the intentional glitch I mentioned earlier). The lofting process analyzes the shapes on the path and connects the first vertex of each shape, and then it creates new edges along and around the loft for each vertex, path step, and shape step setting, resulting in a 3D mesh.

To try to correct the problem, you would turn off Get Shape, and then you could select the sloped shape, choose the Vertex sub-object level on the Modify panel, and then select the upper-right vertex and click the Make First button. Placing the first vertex on each shape in the same relative position definitely takes the twist out of the loft, but it still doesn't look like a handicap ramp. The beginning of the sidewalk is rectangular, but it starts to slope immediately at the beginning and gradually transitions to the full slope at 12 feet.

What would work better is to get the original rectangular shape at 12′0″ to hold that cross section for the first 12 feet. Then in Path Parameters rollout, you'd enter *13′0″*. At that level, you'd select Get Shape and the sloped shape (**Figure 5.17**). Then to remove shading artifacts, deselect Smooth Length and Smooth Width in the Surface Parameters rollout.

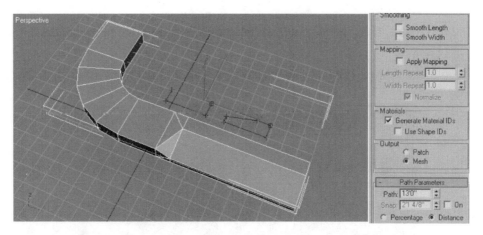

FIGURE 5.17 *To hold the rectangular cross section for 12 feet and then have it slope within a distance of one foot, use Get Shape to place the original rectangular shape at 12'0", and then set the Path level to 13'0" and use Get Shape to select the sloped shape.*

Next you'd set the Path level at *16'0"* and use Get Shape to place the sloped shape again. This holds the sloped cross section for 3 feet. The last step is to set the Path level to *17'0"* and use Get Shape to place the original rectangular shape. The resulting curb-cut transitions from sloped to rectangular within 1 foot and holds the rectangular cross section to the end of the path (**Figure 5.18**).

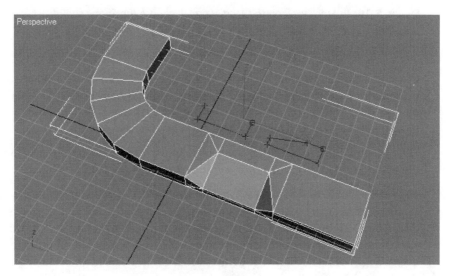

FIGURE 5.18 *The sloped shape is at level 16'0", and the rectangular shape is at 17'0". The handicap ramp is placed at the location you specified.*

The position of the ramp can be easily adjusted at any time to move or resize the ramp. There are two methods of adjusting the position of the shapes on the path.

In Stack view on the Modify panel, select the Shape sub-object level for the selected loft object. The Loft sub-object shapes will turn red when selected (**Figure 5.19**).

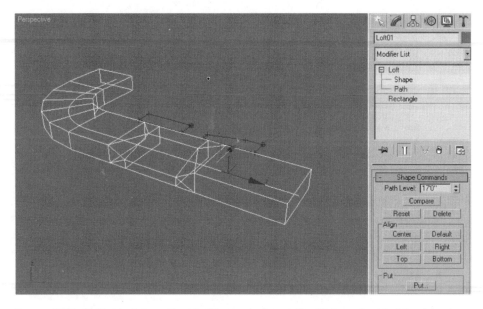

FIGURE 5.19 *In Stack view on the Modify panel, choose the Shape sub-object level, and select the shape on the path (not the original shape) you want to move. It will turn red when selected.*

Once the shape you want to move is selected, the Path Level field in the Shape Commands rollout displays the level where the shape is currently located. All you have to do is type in the new distance from the first vertex that you want that shape to be on and hit Enter. The shape will move to the new position.

The other option is to select the shape or shapes in Shape sub-object-level mode, click the Select and Move button, and simply move the shapes along the path.

To get a feel for how you can easily edit lofted objects on the fly—which isn't always so simple using other modeling methods—try working with some simple exercises of your own. You could quickly add curbstones to the sidewalk by creating a groove near one edge using new vertices on the original shapes. You could chamfer (cut the corner at a 45-degree angle) or fillet (round the corner) the edges to create more detail or quickly alter the size of the sidewalks. Because the shapes are instanced on the path, any modifications you make to the 2D shapes will be automatically applied to the entire sidewalk.

Gaining More Control

Now let's look at how to "clean" mesh objects with lofting. Open **Ch05_equal_vertex01.max** from the CD-ROM if you want to follow along.

Earlier in the chapter you learned that each shape can have as many vertices as you want, and that not all shapes on a path need to have the same number of vertices. If you loft a circle shape at one end of a straight path to a star shape on the other end, you get a complex mesh object (**Figure 5.20**). The circle has four vertices and the star has 12; both shapes have five lofting shape steps that define the mesh surface and the curvature for the loft object.

As you can see in Figure 5.20, the object is what you might expect, but if you look closely you'll see that 3ds max 7 has to make some guesses as it transitions the surface from a few points at the bottom to more points at the top. The result is a somewhat irregular surface that you don't have complete control over.

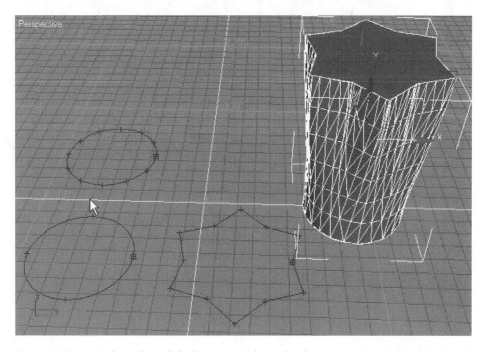

Figure 5.20 *A circle and star lofted on a straight path. The program interpolates the topology of the surface to transition from four vertices with five shape steps at the bottom to 12 vertices with five shape steps at the top.*

To produce a more regular surface, it's often better to use shapes with the same number of vertices along the path because it helps eliminate surface glitches as the software determines the topology. In **Figure 5.21**, you can substitute a circular NGon shape with 12 vertices for the lower circle. With this type of shape, the surface is more regular, it's easier to optimize, and it makes it easier to control the transitions between shapes.

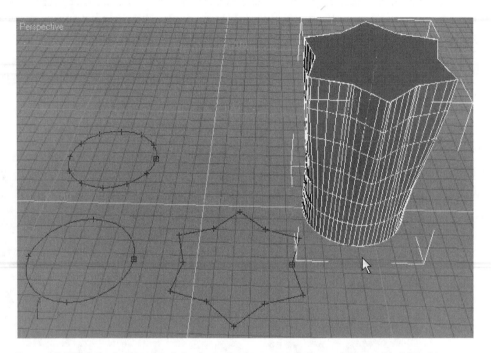

FIGURE 5.21 *Substituting the circle shape for four vertices for an NGon with 12 vertices produces a much cleaner-looking mesh that can be optimized and edited more easily.*

Materials, Mapping, and Lofted Objects

You have seen some of the editing advantages of using lofted objects with multiple shapes along the path. There are also some significant advantages of lofted objects when it comes time to apply materials.

Say, for example, that you want to apply expansion joints to the sidewalk, but you don't want the extra geometry associated with modeling the joints. You could use a Bump map to give the illusion of joints while leaving the geometry as is. In this section, I describe how to do this.

In the Material Editor, you would assign a Gradient Ramp map to the Bump slot. Then in the Gradient Ramp, you'd change the flags to black and white and

note

The map you can use if you want to follow along in the next lofting example is a Gradient Ramp map, which is a standard map type in 3ds max 7. In a Gradient Ramp, white areas of the map create bumps, while black areas have no effect on the surface. You'll learn more about maps and materials in Chapter 12, *Material Editor: Your Palette at a Glance*, and Chapter 13, *Maps: Patterns Before Your Eyes*.

set the Interpolation type to Solid (**Figure 5.22**). Moving the white flag to the left produces a white field with a thin black line along the left edge. To rotate the map 90 degrees, you'd enter *90* in the W: Angle field on the Gradient Ramp Coordinates rollout.

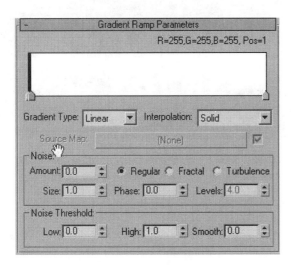

FIGURE 5.22 *A Gradient Ramp map with black-and-white flags and Interpolation set to Solid. The map is rotated 90 degrees in the W axis.*

On the Gradient Ramp level of Material Editor, you would turn on the Show Map in Viewport toggle so that you could see the Ramp on the object in the shaded viewport. It appears as a white sidewalk with a thin black strip at one end.

Then you'd select the loft object and, in the Surface Parameters rollout of the Modify panel, enter *8.0* in the Length Repeat field of the Mapping area. This repeats the black-and-white pattern over the length of the sidewalk loft object (**Figure 5.23**). When rendered, the black becomes an indented expansion joint in the surface of the sidewalk. It only simulates the indentation and does not add much overhead to the rendering time.

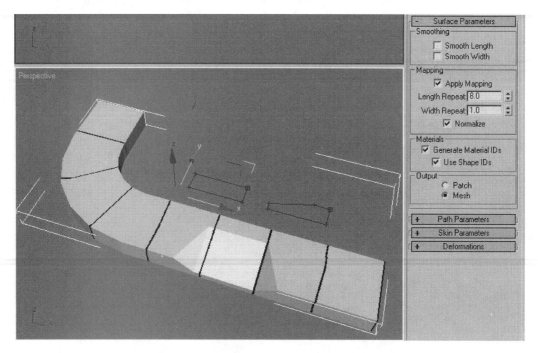

FIGURE 5.23 *In the Surface Parameters rollout on the Modify panel for the lofted object, the Length Repeat field adjusts the number of repetitions of the map along the length of the path.*

Lofting Techniques

As with much of 3ds max 7, if you don't have a fundamental understanding of lofting and then try to figure it out on your own under production deadlines, you most likely will struggle with even the easiest modeling tasks and miss out on the power the software designers have packed into this technique. But armed with a fundamental knowledge of lofting gained by reading and practicing what's been covered in this chapter so far, you should be ready to perform exercises that demonstrate how lofting can be used to set an efficient and flexible modeling scenario similar to what you might find in a production house.

Four lofting exercises are presented in this section. In the first two exercises, you'll learn to model and modify an airplane wing that will be used later with the fuselage you create in Chapter 7. You'll also learn about new tools in 3ds max 7 that let you deform the basic loft object for more control of the end result.

In the last two exercises, you'll create and modify an efficient bridge to use later in an outdoor scene you'll create in Chapter 8, *More Modifiers: Orderly Progression*. The object of the exercises is to create models that are easy to change and will add minimum overhead to the scene.

Lofting an Airplane Wing

In this first exercise, you'll use the 2D shape you modified from a rectangle into an airplane wing profile in Chapter 3 as the loft shape of a 3D wing. You'll learn to reposition the pivot point of the 2D shape to control where the loft shape attaches to the loft path, as well as a method of changing the length of the loft path (a line) so that you can see the actual length as you edit the line. This may seem like a simple process. However, a line is not a parametric shape, so it has no numeric adjustments.

In Exercise 5.2, you'll learn to use the Loft Deformation tools to scale the wing tip for a more rounded effect. The scale deformations are an integral part of the lofting process, and the deformations do not affect the original 2D shapes. So you can experiment and still be able to cancel your actions without changing the base object.

Exercise 5.1: Modeling the Wing

1. Open **Ch05_wing01.max** from the CD-ROM and save it to your project folder with the name *Ch05_wing02.max*. You can use the File > Save As command and click the plus sign in the Save File As dialog to automatically increment the file name while saving the new file. This file contains two 2D shapes: the wing profile from Chapter 3 that will be the cross-section shape, and a line that will be the loft path.

2. In the Perspective viewport, select the line called *wing_path*. In the Geometry category of the Create panel, click the Standard Primitives field and choose Compound Objects from the drop-down list. In the Object Type rollout, click the Loft button. In the Creation Method rollout, click Get Shape (**Figure 5.24**).

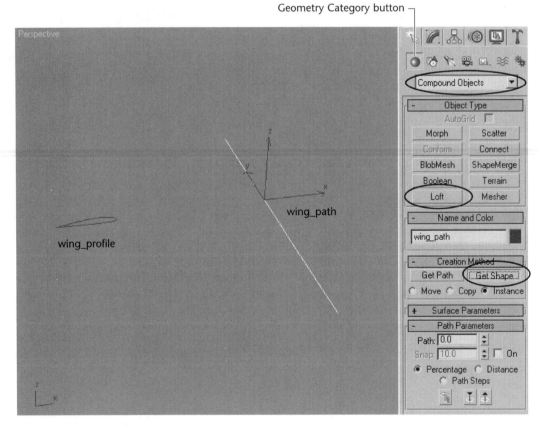

FIGURE 5.24 *Select the line called* wing_path *and click Get Shape in the Loft panel. The lofted object is created along this line.*

3. Click wing_profile in the Perspective viewport when you see the Get Shape cursor appear over the edge of the shape. The result is an airfoil mesh object. Look at the orientation of the wing on the path and compare it to what you learned at the beginning of this chapter. The pivot point of the shape attached itself to the first vertex of the path with the local positive Z axis of the shape projecting down the path, and the local positive Y axis of the shape aligning with the local positive Z axis of the path (**Figure 5.25**). On the Modify panel, rename the loft object *Wing*. You will need the detail provided by the path and shape steps in this model in Exercise 5.2; otherwise it might be prudent to adjust those at this point in time to optimize the wing.

note

It would be possible to rename the loft object to *Wing* from the Create panel, except that you wouldn't be able to exit Get Shape mode by re-toggling the Get Shape button. Thus, you wouldn't be able to select the wing_profile object in the first place. Clicking and re-clicking on Get Shape works for toggling the function on the Modifier panel only. To first exit the loft creation mode, you must either right-click in a viewport or activate the Modifier panel, and do all the editing from there.

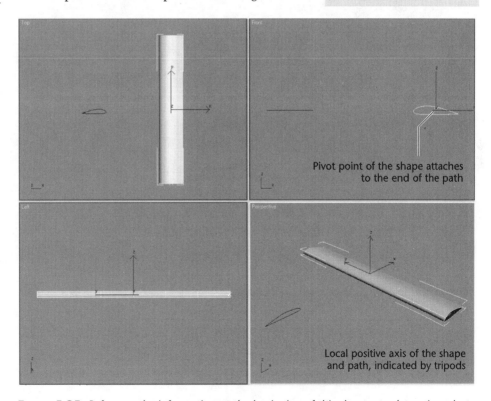

FIGURE 5.25 *Reference the information at the beginning of this chapter to determine what affects the placement and orientation of the loft shape on the loft path.*

4. Assume the shape should actually attach itself to the path more toward the leading edge of the shape. In the Top viewport, select the wing_profile 2D shape and zoom in so that it fills the viewport. On the Hierarchy panel, click the Affect Pivot Only button. Click the Select and Move transform button on the main toolbar and move the pivot point right along the *X* axis to a position similar to where the pivot point is located in **Figure 5.26**. Click the Affect Pivot Only button to exit that mode.

Notice the Wing loft object didn't change to reflect the edit made to the shape, even though the Instance option was used to create the loft object. This is because the change you made to the pivot point is a transform, not a modification, and only modifications are part of the instance-cloning process.

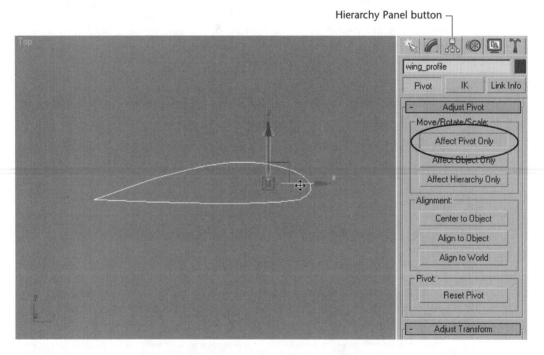

FIGURE 5.26 *You can reposition the pivot point of an object using the Hierarchy panel.*

5. To update the wing, select it in the Perspective viewport and, on the Modify panel, Creation Method rollout, click Get Shape, and pick the wing_profile shape in the viewport. The wing will shift position on the path. Click the Get Shape button to exit that mode.

Next you'll lengthen the wing by adjusting the path at the Vertex sub-object level, but you'll also learn to use the Measure utility to view the length as you make the changes.

6. Right-click in the Top viewport to activate it, and then click Zoom Extents in the viewport navigation tools to see the whole display. Click the Select By Name button in the main toolbar and select wing_path from the list. In Stack view on the Modify panel, expand Line and highlight the Vertex sub-object mode. Select the vertex at the top of the path by dragging a window around it (**Figure 5.27**).

tip

To zoom in on a selected object or objects, you can use the Zoom Extents Selected button for the active viewport or Zoom Extents All Selected button. Clicking and holding the mouse on the Zoom Extents or Zoom Extents All button at the lower right of the display allows you to choose from the flyout buttons that appear.

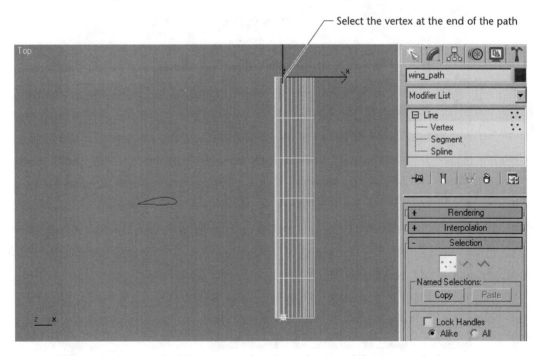

FIGURE 5.27 *In the Vertex sub-object mode, select the end vertex of the wing_path shape.*

7. You could move the vertex in the Top viewport's positive *Y* axis to lengthen the line, but you wouldn't know how long it is. You could also type in a specific value in the Transform Type-in fields at the bottom of the display, but it would only specify a coordinate point in 3D space and would not indicate the length of the line. An easier and more accurate way to lengthen the line would be to click the Measure button on the Utilities panel and then select Lock Selection in the Measure dialog. Click the New Floater button at the bottom of the dialog, and the length of the shape is displayed in the Shapes section on the left side (**Figure 5.28**).

> **caution**
>
> You should still be in Select and Move mode, so it's easy to move something inadvertently. Select and Move is a tool that enhances workflow by eliminating a separate selection step, but you must be aware of what you are doing at all times.

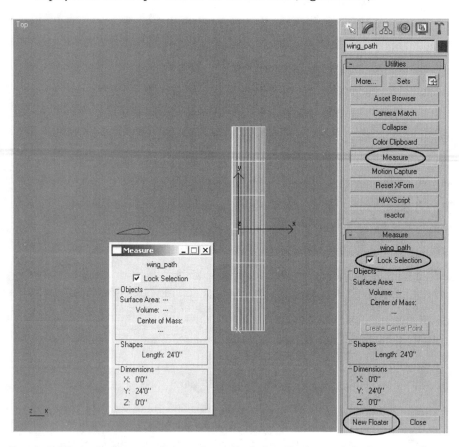

FIGURE 5.28 *In the Measure dialog, you can lock the selection and display a new floater dialog that notes the length of the object.*

8. In the Top viewport, press *G* to activate the grid and *S* to turn on Snap. In Stack view on the Modify panel, highlight the Vertex sub-object mode again and, in the Top viewport, click and drag the *Y*-axis restrict arrow to move the vertex in the positive *Y* axis until the Measure floater reads *30'0"* (**Figure 5.29**). Select Lock Selection in the Measure floater and close the dialog. Exit sub-object mode in Stack view by clicking on Line. Press *S* to exit Snap mode or toggle the Snap button in the main toolbar.

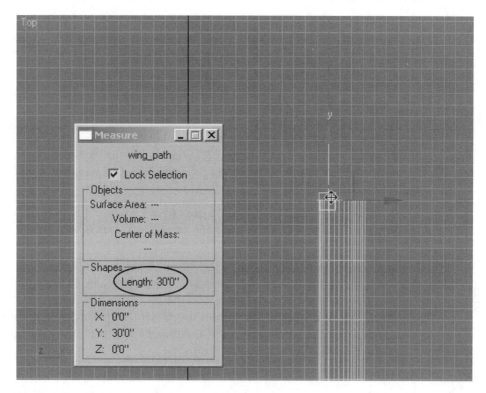

FIGURE 5.29 *To lengthen a line to a specific amount, you can use the Measure utility in Lock Selection mode, with a floater and grid snaps.*

9. Save the file. It should already be named
    Ch05_wing02.max.

You have lofted and modified a wing from two simple 2D shapes and changed the orientation of the
shape on the path by adjusting the pivot. You also
adjusted the length of the path with the help of a
locked Measure utility.

tip

If you come to the edge of the
viewport while moving the
vertex in Step 8, you can press
the *I* key to interactively pan the
view and center the cursor while
still in Select and Move mode.

The result of this exercise is a relatively complex
mesh object that might have been more difficult to create using other modeling techniques, and wouldn't possess the flexible editing capability that this one does.

Exercise 5.2: Editing Mesh Objects Using Loft Deformations

Scale Deformation tools give you another level of control over loft objects to create
more complex objects using simple 2D shapes. In this exercise, you'll use Scale
Deformation tools to round the wing tips of the 3D lofted wing you worked with in
the last exercise.

1. Open the file called **Ch05_wing02.max** from Exercise 5.1 or from the CD-ROM.
    Save it to your project folder using the name *Ch05_wing03.max.* This is a straight
    wing that needs more work.

2. In the Top viewport, select the wing 3D mesh object. In the Deformations roll-
    out of the Modify panel, click the Scale button. The Scale Deformation dialog
    appears with a red line indicating that the shapes are 100 percent of their origi-
    nal size along the entire loft path in the *X* axis. The Make Symmetrical button
    is selected by default to ensure the *X*-axis and *Y*-axis scaling are the same
    (**Figure 5.30**).

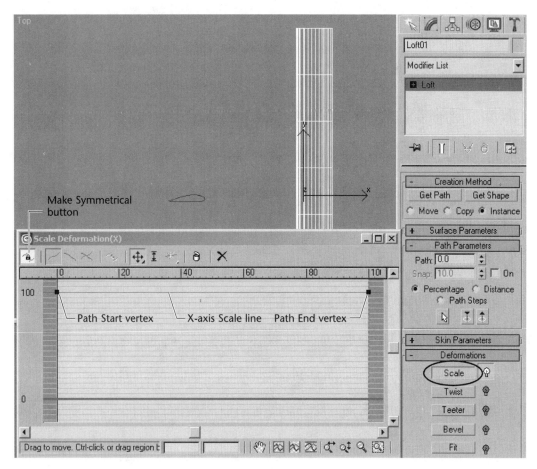

FIGURE 5.30 *In the Scale Deformation dialog, the red line represents the scaling of shapes along the path in the X axis, the black squares are the path vertex control points, and the Make Symmetrical button is selected by default for equal scaling in the X and Y axis.*

3. In the Scale Deformation dialog, select and move the right black control point down near the heavy gray horizontal line. The loft object tapers to almost 0 percent in the *X* and *Y* axis (**Figure 5.31**). Click the Reset Curve button (a black *X*) in the dialog toolbar to reset the scaling to 100 percent.

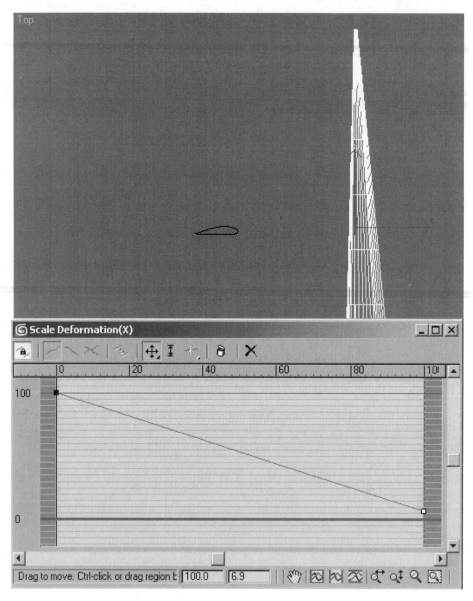

Figure 5.31 *Moving the right black control point near 0 tapers the wing in both axes.*

4. Toggle the Make Symmetrical button off—you only want to round the wing tips in the *X* axis. Click the Insert Corner Point button on the toolbar in the dialog, and click on the red line near the 20 percent path area (use the horizontal ruler above the red line) and again near the 80 percent path area to add two points to the scale line. Click the Move button on the toolbar and highlight the new point near 20 along the horizontal ruler. In the left numeric field at the bottom of the dialog enter *20*. Press Enter (**Figure 5.32**). Then select the point on the red line near 80 and enter *80* in the left numeric field. The right numeric field for each point is the scale factor and will be adjusted in Step 5.

> **note**
>
> Adding control points to the scale line is similar to adding vertices to the path. Extra geometry is generated between control points based on the Path Steps setting. This can cause extremely dense geometry, so add only as many control points as you think you need, and always keep in mind the complexity of the model you're creating.

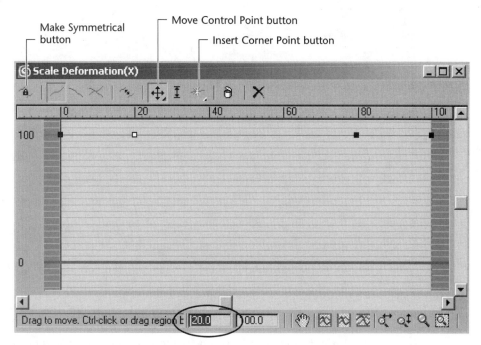

FIGURE 5.32 *Add two new control points to the X-axis scale line and enter 20 for the left control point in the left numeric field in the lower center of the dialog.*

5. Highlight the two end control points by drag-
    ging a selection window around them. Then
    move them by entering *10* in the right numeric
    field at the bottom of the dialog. This scales
    each end to 10 percent of its original size in
    only 20 percent of the path at either end
    (**Figure 5.33**).

tip

The scale center is the pivot
point of the shape—in other
words—the path of the loft
object.

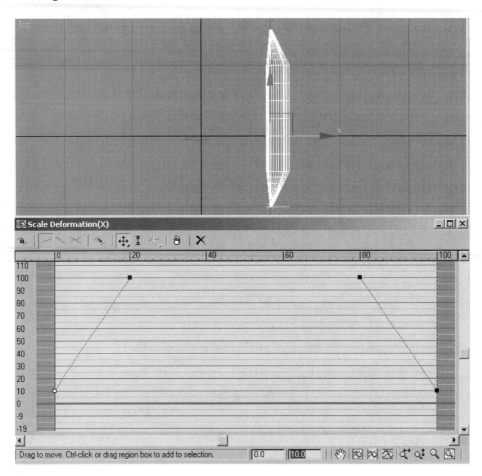

FIGURE 5.33 *Move the end control points on the scale line to taper the first and last 20 percent of the wing to 10 percent of the original size, in only the X axis.*

6. Highlight all the control points by dragging a window around them, right-click on any one, and choose Bezier Corner from the menu (**Figure 5.34**). Black Bezier handles appear for each control point, which you can use to adjust the tangency of the curves.

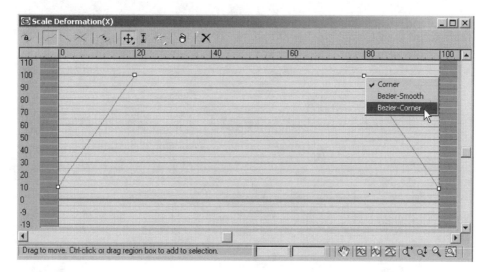

FIGURE 5.34 *You can change the tangency of highlighted control points by right-clicking on the control point and choosing from the menu.*

7. For a rounder and more streamlined wing tip, adjust the Bezier handles so that they look similar to the ones in **Figure 5.35** on the next page. Closely examining the ends of the wing in the Perspective viewport reveals pinching at the ends, caused by 100-percent scaling in the *Y* axis. You can fix this by scaling the *Y* axis.

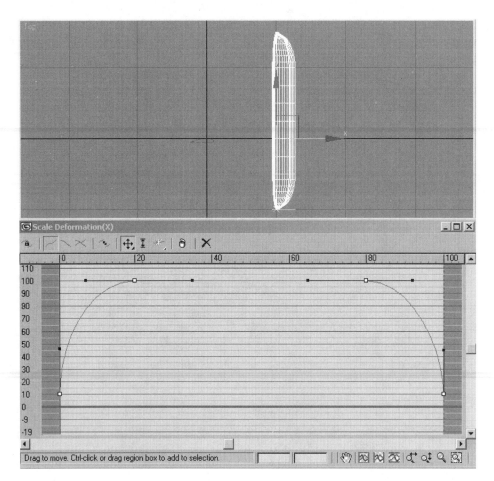

FIGURE 5.35 *Moving the Bezier handles into horizontal and vertical positions rounds the wing tips for a more streamlined effect.*

8. Click the Display *Y*-Axis button in the Scale Deformation dialog to show the green line of the *Y*-axis scaling in the dialog. Add new control points at 5 percent and 95 percent, scale the ends down to 30 percent, and adjust the curves (**Figure 5.36**).

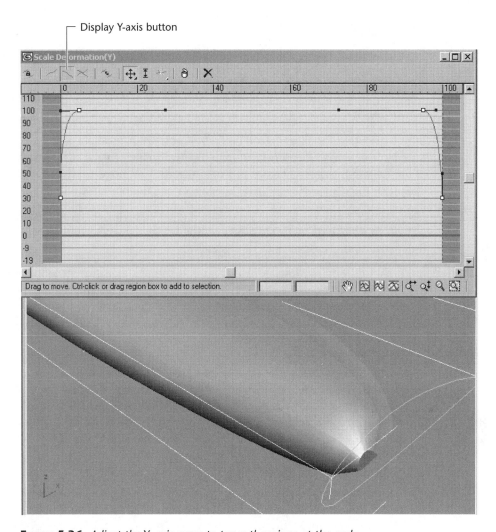

Display Y-axis button

FIGURE 5.36 *Adjust the Y-axis curve to taper the wings at the ends.*

9. Close all dialogs and save the file. It should already be called *Ch05_wing03.max*.

You have learned to modify the scaling independently in the *X* and *Y* axes of the loft object without affecting the original shape or path.

Lofting with Multiple Shapes

As mentioned in the beginning of this chapter, you can loft as many shapes on a single path as you want. The only limits come from a practical standpoint rather than a technical one. And as you already know, new users to lofting often get confused by a twisting in the lofted mesh caused by misaligned first vertices of multiple shapes on the path.

In the next two exercises, you'll learn to recognize a problem intentionally introduced in this example and how to manipulate a shape's first vertex to correct it. The example used in these exercises is a roadway with a bridge that you'll use again in Chapter 8 to create a crossing over a small stream in your airport scene.

The roadway will be straight for a distance and then, within a fairly short distance, will widen to include wider sidewalks on the bridge. On the other side of the bridge, the roadway will taper back to its original width.

After you loft the roadway and bridge, you'll learn different methods for optimizing the number of faces in the mesh. Your ability to recognize unnecessary mesh density and eliminate it will be of great benefit in a production environment.

Exercise 5.3: Correcting Lofting Twisting

1. Open the file from the CD-ROM called **Ch05_Bridge01.max** and save it to your project folder with the new name *Ch05_Bridge02.max*. The scene contains three shapes: a long line, representing the path, and two cross-section shapes, one with wider sidewalks in the area that will become the bridge.

2. Activate the Top viewport, and use the Select by Name option to select the shape called *road_centerline*. To zoom out so that you can see the entire line in the viewport, use the Zoom Extents Selected option with the navigation tools. In the Geometry category on the Create panel, click Standard Primitives, and choose Compound Objects from the drop-down list. In the Object Type rollout, click the Loft button. In the Creation Method rollout, click the Get Shape button, and in the viewport select road_shape, which is the cross-section shape on the left. Click the Select button in the main toolbar to exit Get Shape mode. The result is a long straight lofted object (**Figure 5.37**).

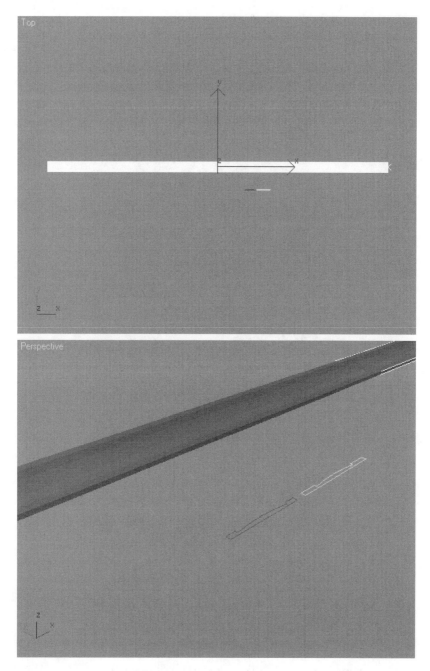

FIGURE 5.37 *Lofting a single shape on a path results in a long straight roadway with sidewalks.*

3. With the loft mesh selected, change its name to *Roadway* on the Modify panel. The bridge will be positioned between 45 and 65 percent along the roadway. In the Path Parameters rollout, enter *45* in the Path field and press Enter. In the Creation Method rollout, click the Get Shape button and select bridge_shape in the Top viewport. Click Select in the main toolbar to exit Get Shape mode. The lofted object tapers ever so slightly from the right end to about the center, but then it becomes twisted because the first vertex in each of the two shapes isn't aligned (**Figure 5.38**).

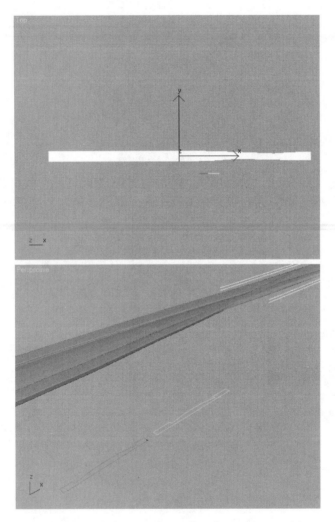

FIGURE 5.38 *With the new shape placed at 45 percent along the path, the mesh object is slightly tapered and very twisted.*

4. In the Top viewport, select both road_shape and bridge_shape. Right-click in the viewport and choose Properties in the menu. In the Object Properties dialog, select the Vertex Ticks option, located in the Display Properties area (**Figure 5.39**). This displays vertex ticks for the selected objects without being in Vertex sub-object mode.

Notice that the two shapes in the Top viewport are similar, except for the side walks and the location of the first vertices. The first vertex of road_shape is located in the upper right, while the first vertex of bridge_shape is in the upper middle. This difference is causing the twisting because both shapes use the same alignment on the path. We need to change the location of the first vertex in bridge_shape so that its first vertex is aligned with the first vertex of road_shape. Click OK to close the Object Properties dialog and in the viewport navigation controls, choose Zoom Extents Selected from the Zoom Extents flyout.

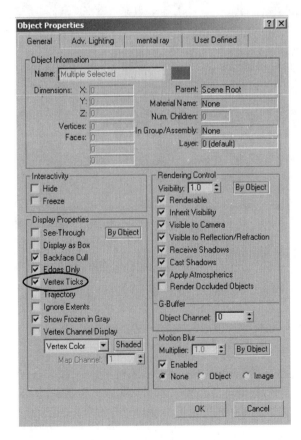

Figure 5.39 *Selecting the Vertex Ticks option lets you view vertices in the viewports without being in Vertex sub-object mode.*

5. Select bridge_shape in the Top viewport. In Stack view on the Modify panel, highlight the Vertex sub-object mode. In the Top viewport, select the upper-right vertex of the shape. Right-click and choose Make First from the quad menu (**Figure 5.40**). This takes the twist out of the road. In Stack view, click Editable Spline to exit sub-object mode.

    The problem now is that the roadway starts to taper at the start and ends at 45 percent (where bridge_shape was inserted). The roadway needs to stay narrow to 40 percent, and then widen between 40 and 45 percent. The bridge width should continue to 55 percent and quickly taper between 55 and 60 percent. The rest of the roadway will be narrow like the beginning.

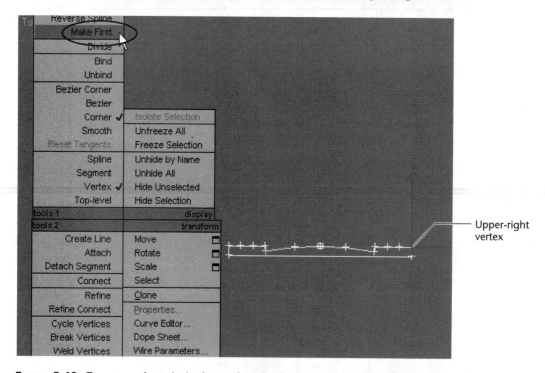

FIGURE 5.40 *To remove the twist in the road, make the upper-right vertex of bridge_shape the first vertex.*

6. To change the taper, insert another clone of the road_shape at 40 percent along the path. In the Top viewport, zoom out and select the Roadway object. In the Path Parameters rollout on the Modify panel, enter *40* in the Path field and press Enter. Click the Get Shape button and pick road_shape in the Top viewport. The Roadway now tapers within just 5 percent of the length of the path (**Figure 5.41**).

FIGURE 5.41 *Inserting road_shape at 0 percent and 40 percent and then inserting bridge_shape at 45 percent confines the tapering to 5 percent of the path length.*

7. To maintain the width across the bridge, choose Get Shape to insert bridge_shape at 55 percent. Then to taper the road back to the normal width, insert road_shape at 60 percent (**Figure 5.42**).

Notice a wrinkling in the tapered areas of the shaded Perspective viewport. We'll remove this in the next exercise.

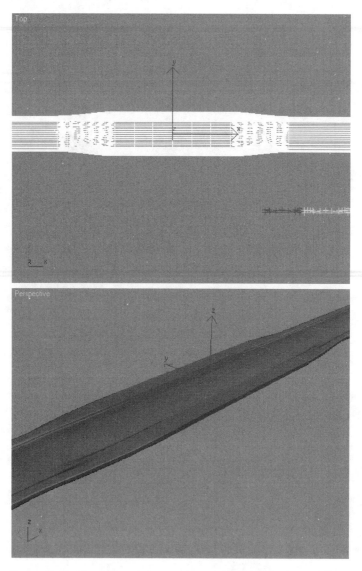

FIGURE 5.42 *By placing the same shape at multiple locations along the path, you can control the areas of transition from one shape to another.*

8. Save the file. It should already be called *Ch05_Bridge02.max*.

You have learned to apply multiple shapes on a path and to use the same shape multiple times to control changes in the lofted object. You also learned to remove twisting by matching the relative position of the first vertex of each shape used.

Learning about the function of the first vertex in lofting is an important step in gaining the control you need to create complex geometry. And, knowing that you can insert the same shape multiple times along a path to control exactly where the loft object transitions from one shape to the next can increase the usefulness of lofting significantly.

Cleaning Up and Optimizing the Lofted Mesh

The lofted roadway from the previous exercise shows some wrinkling of the surface at the tapering transition areas, caused by a different number of vertices in the sidewalks of the 2D shapes. 3ds max 7 is interpolating as best it can between shapes with different numbers of vertices. In addition, the model and mesh contain many unnecessary faces that affect the overall performance of your computer. On a fast computer with only this object in the scene, you won't notice the overhead. However, to be effective in production, you must identify and eliminate any detail that is not directly contributing to the quality of the final images.

This exercise will help you identify suspect areas and remedy the problem using some simple edits.

Exercise 5.4: Optimizing the Mesh

1. Open the file called **Ch05_Bridge02.max** from your project folder or from the CD-ROM. Save a copy to your project folder with the name *Ch05_Bridge03.max*. We'll remove the unnecessary vertices to reduce overhead.

2. Select the roadway loft object in the Top viewport, right-click, and choose Properties from the quad menu. Notice the roadway has 4,662 faces.

3. In the Top viewport, select the bridge_shape 2D shape. Notice the shape has two extra vertices in the segment that defines the top surface of the sidewalk, while the corresponding segment in road_shape does not (**Figure 5.43**). In Stack view on the Modify panel, highlight the Vertex sub-object level. Select the two intermediate vertices for each sidewalk top and press Delete to remove them. Exit sub-object mode and notice the wrinkling in the mesh object is gone (**Figure 5.44**).

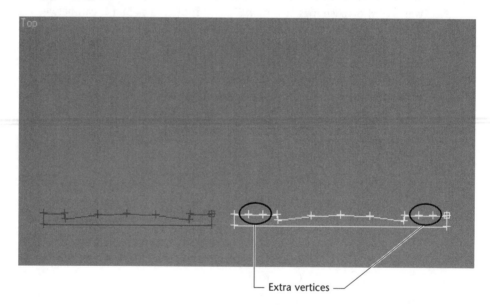

FIGURE 5.43 *Extra vertices in one shape cause interpolation problems to the other shape without contributing useful geometry to the mesh.*

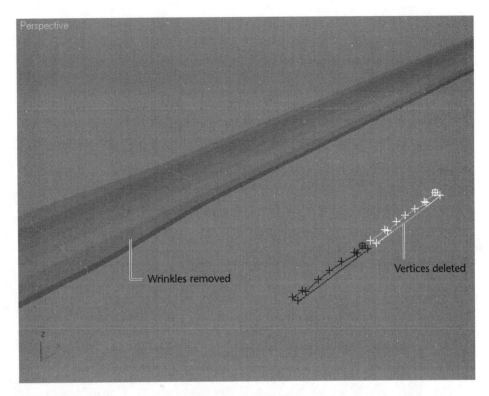

FIGURE 5.44 *Removing the extra vertices creates cleaner geometry.*

4. If you select Roadway, right-click, and open the Properties dialog, you'll see
    that the density of the mesh has been reduced by 574 faces. Every little bit
    helps. Again, remember the definition of shape steps and path steps in lofting.
    They are intermediate steps between vertices that define curvature. There are
    no curves in this roadway object, so the default steps settings can be reduced.
    Select Roadway and, in the Skin Parameters rollout on the Modify panel, set
    the values of Shape Steps and Path Steps to *0*. The Object Properties dialog now
    shows that the mesh contains only 128 faces (see **Figure 5.45** on the next
    page). Click OK to close the dialog.

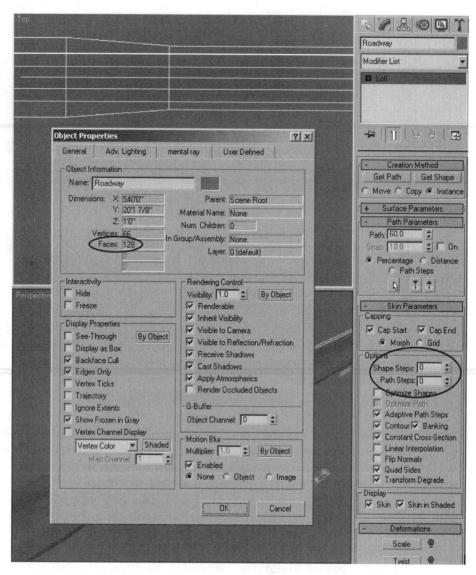

Figure 5.45 *Setting the Path Steps and Shape Steps to 0 on the Modify panel reduces the number of faces to a mere 128 for this straight roadway and bridge, a very significant difference.*

5. Save the file; it should already be called *Ch05_Bridge03.max.*

Minor changes in the 2D shapes and in the parameters of the loft object has created a higher quality and more efficient lofted roadway with bridge.

Paying attention to these small details early in your learning curve with 3ds max 7 is important. By making these techniques an integral part of your workflow, you'll become a more productive modeler.

Summary

In this chapter, you learned how to do the following:

- Create and manipulate lofted objects.
- Use shape and path step controls to significantly reduce the overhead of lofted objects by reducing the number of faces in the model.
- Edit the 2D shape and path without having to deal directly with complex 3D geometry.
- Apply multiple 2D shapes to the same loft path to increase the complexity of the 3D geometry, while retaining simple editing capabilities at the shape level.

This chapter also presented the advantages of lofted objects when you need to apply materials with patterns that can follow the curvature of the lofted objects. Lofting is the only modeling technique that provides a high level of control when applying materials, so it is often worth considering lofting even if there are other modeling techniques that would get the job done. Lofting Deformations, in this case, scaling the ends of an airplane wing, is a method presented in this chapter that gives secondary control to extend the capabilities of lofting.

I encourage you to review the information on lofting in Chapter 2 and, together with the methods learned in this chapter, practice lofting various objects on your desk or in your office until you become very comfortable with this modeling technique.

CHAPTER 6

3D Primitives:
Building Blocks

In This Chapter

So far in this book you've learned to create and modify 2D shapes, to use 2D shapes for lofting, and to use modifiers, such as Extrude and Bevel Profile, to generate complex 3D objects.

In this chapter, you'll learn about another drag-and-click method of creating 3D primitive objects, in which 3ds max 7 does some of the preliminary work for you by providing basic 3D objects with editable parameters. By creating 3D primitive objects, you can modify the objects by changing specific parameters on the Modify panel, such as the length, width, height, and number of segments for each direction.

The first part of this chapter walks you through the creation of several commonly used primitives, to which you'll apply and adjust some modifiers, so that you can gain some hands-on experience with the value of quickly creating objects that have a lot of editing capability.

Later in the chapter you'll create a scene containing several 3D primitives. You'll learn how to use compound objects to edit the primitives, convert a primitive to an editable mesh, and modify the 3D primitive at the sub-object level—Vertex, Edge, Face, Polygon, or Element—to make more complex changes. You'll also learn to use the Edit Mesh modifier to access sub-object-level editing to gain added flexibility, albeit at a potential cost to computer performance.

In the exercises near the end of the chapter, you'll create a landscape with a small airport runway cut into the surface, and a sky that will be the basis for the outdoor scenes used in later chapters. As you perform the exercises, make sure you look beyond the individual steps of each exercise so that you develop some comprehension of the concepts being presented and the workflow introduced. This way you'll be able to apply the processes to your own projects.

This chapter covers the following topics:

- **3D primitives.** You'll learn the process of creating 3D primitives to use as the building blocks for more complex models.
- **Modifiers.** You'll learn to apply and change modifiers to edit the 3D primitives and provide a more flexible workflow.
- **ShapeMerge.** You'll learn how this powerful tool lets you project 2D shapes onto a 3D surface to define new edges and faces for editing.
- **Named selection sets.** You'll learn how you can create selections and name them using named selection sets for fast retrieval at any time, which is particularly convenient at the sub-object level.
- **Face normals.** You'll learn how to take advantage of face normals to control the visibility of parts of 3D objects.
- **Xform modifier.** You'll learn how to use this "transform" modifier to make transforms, particularly scaling, at specific levels in the Modifier stack. The Xform modifier helps avoid distortion problems later in the editing process that are caused by the evaluation order of modifiers and transforms.

Key Terms

- **ShapeMerge.** This tool can be used to cut new edges that define a new set of faces, which then can easily be selected later for further modification.
- **Face normal.** Each face or polygon of a 3D object has an imaginary vector that is perpendicular to the surface. If a face normal points in the viewer's direction, the face is visible; otherwise, it is invisible. A material attribute called *2-sided* can be used to make the face visible, regardless of the direction of the face normal.

Creating and Modifying 3D Primitive Objects

Here we take the first steps toward creating a landscape and sky scene that will be used in other chapters of the book. In this section, you'll create a single concrete pylon that will be used in Chapter 8, *More Modifiers: Orderly Progression*, to divert traffic along a roadway.

This section of the chapter stresses the importance of the order in which modifiers are applied to objects. The exercises within it are basic, allowing you to focus on the process of editing using modifiers. Again, learning the process and workflow for using the Modifier stack to adjust the object you've created is more important than creating the object itself.

Exercise 6.1: Creating 3D Primitives

1. Open 3ds max 7 to a fresh scene, or choose File > Reset, and in the dialog that appears, click Yes to reset the scene to the default settings. If you have made changes to the current scene, you'll first be presented with a dialog asking if you want to save the current changes. After choosing Yes or No, a dialog appears asking if you want to reset. Click Yes (**Figure 6.1**).

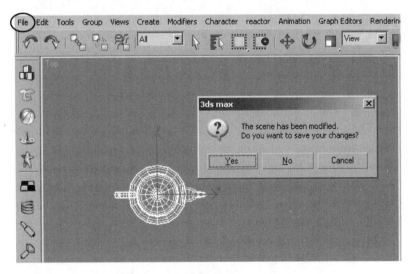

FIGURE 6.1 *To reset the scene to the default settings, choose File > Reset. You'll be prompted to save the current changes if you have made any, and then you need to click Yes to reset.*

Next you'll create a few 3D Primitive objects in the scene that you probably won't need to keep. Using the Edit > Hold and Edit > Fetch feature from the main menu is a convenient method for holding your place in the scene when you want to experiment but still be able to return to the current scene if necessary.

2. From the main menu, choose Edit > Hold (**Figure 6.2**). This stores the current scene in a buffer file that can be retrieved using Edit > Fetch at any time. Only one Hold file can be stored at any one time, so a subsequent Hold operation will overwrite the currently saved file.

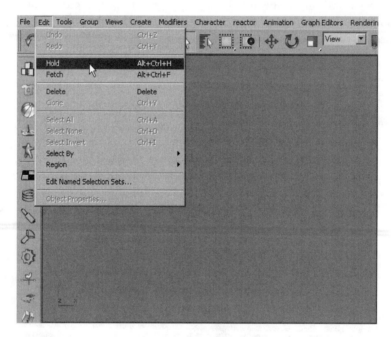

FIGURE 6.2 *The Edit > Hold command saves the current file on your hard drive so that you can retrieve it at any time using Edit > Fetch. This technique is useful when you want to experiment with changes you're not sure you'll keep.*

3. On the Create panel, Geometry category, Standard Primitives Object Type roll-out, click the Box button. In the Top viewport, click and drag near the upper left of the viewport toward the lower right to define the base of the 3D box (**Figure 6.3**). Release the mouse button, push the mouse forward to define a positive height value of the box, and click to set the value. Don't be concerned with the size of the box; you can modify it later.

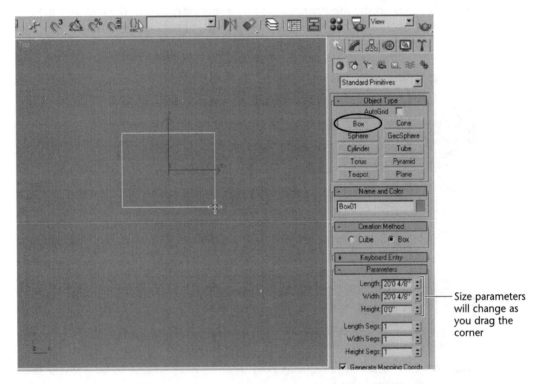

Size parameters will change as you drag the corner

FIGURE 6.3 *Creating a 3D box requires three steps: click and drag in a viewport to define the base, release and push the mouse to define the height, and then click to set the height.*

4. Click the Cylinder button in the Object Type rollout. In the Top viewport, click and drag to set the radius of a cylinder, release and move the mouse forward to define a positive height, and click to set the height. Again, the size of the cylinder doesn't matter in this case. Just concentrate on the process of creating the various types of primitives.

5. In the Top viewport, create a sphere, a tube, and a cone primitive. The method you'll use to create each will vary, depending on the object's parameters. The basic process, however, is to click and drag, and then release, followed by a move and then click if necessary. The move and click is repeated as many times as necessary to create the object.

6. After creating the cone primitive, and while it's still selected, enter the following parameters on the Modify panel to resize the cone: *2'0"* in the Radius 1 field, *1'0"* in the Radius 2 field, and *3'0"* in the Height field (**Figure 6.4**).

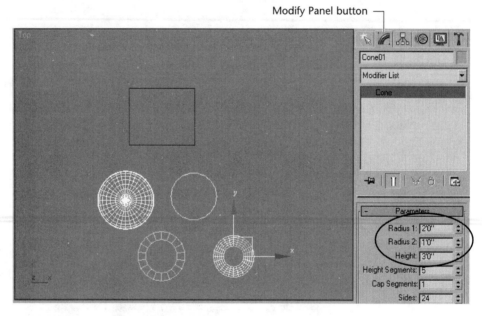

FIGURE 6.4 *On the Modify panel, enter exact amounts in the Parameters fields to change the size of the selected object.*

You've created several primitives—now it's time to clear the scene so that you can create a pylon object for your airport.

7. In Step 2, you performed an Edit > Hold operation to store a file with no objects on the hard drive. Now let's return to that file. Choose Edit > Fetch. In the About to Fetch dialog, click Yes to retrieve the empty scene (**Figure 6.5**).

Get in the habit of using Hold and Fetch anytime you think you may want to return to a particular state in your scene.

Because the purpose of this exercise was to refresh your memory in creating 3D primitives and to learn to use the Hold and Fetch options in 3ds max 7, there's no need to save the current file.

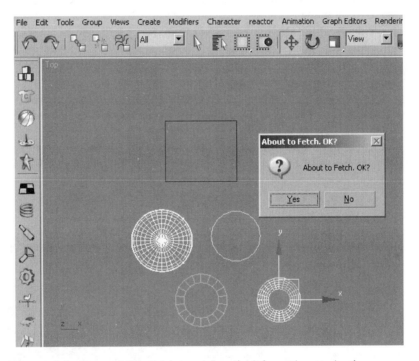

Figure 6.5 *Choose Edit > Fetch to retrieve the information previously stored in the Hold file on your hard drive.*

Modifying 3D Primitives

In this exercise, you'll create a cylinder primitive, set it to a pre-determined size on the Modify panel, and add modifiers to turn it into a conical shape that is bent 90 degrees. It will act as a serious traffic barrier to keep cars off the airport runway in Chapter 8.

This exercise could use a cone primitive as the base object, but it instead asks you to create a cylinder and taper it into a cone shape using a modifier. Doing it this way will help you understand the importance of applying multiple modifiers in a specific sequence to get the end result you want. It will also introduce you to some editing capabilities within the Modifier stack that allow you to easily make changes.

Exercise 6.2: Creating and Modifying a Concrete Pylon

1. Open a new scene in 3ds max 7, or choose File > Reset. Choose File > Save As. In the Save As dialog, navigate to your project folder and save the file using the name *Ch06_Pylon01.max*. Note that you don't need to type *.max* in the name—it will automatically be appended when you save anyway (**Figure 6.6**). Click Save.

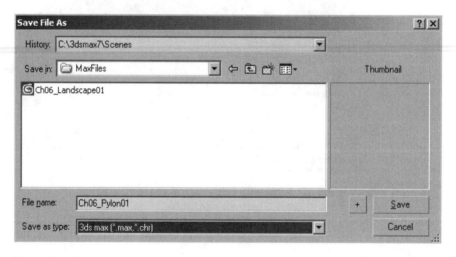

FIGURE 6.6 *Save a new scene to your project folder with the name Ch06_Pylon01.max.*

2. On the Create panel, click the Cylinder button. In the Top viewport, click and drag to set the Radius of a cylinder, release and push the mouse forward to define a positive height, and click to set the height. Don't worry about exact sizes right now.

3. On the Modify panel, change the object name to Pylon01, and enter *2'0"* in the Radius field and *6'0"* in the Height field. Leave the rest of the parameters at their default settings (**Figure 6.7**). Remember to press Enter after entering the last data in a field to see the results in the viewports.

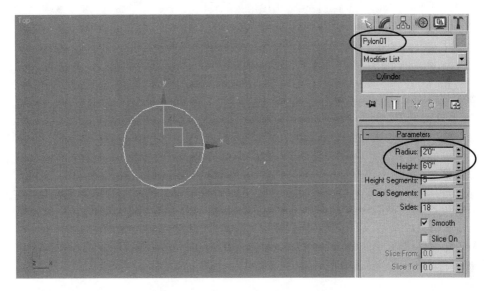

FIGURE 6.7 *Modify the cylinder primitive by changing the name on the Modify panel to* Pylon01 *and setting the Radius and Height fields to 2'0" and 6'0", respectively.*

4. On the Modify panel, choose Bend from the Modifier List (**Figure 6.8**). Then in the Parameters rollout, enter *90* in the Bend Angle field and press Enter. The cylinder will bend from its base at a 90-degree angle (**Figure 6.9**).

FIGURE 6.8 *From the Modifier List, apply a Bend modifier to the cylinder.*

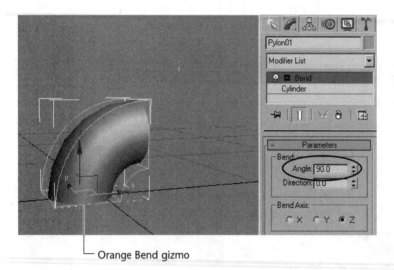

└─ Orange Bend gizmo

FIGURE 6.9 *Enter 90 in the Bend Angle field and press Enter. The cylinder bends. Notice the orange Bend gizmo surrounding the cylinder and that the active Bend modifier is highlighted gray in Stack view.*

5. The added angle would certainly deter traffic, but you also want the pylon to have a taper toward the top. On the Modify panel, Modifier List, choose Taper modifier. A new gizmo appears around the cylinder in the viewports. Enter *-0.5* in the Taper Amount field and press Enter.

   The cylinder takes on a strange distorted appearance in the viewports and may not be at all what you expected (**Figure 6.10**). While the modifiers you have applied—first the Bend and then the Taper—are valid modifiers with valid settings, the order in which they were applied produces unwanted results.

6. To remedy these results, in Stack view, click and drag the Taper modifier from the top of the stack to just below the Bend modifier. Release the mouse button when you see the blue line appear below Bend (**Figure 6.11**), and Taper will be moved below the Bend modifier.

   The Taper modifier is now applied before the Bend modifier, resulting in a better pylon for your airport.

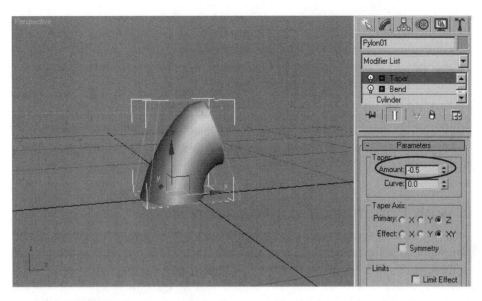

FIGURE 6.10 *Applying a Taper modifier to the cylinder and entering a negative Taper amount produces a distorted object.*

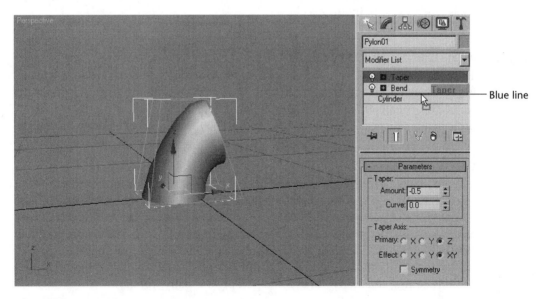

FIGURE 6.11 *You can drag and drop modifiers in the stack to change the editing results of objects. The blue line will indicate where the modifier will be applied as you drag it up and down the stack.*

7. In Stack view, highlight Cylinder to drop to the parameters of the cylinder. Enter *1'0"* in the Radius field and press Enter. The cylinder remains tapered and bent, but the size changes. Again in Stack view, highlight Bend at the top of the stack to return to that level. It is good practice to remember to return to the top of the stack after editing at lower levels.

8. Save the file. It should already be called *Ch06_Pylon01.max*.

As you can see, the order the modifiers are applied to an object can greatly affect the end result. However, modifiers can be moved up or down the stack to change the order.

Working with Primitives in an Outdoor Scene

Many other modifiers and workflow techniques can be used with 3D primitives. You'll learn just a few of these in the next set of exercises as you create a landscape and sky for the airport scene. In this and the next sections, you'll use ShapeMerge to define a runway and then modify a hemisphere primitive by flipping the face normals toward the viewer so that the hemisphere is visible when looking up, away from the land.

You'll also get some practice using the Modifier stack and modifiers to gain editing flexibility and hopefully reduce overhead for faster production, both very important goals when working in 3ds max 7.

Using the ShapeMerge Compound Object

The scene you open next contains a plane primitive object used as a landscape. There is a 2D shape in the scene that you'll use to define the edges of the runway and taxiway of this small airport. The shape is placed below the landscape so that it can be projected in its Local *Z*-axis onto the plane. If you need a refresher on the Local reference coordinate system, see Chapter 2, *Fundamental Concepts*.

Once you've defined the edges of the runway and taxiway, you'll select the new faces defined by the ShapeMerge operation and create a named selection set that lets you reselect the set of polygons at any time without having to manually select each polygon or group of polygons. The ability to reselect polygons will be very important for efficiently assigning materials to the scene in Chapter 12, *The Materials Editor: Your Palette at a Glance*. Thinking ahead to anticipate processes is an important part of working with 3ds max 7. Once you learn the fundamentals of the tools, anticipating possible editing situations will become part of your daily workflow.

The landscape plane has also been created 5 feet lower than the World Grid. You'll use an Align tool to raise the entire runway 5 feet and then rotate its polygons to form a ramping runway.

Exercise 6.3: Using ShapeMerge and Named Selection Sets

1. Open the file called **Ch06_Landscape01.max** on the CD-ROM. Choose File > Save As and click the plus button to save an incremental file called *Ch06_Landscape02.max* to a project folder on your hard drive. Click the Select button on the main toolbar and, in the Top viewport, select the plane primitive called *Landscape* in the scene. From the Modify panel, notice that the parameters are set to 2,000 feet square, and that the default settings are in effect for the rest of the fields (**Figure 6.12**). Also notice a 2D shape in the lower center in the Top viewport.

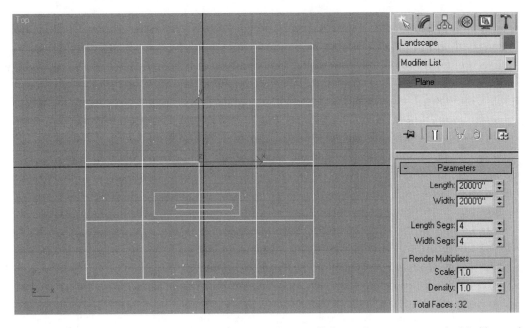

Figure 6.12 *Select the Landscape plane and observe the overall size and parameters on the Modify panel.*

2. You need to define the edges of the runway or taxiway on a plane that has a limited number of faces and vertices, which can be used to edit the object. Instead of directly selecting and working with the faces and vertices in the plane object, you'll use the ShapeMerge Compound Object tool to project the shape onto the plane. It is important that the 3D object—in this case, Landscape—is selected. On the Create panel, click Standard Primitives and choose Compound Objects from the list (**Figure 6.13**).

FIGURE 6.13 *On the Create panel, choose Standard Primitives > Compound Objects to access a rollout of Compound Object tools, including ShapeMerge.*

3. On the Create panel, Object Type rollout, click the ShapeMerge button. In the Pick Operand rollout, click the Pick Shape button. In the Top viewport, pick the edge of the runway 2D shape. The shape looks like it turns white in the viewport. (It doesn't actually turn white; instead the new edges are being cut into the plane as the shape is projected up onto it.) The name *Shape 1: runway_shape* appears below Mesh: Landscape in the Operands window. Click the Pick Shape button again to exit that mode (**Figure 6.14**).

You can verify that ShapeMerge successfully projected the shape by clicking the Cookie Cutter radio button in the Operation area of the Parameters rollout (**Figure 6.15**). The new polygons will be subtracted from the plane, leaving a hole. To return the polygons to the plane, click the Merge radio button (the default setting).

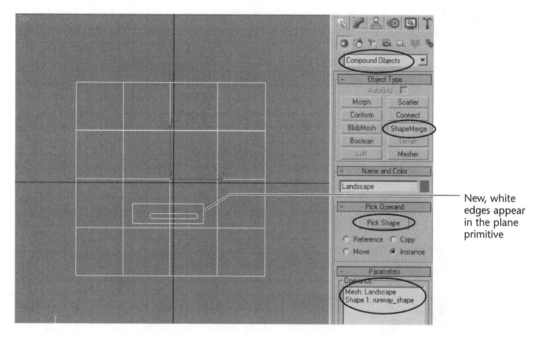

New, white
edges appear
in the plane
primitive

FIGURE 6.14 *ShapeMerge projects the shape, which is below the plane, up onto the plane to define new edges and polygons. The shape is still in its original position and has not been modified.*

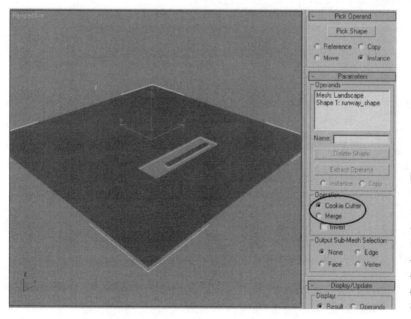

FIGURE 6.15
Use the Cookie Cutter Operation mode of ShapeMerge to verify that ShapeMerge was successful. Return immediately to Merge mode once you see the results.

4. If you used the Cookie Cutter to test ShapeMerge, make sure you're back in Merge mode. You must now select the new polygons defined by the ShapeMerge operation. To access the Polygon sub-object level, right-click on Landscape in the Top viewport and choose Convert To > Convert to Editable Mesh in the quad menu that appears (**Figure 6.16**). This "bakes" the ShapeMerge operation into the mesh and gives you access to sub-object-level editing.

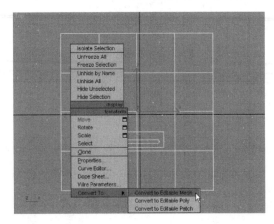

FIGURE 6.16
Converting the object to an editable mesh reduces the overhead of ShapeMerge and provides access to the sub-object levels.

5. On the Modify panel, expand Editable Mesh in Stack view and highlight Polygon sub-object mode. The polygons generated by ShapeMerge will automatically be selected and appear red (**Figure 6.17**).

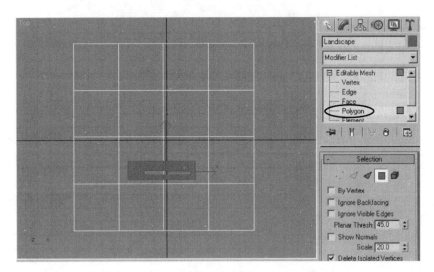

FIGURE 6.17 *Converting a ShapeMerge object to an editable mesh object and accessing the Polygon sub-object mode selects the new polygons created by ShapeMerge.*

6. On the main toolbar, enter *Runway* in the Named Selection Set field and press Enter (**Figure 6.18**). Pressing Enter after typing the name is important to ensure the naming of the selection set is complete. Click an empty space in the Top viewport to clear the current selection set. In Stack view, highlight Editable Mesh to exit Polygon sub-object mode. Editable Mesh in Stack view turns gray.

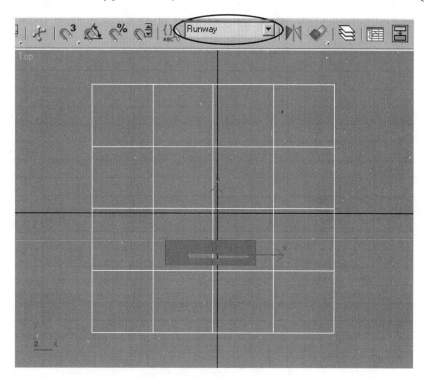

FIGURE 6.18 *When you have a selection set at any sub-object level, you can type a name for the selection set in the Named Selection Set window on the main toolbar and press Enter. Naming the set enables you to reselect the previously selected faces easily at a later time by going to sub-object mode and choosing the name from the list.*

The next step involves raising the polygons that make the runway and taxiway higher than the ground around them using an alignment tool built into editable mesh objects at the sub-object level.

7. Select the Landscape plane in the Perspective viewport and click the Select and Move button on the main toolbar. Read the *Z*-axis position, in absolute coordinates, of the pivot point of the plane at the lower center of the display. It shows the pivot is *-5'0"* or 5 feet below the current World Grid (**Figure 6.19**).

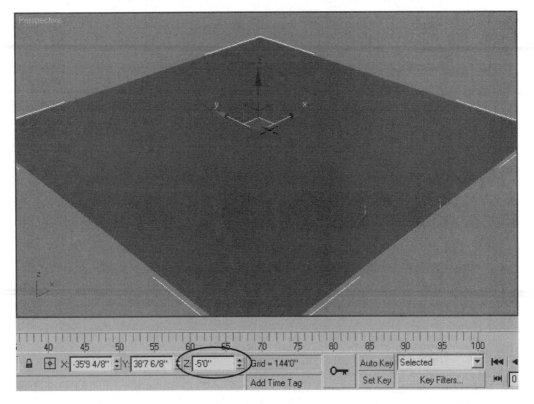

FIGURE 6.19 *With an object selected and the Select and Move option active, you can read the current coordinates of the object's Pivot Point in the Transform Type-in display.*

8. To align the runway polygons to the current World Grid, you need to reselect them. On the Modify panel, highlight the Polygon sub-object level in Stack view. Notice that nothing high-lights in the viewport. This is because we cleared the selection set by picking an empty space in Step 6. If you had not had the fore-sight to create a named selection set, this would be a problem. Click the arrow to the right of the Named Selection Set field on the main tool-

tip

You must be in the sub-object mode for the type of named selection set you had originally created. For example, if I were in Vertex sub-object mode, Runway would not appear in the Named Selection Set list.

bar and choose Runway from the drop-down list (**Figure 6.20**). This reselects the runway polygons and they turn red in the viewports.

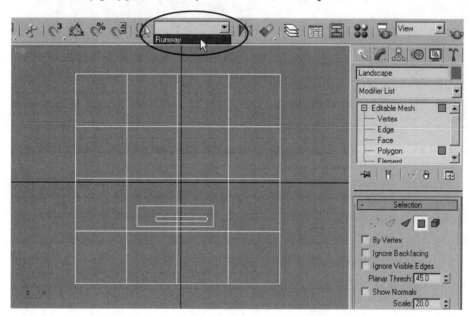

FIGURE 6.20 *When Landscape is selected and you are in Polygon sub-object mode, you can use named selection sets to reselect the runway polygons.*

9. Make sure the Perspective viewport is still active. On the Modify panel, Edit Geometry rollout, click the Grid Align button. This moves the selected polygons 5 feet in the positive Z-axis, creating a slightly ramped apron to the surrounding landscape. The ramping can be clearly seen by zooming in on the runway in the Left viewport (**Figure 6.21**).

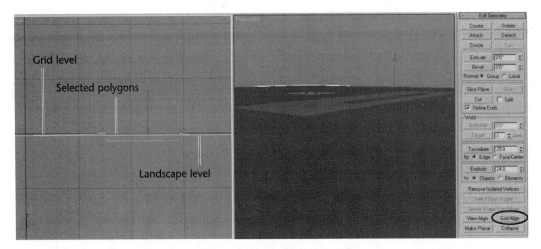

FIGURE 6.21 *Grid Align moves the selection set in a straight line to the active grid for the current viewport.*

10. In Stack view on the Modify panel, highlight Editable Mesh to exit sub-object mode. Save the file; it should already be called *Ch06_Landscpape02.max*. Selecting the polygons of the runway without a named selection set would have been a complex task.

In this exercise, you used

- ShapeMerge, an important tool for creating complex sets at the sub-object level for more editing control
- Named selection sets, which let you easily reselect the sub-object level sets later in the production cycle
- Align tools (the Grid Align tool in this case), which at the sub-object level let you manipulate your mesh objects in ways that would be much more difficult manually

Don't forget to think proactively and generate the named selection sets in advance, even if you're not sure you'll use them later. If you do need to reselect complex sets, named selection sets will save you a lot of time.

Using Modifiers for a Flexible and Efficient Workflow

In the next exercise, you'll practice a flexible and efficient method for creating the sky for the outdoor scene. Of course, there are other methods you could use—you could apply a photo of a sky as the background image or map a panoramic sky photo around the inside of a sphere or cylinder. But the method presented here emphasizes optimum workflow, which is what you want to always keep in mind.

You'll create a geosphere primitive object, which is a spherical object made of geodesic polygons containing an evenly distributed pattern of vertices over the surface. The geosphere will be made into a hemisphere and, for efficiency, you'll remove the unnecessary faces that cap the bottom.

By default, the face normals of a sphere point outward from the center. However, from the point of view of someone standing inside the sphere looking up at the "sky," the faces would be invisible. So you must flip the faces to point the face normals toward the viewer. This could also be done by converting the geosphere to an editable mesh and using the built-in tools to delete some faces and flip others. However, if you later decide that the dome should change size or not have the bottom cap faces deleted, you would have limited options for changing it.

You'll also utilize the Modifier stack in this exercise to allow changes at many levels in the process at any time. This is a workflow that takes advantage of the power of the Modifier stack and parametric modifiers.

You will also learn to scale objects using the Xform modifier. Directly scaling an object sometimes causes unwanted distortion when the object is modified later because 3ds max 7 evaluates the Modifier stack first before evaluating any transforms, such as Move, Rotate, and Scale.

Creating a Skydome

The first step in making a flexible sky for your outdoor scene is to start with a geosphere primitive and modify it so that it's visible to a viewer when standing on the ground in your scene.

I can't say it often enough— *flexibility and efficiency are something you should always strive for.* Rebuilding mesh objects from scratch and having objects with too many unnecessary faces waste valuable time in production and are the primary reason why users suffer from low productivity.

Exercise 6.4: Using Face Normals and Extra Faces

1. Open the file called *Ch06_Landscape02.max* from the last exercise or from the CD-ROM. Save the file to your project folder with the name *Ch06_Landscape03.max*. It is the landscape scene in which you used ShapeMerge to add a runway.

2. If you're continuing from the previous exercise, on the Create panel, Geometry category, Object Type rollout, click the Geosphere button. In the Top viewport, click near the center of the landscape plane and drag to the right edge of the plane. This creates a geosphere centered near the middle of the landscape (**Figure 6.22**).

note

The geosphere may seem to disappear in the Top viewport because of a process called *viewport clipping*, which speeds working in the viewports by cutting the display of geometry that is closer than certain distances from the viewer. It is only a visual effect—it doesn't affect the geosphere itself, which you can observe in the other viewports.

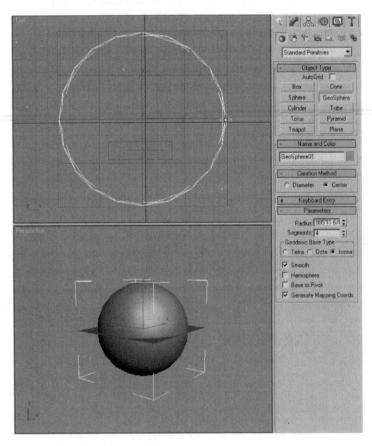

Figure 6.22
Create a geosphere primitive that covers the landscape plane.

3. On the Modify panel, Parameters rollout, select the Hemisphere option to remove half of the geosphere and create a cap of faces to close the bottom of the geosphere. The face normals of the geosphere point outward from the center, making the bottom cap visible in the shaded Perspective viewport.

4. On the Modify panel, in the Modifier List, choose Normal. This flips the face normals and the geosphere turns "inside out" (**Figure 6.23**). Notice in the Perspective viewport that the flipped cap faces are coplanar with the landscape surface. This is unnecessary geometry and will cause problems because 3ds max 7 can't know which set of coplanar faces we want to see.

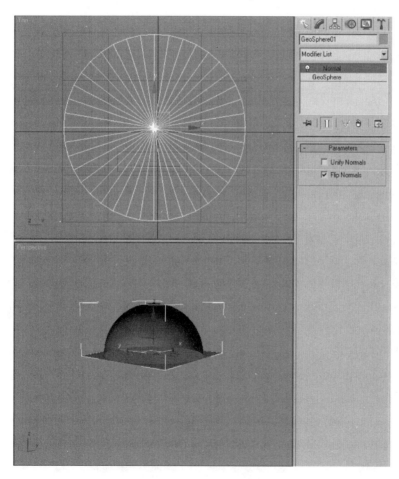

FIGURE 6.23

Applying a Normal modifier flips the direction of the face normals, making them point inward toward the landscape so that viewers standing on the landscape can see the faces.

5. You could convert the geosphere to an editable mesh and delete the cap faces, but then you wouldn't be able to adjust the parameters of the geosphere if you later changed your mind. Again, flexibility is an important part of what you are trying to achieve here. Instead, you'll use two modifiers, MeshSelect and Delete Mesh, to accommodate later changes, if necessary. In the Modifier List, choose the MeshSelect modifier. Expand the modifier in Stack view and highlight Polygon mode. Click the Select button on the main toolbar and make sure you're in Window Selection mode. In the Front viewport, drag a window around the bottom edge of the hemisphere. The cap faces become highlighted in red (**Figure 6.24**).

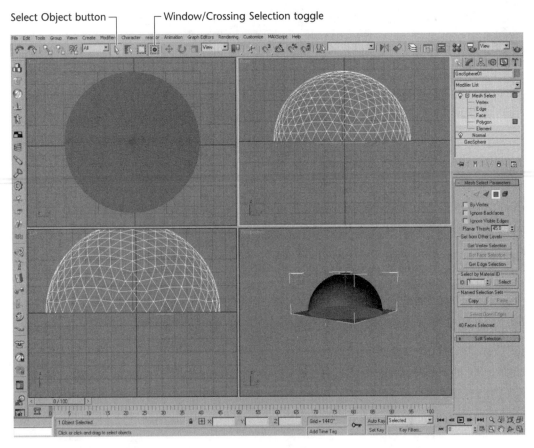

FIGURE 6.24 *With a MeshSelect modifier in the stack, you can choose Polygon sub-object mode and select the bottom cap faces of the hemisphere.*

6. The MeshSelect modifier lets you select at only the object or sub-object level, and then passes the selection up to the next modifier in the stack. In the Modifier List, choose the DeleteMesh modifier to delete the cap faces. Then apply another MeshSelect modifier to end the sub-object selection and return control to the whole mesh. After doing this, you can disable or remove the lower MeshSelect or the DeleteMesh to easily get the faces back if you need to. You can also adjust the Normal modifier or the base Geosphere parameters.

7. Now it's time to scale the geosphere so that the top of the sphere is lower to the ground, which makes a more effective sky for viewers who are looking toward the horizon. Always use an Xform modifier to scale objects at a specific level in the Modifier stack so that the information is passed up the stack correctly. (See the Caution note on this page for more information.) In the Modifier List, choose the Xform modifier.

8. The Xform modifier is automatically in sub-object Gizmo mode. Click the Select and Scale button on the main toolbar and, in the Front viewport, click and drag downward on the Y-axis restrict arrow to produce the Scale Transform gizmo. Observe the Transform Y field at the bottom of the window, and drag until the field reads approximately 75 percent (see **Figure 6.25** on the next page). Click on Xform in Stack view to exit the sub-object Gizmo mode.

note

If you try to drop below the lower MeshSelect modifier in the stack, a warning will display that says, "A modifier exists in the Stack that depends on topology. Changing parameters may have undesirable effects." Always use the Hold/Yes button to store the current scene so that you can use Edit > Fetch to retrieve it. However, in this case, you have not changed the topology of the geosphere in a way that would cause any problems and, theoretically, you could ignore the warning.

caution

Do not scale objects in 3ds max 7 at the object level. You need to apply an Xform modifier. It is possible to scale at any sub-object level without problems, however.

Scale along the Y axis using the Transform gizmo arrow

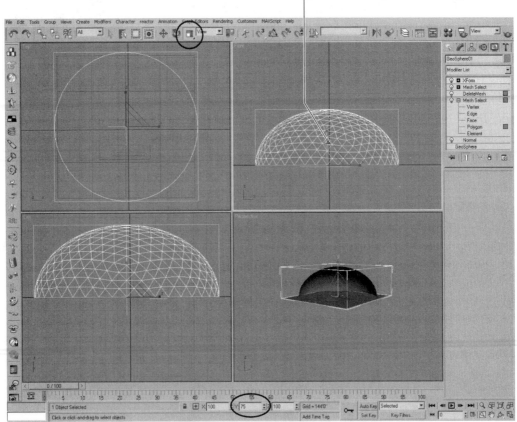

FIGURE 6.25 *Using the Xform modifier, you can safely scale the hemisphere to 75 percent of its original height in the Y-axis in the Front viewport. Always exit the Gizmo sub-object mode of Xform modifiers after you make your changes.*

9. Save the file. It should already be called *Ch06_Landscape03.max*.

In this short lesson, you've learned some critical techniques and workflows that can greatly increase your efficiency and flexibilty. The Normal modifier makes you more efficient by allowing you to make the faces more visible for the viewer by adjusting the face normals, rather than assigning the object a thickness, for example, which would increase the number of faces significantly. And using the MeshSelect and the DeleteMesh modifiers gave you the flexibility to bring the polygons back by disabling or deleting the modifiers.

Summary

In this chapter, you learned to create primitive 3D objects and apply modifiers to them, creating a history of discrete operations in the Modifier stack through which you can navigate to make changes later if you need to.

You were also introduced to some other production techniques, such as the ShapeMerge tool and the Xform modifier, as well as such concepts as face normals and named selection sets, which you'll use regularly when working with 3ds max 7.

CHAPTER 7

The Editable Poly: Box Modeling

In This Chapter

So far you've learned to model 2D shapes, using modifiers and lofting, and 3D primitives, using modifiers.

In this chapter, you'll learn how to apply a modeling technique that's commonly referred to as *box modeling* because the process often involves using a simple 3D box primitive that is converted to an editable poly or has the Edit Poly modifier applied. You then manipulate the object (it doesn't have to be a box—any 3D object can be used) at the sub-object level, much as a sculptor would work a block of clay—pulling here, pushing there—until the desired results are achieved.

The biggest advantage of box modeling over other modeling techniques is that you have explicit control over the number of polygons in the object, so you gain greater efficiency. And efficiency is one of the main reasons that box modeling is very popular with designers in the computer games industry.

The downside of box modeling is that you do not have a process history through which you can navigate to make changes at various levels in the Modifier stack or when lofting. Once you have committed to a command, flexible editing is not an option. The best way to decide if box modeling is for you is to learn the fundamentals of this method so that you can compare it to the other techniques presented in this book. Then you can make an informed decision in regard to your particular style and workflow.

The first few exercises in this chapter have you practicing and focusing on a very fundamental workflow as you create a couple of whimsical objects, allowing you to familiarize yourself with the power of box modeling without having to be concerned with the outcome. Subsequent exercises walk you through the creation of one-half of the fuselage of a small airplane, requiring you to pay close attention to the steps so that you can produce an object that will work in the outdoor scene you created in the last chapter.

You'll also learn about and use two more modifiers: Symmetry and Lathe. The Symmetry modifier will help you create a whole fuselage out of the half that you create; the Lathe modifier will help you turn a 2D shape into the nose bezel of the airplane. You'll also learn to merge objects from other scenes by utilizing the airplane wing you lofted in Chapter 5.

This chapter covers the following topics:

- **Editable poly.** Also known as *Epoly*, an editable poly is a 3D object composed of quad, or four-sided, polygons instead of the triangular faces that make up an editable mesh.

- **Symmetry modifier.** This powerful modifier lets you create half an object, and then it copies a mirror image of it, trims it, and combines the halves into a whole integral mesh.

- **Lathe modifier**. Using the Lathe modifier to lathe, or revolve, a 2D shape around a center to create a 3D surface is a flexible workflow.

- **Merge.** Merging provides an opportunity to import objects from other 3ds max 7 scenes, which increases productivity, especially in a collaborative work environment.

Key Terms

- **Quad polygon.** This four-sided surface definition lets tools be included in the editable poly object and Edit Poly modifier that would be impossible to access using standard triangular mesh surfaces.

- **Settings dialog.** Specific to Editable Poly objects and the Edit Poly modifier, the Settings dialog lets you preview or cancel changes to objects before committing the command.

- **NURMS.** Non-Uniform Relational Mesh Surface is 3ds max 7 jargon for a surface algorithm that adds geometry to round the corners of low-polygon objects.

Understanding the Basics

Box modeling is a very straightforward way to edit simple 3D objects into more complex forms that maintain a low polygon count. Box modeling does, however, require that you have good perception of 3D space, much like a fine-art sculptor does.

The Edit Poly modifier is new in version 7 of 3ds max, and the functionality of the editable poly object has been enhanced. Both have similar functionality. You can learn more about how they are alike and different from each other by choosing Help > User Reference from the main menu. For the purposes of this chapter, however, you just need to become familiar with the fundamental workflow for box modeling techniques, so that you can use the objects that have been converted to editable poly.

Some of the work you do with box modeling is accomplished in the Perspective or User viewport where you can see the object at an angle for reference. Work slowly at first and verify your progress by looking at the orthographic viewports to make sure "what you see is what you get." It's imperative that you use the Transform gizmo to restrict transforms to a particular axis.

With a little practice, box modeling will become a very fast and intuitive method of creating objects such as outbuildings, furniture, and characters, or boats and airplanes that don't require engineering accuracy.

Getting Started with the Tools

In this section, you'll be designing a small building that could be used as a playhouse for children. The actual sizes of the building are not important at this time; instead you should concentrate on the workflow and the tools being introduced in 3ds max 7.

You'll open a file with a box in the form of a cube. The file already has Edge Faces turned on in the Perspective viewport, so you'll be able to view the wireframe and shaded object simultaneously, making it much easier to work.

Then, by editing the box at the sub-object level of an editable poly, you'll manipulate edges and polygons to form a low-polygon house with windows in the front. At the end of the exercise, you'll enable a feature of editable poly that illustrates the flexibility of box modeling.

Exercise 7.1: Designing a Playhouse

1. Open **Ch07_Box01.max** from the CD-ROM and save it to your project folder with the name *Ch07_Box02.max*. Click the Select Object button on the main toolbar and select the cube in the Perspective viewport. Notice the Edged Faces option is enabled so that you can see the visible edges and the shaded object. Right-click in the Perspective viewport and choose Convert To > Convert to Editable Poly from the quad menu (**Figure 7.1**).

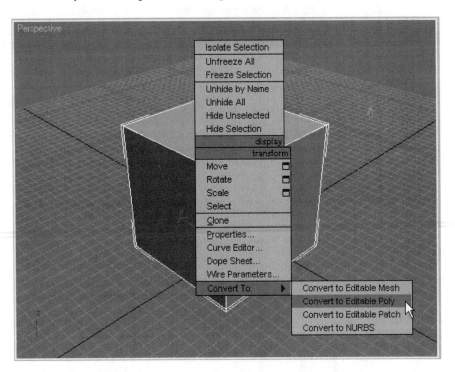

FIGURE 7.1 *Select the cube and right-click to convert to editable poly.*

2. On the Modify panel, expand Editable Poly in Stack view and highlight the
    Edge sub-object in the stack. Select the vertical corner edge nearest you in the
    Perspective viewport. It will turn red when selected. On the Modify panel,
    Selection rollout, click the Ring button. This button aids the selection at the
    sub-object level of similar edges around the object that share common poly-
    gons (**Figure 7.2**). Notice that four edges are selected (displayed just below the
    Ring button), and all four have similar vertical edges.

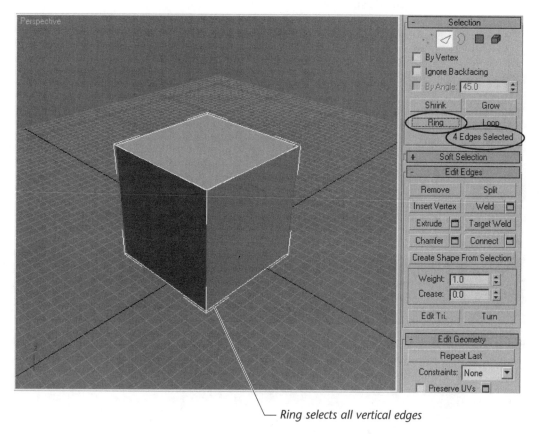

— Ring selects all vertical edges

FIGURE 7.2 *When you select an edge at the sub-object level and click the Ring button, 3ds max 7
selects all similar sub-objects that share adjacent polygons.*

3. Now you need to cut two new edges that connect the four vertical edges. On the Modify panel, Edit Edges rollout, click the Settings icon, located just to the right of the Connect button. The Connect Edges dialog appears. You can preview the potential changes in the viewports before committing to the edit. In the Connect Edge Segments field of the dialog, enter 2. This cuts two equally spaced edges connecting each of the selected vertical edges, which you can also preview in the viewports. Click OK in the Connect Edges dialog to finalize the edit (**Figure 7.3**).

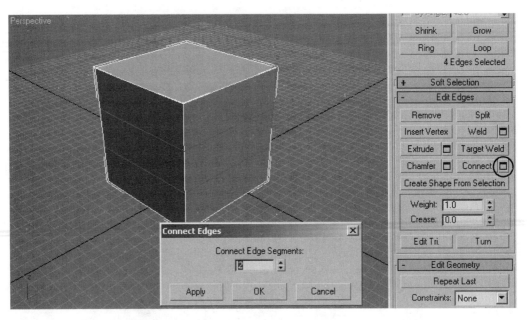

FIGURE 7.3 *The Settings icon lets you preview changes before committing to the final result.*

4. Click an empty area in the Perspective viewport to clear the current selection set. At the top of the Selection rollout, select the Ignore Backfacing option. This will prevent you from accidentally selecting edges you cannot see. Select the front right and back left edges at the top of the cube. Use the Ctrl key to add to a selection set. Click the Settings icon again, and in the Connect Edges dialog that appears, set the Connect Edge Segments field to *1*. This creates one new segment from midpoint to midpoint of the selected edges (**Figure 7.4**). Click OK to commit to the edit.

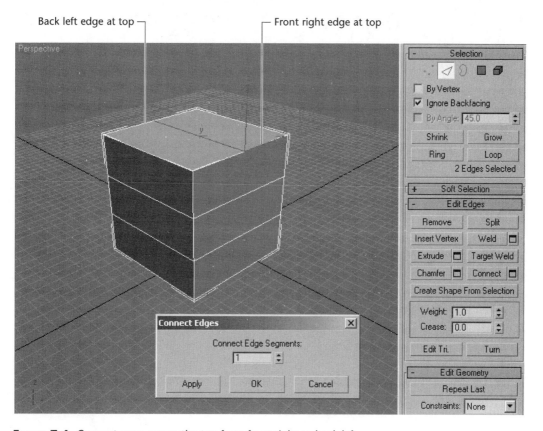

FIGURE 7.4 *Connect once across the top from front right to back left.*

5. Click any empty space in the Perspective viewport to clear the edge selection. Select only the new edge that divides the top polygon. Click the Select and Move button on the main toolbar. Toggle on Offset mode from the status bar and enter *5* in the Z-axis field. Press Enter. A peaked roof will be formed for your house (**Figure 7.5**).

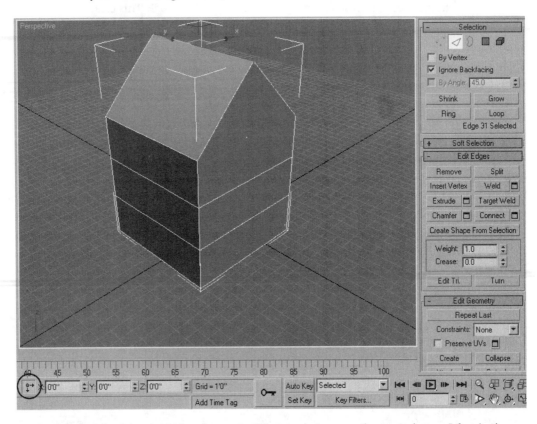

FIGURE 7.5 *Use the Select and Move button in Offset mode to move the new edge up 5 feet in the Z-axis to form a roof.*

6. Now let's add a European look to the roof. Highlight Vertex sub-object mode in Stack view. Using the Ctrl key, select the two vertices at the ends of the roof peak. In the Edit Vertices rollout, click the Settings icon to the right of the Chamfer button. In the Chamfer Vertices dialog, enter 4 and press Enter. The roof vertices are chamfered (**Figure 7.6**). Click OK to finalize the command.

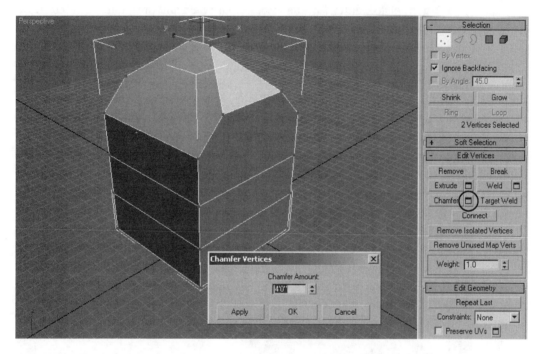

FIGURE 7.6 *Chamfer the two peak end vertices 4 feet for a European look.*

7. At the Polygon sub-object level, you'll add two large depressed areas to the front of the playhouse for windows. In Stack view, highlight Polygon sub-object mode. In the Perspective viewport, use the Ctrl key to select the top and middle polygon on the right side of the house. They will both turn red. In the Edit Polygons rollout, click the Settings icon beside the Inset button. In the Inset Polygons dialog, enter *1* in the Inset Amount field and press Enter. This creates a new polygon that is inset 1 foot from the previous polygon's edges (**Figure 7.7**). This is not quite what you want, however.

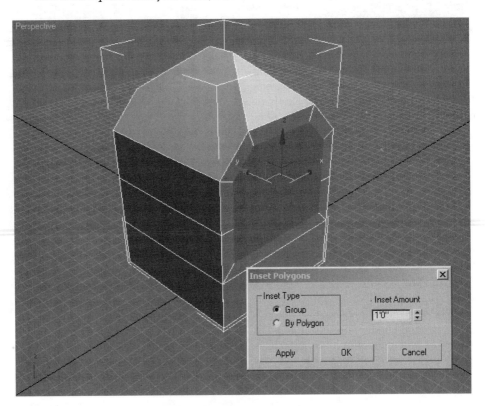

FIGURE 7.7 *Select the two upper polygons on the right side and use the Inset Polygons dialog to inset the new polygon by 1 foot.*

8. Click the By Polygon radio button in the Inset Polygons dialog. This insets each selected polygon on its own center (**Figure 7.8**). Click OK to close the dialog and finalize the edit.

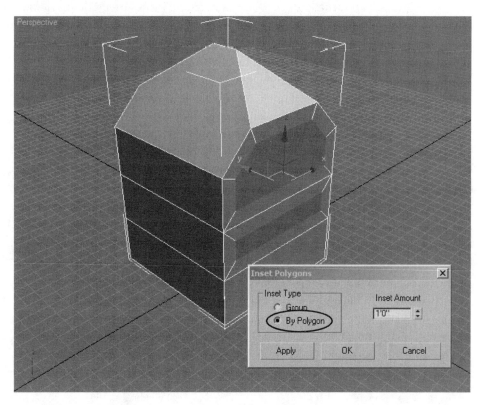

FIGURE 7.8 *The By Polygon option insets each selected polygon on its own center, rather than centering on the selection set as a whole.*

9. Click any empty space in the viewport to clear the selection set. Select the new lower polygon you created in Step 8. In the Edit Polygons rollout, click the Settings icon to the right of the Extrude button. In the Extrude Polygons dialog, enter *-1* in the Extrusion Height field and press Enter. The polygon is pulled 1 foot into the playhouse with newly created polygons at the edges (**Figure 7.9**). Click OK.

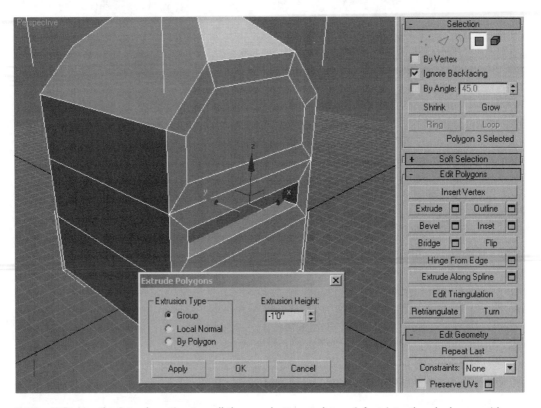

FIGURE 7.9 *Use the Extrude option to pull the new bottom polygon 1 foot into the playhouse with newly created polygons at the edges.*

10. Select the upper polygon you created in Step 8. In the Edit Polygons rollout, click the Settings icon located beside the Bevel button. In the Bevel Polygons dialog, enter *-1* in both the Height and Outline Amount fields and press Enter. The selected polygon is moved into the playhouse, and new sloped sides are added to the surface (**Figure 7.10**). Click OK in the Bevel Polygons dialog.

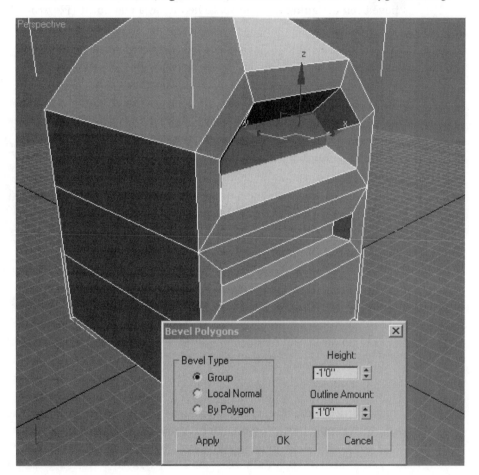

FIGURE 7.10 *Use Bevel to move the top polygon inward with sloped sides, keeping it connected to the original surface.*

So far you've been taking steps to create a 3D playhouse, but the workflow could be the same for a variety of objects. Let's try something different.

11. Exit sub-object mode by highlighting Editable Poly in stack view. On the Modify panel, Subdivision Surface rollout, select the Use NURMS Subdivision checkbox and clear the Isoline Display checkbox. Enter *2* in the Display Iterations field and press Enter. This applies a smoothing algorithm to your model to add extra polygons that round the edges. You could just as easily have been designing an alien space helmet as a playhouse (**Figure 7.11**).

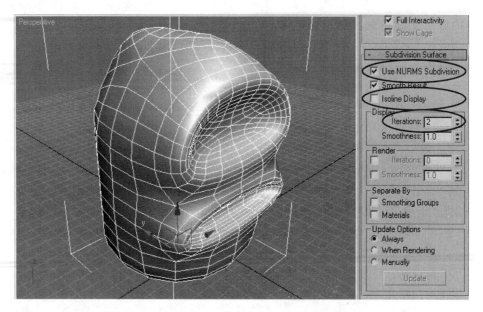

FIGURE 7.11 *By enabling the Use NURMS Subdivision option, your playhouse can be changed to something resembling an alien space helmet.*

12. Save the file. It should already be called *Ch07_Box02.max*.

You have learned some of the fundamentals of box modeling and have seen that by starting with simple blocky objects and turning on the NURMS Subdivision option you can also create much more complex rounded models. Of course, if it was a playhouse you wanted, then editing the edges and polygons would be all you needed.

When using the NURMS Subdivision option to round the edges of the boxy low-polygon model into a more flowing organic form, you'll have to practice with the relationship of edges to generate the proper amount of rounding. You'll also need to plan ahead before you start editing because it's difficult to undo more than one or two steps as the work progresses.

Using Box Modeling to Create a Fuselage

In this section, you'll use box modeling techniques similar to the ones you just practiced in the previous exercise to create half an airplane fuselage. While the size of the house you created earlier didn't really matter, you'll want the fuselage to be a certain size to match the rest of your scenes throughout the book.

The scene for Exercise 7.2 has been set up to allow you to trace over a set of plans for a Turner Special airplane that I found on the Internet. The plans show a side, top, and front view of the fuselage along with several cross sections (**Figure 7.12**).

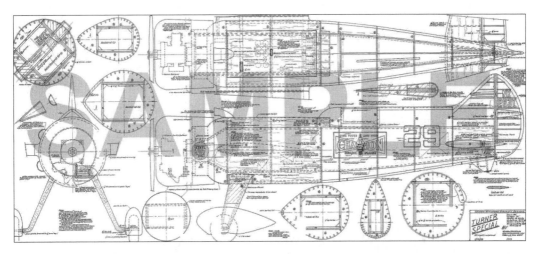

FIGURE 7.12 *A plan for a Turner Special airplane found on the Internet will be used as a guide for creating a model.*

The scene has been set up for you so that you can concentrate on the box modeling. Three intersecting planes have a material applied that uses the fuselage plans as a color map. The maps have been enabled to show in the viewport. A segmented box has been placed in the scene. It has been sized and aligned to match the side, top, and front views of the airplane and converted to an editable poly object. The material has mapping coordinates assigned, which retains the original aspect ratio of the image to keep it from distorting the plans.

tip

The fuselage exercises require that you often work in the Perspective viewport and that you utilize the Transform gizmos to ensure you're moving sub-object selections in the desired axis. New users to 3D modeling often find it difficult to visualize where they are in 3D space. Earlier chapters in this book have suggested working only in orthographic viewports, Front, Top, Left, Right, Back, and Bottom until you become orientated in 3D space.

Start slowly with this exercise and make sure you understand each step as you perform it. As mentioned earlier, planning this sort of modeling in advance can help you avoid working yourself into a corner that is hard to undo later. I have tried to keep the steps simple so that you can learn from them, but it may still be confusing as to which vertex or edge must be selected for each step.

Exercise 7.2: Creating the Turner Special Fuselage

1. Open **Ch07_Plane01.max** from the CD-ROM and save it to your project folder as *Ch07_Plane02.max*. This file is the scene containing a box that is aligned with three intersecting planes, and the fuselage plans have been applied as a material. Select the Fuselage box in the Top viewport. Right-click and choose Properties from the quad menu. On the General tab of the Object Properties dialog, select the See-Through option in the Display Properties area (**Figure 7.13**). Click OK to close the dialog. This allows you to see the plans through the box for easier editing (**Figure 7.14**).

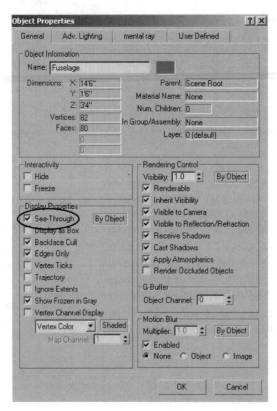

FIGURE 7.13 *Set the properties for seeing through the box.*

FIGURE 7.14 *The box becomes transparent gray in the viewports.*

tip

If your plans appear very pixilated in the viewports and hard to read, you may need to adjust your graphics card drivers for 3ds max. Choose Customize > Preferences, and then in the Preference Settings dialog, select the Viewport tab. In the Display Drivers area, click the Configure Drivers button.

Keep an eye out for options such as Background Texture Size and Download Texture Size. For the Match Bitmap Size option, select Closely as Possible or set it to the highest resolution option. Each graphics card and driver is different, so the wording may be similar but not exactly the same.

You'll need to exit 3ds max 7 and open it again to have the changes take place.

It may also help to turn on Texture Correction in the Viewport options by right-clicking the viewport label and toggling it in the menu.

2.   Right-click in the Top viewport to activate it. Maximize the viewport by click-
     ing the Maximize Viewport toggle or using the Alt + W keyboard shortcut. The
     Fuselage box is covering half of the top plan.

     In the next several steps, you'll move sets of vertices to match the curve of the
     plan as it tapers toward the back. Each horizontal row of vertices must be edit-
     ed, with the exception of the row at the center of the plan, so that the whole
     tail tapers to the back.

3.   Expand Editable Poly in Stack view and highlight Vertex sub-object mode.
     Click the Select Object button on the main toolbar and make sure Window
     Selection mode is active. Drag a selection window around the vertices on the
     far right in the second row from the top. There should be five vertices selected
     and indicated in the Selection rollout (**Figure 7.15**). It will appear as if only
     one vertex is selected (red), as the others are directly below it.

Select Object button

Window/Crossing Selection toggle

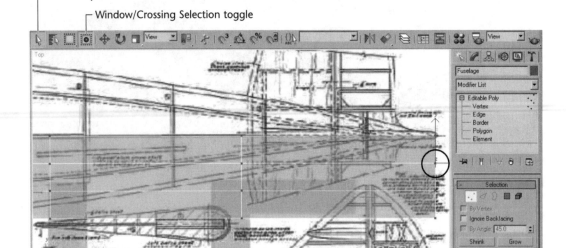

FIGURE 7.15 *Use Window selection mode to select the five stacked vertices in the second row from the
top at the far right of the box.*

4. Click the Select and Move button on the main toolbar and use the *Y*-axis restrict arrow to move the five vertices up very close to the corner of the box (**Figure 7.16**).

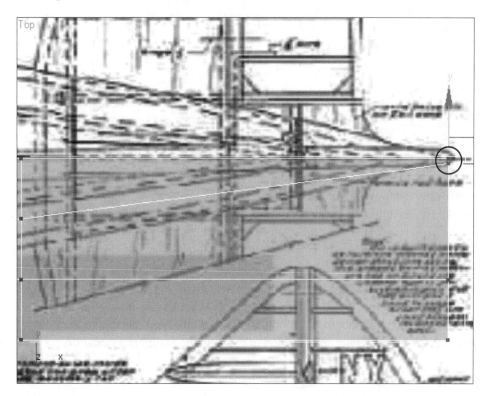

FIGURE 7.16 *Move the five vertices in the Y-axis almost to the upper-right corner of the box.*

5. Repeat Step 3 for the next five vertices at the far right of the box, and then for the five vertices at the lower-right corner to taper the tail (see **Figure 7.17** on the next page). You may need to zoom in to get the sets of vertices close to each other without overlapping them.

6. Now move each of the other tail vertices into place to align the vertices with the lines in the plan so that the whole tail is tapered smoothly from left to right (see **Figure 7.18** on the next page). All the outer sets of vertices will have five vertices, but the interior sets will have only two vertices each, one at the top of the box and one at the bottom.

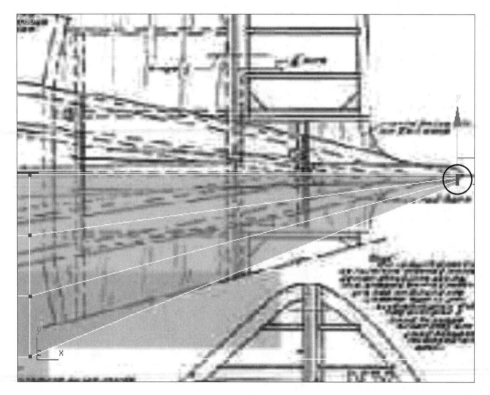

FIGURE 7.17 *Move each set of five vertices at the right side of the box to taper the tail to a point.*

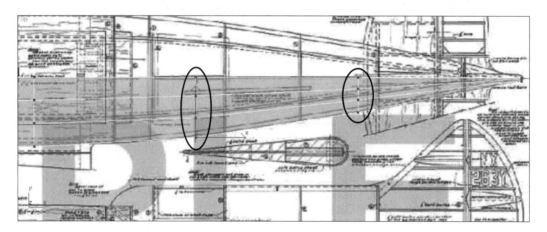

FIGURE 7.18 *Move the other tail vertices into place using the lines of the plan as a guide.*

7. Exit Vertex sub-object mode and save the file; it should already be named *Ch07_Plane02.max*. You have begun the process of using box modeling to rough out the shape of half a low-polygon fuselage.

By tracing an image that is mapped to planes in the scene, you can fairly accurately edit a box into a more useful form. An important part of the process is remembering to select only the vertices you want to move in any step. Using a viewing technique called See-Through makes the editing much easier.

Editing Using Multiple Viewports

Your ability to quickly and accurately select the sub-object components you want to edit will affect your productivity throughout the box modeling process. In Exercise 7.2, you were able to easily work directly in the Top viewport to align all the vertices with the fuselage plans. In many cases, however, it will be easier to select vertices in one viewport and move them into position in another viewport.

In the next exercise, you'll edit across multiple viewports to gain more accuracy and speed in the editing process.

Allow yourself some time for this exercise and save your file often as you progress so that if you make a mistake you can recover more easily.

Exercise 7.3: Increasing Selection and Editing Control

1. Open **Ch07_Plane02.max** from the last exercise or from the CD-ROM and save it to your project folder as *Ch07_Plane03.max*. In the Top viewport, select the Fuselage box. It has been edited in the Top viewport, so its edges and vertices follow the curvature of the plans. It will be easier to see all the vertices if you hide the Top_view plane, so select it by clicking the Select by Name button on the main toolbar and double-clicking Top_view in the list. Right-click in the viewport and choose Hide Selection from the quad menu (see **Figure 7.19** on the next page). The object is still roughly box shaped, however, while the fuselage is rounded, as viewed from the front. Use the Maximize Viewport toggle or press Alt + W to switch to the four-viewport display. Select the Fuselage and on the Modify panel in Stack view, highlight the Vertex sub-object level.

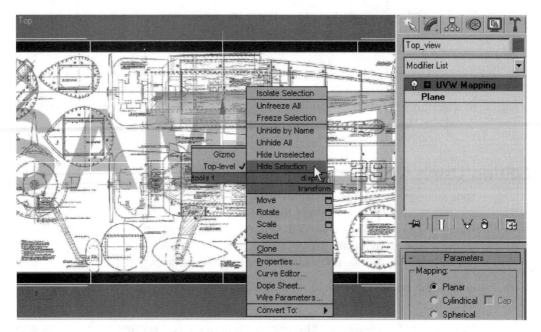

Figure 7.19 *Use the Select by Name dialog to select Top_view, and then right-click in the viewport to choose Hide Selection from the quad menu. This allows you to select and move the vertices at the bottom of Fuselage.*

Selecting vertices using Window Selection mode is not an option for this step because the vertices taper from front to back and are no longer in a straight line. To edit accurately, you must select the vertices individually in the Perspective viewport and then move them into place in the Left viewport to match the plan. The Lock Selection toggle is a helpful tool here because it locks the selection so that you cannot accidentally select something else when you switch viewports. You can access the Lock Selection toggle most easily by pressing the spacebar on the keyboard to toggle it on or off. When locked, the lock icon turns yellow at the bottom center of the display.

2. Starting at the front of the Fuselage object in the Perspective viewport, select a vertex, lock the selection, activate the Left viewport, and align the vertex to the plan (**Figure 7.20**). Then unlock the selection using the Lock Selection toggle and activate the Perspective viewport.

Move vertex in this viewport and unlock selection   Select vertex in this viewport and lock selection

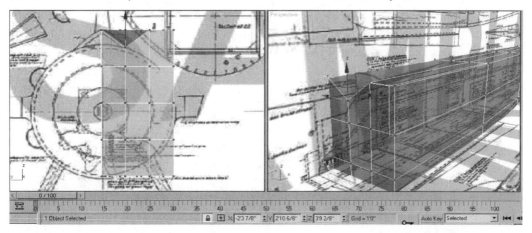

Figure 7.20 *Select and lock vertices in their original position in the Perspective viewport. Then activate the Left viewport to move the selected vertex to align with the plan. Unlock the selection again by toggling the spacebar.*

3. Repeat Step 2 until you have all the vertices moved into position. Work slowly and carefully. To make sure you're selecting the correct vertices, use the Zoom, Pan, and Arc Rotate tools, which are part of the navigation buttons located at the lower-right of the display, or use the middle mouse button. Verify your edits make sense by reviewing in all four viewports. Save the file often. As you work your way back along the fuselage, it should look similar to **Figure 7.21** on the next page.

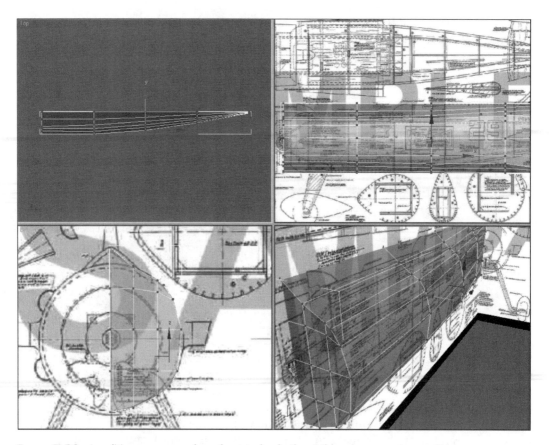

FIGURE 7.21 *As editing progresses from front to back, the visible edges remain parallel and the shape of the fuselage in the plans is emerging in the four viewports.*

4. In the Front and Perspective viewports, move the vertices in the tail area of the fuselage to match the angle of the plans (**Figure 7.22**). Remember to check in each viewport to make sure you are not moving the wrong vertex and that the surface is not overlapping itself anywhere. The visible edges are your best cue that all is well.

5. Make sure you clear the Lock Selection toggle, exit sub-object mode in Stack view, and save the file. Right-click in a viewport and choose Unhide All from the quad menu to unhide the Top_view plane. Save the file. It should already be named *Ch07_Plane03.max*.

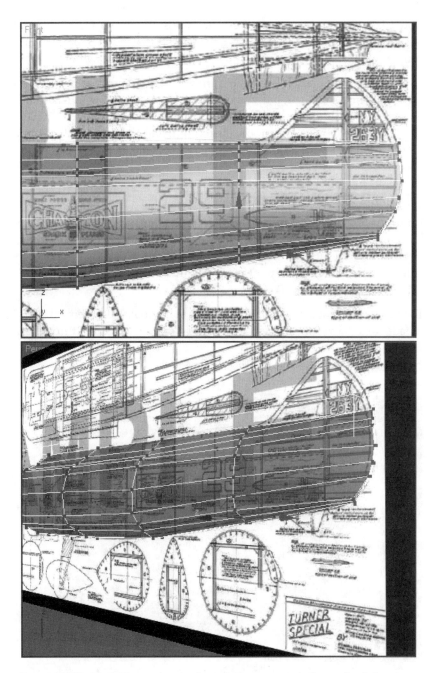

FIGURE 7.22 *Move the vertices in the tail zone to match the angle of the plan and clean up any areas that you think need it.*

Now take a break; this has probably been a stressful exercise. You might even open the original file and start again. This is a modeling style that requires some practice, but once you are comfortable in 3D space you'll be able to quickly rough out complex models.

Box modeling is a perfect example of how repetitive practice helps. The editing of vertices is simple enough, but visualizing what you are doing in relation to 3D space presented in multiple views can make it seem confusing at first. Do not become discouraged and abandon the process as too difficult. It's a valuable tool in 3ds max 7 that will increase your productivity.

Adding Detail to the Model

Up to this point, you've mainly been adjusting vertices in the back half of the fuselage to shape the model in the tail portion. However, as you were working, you may have noticed the lack of vertices in the cockpit area in the top middle of the fuselage and considered the difficulty of modeling the change of direction where the windshield curves to the nose (**Figure 7.23**).

To remedy this problem, you'll use the Slice Plane tool at the Element sub-object level to add detail by cutting new edges and vertices vertically through the model.

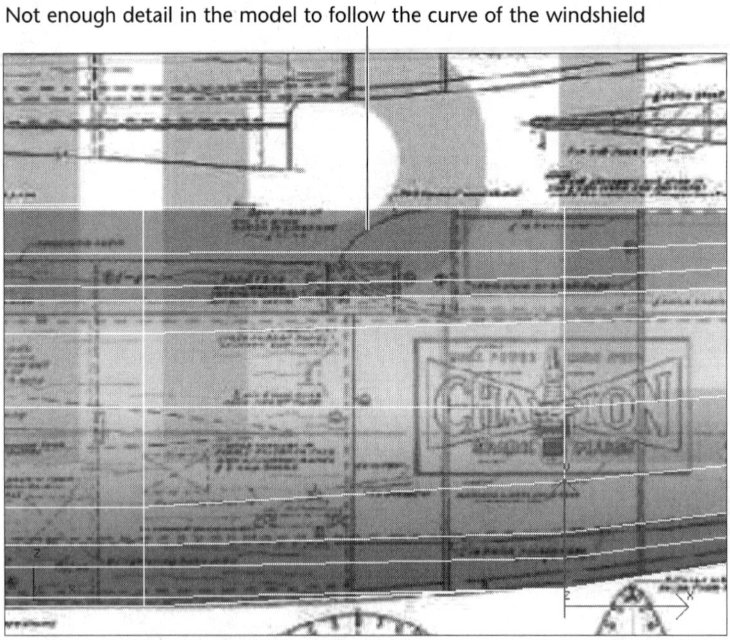

Not enough detail in the model to follow the curve of the windshield

FIGURE 7.23 *You need to add extra detail in the area of the cockpit to create the curved windshield.*

Exercise 7.4: Using the Slice Plane Tool to Add More Detail

1. Open **Ch07_Plane03.max** from the last exercises or from the CD-ROM. Save it to your project folder as *Ch07_Plane04.max*. Activate the Front viewport and zoom in on the midsection of the fuselage. Select the fuselage and in Stack view, highlight the Element sub-object level and click on the fuselage again. The entire model is one element that turns red when selected and is no longer transparent. Press the F2 key on the keyboard to toggle highlighting off for that viewport. The visible edges are now red, but the object is transparent.

2. In the Edit Geometry rollout, click the Slice Plane button. A yellow plane appears running horizontally through the geometric center of the fuselage. It needs to be rotated to define a vertical slice. Click the Select and Rotate button on the main toolbar and, in the status bar, enter *90* in the Z-axis Transform Type-in field. Press Enter. Click the Select and Move button on the main toolbar and move the Slice Plane left in the *X*-axis to the top rear of the curved windshield (**Figure 7.24**).

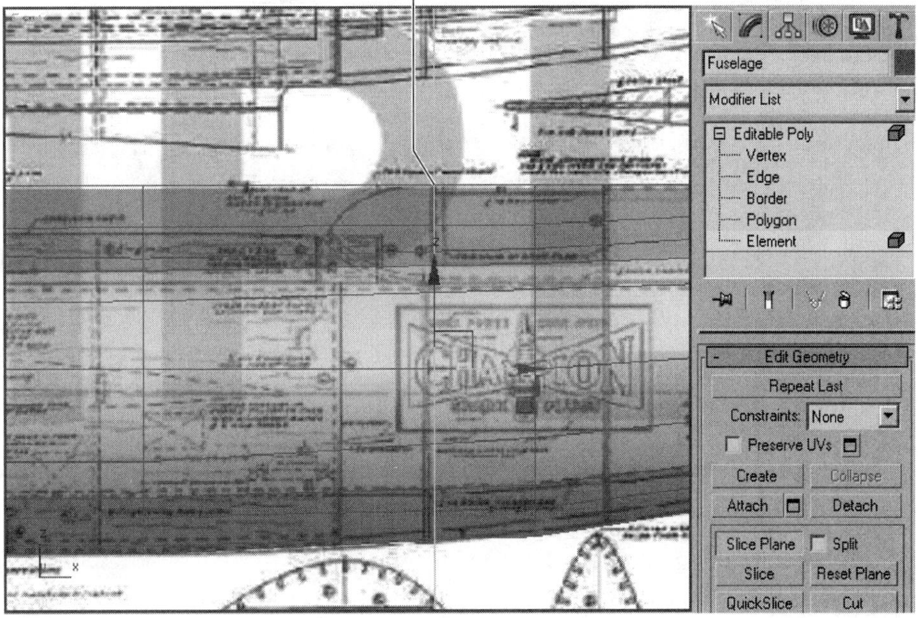

Rotate, then move the yellow Slice Plane gizmo to the back edge of the windshield

FIGURE 7.24 *Activate the Slice Plane, then rotate it and move it to the back of the curved windshield.*

3. Click the Slice button just below the Slice Plane button to cut the new edges and vertices into the model. Move the Slice Plane left to the middle of the curved windshield and click Slice again. Move the Slice Plane to the left edge of the curve and click Slice again. Click the Slice Plane button to exit that mode. You now have three new sets of edges and vertices to create the curve.

4. In Stack view, highlight Vertex sub-object mode. Click any empty space in the Front viewport to deselect the new vertices, and then move the new vertices to form the windshield (**Figure 7.25**). Exit sub-object mode in Stack view, a good habit to develop when you are finished editing in sub-object mode.

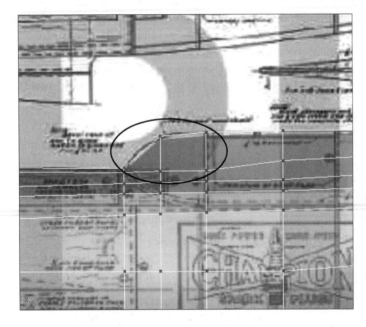

FIGURE 7.25 *You can now move the new vertices into place to finish the curved windshield and nose of the fuselage.*

5. Save the file. It should already be called *Ch07_Plane04.max*. You have learned to add extra vertices using the Slice Plane tool when you need more detail.

Adding extra detail is often necessary to rough out the model you need. However, always keep in mind that the lower the polygon count, the better the quality in general. Make sure the extra detail adds to the quality of the model for the uses intended.

Putting a Tail on the Fuselage

The plans of the plane show a short tail that is not part of your model at this stage of development. You'll now use Polygon sub-object editing to add several segments vertically, then adjust the vertices to fit the curvature as seen in the Front viewport.

Exercise 7.5: Adding a Tail

1. Open **Ch07_Plane04.max** from the last exercise or from the CD-ROM. Save it to your project folder with the name *Ch07_Plane05.max*. Select the fuselage and zoom in to the tail area in the Top, Front, and Perspective viewports.

2. On the Modify panel in Stack view, highlight Polygon sub-object mode. Click an empty space in the Top viewport to clear the current selection. Select the top, inside polygon at the tail. It's probably at an angle that matches the curve of the fuselage. Make sure the Top viewport is active. In the Edit Geometry rollout, click the View Align button to flatten the polygon so that it's perpendicular to the current viewport (**Figure 7.26**).

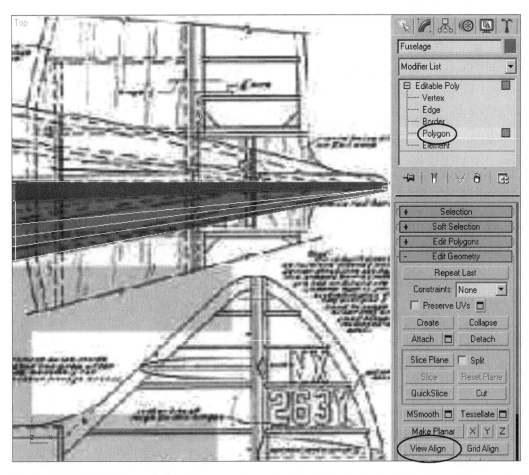

FIGURE 7.26 *Select the top inside polygon and use the View Align button to flatten the polygon so that it's perpendicular to the active Top viewport.*

3. In the Edit Polygons rollout, click the Settings icon beside the Extrude button. In the Extrude Polygons dialog that appears, enter *0'4 4/8"* or *4.5"* in the Extrusion Height field. This extrudes the polygon about one quarter of the way up the tail (**Figure 7.27**).

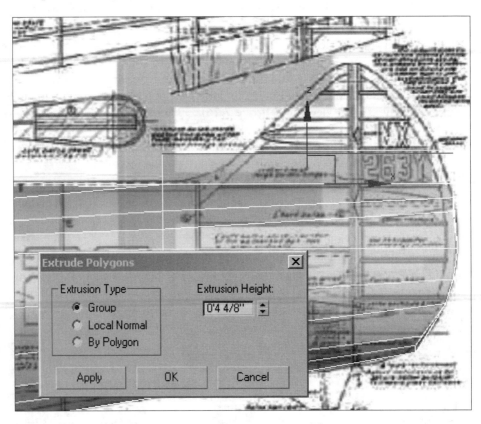

FIGURE 7.27 *Use the Settings icon to extrude the selected polygon approximately 4.5 inches up the tail.*

4. Click the Apply button in the Extrude Polygons dialog to repeat the extrusion three more times until it reaches the top of the tail (**Figure 7.28**). Click OK.

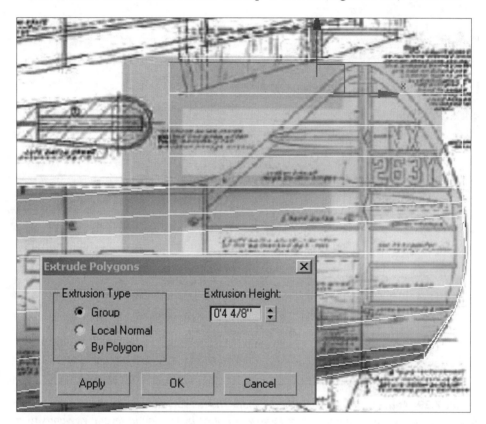

FIGURE 7.28 *You can use the Apply button in Extrude Polygons dialog to add three more segments with the same height as the original.*

5. In Stack view, highlight Vertex sub-object mode and, in the various viewports, move vertices to form the curvature of the tail (**Figure 7.29** on the next page). Use the blue and red (selected) vertices to define the shape of the tail. The gray-shaded polygons may disappear behind the map plane and make it seem as if the model is losing polygons. It may help to temporarily switch the viewports to Wireframe to verify the vertex placement.

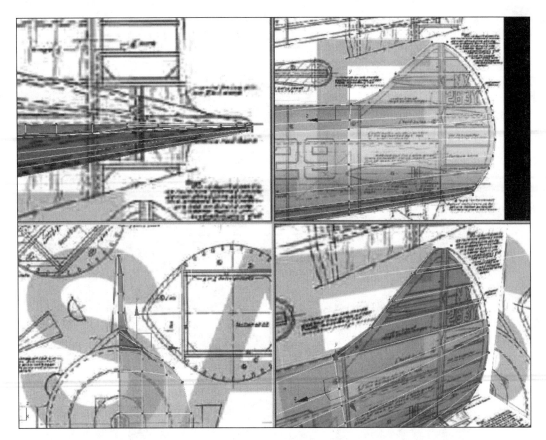

FIGURE 7.29 *At the Vertex sub-object level, shape the tail curvature using the plans as a guide. Use all four viewports as you work and remember to verify often by viewing in several viewports to ensure you are editing correctly.*

6. Exit sub-object mode in Stack view. Save the file; it should already be called *Ch07_Plane05.max*. Half the fuselage is now roughed out. While it may have taken some time for you to create this model, the next one will be that much easier now that you understand some of the fundamental workflow involved in box modeling.

Feel free to continue to work on the half fuselage to tweak it into a form you are happy with. As mentioned before, save the file often as you edit as there is no history that you can drop back in to recover from major mistakes.

Making a Whole from a Half

In this section, you'll merge a 2D shape from another file and apply and adjust the Lathe modifier to create a nose cone for the fuselage.

You have created only half a fuselage but need to turn it into a symmetrical model to have a decent airplane. You'll learn to use the Symmetry modifier that performs several steps while creating a whole symmetrical object. It mirrors the object, slices the two halves, and then welds the vertices at the slice to make a closed surface.

Finally, you'll merge the wing you created using lofting in Chapter 5.

Exercise 7.6: Adding Some Final Touches

1. Open **Ch07_Plane05.max** from the last exercise or from the CD-ROM and save it to your project folder with the name *Ch07_Plane06.max*. You are finished with the plans for the moment, but do not want to delete them. Select the Fuselage box in the Front viewport and, from the Tools pull-down menu, choose Isolate Selection. You can also use the keyboard shortcut Alt + Q. This hides all but the selected object or objects and leaves a Warning: Isolated Selection dialog in the center of the display. You can move this dialog off to one side. Click the Zoom Extents All button to fill all viewports with the fuselage.

2. Choose File > Merge. In the Merge File dialog, locate the file called **Ch07_Nose_cone.max** on the CD-ROM and highlight it. Click the Open button and highlight the Nose_cone object in the list (see **Figure 7.30** on the next page). Click OK to merge the shape into your scene.

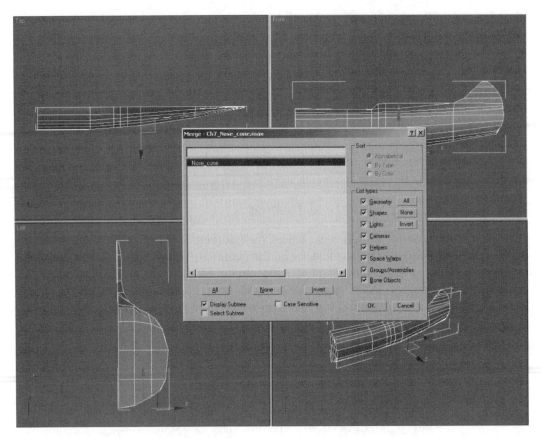

FIGURE 7.30 *Isolate the fuselage, and then merge the Nose_cone 2D shape from a .max file on the CD-ROM called* **Ch07_Nose_cone.max.**

3. Zoom and pan if necessary to see the new selected shape located near the top front of the fuselage. Activate the Front viewport. On the Modify panel, Modifier List, click the Lathe modifier. The shape will lathe, but not in the correct orientation. In the Direction area of the Parameters rollout, click the X button. This lathes or rotates the shape about the shape's own local X-axis (**Figure 7.31**).

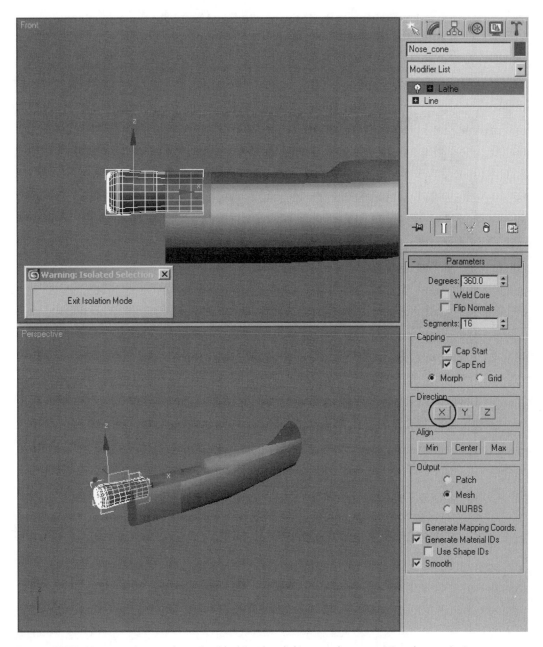

FIGURE 7.31 *You can change the axis of lathing by clicking on the appropriate button in Parameters rollout—in this case, the X button.*

4. In Stack view, expand the Lathe modifier and highlight the Axis sub-object
    level. In the Front viewport, move the Axis gizmo down in the viewport's Y-axis
    until the nose cone is slightly larger than the front of the fuselage (**Figure 7.32**).
    Exit Axis sub-object mode and move the whole nose cone up slightly to center
    it on the fuselage.

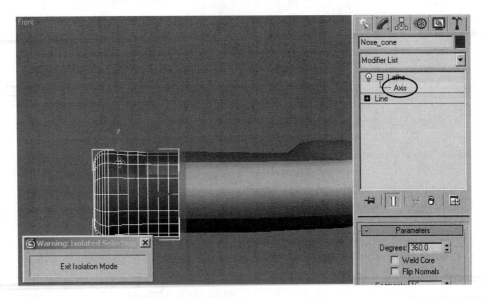

Figure 7.32 *In Axis sub-object mode, move the axis in the negative Y-axis of the Front
viewport to make it larger than the fuselage.*

5. Select the Fuselage box in the Front viewport. From the Modifier List, select the
    Symmetry modifier. The fuselage is mirrored, sliced, and welded, but again in
    the wrong axis (**Figure 7.33**). In the Mirror Axis area of the Parameters rollout,
    click the Y radio button and select the Flip option. The fuselage is now facing
    the right direction, but it's still not correct because it is not mirrored about the
    inside center to make a complete fuselage.

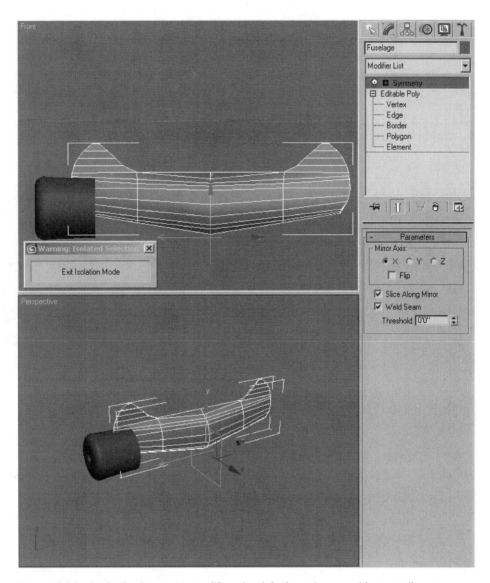

Figure 7.33 *Apply the Symmetry modifier; the default settings provide two tails.*

6. Expand Symmetry in Stack view and highlight the Mirror sub-object level. Click the Select and Move button and, in the Top viewport, move the mirror plane in the positive *Y*-axis until you have a complete fuselage and tail (**Figure 7.34**). If you move the Mirror plane too far, you'll produce a gap; not moving it far enough will slice away part of the tail. Zooming in the Top viewport on the Mirror plane will increase the degree of accuracy when moving the mirror plane. Exit sub-object mode. You now have a complete fuselage that is a continuous, closed surface. Click the yellow Exit Isolation Mode button to unhide the other objects in the scene.

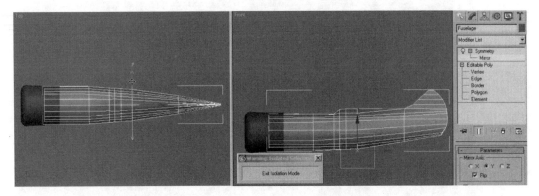

FIGURE 7.34 *Activate the Y mirror axis and select the Flip option, and then move the mirror plane to slice and weld the two halves into a whole fuselage.*

7. Choose File > Merge. Highlight **Ch07_wing03.max** on the CD-ROM. Click the Open button and highlight Wing in the Merge dialog that appears. Click OK, and the lofted wing you created in Chapter 5 will appear. Use the Select and Move button to position the wing based on the plans (**Figure 7.35**).

8. Save the file; it should be called *Ch07_Plane06.max*.

You now have a rough airplane minus the rear elevator wings. Use any of the methods you have learned so far in the book to create something suitable for this airplane. You are the artist.

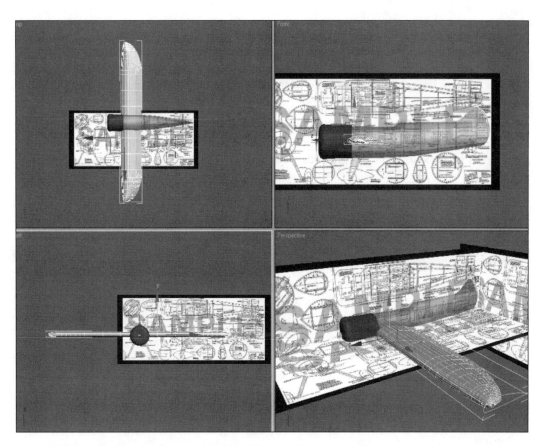

FIGURE 7.35 *Merge the lofted wing and reposition it similar to the plans.*

Summary

This chapter introduced you to box modeling, which involves selecting a simple primitive object—often a box—and then adding detail at the sub-object level and manipulating it into the final object.

Box modeling gives you explicit control over the number of faces in your object, thus enhancing the efficiency of the model. However, box modeling also tends to be a one-way street—as the detail increases and the object takes shape, it is very difficult to go back and edit the previous steps.

You also learned about two modifiers, the Symmetry modifier and the Lathe modifier. The Symmetry modifier enhances production by letting you create only half of the object and then generating a mirror image and connecting the two to form a symmetrical object. The Lathe modifier revolves a 2D shape around the axis to generate the 3D mesh, which you can easily edit by manipulating the original 2D shape.

CHAPTER 8

More Modifiers: Orderly Progression

In This Chapter

So far in this book I've been stressing the need to keep the face count of your modeling to an absolute minimum for efficient use of computer resources. However, there are times when you have to add more faces to a model to get the detail you need in the final images. Knowing how to add extra detail with a minimal impact on the system is an important part of the process of efficient modeling. The concepts presented in this chapter not only address adding that detail, but also how to control the number of faces for optimized models.

The tools presented in this chapter will help you add detail to the landscape you created in Chapter 6, *3D Primitives: Building Blocks*. We'll look closely at the Hierarchical Subdivision Surfaces (HSDS) modifier and displacement mapping, two tessellation techniques that increase the number of faces in a mesh while controlling optimization. We'll also delve deeper into some advanced functionality of the Edit Poly modifier to extract information from existing models that can be used to distribute objects throughout a scene.

In addition, you'll learn about the XRef method of merging information from other max files while retaining a connection to the original files for both efficiency and control, especially in a collaborative work environment. And finally, you'll practice using the Shell modifier to assign a given thickness to walls you create that contain a single face.

This chapter covers the following topics:

- **HSDS modifier.** The Hierarchical Subdivision Surfaces modifier lets you add multiple levels of detail to specific areas of a model.
- **Paint Deformation.** You can deform mesh objects by painting over a surface to affect the position of the vertices using the Paint Deformation option in the Edit Poly modifier.
- **Displacement mapping.** Grayscale images may be used to physically displace vertices in space based on the luminance values (whiteness) of pixels.
- **Displace Mesh modifier.** This World Space modifier lets you view and optimize the results of displacement mapping in the viewports and the rendered scene.
- **Snapshot tool.** The Snapshot tool lets you create a copy of a mesh object and helps free computer resources by "baking" edits into the mesh.
- **Epoly modifier.** This modifier provides the functionality and tools of Editable Poly surfaces at specific levels in the Modifier stack.
- **Distance Spacing tool.** Using this tool, you can place objects throughout a scene based on specific distances along a spline that is used as a path.
- **XRef files.** This option enables you to merge files as "external references" by retaining an editing link to the original file for both convenience and efficiency in 3ds max 7.
- **Shell modifier.** This modifier adds thickness to thin-walled objects.

Key Terms

- **Tessellate.** A method of dividing faces to add detail to a mesh object.
- **Deformation.** Moving vertices in space to change the shape of a surface.
- **XRef.** External References from a merged mesh to the original file that create a one-way link for editing. If you change the original, the XRef clone changes too.

Using Modifiers to Add Detail to 3D Objects

In Exercise 8.1, you'll practice tessellating surfaces using an HSDS modifier at the sub-object level. Once you have increased the localized detail in the model with the HSDS modifier, you'll use the Paint Deformation option of the Edit Poly modifier to create hills in the landscape containing the extra vertices generated by the tessellation.

Another method of adding detail to 3D objects is to use displacement mapping. In Exercise 8.2, you'll create a streambed using the Displace Mesh modifier and grayscale displacement maps in materials to automatically tessellate surfaces based on the luminance value (the whiteness) of the pixels in a map. Then you'll learn to utilize options in the Displace Mesh modifier to limit the number of new faces while maintaining the visual detail.

Exercise 8.1: Adding and Painting Detail

1. Open **Ch08_Mountains01.max** and save it to your project folder with the name *Ch08_Mountains02.max*. This is a landscape file similar to the one in Chapter 6. In the Top viewport, select the Mountains object.

   The Mountains object has too few vertices and faces to create convincing mountains on the horizon by manipulating vertices. By tessellating two of the polygons, you'll provide enough detail in that area to create convincing mountains without adding unnecessary overhead to the rest of the model.

2. On the Modify panel, click Modifier List and choose HSDS from the list. Expand HSDS in Stack view and highlight the Polygon sub-object level. In the Top viewport, select the two polygons in the center of the top row (**Figure 8.1**).

Select two polygons at the top center

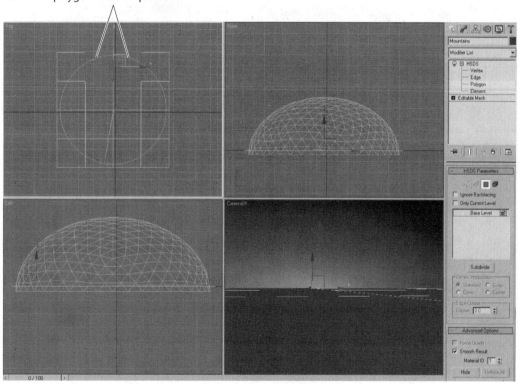

FIGURE 8.1 *At the Polygon sub-object level of the HSDS modifier, select the two polygons in the center of the top row (in the Top viewport).*

3. These polygons are at the Base Level of selection before any tessellation is applied. Click the Subdivide button in the HSDS Parameters rollout to tessellate the polygon into four new polygons at Level 1. Click the Subdivide button three more times for a total of four levels of tessellation above the base level (**Figure 8.2**). The result is that the greatest extra detail has been added in the location where you want the mountain, and the tessellation tapers off away from the selected polygons.

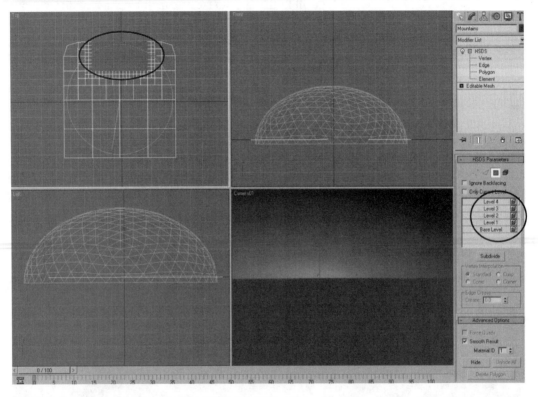

FIGURE 8.2 *Clicking four times on the HSDS Subdivide button tessellates the selected polygon with minimal disturbance to the surrounding polygons.*

4. In Stack view, select HSDS to exit sub-object mode. From the Modifier List, choose the Edit Poly modifier. Expand Edit Poly and highlight the Polygon sub-object level in Stack view. Click the Select button on the main toolbar and drag a window around the two smaller sets of tessellated polygons. Use the Zoom Extents All Selected button to zoom in on the tessellated polygons in the Top viewport (**Figure 8.3**). You can access flyout buttons by clicking and holding on any button with a small black triangle in the lower-right corner.

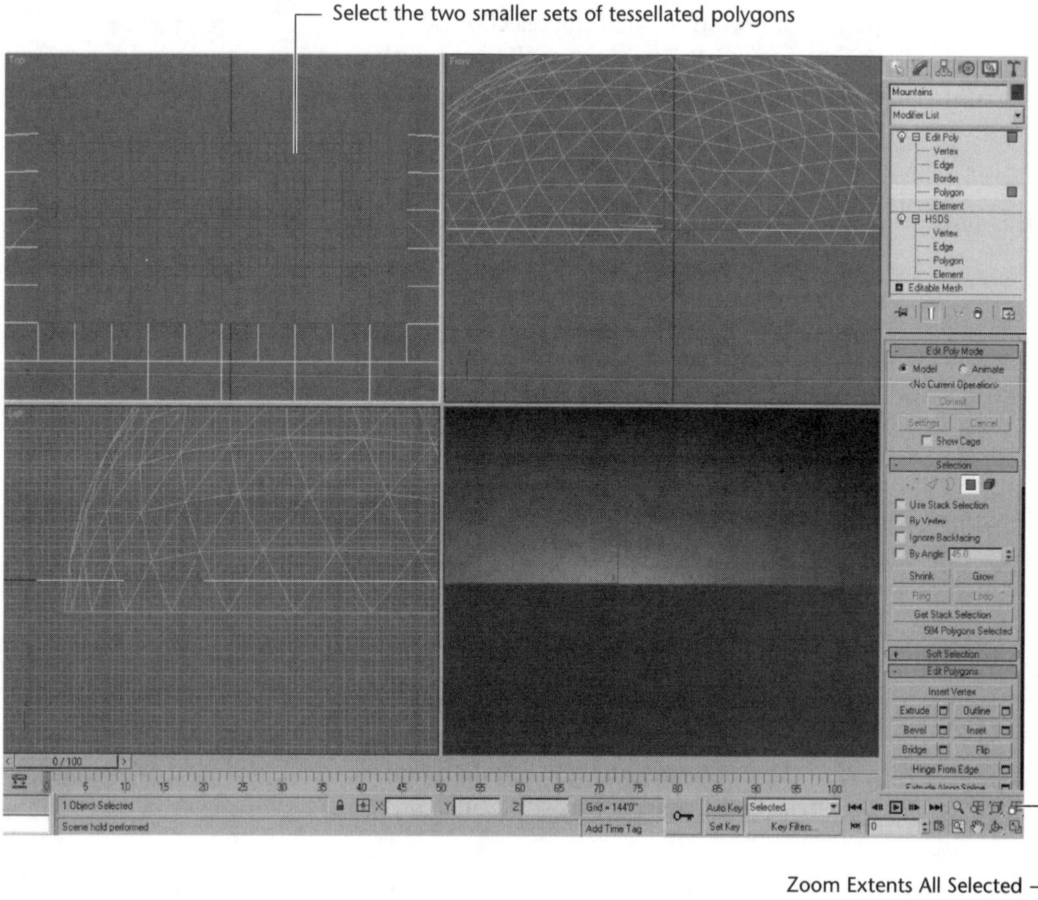

Select the two smaller sets of tessellated polygons

Zoom Extents All Selected

FIGURE 8.3 *In the Edit Poly modifier, select the two smaller sets of tessellated polygons you want to raise to form hills.*

5. On the Modify panel, expand the Paint Deformation rollout at the bottom of the panel. In the Push/Pull Value field, enter *20* and press Enter. This value causes each vertex to be deformed 20 feet. In the Brush Size field, enter *100* and press Enter to obtain a brush diameter of 100 feet. Click the Push/Pull button in the rollout. You are now ready to paint over the select polygons, from the top of the selection set to the bottom in the Top viewport (**Figure 8.4**).

6. From the Edit pull-down menu, press Hold to save the current scene in a buffer file in case you need to recover from editing mistakes you may make later in the process. In the Top viewport, press and hold the left mouse button and paint from the top edge of the selection back and forth toward the bottom edge. The vertices you paint will deform upward in their original Z-axis direction. Watch carefully in the other viewports to see the progress. Repeat the process several times until you raise hills that look similar to those in **Figure 8.5**. To deform vertices in the negative Z-axis, enter a negative number in the Push/Pull Value field. To switch to Revert mode, which will erase your most recent painting changes, paint while pressing and holding the Ctrl key.

Using the Edit Poly Paint Deformation tools, paint strokes over the surface are deformed in a progressive manner, depending on the brush size and deformation strength. You should monitor the effects in all viewports as you paint.

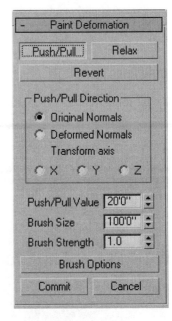

FIGURE 8.4 *Using the Push/Pull Value and the Brush Size settings, you can control the amount each vertex will be deformed when painted in the viewport.*

tip

The Paint Deformation option lets you use pressure-sensitive pens and tablets so that you can gain more control over the deformation of sub-object selection sets.

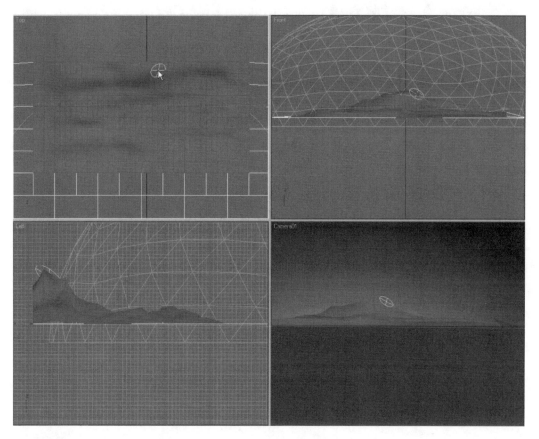

FIGURE 8.5 *You can paint back and forth, moving from the top of the selection set down over the surface of the selected polygons to displace the vertices upward with every stroke.*

7. On the Modify panel, Stack view, select Edit Poly to exit the sub-object level. Save the file; it should already be named *Ch08_Mountains02.max*. You've succeeded in raising random hills from a flat plain that are both convincing and efficient—something to strive for in all your work.

Low-polygon objects should be tessellated using the HSDS modifier only in the areas that you determine need the extra detail. The modifier should be applied early in the editing process for the most flexibility.

note

There is a process in 3ds max materials called Bump mapping that creates the illusion of deformed geometry at render time, but doesn't actually create any new detail. Bump mapping is very efficient, but somewhat limited in scope and application. You will learn more about Bump mapping in Chapter 13, *Maps: Patterns Before Your Eyes.*

Another method of adding detail to 3D objects is using displacement mapping, which utilizes the luminance value of pixels in a map to tessellate and displace vertices. The next exercise will walk you through the process of assigning a material with a displacement map to create a streambed at the foot of the hills. Then you will need to apply a Displace Mesh modifier to see the results of the displacement map.

After creating the streambed, you'll have a mesh object with many faces and you'll have learned how to optimize the mesh for maximum efficiency.

Exercise 8.2: Creating a Streambed Using Displacement Mapping

1. Open **Ch08_Ditch01.max**. Save it to your project folder with the name *Ch08_Ditch02.max*. The scene is the landscape with mountains from Exercise 8.1 with a new camera angle and with a material assigned to the Mountains object.

2. Choose Select by Name from the main toolbar, and then select Mountains. Click the Material Editor button on the right of the main toolbar or press *M* to open the Material Editor. The active material in the Material Editor has a map assigned in the Displacement slot on the right side of the Maps rollout. Notice in **Figure 8.6**, however, that the Displacement map is inactive, because the Displacement Map option on the left is not selected.

caution

Displacement mapping creates objects with many faces, so this exercise will be slow on computers with slower processors or minimum amounts of memory.

White corners in the sample window   Material Editor button

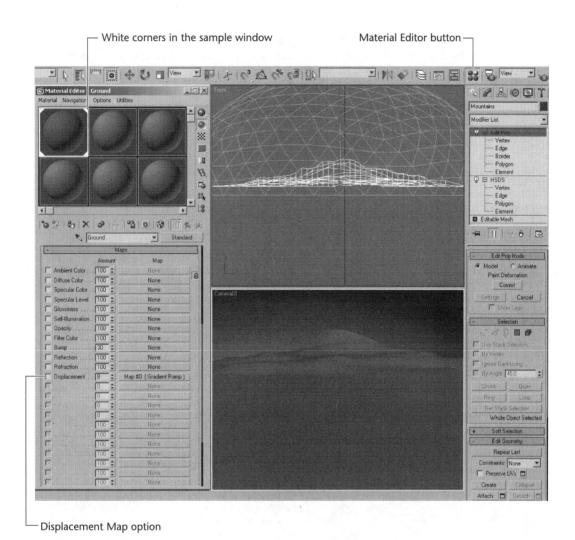

Displacement Map option

FIGURE 8.6 *The Material Editor reveals that a material called* Ground *has a disabled Displacement map and is assigned to an object in the scene. The white triangles in the corners of the sample window indicate the material is assigned in the scene.*

3. In the Material Editor, select Displacement, and then click the corresponding Map button immediately to the right to be directed to that level in the material. The Displacement Map level displays a grayscale Gradient Ramp map that is mostly white with a thin vertical band. White in the map displaces vertices, while black has no effect. In the Material Editor, toggle on the Show Map in Viewport button. This displays the map on the Mountains object in the Camera01 viewport (**Figure 8.7**). Nothing happens to the mesh yet, however. It needs a Displace Mesh modifier to display the displacement.

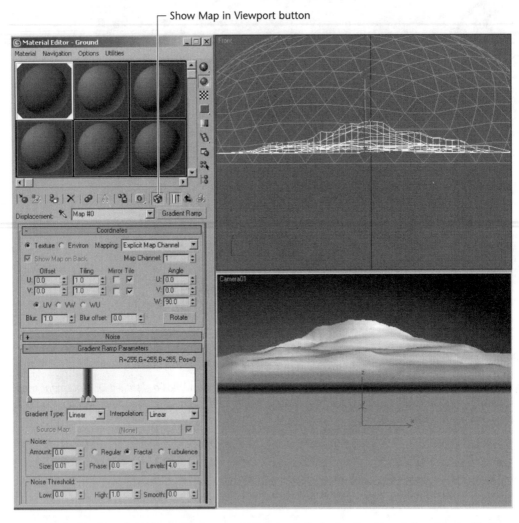

FIGURE 8.7 *The Material Editor's Displacement Map level displaying the Mountains object with the Gradient Ramp applied in the Camera01 viewport.*

4. On the Modify panel, choose Modifier List and then Displace Mesh (WSM) (**Figure 8.8**). This modifier is a World-Space modifier that functions in the World coordinate system rather than in the object's Local coordinate system for Object-Space modifiers, which you've been using up until this point. You might see a change in the scene, but it will only appear as if the mountains have moved in the positive Z-axis. The Displace Mesh modifier is not applying enough detail to the surface for good definition of the displaced values. Now close the Material Editor.

5. On the Modify panel, Displacement Approx. rollout, select Custom Settings, a custom subdivision setting that controls the tessellation of the mesh and displays more detail in the displaced areas. In the Subdivision Presets section, click the High button for more detail. Click the Quick Render button on the right side of the main toolbar to see the new streamed in front of the hills (see **Figure 8.9** on the next page).

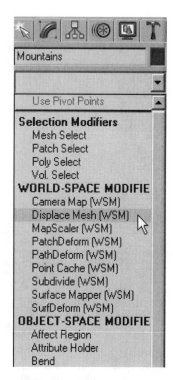

FIGURE 8.8 *The Displace Mesh modifier is a World-Space modifier found near the top of the Modifier List.*

The World-Space modifiers are always listed at the top of the Modifier stack and are called *bindings*. You can see the effect of this modifier by toggling the Light Bulb icon to the left of Displace Mesh Binding at the top of Stack view. Be sure to leave it toggled on.

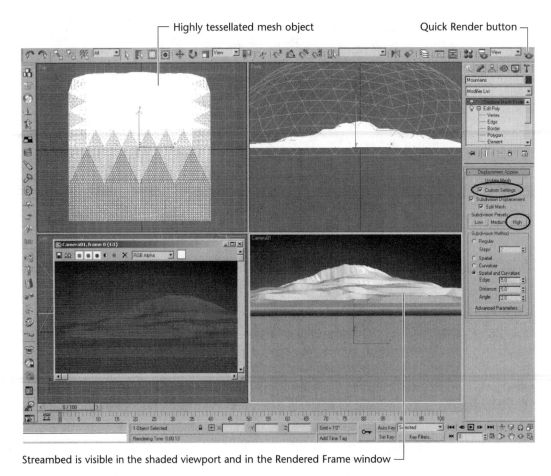

Highly tessellated mesh object   Quick Render button

Streambed is visible in the shaded viewport and in the Rendered Frame window

FIGURE 8.9 *The Top viewport shows the tessellated mesh, while the Rendered Frame window shows the displaced mesh.*

Next you'll use settings in the Displace Mesh modifier to optimize the tessellated mesh based on the curvature of the surface. Areas that require faces to show the curves will be optimized less than areas that are flat.

6. In the Displacement Approx. rollout, Subdivision Method section, click the Curvature radio button. After a few seconds of calculation, the mesh, visible in the Top viewport, will reduce the tessellation in the flat areas. Click on the Quick Render button to see in the Camera01 viewport that there's very little difference between the quality of the previously rendered image and the one with lower tessellation (**Figure 8.10**).

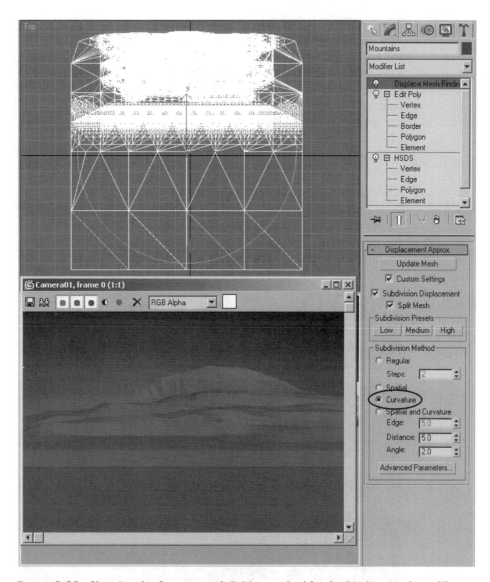

FIGURE 8.10 *Choosing the Curvature subdivision method for the Displace Mesh modifier greatly reduces the number of faces without significantly affecting the rendered image.*

You may have noticed displacement mapping and the Displace Mesh World-Space modifier use a high degree of computer resources, as evidenced by the slowing of most computers during these operations. Next we'll reduce this overhead using a tool called *Snapshot*, which creates a new copy of the mesh with the displacement "baked" into it. You can then delete the original mesh and remove the displacement mapping to save even more resources.

7. Choose Tools > Snapshot. In the Snapshot dialog, click OK to accept the default settings (**Figure 8.11**). Press the Delete key to delete the mountains from the scene.

tip

Using the curvature subdivision method on my test computer, the number of faces in the mesh dropped from 338,944 to 175,492 and the rendering time dropped from 12 seconds to 6 seconds. Remember to always do what you can to reduce the number of faces while retaining adequate visual quality for increased productivity.

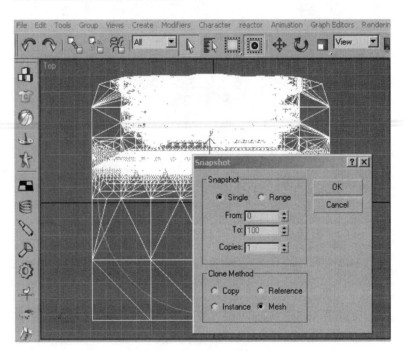

FIGURE 8.11 *Choose Tools > Snapshot to create a mesh copy of mountains, called* Mountains01, *with the displacement baked into the mesh.*

8. The Modifier stack now shows the object is an editable mesh with no modifiers. Open the Material Editor by pressing *M*. Click the Map/Materials Navigator button on the lower-right of the sample windows and choose Ground (Standard) in the navigator to return to the top of the material. In the Material Editor, Maps rollout, clear the Displacement checkbox to disable the map (**Figure 8.12**).

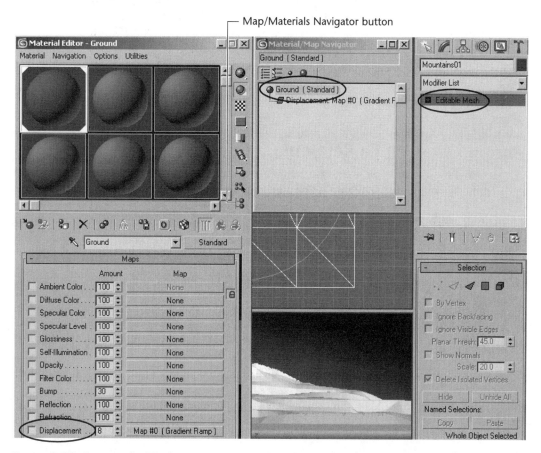

FIGURE 8.12 *Because the Displacement map uses lots of computer resources when it is active and the mesh has a Displace Mesh modifier, it is a good idea to disable the map to avoid displacing the mesh with this material again by mistake.*

9. Close all dialogs. Save the file; it should already be called *Ch08_Ditch02.max*. The landscape is now a simple editable mesh object that has been optimized but still has the necessary detail to be visually acceptable in the scene.

As with all modeling, paying attention to the optimization of faces and vertices in the model is the single most productive tool you have available. Tessellation is often a good method for creating detail, but always try to reduce any unnecessary detail when the editing is finished and your object appears correct in the scene.

caution

Making a Snapshot mesh is a permanent change, so you'll lose the ability to go back and alter the parameters you have adjusted. Before using the Snapshot tool and deleting the original, make sure you save a copy of the original if you think you may need to edit your modifiers.

Merging Files While Retaining a Connection

In this section, you'll use the Edit Poly modifier to extract a line from the lofted bridge object you created in Chapter 5, *Lofting: Control is Everything*. You'll use that line in conjunction with the Spacing tool to distribute evenly spaced pylons along the roadway you created in Chapter 6, *3D Primitives: Building Blocks*. To merge these two models, you'll use the XRef method, which allows you to maintain a connection to the original file to facilitate editing. You'll also use the Shell modifier to edit the object locally without affecting the original file.

Extracting Data Using Modifiers

Exercise 8.3 involves a scene similar to Exercise 8.2, with a bridge over the new streambed and a new camera looking down the road.

The lofted roadway travels up and over the streambed and needs guardrails to be safe. You have already created a pylon in Chapter 6 that can be used as a guardrail post. You will merge that into the scene and then distribute copies along the edge of the road and bridge at specific intervals using the Spacing tool.

The roadway is a lofted object and may need to be altered later, so you do not want to convert it to an editable object to extract lines from the loft that can be used as a guide for the Spacing tool. Instead you will use the Edit Poly modifier to "borrow" the lines without altering the lofted object. The Edit Poly modifier is used instead of the Edit Mesh modifier because it allows you to choose edges using the Loop and Ring options; whereas with the Edit Mesh modifier, you'd have to select the appropriate edges manually.

Exercise 8.3: Using the Edit Poly Modifier to "Borrow" Lines

1. Open **Ch08_Road01.max** from the CD-ROM. Save it to your project folder using the name *Ch08_Road02.max*. The Camera02 viewport shows a view from the road, looking down it and over a bridge toward the hills on the horizon. To merge a pylon into this scene, choose File > Merge. In the Merge File dialog, highlight a file called **Ch08_Pylon01.max** on the CD-ROM. In the Merge dialog that appears, highlight Pylon01 in the object list (**Figure 8.13**). Click OK to merge the object into your scene.

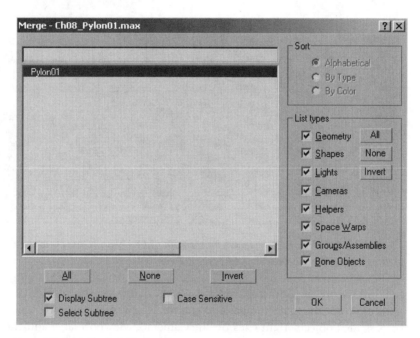

Figure 8.13 *Choose File > Merge, open* **Ch08_Pylon01.max**, *and merge the Pylon01 object from the file into your scene.*

2. The Pylon01 object is merged into the current scene with its pivot located in the same relative position as the original object. It has been positioned to be visible in the Camera02 viewport of this scene (see **Figure 8.14** on the next page).

Figure 8.14 *Merging the Pylon01 object from Ch08_Pylon01.max into the current scene places it near the roadway in the Camera02 viewport.*

3. Make sure the Camera02 viewport is the active viewport. Click the Select button from the main toolbar and choose Roadway. To view the visible edges and shaded objects, right-click on the Camera02 viewport label and choose Edged Faces in the menu that appears. On the Modify panel, Modifier List, choose the Edit Poly modifier. In Stack view, expand Edit Poly and highlight the Edge sub-object level (**Figure 8.15**).

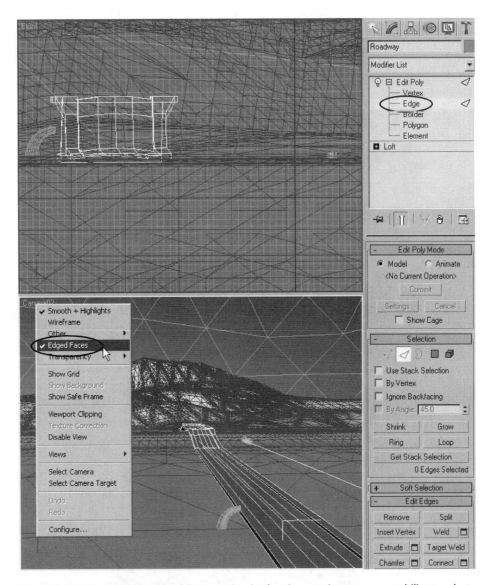

FIGURE 8.15 *Enabling the Edged Faces option in the viewport improves your ability to select edges using the Edit Poly modifier.*

4. Select one of the edges at the top of the roadway that is closest to you. It will turn red. On the Modify panel, Selection rollout, click the Loop button to select all edges along the top of the roadway that touch the end of the selected edge. It should report 9 Edges Selected (**Figure 8.16**).

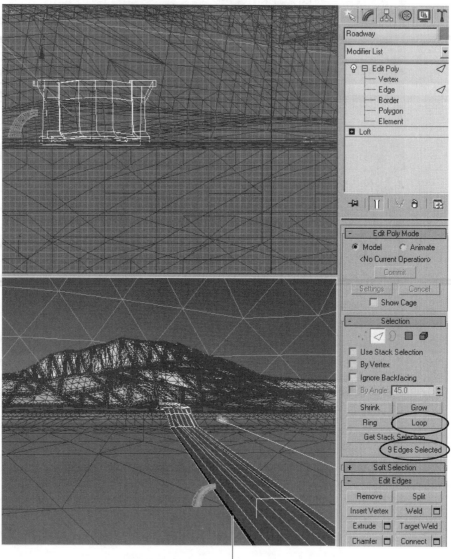

Select this edge first

FIGURE 8.16 *Selecting one edge nearest you at the top of the Roadway object and clicking the Loop button will select all nine edges along the roadway.*

5. In the Edit Edges rollout, click the Settings icon beside Create Shape. In the Create Shape dialog, enter *rail_path* in the Shape Name field, and make sure the Linear radio button is selected to keep the new line straight (**Figure 8.17**). Click OK. A new line has been created.

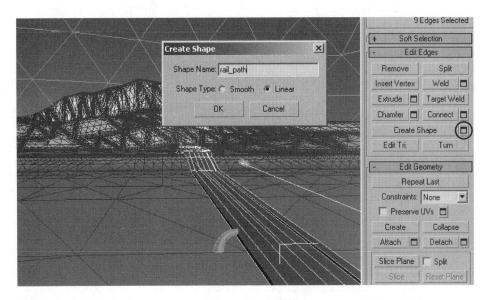

FIGURE 8.17 *Use the Create Shape dialog in the Edit Poly modifier to turn a selection of edges into a new line object.*

6. Click any empty space to clear the selection set. Repeat Step 5 on the other side of the roadway object to create a shape named *rail_path02*. Exit sub-object mode by highlighting Edit Poly at the top of Stack view. Click the Remove Modifier from Stack button to delete the Edit Poly modifier. The new objects have been created, so the modifier is no longer needed. Removing it frees up valuable computer resources (**Figure 8.18**).

Remove Modifier from Stack button

FIGURE 8.18 *After using Edit Poly Create Shape to create a line on the other side of Roadway, you can remove the Edit Poly modifier to save computer resources.*

7. In the Camera02 viewport, select Pylon01. From the Tools menu, choose
    Spacing Tool. In the Spacing Tool dialog, click the Pick Path button. Press *H*
    to display the Pick Object dialog. Highlight rail_path in the list and click the
    Pick button (**Figure 8.19**). This places three equally spaced clones along the
    line; however, notice they bend inward toward the road. You want them to
    bend outward.

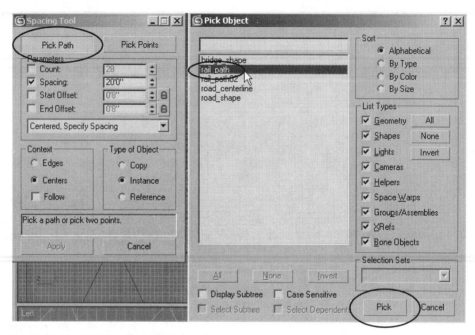

FIGURE 8.19 *The Spacing tool places three clones of the Pylon01 along the rail_path.
However, they are facing inward toward the center of the road, which is not what you want.*

8. In the Spacing Tool dialog, select the Spacing option and clear the Count
    checkbox in the Parameters section. Enter *20* in the Spacing field and press
    Enter. Notice that the default setting in the Type of Object area is Instance,
    which provides clones with a two-way link connection (**Figure 8.20**). The
    two-way Instance link will enable you to affect all clones by making changes
    to any one of them.

    You should now have 28 objects on 20-foot centers along the entire edge of
    the road. Click the Apply button to finalize the Spacing Tool. Close the dialog.

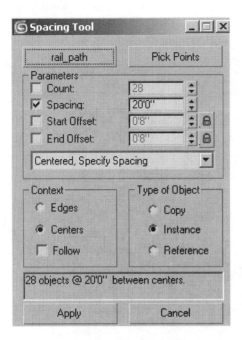

FIGURE 8.20 *Clearing the Count checkbox, checking Spacing, and entering 20 in the Spacing field places 28 Instance pylons 20 feet apart along the line.*

9. Repeat Steps 7 and 8 using the line on the other side of the roadway called *rail_path02*. You now have 56 clones that are bent and too large. Press Delete to delete the original Pylon01—you no longer need that, and you'll be fixing the others so that they are straight, smaller, and more efficient.

10. Select any one of the 56 pylons in the Camera02 viewport. On the Modify panel, Stack view, notice that the names of the object and modifiers are in bold text. This indicates it's an Instance clone with a two-way connection between the editing parameters of all similar clones. Changing any one affects all the others (see **Figure 8.21** on the next page).

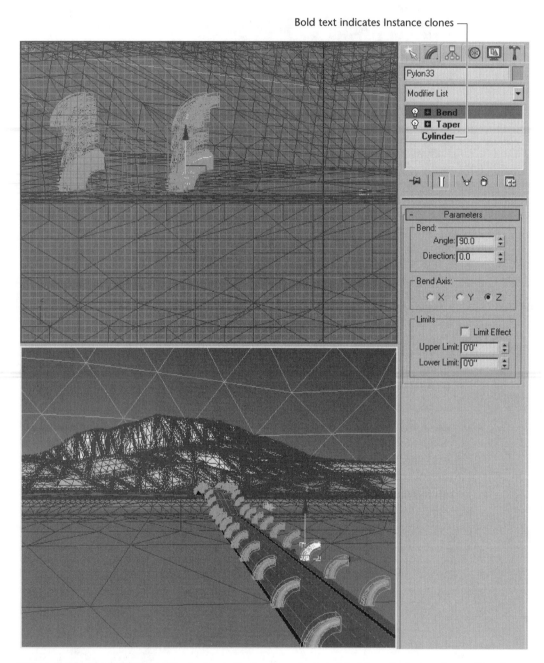

FIGURE 8.21 *The bold text in Stack view indicates the selected object is an Instance clone with a two-way connection to other clones.*

11. Make sure the Bend modifier is highlighted in the Stack view and click the Remove Modifier from Stack button, located below the Stack view. This removes all Bend modifiers from all clones. Highlight Cylinder in the Stack view. In the Parameters rollout, enter the following: *0'6"* in the Radius field; *3'0"* in the Height field; *1* in the Height Segments field; *1* in the Cap Segments field; and *12* in the Sides field (**Figure 8.22**).

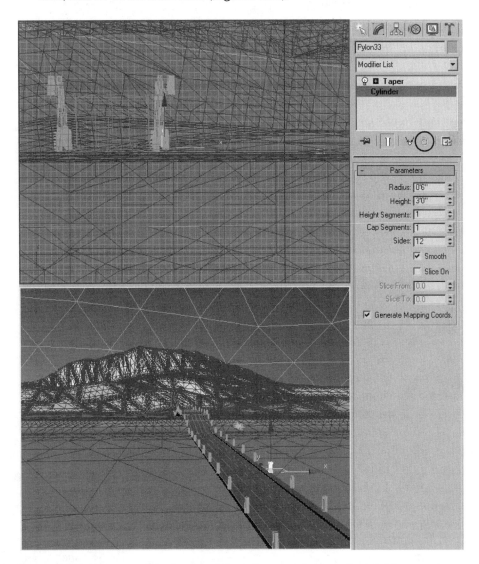

FIGURE 8.22 *You can reduce the size of the pylons and decrease the total face count by more than 9,000 simply by editing only one Instance clone.*

12. Highlight the Taper modifier at the top of Stack view to return to that level. Save the file. It should already be called *Ch08_Road02.max*.

You have learned to borrow geometry from existing objects and use that new geometry for other purposes, in this case with the Spacing tool to replicate multiple clones in a scene with specific spacing requirements. You have also learned some of the advantages of Instance cloning to facilitate easy editing of objects.

As with all lessons in the book, it is important that you learn the concepts and workflow behind the simple exercises. Cloning, for example, lets you edit multiple objects at once, while using fewer computer resources, because each clone requires less than the original object.

Merging External Reference Objects for Editing Control

You know how to merge objects from one file into another and you have learned to use Instance clones that have a two-way link to all similar clones in the scene. In the next exercise you will use XRef (external reference) to merge a hanger building with a one-way link from the object in the original file to the merged object in the current file.

This is an especially powerful feature to use in an office where many people are working on a complex scene. Each team member can keep track of his or her own work, while a master file is created and automatically updated.

Exercise 8.4: Collaborating Using XRef Objects

1. Open **Ch08_Road02.max** from the last exercise or from the CD-ROM. Save it to your project folder as *Ch08_Road03.max*. Choose File > XRef Objects (**Figure 8.23**).

2. Copy **Ch08_Xref_Hanger.max** from the CD-ROM to your project folder. Next you'll merge a building with three parts—the foundation, walls, and roof that you created in Chapters 3 and 4.

FIGURE 8.23 *XRef Objects can be accessed from the File menu.*

3. In the Add/Set area of the XRef Objects dialog, click the Add button and, from your project folder, open the file called *Ch08_Xref_Hanger.max* that you copied from the CD-ROM in Step 2. In the Xref Merge dialog, click the All button to highlight the three objects in the scene (**Figure 8.24**). Click OK to merge the objects into your scene. The name of the merged file appears in the top pane, and the names of the merged objects appear in the bottom pane of the XRef Objects dialog (see **Figure 8.25** on the next page). Click the Close button.

The XRef Scene command on the File menu functions much the same way that the XRef Objects command does, but it doesn't allow access to the individual objects in the merged scene for further editing like XRef Objects does. XRef Scene can be used to merge environments that you will not need to edit for your scene, but may be changed in the original file.

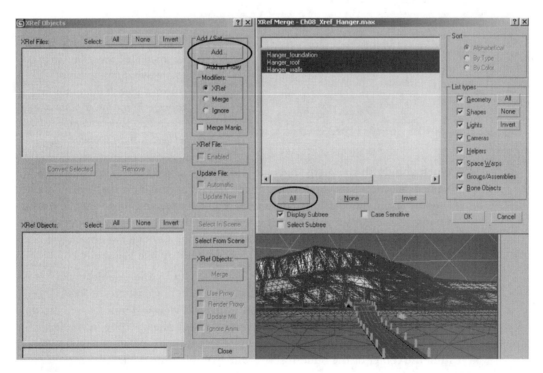

FIGURE 8.24 *You choose the file and the objects from the file that you want to merge in the XRef Objects dialog.*

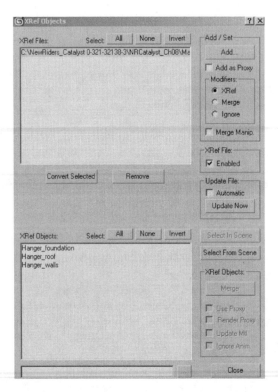

FIGURE 8.25 *The name of the merged file appears in the upper pane, while the names of merged objects from that file appear in the lower pane of XRef Objects. Your path name will be different than shown here.*

4. When you finish the merge operation, the three objects are selected. In the Named Selection Sets window in the main toolbar (the large blank drop-down window at the right of the main menu), enter *Hanger* and press Enter. Creating a named selection set will make it easier to select the objects as a group later if you need to. Working in the Top and Left viewports, move the objects into position near the roadway so that it looks something like **Figure 8.26**.

5. On the main toolbar, click the Select by Name button and double-click {Hanger_walls} in the Select Objects list. Names in braces indicate XRef Objects in the list (**Figure 8.27**). Notice in the Camera02 viewport you can see through the back wall of the hanger when looking through the opening in the front. The walls are single-thickness faces whose face normals point outward away from the center of the building. You will give the walls thickness.

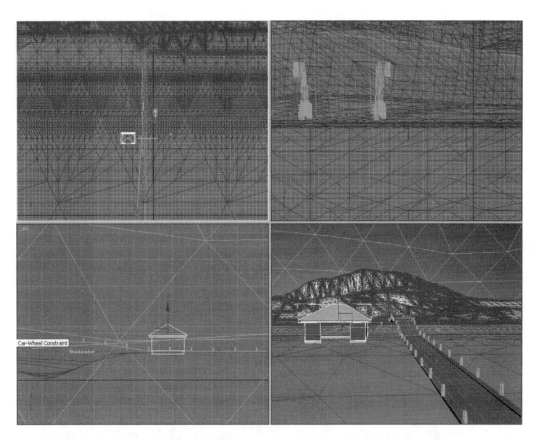

FIGURE 8.26 *Move the selected objects above the ground and to the left of the roadway, as seen from Camera02.*

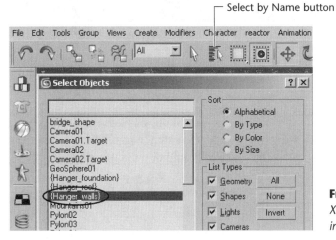

FIGURE 8.27 *The names of Xref Objects will be enclosed in braces in name lists.*

6. On the Modify panel, click Modifier List and choose Shell from the list. In the Parameters rollout, enter *6* in the Inner Amount field and *0* in the Outer Amount field. Press Enter. At the bottom of the rollout, select the Straighten Corners option. This gives the wall a 6-inch thickness toward the inside. You can no longer see through the walls (**Figure 8.28**).

Walls have thickness

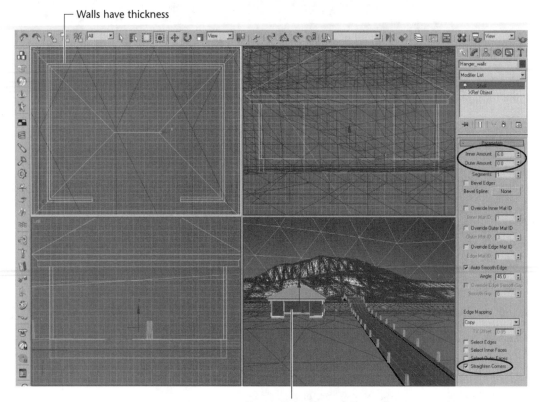

You can't see through the walls now

FIGURE 8.28 *Applying a Shell modifier gives the Hanger_walls thickness.*

7. Save the file; it should already be called *Ch08_Road03.max*.

You have merged three objects with XRef Objects, edited one of the merged objects, and saved the file. XRef Objects is a one-way connection that allows edits to flow from the original to the merged copy, but not back, as you will see in the next exercise.

Checking the Functionality of XRef Objects

To see how the XRef Objects method works, you'll open the original file to observe that using the Shell modifier does not result in having the changes incorporated into the original file. You will then edit the roof in the original file, save it, and open Ch08_Road03.max again. This will update the XRef and you will see the edits have been passed from the original to the merged objects in your scene.

Exercise 8.5: Making the Roundtrip with XRef Objects

1. Open **Ch08_Xref_Hanger.max** from your project folder. Notice in the Perspective viewport that the walls are still one-face thickness. The edits you made in Ch08_Road03.max have not been passed to this file (**Figure 8.29**).

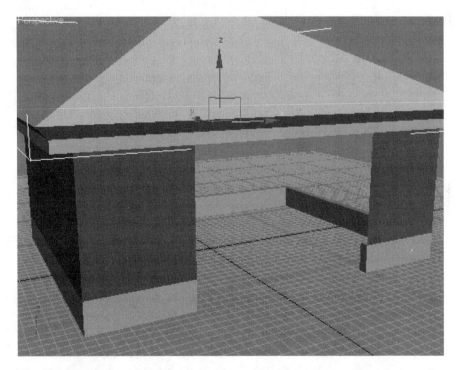

Figure 8.29 *Because of the direction of face normals, you can see through the walls in the original file.*

2. In the Perspective viewport, select Hanger_roof. On the Modify panel, Bevel
    Values rollout, enter *15* in the Level 3 Height field of the Bevel modifier. This
    raises the peak of the roof (**Figure 8.30**).

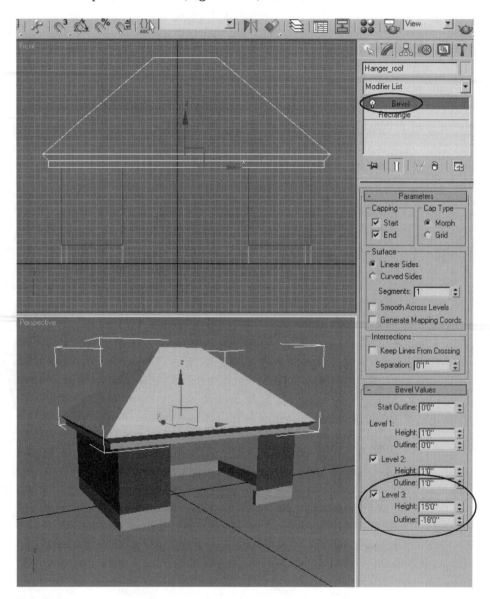

FIGURE 8.30 *Edit the Bevel modifier for Hanger_roof to raise the peak 5 feet by entering* 15
in Level 3 Height field and pressing Enter.

3. Save the file. It should still be called *Ch08_Xref_Hanger.max*. The changes have been made and the file has been saved to overwrite the original.

tip

XRef Objects may also be updated manually at any time via the XRef Objects dialog, accessed by choosing File > Xref Objects. This method is convenient when there are ongoing changes in a production workflow.

4. Open the file from the CD-ROM called **Ch08_Road03.max**. In the process of opening the file, 3ds max 7 checked for XRefs in the scene and automatically updated the current file with the new changes. You can see in **Figure 8.31** that the roof peak is higher than it was originally. Save this file; it should still be called *Ch08_Road03.max*.

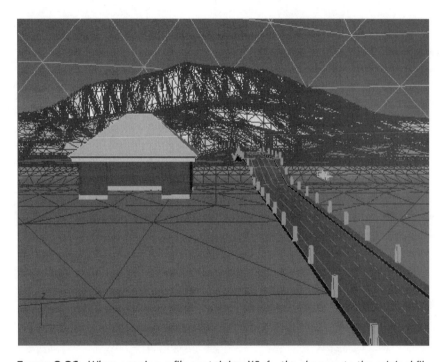

FIGURE 8.31 *When opening a file containing XRefs, the changes to the original file are automatically updated in the current file.*

XRef merging allows many team members to collaborate while keeping all edits current in a master file. The merged XRef Objects and XRef Scenes also take up less memory than when they are merged straight into the scene.

Practice with XRef to find a balance in your work where XRef can speed production by easing the management of max files from various sources.

Summary

One of the main themes of this book is to show you how to increase workflow efficiency when using 3ds max. Reducing the number of faces in 3D mesh objects is key in achieving this goal. However, sometimes you need extra faces to show necessary detail in your models. In this chapter, you've learned to add detail with minimum impact using Displacement mapping and HSDS tessellation.

You also learned about a collaborative workflow method using XRef Objects, which allows you to link objects from external files for more efficient use of computer resources. With XRef Objects, you can modify the original files and have them automatically update the objects in your scenes.

PART III

Lighting and Cameras

CHAPTER 9

Cameras:
Placement and Movement

In This Chapter

Creating cameras and adjusting their parameters is simple in 3ds max 7. However, placing and moving cameras effectively is foreign to almost anyone who isn't formally trained as a photographer. For most 3D animators, the placement and movement of cameras ends up looking more like hit and miss experimentation.

In this chapter, you'll learn some of the common techniques of camera placement and movement used by the film industry, which can be useful to apply to your own scenes.

This chapter covers the following topics:

- **Camera types.** Two types of cameras are available in 3ds max 7: target and free.

- **Creating and adjusting cameras.** You will learn to create and make simple adjustments to both the target and free camera types.

- **Camera composition.** Placement of cameras in a scene can greatly affect the perception of the viewer. You will learn some fundamentals of traditional still and film camera placement techniques that can be applied to 3ds max 7 scenes.

- **Camera movement.** Camera movement in animation must be done carefully to convey the appropriate message to viewers, either by making them comfortable or disturbing them.

Key Terms

- **Focal length.** As it relates to the traditional camera, *focal length* describes the distance from the lens to the film plane, measured in millimeters. However, with cameras in 3ds max, the term is used differently. It describes whether a wide angle or telephoto lens has been used to control perspective and only simulates the effect of focal length adjustments in a real camera.

- **Field of view.** By default, the horizontal width of the camera view, expressed in degrees.

- **Cut edit.** A sudden change from one scene to the next, used in traditional film and television animations.

- **Fade or dissolve edit.** A slower transition from one animated scene to another, used to convey the passage of time or distance.

Camera Basics

Because of the years invested in watching film and television, most people are at least somewhat familiar with camera placement and movement. However, few have actually become "students" of camera work and have spent time consciously analyzing the effects of perspective and movement. If you intend to control the viewer's perception of your scenes, you must make sure you have a thorough understanding of these topics. For example, slight changes in cameras can create a pleasing or disturbing emotional response in the viewer, so you don't want to accidentally mix such disparate emotions as these.

In general, target cameras are employed as still cameras or animated cameras that focus on a fixed point in the scene. Free cameras tend to be used for moving through the scene. Keep in mind that these are only the more common uses. You can use either type of camera to meet your needs for a particular scene.

It's very important to know and remember that 3ds max 7 cameras represent single lens cameras that provide no peripheral vision. While most people are very aware of the fact that there is no peripheral vision in the real world of film and photography, it's often forgotten when employing cameras in 3ds max 7. As a result, it's not unusual to see wild camera positions and camera movements in some projects that create tension and make many viewers uncomfortable.

Finally, the cameras in 3ds max 7 are designed to represent a similar viewpoint to that of a typical 35mm film camera in the real world.

Camera Types

Both target and free camera types are created via the Cameras category on the Create panel (**Figure 9.1**):

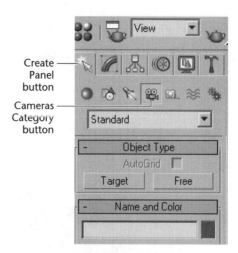

- **Target cameras.** Target cameras have two components: the camera and a target. The camera is always pointed toward the target that is placed some distance away.

- **Free cameras.** Free cameras have a single camera component, which can rotate freely in space, much like a real camera.

FIGURE 9.1 *To create cameras, open the Create panel and click on the Cameras Category button to display the Object Types rollout, which contains the buttons for target and free cameras.*

Target cameras are analogous to big studio cameras used in film and television that are mounted on heavy tripods or stands and have limited range of movement. Free cameras are more like the newer and lighter handheld cameras that give photographers much more flexibility in positioning.

Unless you're very comfortable with the coordinate systems and work planes of 3ds max 7, it's best to create target cameras in the Top viewport of the scene. The Top viewport provides a "ground plane" from which to work comfortably on most scenes. You can adjust the position of the target camera in the other viewports.

Free cameras, on the other hand, can be created in any viewport because they'll always point away from the viewer in the orthographic viewports or straight down in nonorthographic viewports. They can then be moved and rotated into the best orientation to suit your needs.

You can have as many cameras of either type in the scene that you need, but you can render only one camera at a time. Because each viewport in the graphic display can be set to any camera, it's possible to see up to four camera viewports at any one time.

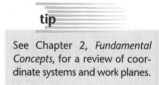

tip

See Chapter 2, *Fundamental Concepts,* for a review of coordinate systems and work planes.

Placing a Target Camera

In Exercise 9.1, you'll practice creating a target camera in an outdoor scene and then switching the current Perspective viewport of that scene to a Camera viewport so that you can manipulate the camera using the Select and Move tool.

Exercise 9.1: Creating and Positioning a Target Camera

1. Open **Ch09_Camera_motion01.max** on the CD-ROM. Save the file to your project folder with the name *Ch09_Camera_motion02.max*. The file displays a snowy mountain landscape with trees scattered at the base of the mountain (**Figure 9.2**).

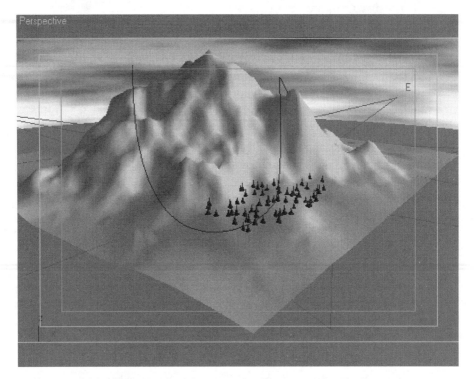

FIGURE 9.2 *Ch09_Camera_motion02.max needs a camera for a more convincing view—this overhead shot revealing the edges of the "world" is obviously not very realistic. The camera will place the viewer in the scene.*

2. Right-click in the Top viewport to activate it. The lowest points of the landscape are on the World Grid, which is the currently active grid and work plane in the Top viewport. On the Create panel, Cameras category, click the Target button. In the Top viewport, click near the bottom of the landscape and the middle of the trees and drag the camera target upward to the far side of the trees. Release the left mouse button to place the target (**Figure 9.3**). The default target camera has a lens focal length of 43.456mm, which represents a typical point of view if you have one eye closed.

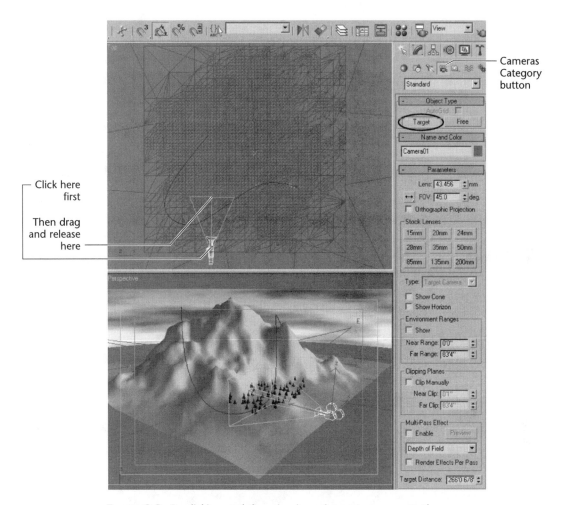

Click here
first

Then drag
and release
here

Cameras
Category
button

FIGURE 9.3 *By clicking and dragging in a viewport, you create the camera and drag it to the target position. Releasing the mouse button places the target.*

3. To see the actual viewpoint of the camera, right-click in the Perspective viewport and press *C* (for camera). The Perspective viewport switches to Camera01 and presents an odd view. This is because you're looking partially under and partially above the World Grid plane and the bottom of the landscape.

4. Notice, however, that the eight navigation buttons at the lower-right of the display have changed to camera navigation tools. Click on the Truck Camera button, which looks like a hand, and in the Camera01 viewport, pick and drag downward (you are trucking the viewport) to move the camera up until the trees are somewhat centered in the viewport (**Figure 9.4**).

note

If you're wondering why the camera parameters have disappeared from the Command panel, it's because you've exited the camera-creation process in 3ds max. To change camera parameters, you must have the camera selected and choose the Modify panel.

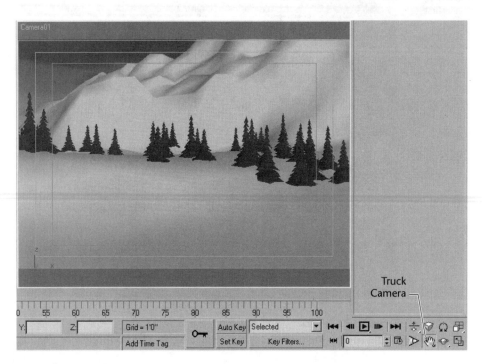

FIGURE 9.4 *Pressing C to switch from the Perspective to the Camera01 viewport and using the Truck Camera tool to raise the camera lets you compose the scene with the trees near the center of the viewport.*

5. Save the file. It should already be called *Ch09_Camera_motion02.max*. Placing the target camera in the Top viewport lets you work from a familiar position to make adjustments to the viewpoint of that camera.

Placing a target camera in a scene is a simple click-and-drag process. You can then position the camera or the target by moving the object using the Select and Move command or the eight camera viewport navigation buttons at the lower-right of the display.

Placing a Free Camera

Because it has no target, placing a free camera requires a simple click in any viewport to create the camera. If you click in an orthographic viewport—

tip

Some of the navigation buttons have a black triangle at the lower-right corner, indicating flyout buttons that feature variations on the default command. Click and hold on a button to access the flyout buttons.

Top, Bottom, Back, Front, Left, or Right—the camera points in the same direction you're looking. If you click in a nonorthographic viewport—Perspective, User, Camera, or Light—the camera is created on the current work plane pointing in the negative Z-axis. You can then use the camera navigation buttons or the Move and Rotate transforms to adjust the view.

In the following exercise, you'll practice matching the selected camera's view to an existing Perspective viewport.

Exercise 9.2: Creating and Positioning a Free Camera

1. Open **Ch09_Camera_place01.max** on the CD-ROM and save it to your project folder with the name *Ch09_Camera_place02.max*. The scene is a small retail display of furniture, dishes, and pottery. For the purposes of this exercise, assume that you have already zoomed, panned, and rotated the Perspective viewport to produce the view that you now see.

   If you were to select one of the Zoom Extents tools now, the current view would be lost. You would need to navigate the viewport again, and it would probably be difficult to match exactly what you currently see.

2. On the Create panel in the Cameras category, click the Free button. In the Perspective viewport, pick on the floor midway between the large pot and the rocking chairs. The camera icon will appear facing directly down on the floor (see **Figure 9.5** on the next page). With Camera01 selected, press the Delete key to delete the camera from the scene.

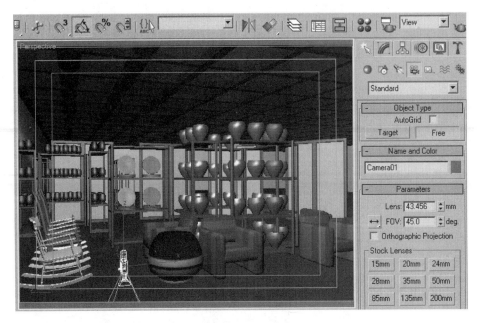

FIGURE 9.5 *Create a free camera on the floor between the large pot and the rocking chairs. It faces downward from floor level. Then delete the camera you just created.*

3. You now have a Perspective view that is a good starting point for your scene. Let's say you'd like to use it to define the camera view. With the Perspective viewport active, choose Views > Create Camera From View or press Ctrl + C (**Figure 9.6**). This places a target camera in the scene pointing in the direction that matches the perspective of the Perspective viewport and switches the viewport to Camera01. On the Modify panel, notice that the Lens field isn't set to the default focal length, but is adjusted for the field of view of the Perspective viewport (**Figure 9.7**).

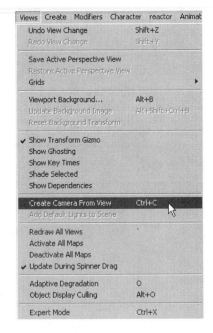

FIGURE 9.6 *To match the perspective of the current viewport, from the main toolbar choose Views > Create Camera from View, or just press Ctrl + C.*

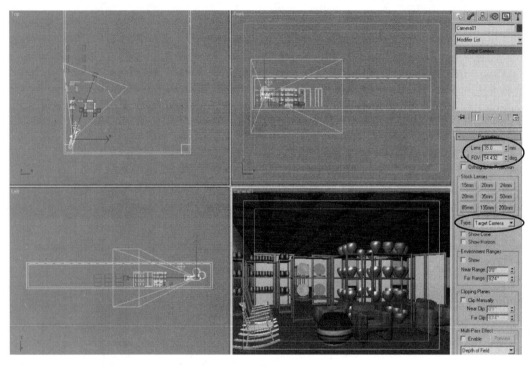

FIGURE 9.7 *The newly created camera matches the focal length and field of view of the current Perspective viewport.*

4. Save the file; it should already be named *Ch09_Camera_place02.max*.

    You have placed a target camera that is positioned to provide the same viewpoint as the current active Perspective viewport in one step with the Create Camera From View command. Alternately, you could have matched an existing camera, either free or target, with the current Perspective viewport by selecting the camera and pressing the keyboard shortcut Ctrl + C.

If you have a target or a free camera and decide at some point that it is the wrong type, you can switch to a different one in the Parameters rollout on the Modify panel. Choose the camera type that you'd like to switch to from the Type drop-down list (Figure 9.7).

You could have used either a target or a free camera in Exercise 9.1 or 9.2. However, you have created one of each type, which you'll use in the exercises that follow.

Remember to use the online reference files in the Help pull-down menu or the shipping manuals to find more controls for cameras in 3ds max 7 scenes.

Camera Composition

The process of creating either type of camera, target or free, is not a difficult task. What does become more difficult, however, is placing the camera in the scene to achieve the greatest effectiveness in communicating the desired message to the viewer. Unless you are aware of some fundamental composition concepts, you're apt to point the camera directly at the main subject in your scenes, which produces a static and often boring image or animation.

The following are some basic composition techniques you should be aware of when setting up cameras in a scene, both for still and animated cameras:

- **The Rule of Thirds.** This basic rule of composition divides the view into nine areas.
- **Camera angle.** Tilting cameras can affect the mood of the scene.
- **Field of view.** This method of "cropping" with the camera controls what the viewer sees.

The Rule of Thirds

The Rule of Thirds is an age-old rule of traditional composition. It should be the first thing you think of when adjusting your camera viewpoint.

When applying the Rule of Thirds, you divide the scene into nine areas: three vertical and three horizontal. The important object in your scene should always be positioned at the intersection of the divisions on the left or right, but not in the center.

Subjects in a scene that are centered are very static, so the viewer tends to look directly at them without perceiving the rest of the scene. Moving the important subject or subjects to the intersections of the grid helps viewers find the subject quickly but also notice the context in which the subject is being presented.

The next exercise demonstrates the Rule of Thirds in a retail scene that is promoting a large terra cotta pot, among other products.

Exercise 9.3: Applying the Rule of Thirds

1. Open **Ch09_Camera_place02.max** from the CD-ROM or from your project folder. Save it to your project folder with the name *Ch09_Camera_place03.max*. The Camera01 viewport should be active. Use the Truck Camera navigation tool to place the large pot near the center of the viewport. Use the Quick Render button in the main toolbar to render the scene (**Figure 9.8**).

FIGURE 9.8 *The scene with the main subject centered in the view is static and uninteresting.*

2. Imagine the Camera01 viewport is divided into three horizontal and three vertical sections. Truck the camera so that the pot is located at the lower left intersection of the imaginary grid. Quick Render the viewport, and you'll see a much more pleasing balance. The eye is encouraged to wander a bit, but still comes to rest on the pot. Another benefit of this repositioning is that the large expanse of distracting floor has been eliminated (see **Figure 9.9** on the next page).

3. Save the file; it should already be called *Ch09_Camera_place03.max*.

FIGURE 9.9 *Applying the Rule of Thirds to the pot creates a more balanced and interesting perspective for the viewer.*

Remember to use this very basic scene-composition technique on all your renderings, and the audience will respond favorably without realizing what you have done.

Take the time to study more traditional forms of media, especially still photos or paintings, so that you gain some practice determining how the fundamental Rule of Thirds is being applied. Then try to work the technique into your daily work, to the point where it becomes automatic.

tip

It's OK to break the rules of art and visualization occasionally if it serves a purpose in your presentation. But just make sure you are aware of the rules and how they are applied before you break them. Otherwise, you risk creating a scene that doesn't have the effect on viewers that you intended.

Camera Angles and Viewer Perception

Just as the position of the subject in the scene influences viewers' perceptions, adjustments to the angle of the camera on the subject can also greatly affect perceptions. Slight changes to the camera angle, especially in the up and down axis, can greatly affect the viewer's emotional response to an image. For example, a horizontal camera produces an effect similar to that of centering the main subject in the viewport. It conveys a sense of quiet and calm, approaching the point of boredom.

In the next exercise, you'll experiment with two variations on the camera angle to witness their effect on viewers' perceptions.

Exercise 9.4: Adjusting Camera Angles

1. Open **Ch09_Camera_place03.max** from the CD-ROM or from your project folder. Save it to your project folder with the name *Ch09_Camera_place04.max*. Adjusting the camera on this scene will produce a more dynamic viewpoint.

2. Adjust the Camera01 viewport using the navigation buttons to zoom (using the Field of View button), truck, orbit, and dolly (which means to move in and out along the view line), so that the pot is still near the lower left intersection, but the point of view of the camera is low to the ground and looking up (**Figure 9.10**). (You'll

> **tip**
>
> If you want to simulate a view camera that has the kind of adjustable film and lens planes used in architectural photography, do the following: Select a camera in the scene, and from the Modifiers menu on the main toolbar apply a Camera Correction modifier. This modifier lets you straighten the converging vertical lines in the scene. The Camera Correction modifier is available only from the Modifier menu.

need to orbit the camera until it moves below the floor, then truck to move the camera above the floor.) The result is a decidedly different perception of the image.

FIGURE 9.10 *A low camera angle looking upward creates a sense of dynamic motion in a still image.*

3. Now adjust the Camera01 viewport so that the pot is viewed from a similar angle, but this time looking downward from above. You can move the camera and target in the Left or Front viewport or use the navigation tools, but try to keep the pot in the same relative position and at the same relative size. Render the image. Notice that there's a much more calm and relaxed feel to the scene (**Figure 9.11**).

It's a good idea to experiment with more camera angles so that you get good at noticing the feelings that each variation evokes. You can also show the different angles to friends and colleagues to get their reactions to the changes.

FIGURE 9.11 *The same scene viewed from above is much less dynamic and is calming to the viewer.*

4. Save the file. It is already called *Ch09_Camera_place04.max.*

Even slight changes to camera angles can affect the viewer in totally different ways, so you should always try several shots to find the one that best suites your purposes.

As mentioned earlier, you should use traditional forms of visualization like photos and paintings to develop a sense of what is being done in other fields that can be applied to your work. The examples here are somewhat extreme to illustrate the point, but the rules apply to all visual arts.

Field of View as a Perception Tool

Looking through a paper towel tube gives you a completely different outlook on the world compared to looking through a shorter toilet paper tube. You don't see as much through the longer tube (there's less field of view) and are more focused on the subjects, while your eye has more area to wander with the short tube (more field of view). The perception of your scene is quite different in each case.

The next exercise has you experiment with changing the field of view while keeping the pot in the same relative position.

Exercise 9.5: Adjusting the Field of View

1. Open **Ch09_Camera_place05.max** from the CD-ROM. Save it to your project folder with the name *Ch09_Camera_place06.max*. Use the Select by Name tool on the main toolbar to select Camera01. Another way to select the camera set to a viewport is to right-click the viewport label and choose Select Camera from the menu. This file shows the camera repositioned so that the pot is located in the lower-left intersection of the grid. The camera is set to use a 35mm lens with a field of view of around 54 degrees in the horizontal (**Figure 9.12**).

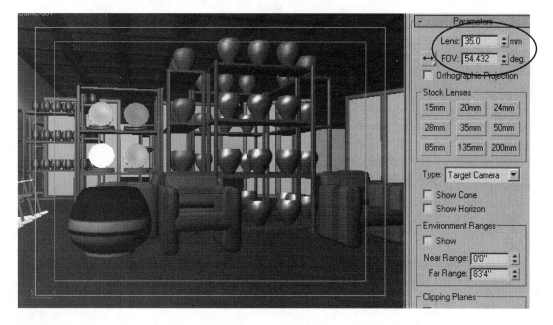

FIGURE 9.12 *The scene as it appears with a lens length of 35mm and a field of view of about 54 degrees, as determined by the camera parameters.*

2. In the Parameters rollout on the Modify panel, click the 85mm button in the Stock Lenses section. Now dolly and truck the camera until the pot is centered on the lower-left intersection. You can only dolly back so far and still stay inside the room. Render the scene.

    Notice you've produced a crowded and compressed view that feels confining, but focuses attention on the pot (**Figure 9.13**). There is little apparent depth to the scene with a field of view of only around 24 degrees.

FIGURE 9.13 *A narrow field of view compresses and flattens the scene.*

3. In the Parameters rollout on the Modify panel, click the 20mm button in the Stock Lenses section to obtain a field of view of around 84 degrees. In the Camera01 viewport, dolly in until the pot is repositioned at the lower-left intersection and is roughly the same size as before. Render the image (**Figure 9.14**).

    The pot takes on a much more important role in the scene and stands out from its surroundings. The scene has much more apparent depth. Try some other variations on field of view and draw your own conclusions on the effects to the mood of the scene.

FIGURE 9.14 *A wide field of view opens up the scene and adds depth while calling attention to the pot.*

4. Save the file. It should already be called *Ch09_Camera_place06.max*.

Remember to use field of view in your scene composition to either calm the viewer using long views or create tension using wider-angle views.

With all the technology we have at our disposal, it's still critically important to learn and practice the fundamentals of good visualization that have been developed over the centuries. Software doesn't envision art—the concept and execution is still up to the individual artist. Many of us, especially from the more technical areas of engineering or architecture, may not be fully aware of these traditional concepts of visualization and will have to put some effort into researching them and applying those principles to our own work. It's not difficult, but you must practice these techniques before they will become an automatic part of your daily routine.

Cameras in Motion

The techniques you have just learned about in this chapter were used to compose still images. The same rules apply to motion pictures or animations, of course, but the camera motion adds another dimension to the problem of "entertaining" your viewer.

A popular reason, especially among architects, for using 3ds max 7 is to provide architectural walk-throughs using either a free or target camera. However, you should avoid this style of animation in most cases. It's difficult to animate this "one-eyed" camera through a building or street scene without upsetting the audience with the lateral swings of the camera as it turns corners. This discomfort is due to the lack of peripheral vision.

If you want to learn to use camera motion techniques, you should again turn to the professionals in traditional fields of film and television, who create short clips of animation and edit them together into a coherent story using programs like Discreet Combustion, Adobe Final Effects, or Adobe Premier.

In this section, I'll briefly introduce you to the following fundamental concepts of camera movement:

- **Dollying and zooming.** The forward and backward movement of cameras.
- **Crabbing and panning.** Lateral or side-to-side movement.
- **Basic scene editing.** Assembling short scenes into an animation.

This section is not intended to be a lesson in the techniques of animation, but to make you aware of proven methods of moving cameras. You'll need to research these concepts further if you want to become a better animator.

Dollying and Zooming Cameras

The forward and backward motion of cameras in a scene can be accomplished by moving the camera closer to or farther from the subjects. However, to achieve a wider angle or more telephoto view of the scene, another effective technique is to animate the zooming of the lens. Both can have a similar effect on the audience, but the changes in perspectives caused by zooming the field of view over time can be made significantly more dramatic by changing the relative size of the objects in the view more rapidly than by moving the camera.

As you watch films, see if you can tell when a camera has been dollied or moved to focus the viewer's attention on a subject, or to open the view to show the context in which the subject exists.

Crabbing and Panning a Camera

Lateral or sideways motion of cameras is probably the trickiest movement to execute successfully. Crabbing a camera straight to the left or right must be done very slowly and smoothly to keep viewers from becoming uncomfortable, both with the motion and with the anticipation of not knowing exactly where they're headed. It adds an element of suspense to the view and can be used to bring new important subjects into the scene, for example.

Panning is the process of rotating the camera around the vertical axis. It should be used judiciously. Because the camera is a single lens with no peripheral vision, viewers can quickly become disoriented and lose their sense of direction. Very seldom do you see panning in films unless it is very, very slow or is used to track a moving subject in the scene.

Many architectural walk-throughs are ruined by panning because the camera has been animated along a path that swings wildly as the path curves through a turn. Remember, in most cases you're probably not striving to provide your viewers with the effect of a wild carnival ride.

Editing Short Scenes into a Coherent Story

Again, tradition film and TV editing can be your guide here, both for a more effective presentation and also as a way to make your work more productive and easy to edit.

Watch a movie and count "one thousand one, one thousand two," and so on, to time the number of seconds any scene is visible on the screen before changing to a new scene. You will be surprised to find that many scenes are only 3 to 5 seconds long before the camera cuts to a new viewpoint. In the United States, animation is 30 frames per second, so a scene can be between 90-150 frames and still convey enough information for the viewer.

If (when) something goes wrong in a 150-frame rendering, it is usually easy to correct the problem and rerender the scene. One the other hand, if something goes wrong in a 4,000-frame animation, it is a lot more difficult to fix the error cost-effectively.

The transition from one scene into the next is usually accomplished using a straight "cut": The first scene ends and the second starts abruptly—something viewers are very comfortable with in the traditional visual arts.

One alternative to a straight cut transition would be to employ a dissolve, in which one scene overlaps and blends into the next scene, or a fade, where the first scene fades down to black just before the next scene appears and comes back to full brightness. This type of edit is usually applied to indicate a change of place or time in the scene.

It's imperative that you take this fundamental information on camera position and motion and investigate it more deeply to help you create scenes that both deliver your intended message with more impact and make your job easier and more productive.

Resources

If you would like more information on film editing and composition, experts in the field have recommended the following:

- http://photoinf.com/General/Robert_Berdan/ Composition_and_the_Elements_of_Visual_ Design.htm
- *The Grammar of the Edit* (Focal Press, ISDN: 0240513401) and *The Grammar of the Shot* (Focal Press, ISDN: 0240513983), both by Roy Thompson
- *Setting Up Your Shots: Great Camera Moves Every Filmmaker Should Know* (Michael Wiese Productions, ISDN: 0941188736), by Jeremy Vineyard

Summary

After doing the exercises in this chapter, you should be comfortable with the fundamental placement and adjustment of free and target cameras in 3ds max 7. More importantly, you should have learned that placing and adjusting cameras without giving any thought to the composition of the scene, as defined by traditional film camera techniques, most likely won't have the effect on the viewer you intended.

Take the time to watch film and television with a more critical eye toward the techniques employed by directors to involve you, the viewer, in the world created by the camera.

For still images, you can refer to books and magazines on architecture or product design to develop a feel for how the focal length and the composition of cameras can affect your perception of the scene.

---

tip

An effective method of creating animations quickly and effectively can be borrowed from Director Ken Burns, who is well-known for his television documentaries on the Civil War and baseball history. Burns often makes his story spring to life initially by moving and zooming a camera across a photograph.

You can use the same method by rendering a high-resolution image in max and applying it to a plane that has flat lighting or self-illumination. Then animate the 3ds max 7 camera, moving and zooming across the image and rendering out as a series of sequential images to create an animated film. As long as you don't turn the camera to change the perspective, the audience will accept the effect and you'll have saved a lot of time by not rendering the camera in the actual scene.

CHAPTER 10

Lighting Methods: Follow the Masters

In This Chapter

Lighting a 3D scene is just as important as, if not more important than, modeling. Newer users of 3ds max 7 often struggle with this concept, and end up spending too much time modeling their 3D scenes and not enough time lighting them. This is a major reason why they can end up with mediocre results in their rendered images.

In particular, newer users in engineering and architecture fields are more inclined to spend too much time creating unnecessary details in their models. Then when they add lighting, they suffer from slow production, primarily because of the overhead of their shadow calculations.

Lighting is very important for defining the mood of a scene and conveying the illusion of depth. Traditional painters often begin their creations by first making a grayscale value sketch to establish the "3D-ness" of the scene. Light-colored areas tend to come forward to the viewer, while darker areas fall back. This visual aid, coupled with camera perspective, is what makes a flat 2D rendering appear three-dimensional to the viewer.

This chapter introduces the concept of lighting in 3ds max 7 by focusing on how the light falls on surfaces rather than on how to position lights based on light sources in the real world. In the exercises at the end of the chapter, you'll light an outdoor scene using a Sunlight system, a spotlight, and several Omni lights that help control the intensity and quality of light falling on the surfaces.

This chapter covers the following topics:

- **Standard lights.** You'll learn to create and adjust efficient standard light types that work with the Scanline renderer to produce a final image in 3ds max 7.

- **Painting with light.** You'll learn to position lights in 3ds max 7 according to where the light must fall on surfaces, rather than where light sources would be located in a real-world scenario.

- **Sunlight system.** You'll learn to place and adjust the direct sunlight according to location and time of day for accurate shadow casting.

- **Casting shadows.** You'll learn methods for adjusting and optimizing shadows to obtain a convincing image produced in an efficient manner.

- **Fill lighting.** You'll learn to simulate the natural phenomenon of light bouncing from surfaces by applying fill lighting.

Key Terms

- **Angle of incidence.** The angle at which light rays strike a surface, which affects the brightness of the light on the surface.

- **Scanline renderer.** This renderer functions with standard lights to efficiently render a final image.

- **Bounced light.** In the real world, a percentage of the light that strikes a surface is bounced back to other surfaces. You will learn to simulate the bounced light using 3ds max 7 standard lights.

note

Lighting and materials function together in 3ds max 7 to create a final impression on the viewer. So when you change either the lighting or the materials, you must allow yourself extra time to adjust the other. You'll learn more about materials in Chapter 12, *Material Editor: Your Palette at a Glance*; Chapter 13, *Maps: Patterns Before Your Eyes*; and Chapter 14, *Mapping Coordinates: Getting the Right Fit.*

tip

A general rule of thumb for creating still images is to spend one third of your time modeling, one third on applying materials, and one third on adding lighting. For animated scenes, you should borrow a little time from each of these three areas for the animation.

As I've said many times already, studying the work of traditional artists and photographers, in this case to see how they applied light and dark values, can be extremely helpful for understanding how these concepts work. The Dutch master Jan Vermeer and American photographer Ansel Adams are good starting points because they are particularly notable for mastering the art of lighting. At the end of this chapter, I've also noted Web sites that you can use as references for further study.

Standard Lights

Standard light types in 3ds max 7 are very efficient lights that calculate direct light from a source to surfaces in the scene. There are several forms of standard lights that cast light in a variety of patterns to give you control of most lighting needs. The standard light types accessible via the Lights category on the Create panel include:

- **Spot.** Spot lights cast light from a single-point light source outward within a cone or pyramid.

- **Direct.** Direct lights are much like a spotlight, except that the light is cast from the source outward within a cylinder or rectangle and parallel to the direction the light is pointing.

- **Omni.** An Omni light casts its light equally in all directions from the source.

The mr Area Omni and mr Area Spot buttons in the Object Type area of the rollout are light types designed for the Mental Ray render engine. The Skylight button is also a light type, designed to be used primarily with the Light Tracer render engine (**Figure 10.1**). Don't use these lights with the Scanline renderer.

The Spot, Direct, and Omni standard lights are designed primarily for rendering with the Scanline render engine in 3ds max 7, one of the fastest renderers in production 3D software.

Because standard lights used in conjunction with the Scanline renderer calculate only the direct light striking a surface and not any light bounced from surfaces, careful placement of the lights is critical to render a convincing image.

All light types can cast shadows from one object onto another in 3ds max 7, but standard light types don't cast shadows by default. So you need to enable this capability. However, shadow-casting lights are an expensive process, mathematically speaking, and judicious use and optimization of shadows is important for making the standard lights as efficient as possible.

FIGURE 10.1 *The Create Lights menu contains both standard lights and Mental Ray lights. Mental Ray lights should not be used with the Scanline renderer used in this chapter.*

> **note**
>
> The other render engines in 3ds max 7 are
>
> **Radiosity.** I cover this renderer in Chapter 11, *Photometric Lights: Bouncing Basics.*
>
> **Light Tracer.** A renderer used with the Skylight light type to simulate light bouncing in the atmosphere.
>
> **Mental Ray.** An advanced renderer used to calculate bounced light and add special effects.

Much of your day-to-day rendering can be accomplished using standard lights. With standard lights, light placement may take longer, but you can achieve faster rendering times and higher overall productivity compared to the shorter initial setup but longer render times with other light types.

Painting with Light

New users to 3ds max 7 have often presumed that if a real-world situation has lights in certain positions—for example, the sun or a light bulb in a lamp—then that is where the lights should be placed in the 3ds max 7 scene.

You have to approach the challenge more like a photographer or even a painter. A photographer doesn't walk into a room with a camera, turn the lights on, snap the picture, and send it to the client. More than likely, the photographer will spend a fair amount of setup time to place spot and flood lights in interior scenes in positions that will highlight or minimize the importance of those areas to the viewer.

For outdoor scenes, photographers use large Mylar or aluminum reflectors to bounce the sunlight onto areas for balance or exaggeration of light values.

As mentioned earlier, painters paint a grayscale value sketch that draws the viewer's gaze to the important areas of the painting and use dark and light values to enhance or minimize the illusion of 3D depth.

Probably the most important feature of standard lights in 3ds max 7 is the fact that, by default, the distance of a light from a surface has no affect on the intensity of the light hitting that surface. Whether an Omni light is positioned 1 inch or 1,000 feet from the object, the amount of light on the surfaces that is perpendicular to the light source is exactly the same.

What *does* affect the intensity or brightness of a light on a surface is the angle of incidence to the surface. To get even light values across an entire surface, the light source will need to be placed far from the surface. For example, to light the box evenly in **Figure 10.2**, the light must be placed high above the box, not a logical position in lighting terms, but the method you use to paint with light in 3ds max 7.

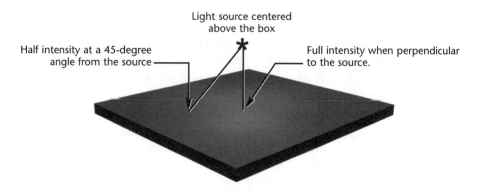

Light source centered
above the box

Half intensity at a 45-degree
angle from the source

Full intensity when perpendicular
to the source.

FIGURE 10.2 *The angle of incidence from source to a surface affects the brightness falling on the surface.*

The Sunlight System

The first light type you'll practice using contains a standard light type, but it's actually a system of components. The Sunlight system in 3ds max 7 consists of a compass that indicates north direction, a standard Target Direct light, and an animation controller that controls position. A Direct light casts its light in a cylinder from the source, resulting in parallel shadows across the lit area. The controller is used to simulate the sun position in real-world terms.

note

You will learn more about animation controllers in Chapter 16, *Controllers and Constraints: More Complexity, More Control.*

You should always create the Sunlight system in the Top viewport for proper orientation. North will always be in the positive Y-World axis, as determined by the compass.

In the exercise that follows, you'll place a Sunlight system in the outdoor scene of an airport similar to the one you created in Chapter 8, *More Modifiers: Orderly Progression*. Then you'll adjust it for a specific time of day and location. The main purpose of using the Sunlight system is to generate direct light from a sun and calculate accurate shadows in the scene—

tip

Clicking and dragging in the Top viewport to create a compass can be a bit tricky the first few times you try it. Moving the mouse a little can create a very large compass that is difficult to see because it is gray against the default gray viewport background. Don't worry, the size of the compass doesn't matter and it can be adjusted later if necessary.

not to light the scene the way the real sun would. You will also learn to adjust the position of the sun and to optimize the shadow-casting calculations.

Exercise 10.1: Creating a Sunlight System

1. Open **Ch10_Airport01.max** from the CD-ROM and save it to your project folder with the name *Ch10_Airport02.max*. It contains the landscape and road from Chapter 8 and has buildings, control tower, and a truck added. Right-click in the Top viewport to activate it.

2. In the Systems category on the Create panel, click the Sunlight button in the Object Type rollout. In the Top viewport, click near the center of the landscape and drag slightly. A gray compass should appear in the viewport. When the compass is slightly larger than the landscape, release the mouse button and move the mouse to adjust the Target Direct light's position from the center of the compass to outside the skydome. Left-click the mouse to set the position of the light (**Figure 10.3**). Don't be overly concerned with the size of the compass or position of the light; they can be adjusted later.

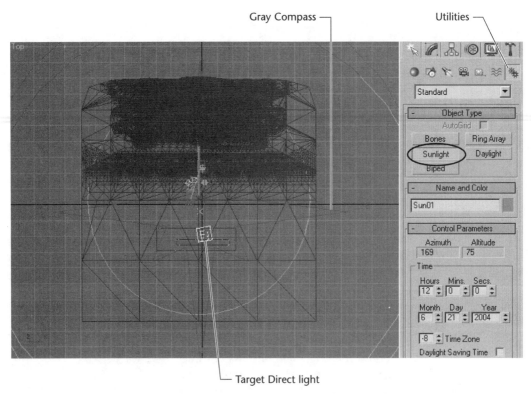

Gray Compass ⌐   Utilities ⌐

Target Direct light

Figure 10.3 *Clicking and dragging to create a compass in the Top viewport and then releasing and moving the mouse to position the light will place a Sunlight system in the scene.*

3. Click the Modify Panel button to verify that the adjustments are for the parameters of the Target Direct light. If you click the Select and Move button on the main toolbar and try to move the Sun01 object, it won't move. This is because an animation controller is controlling its position. With Sun01 selected, click the Motion Panel button. Notice the controls for positioning the Sun01 are based on real data. In the Control Parameters rollout, enter *9* in the Hours field and *9* in the Month field to obtain a time and date of 9 a.m. on September 21, 2005, with a default location of San Francisco, CA (**Figure 10.4**).

4. Right-click in the Camera01 viewport to activate it. On the main toolbar, click the Quick Render button. A dark image with shadows will slowly render. The sky will be almost entirely black, and the shaded sides of objects in the scene will be very black. This doesn't resemble what you would expect it to look like at 9 a.m. in San Francisco (see **Figure 10.5** on the next page). The Scanline renderer is calculating only the direct light from Sun01. In the real world, the scene is flooded with light bounced from moisture and particles in the atmosphere and from the ground and objects in the scene. The bounced light is not calculated with Scanline rendering.

Motion Panel button

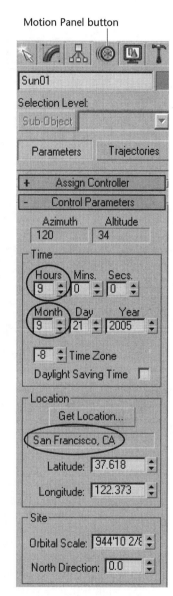

FIGURE 10.4 *The Motion panel is where you adjust the time, date, and location of the sun in a Sunlight system.*

Figure 10.5 *Performing a Quick Render on the Camera01 viewport slowly produces a very dark scene with only direct light from Sun01 visible and with the objects casting shadows.*

5. Close the Rendered Frame window and save the file. It should already be called *Ch10_Airport02.max*.

Creating a Sunlight system calculates the direct light and shadows from a given Sun01 position, which can be adjusted on the Motion panel.

You may be having doubts at this point about the viability of using the Sunlight system to render a convincing outdoor scene. It seems slow and the lighting is terrible. Just remember the purpose of the system is to calculate direct light and shadows, which it has done quite effectively.

tip

3ds max 7 doesn't normally enable shadow casting for standard lights that you create from the Create panel. However, the Sunlight system automatically enables shadow casting.

Optimizing Shadows

The slow rendering in Exercise 10.1 is caused primarily by shadow calculations. In this section, you'll learn how to optimize these calculations so that you can get faster render times.

The default shadow type for the Sunlight system is Ray Traced shadows. The shadows are calculated by mathematical algorithms that shoot rays from the light to the objects in the scene and to the viewer. The process then disables the direct light in areas of interference of those rays, creating shadows. The default math behind the shadow calculations is doing a lot of work even in this simple scene.

One way to reduce the performance overhead is to disable the shadow casting for those objects in the scene that don't cast important shadows and the objects that shouldn't receive shadows. For example, in the scene we've been working on, the landscape doesn't need to have shadows cast into the space below the landscape. And a sky should never receive or cast shadows. We'll practice this technique in Exercise 10.2.

There is also a very important setting in Ray Traced shadows, called the *Max Quadtree Depth value,* that should always be adjusted for best performance. It controls how the rays are calculated for shadows. While the math behind how it accomplishes this is beyond this lesson, I guarantee you will be wasting computer resources for the majority of scenes that use Ray Traced shadows if you do not adjust it. We'll practice using this setting in Exercise 6.3.

In the small scene in the next exercise, you won't see any significant improvement in performance (it might even hurt performance slightly), but controlling the shadow casting on objects, especially in more complex scenes, is a necessary habit to develop.

Exercise 10.2: Controlling Shadows for Faster Rendering

1. Open **Ch10_Airport02.max** from the last exercise or from the CD-ROM and save it to your project folder with the name *Ch10_Airport03.max*. With the Select button active, select Skydome and Mountains01 in the Left viewport.

2. Right-click in the Left viewport and choose Properties from the Quad menu. In the Object Properties dialog, the Name field is set to Multiple Selected. In the Rendering Control area, unselect the Cast Shadows option. This clears shadow casting for all selected objects (see **Figure 10.6** on the next page). Click OK.

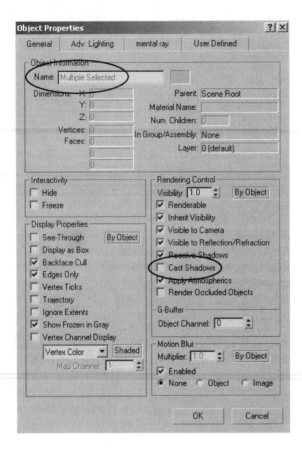

FIGURE 10.6 *You can select multiple objects and turn shadow casting off in the Object Properties dialog for all selected objects.*

3. In the Left viewport, click on Skydome so that only it is selected. Right-click on Skydome and choose Properties in the Quad menu. In the Rendering Control section, clear the Receive Shadows checkbox. Click OK. Now neither Mountains01 nor Skydome can cast shadows, and only Skydome is set not to receive shadows.

4. Save the file; it should already be called *Ch10_Airport03.max*.

Often it's the little things like shadow casting and shadow receiving that adversely affect production. Develop workflow habits for verifying the settings in every scene.

tip

Shadow casting and shadow receiving can also be controlled at the layer level instead of at the individual object level. For example, if you were creating an overall view of a restaurant, you might save significant time by setting all the silverware on the tables onto a layer that has Receive Shadows disabled. For more information on layers in 3ds max 7, refer back to Chapter 2, *Fundamental Concepts*.

As you learn these techniques, practice turning them on and off a few times to help you to remember to do it when you are creating scenes for production. The more you use a tool, the more likely you are to automatically check the settings during your daily routine.

There is no magic number for Max Quadtree Depth that is best; you must try each setting to see which is best for the variables in your particular scene.

Exercise 10.3: Using Max Quadtree Depth for Faster Rendering

1. Open **Ch10_Airport03.max** from the last exercise or from the CD-ROM. The Camera01 viewport renders on my machine, which has a dual 3.2 Xeon processor with 2 gigs RAM, in 1 minute 15 seconds. Your render times will be different. Render your Camera01 viewport and check the rendering time in the Status bar at the lower-left of the display so that you can compare after you change shadow paramenters (**Figure 10.7**).

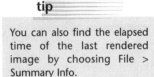

tip

You can also find the elapsed time of the last rendered image by choosing File > Summary Info.

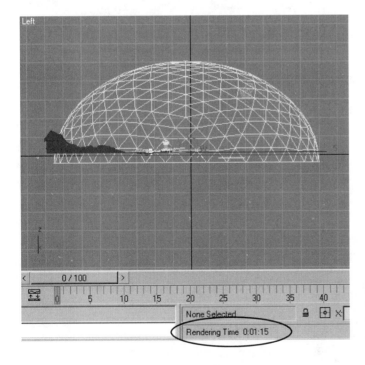

FIGURE 10.7 *After rendering a scene, you can see the elapsed time in the Status bar at the lower-left of the display.*

2. In the Top viewport, select Sun01 or use Select by Name. In the Ray Traced Shadow Params rollout on the Modify panel, notice the Max Quadtree Depth is set to *7* by default (**Figure 10.8**). This default setting is seldom ideal because it usually takes too long to render.

3. Enter *8* in the Max Quadtree Depth field and press Enter. Render the Camera01 viewport. For my machine the render time with the new setting is 32 seconds, less than half what it was at the default setting.

4. Setting the Max Quadtree Depth to *9* and rendering again drops the rendering time to 11 seconds on my machine. This is a significant savings over the previous rendering time. Increasing the Max Quadtree Depth to *10* and rendering the Camera01 viewport again drops the final rendering time to 4 seconds. This setting is critical if you are using the default Ray Traced shadows for the Sunlight system or for any other lights that you set to use Ray Traced shadows.

Where the sun is currently positioned—low and shining right to left in the Camera01 viewport—illuminates only part of the sky near the horizon on the left. Sun01 should not light the sky at all. If it does, the scene would not be convincing as the sun moves to reflect the time of day.

tip

Sun01 still appears to be lighting the skydome at the lower left in the shaded Camera01 viewport. This is a viewport feature to make updating the viewports faster, rather than to calculate all lighting effects. You should always render the scene to test the results of any changes to lights.

FIGURE 10.8 *The default setting for Max Quadtree Depth must always be changed to find the optimum value for your scene.*

5. In the General Parameters rollout on the Modify panel, click the Exclude button. In the Exclude/Include dialog, highlight Skydome in the left Scene Objects column and click the double-right arrow button between the columns to push Skydome into the right Exclude column (**Figure 10.9**). Click OK. The skydome is no longer affected by Sun01 when rendered.

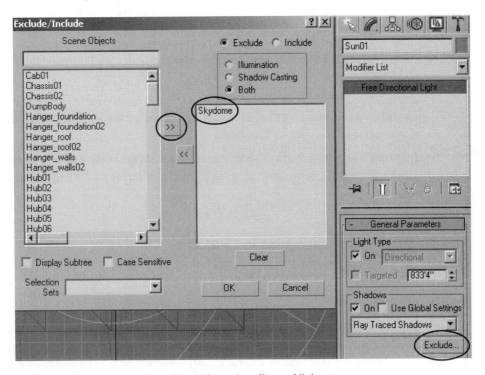

FIGURE 10.9 *You can exclude objects from the effects of light.*

6. Save the file. It should already be called *Ch10_Airport03.max*.

By changing a few simple settings—the shadow casting and receiving of objects, and especially the Max Quadtree Depth of Ray Traced shadows—you have dramatically increased production by cutting the rendering time of your scene.

There is no method of calculating the savings you may achieve by adjusting Max Quadtree Depth for Ray Traced shadows, so you must always try 8, 9, and 10 to find the best results for your particular scene.

Working Toward Even Lighting

The current scene is now rendering much more quickly than with the default shadow parameters for the Sun01 in the scene. You can now proceed with making the lighting in the scene appear more convincing.

The first step will be to control light on the skydome so that it is even across the entire sky. You will learn to use the Exclude feature to make sure the new light only lights the skydome. Next you'll add and adjust lights that will fill in areas in the shaded portion of the rendered scene to bring the light values up to simulate light bouncing off the atmosphere and surrounding objects.

You want the skydome object in the scene to have an even and consistent light over the entire sky coverage. This can be accomplished by taking advantage of the angle of incidence of the light to the inside of the skydome.

The light you add will affect only the skydome. When you add new objects to the scene you don't want to have to manage whether they are affected by this new light or not.

Exercise 10.4: Evenly Lighting the Skydome

1. Open **Ch10_Airport03.max** from the last exercise or from the CD-ROM. Save it to your project folder with the name *Ch10_Airport04.max*. Right-click in the Top viewport to activate it.

2. In the Lights category on the Create panel, click the Onmi button in the Object Type rollout. Then click near the center of the skydome in the Top viewport (**Figure 10.10**). Render the Camera01 viewport to see the skydome and the underside of all objects lit by the new Omni light.

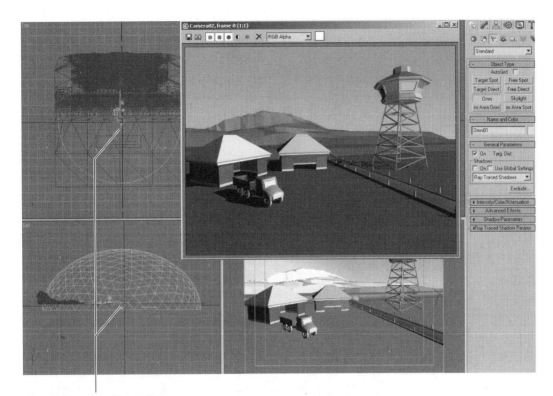

Omni light centered in skydome

Figure 10.10 *An Omni light centered in the skydome in the Top viewport lights everything from below.*

3. In the General Parameters rollout on the Modify panel, click the Exclude button. In the Exclude/Include dialog, highlight Skydome in the left column and click the double-arrow button to move it into the right column. This excludes the skydome from the Omni light, which is not what you want. In the Exclude/Include dialog, click the Include radio button on the upper right of the dialog. Click OK. Only the skydome is lit with the new Omni light, and any new objects added to the scene will automatically be excluded from the effects of this light.

4. Render the Camera01 viewport and notice that the skydome remains evenly lit, but the shaded areas of the other objects have turned completely black again (**Figure 10.11**).

To fill in the shaded areas on the front and left of the objects in the scene, you'll place Omni lights far enough away from the objects to produce an angle of incidence of approximately 90 degrees. This way they will cast an even light on those surfaces. Then you'll adjust the intensity of the lights to simulate bounce light in the scene.

FIGURE 10.11 *Including only the skydome in the Exclude/Include dialog makes the management of Exclude/Include easier as new objects are added to the scene.*

5. In the Top viewport, add an Omni light to the left of the landscape and another at the bottom of the landscape (**Figure 10.12**). The Camera01 viewport will be overly bright.

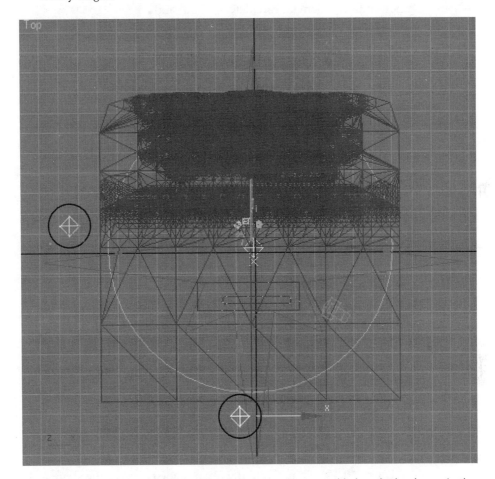

FIGURE 10.12 *Add Omni lights to the left of the landscape and below the landscape in the Top viewport as fill lights.*

6. With Omni03 selected, on the Modify panel enter *0.5* in the Multiplier field on the Intensity/Color/Attenuation rollout. Press Enter. The light will be reduced to half the intensity it was. Click the Exclude button in the General Parameters rollout and exclude Skydome from this light. Click the Select button on the main toolbar and select Omni02 to the left of the landscape. On the Modify panel, enter *0.3* in the Multiplier field to reduce its intensity to one-third the original (**Figure 10.13**). Exclude Skydome from Omni02.

tip

Standard lights are additive, so when two lights with the same intensity strike a surface at the same angle of incidence, the amount of light on the surface is doubled.

Figure 10.13 *Reducing the intensity of the new fill Omni lights and excluding the skydome from them simulates bounced light in the scene.*

7. Render the Camera01 viewport and the scene will appear more convincing (**Figure 10.14**). Eliminating the black shaded areas of the scene with the fill lights simulated light that would normally be bouncing from the atmosphere and other surfaces. Close the Rendered Frame window and save the file; it should already be called *Ch10_Airport04.max*.

Figure 10.14 *The scene has a more natural appearance with the simulation of bounced light and shadows.*

References

To see some examples of traditional 2D images, both paintings and photographs, I've added two Internet Web sites you can view for reference.

Jan Vermeer had to simulate all lights with paint. He used the illusion of light to focus the viewer's attention on the important areas. Ansel Adams, on the other hand, used natural light for his photos but manipulated the development of the film and the prints in the darkroom to gain a wide range of grayscale to enhance the apparent depth of the scene and, again, to focus the viewers' attention where he wanted.

- www.mystudios.com/vermeer/
- www.masters-of-photography.com/A/adams/adams_poster.html

Summary

This is a relatively simple scene, but the process is similar on scenes of any size and complexity. The 3ds max 7 lighting methods are not difficult, but you must first learn to view the world as a traditional painter or photographer so you will know what to create in 3ds max 7.

It may seem to like a lot of steps to add so many lights, adjust them, and keep track of the Exclude/Include feature, but once you have done it a few times it is actually quite straightforward, and it offers you the control you need to paint light on surfaces for the look you want to convey to your viewers.

CHAPTER 11

Photometric Lights: Bouncing Basics

In This Chapter

In the last chapter, you learned to place standard lights in positions that don't correlate to the location of light sources in natural lighting. Standard lighting works differently because the lights don't calculate bounced light when rendered using the Scanline renderer. However, the combination of standard lights and scanline renderering is an efficient method of lighting a scene.

In this chapter, you'll learn to light an interior scene using photometric lights and radiosity rendering. This method of lighting and rendering is more mathematically intensive than the standard-scanline combination because the lights behave according to the laws of physics, interacting with the objects in the scene to create a more natural effect.

The intensity settings for photometric lights are calculated according to values that correspond to real lighting, measured in candelas, lumens, or lux. Don't worry if you are not a lighting engineer who knows what these values mean. For the vast majority of 3ds max 7 users, the final rendered image is "right if it looks right," so you can adjust the intensity settings as desired for your scene.

Not only does the initial intensity of lights behave according to the laws of physics, but the decay of the intensity over distance, known as *attenuation* of light, is also very accurate.

tip

Standard lights also have a manual attenuation adjustment that was not appropriate for the outdoor scene in the last chapter, but which should be used on all standard lights in interior scenes.

What is particularly important when using photometric lighting and the Radiosity renderer is that your models are the proper size. Because the lights are adjusted according to the laws of physics, it would be unreasonable to try to light a very large room with a single standard light bulb. Conversely, a room that is extremely small would be very bright with just a normal light bulb.

This chapter covers the following topics:

- **Placing and adjusting photometric lights.** Placing photometric lights used with radiosity rendering is similar to the way you would place lights in the real world. You let the light bouncing from surfaces act as the fill lighting.

- **Using exposure control.** Exposure control in radiosity rendering is much like photography. You must often adjust the amount of light striking the "film" to have the proper final image.

- **Adjusting meshing parameters.** The radiosity solution, including lighting and shadows, is stored in the vertices of a special mesh object that is generated on top of the mesh to distribute the lighting across the faces of the mesh.

- **Controlling color bleed and reflectance.** You'll learn to apply Advanced Lighting Override materials to control how much color from a surface is allowed to bleed to surrounding surfaces.

- **Making materials act as lights.** You'll learn to make materials give off light in a scene by adjusting the Luminance scale in Advanced Lighting Override material.

Key Terms

- **Attenuation.** Attenuation, or the natural decay of light from its source, is based on the inverse square law of physics. Light intensity diminishes based on the inverse of the square of the distance from the light source (the formula is $1/d^2$, or one over the distance squared).

- **Direct illumination.** Direct light travels directly from the light source to a surface.

- **Indirect illumination.** Indirect light is bounced from one surface to another.

- **Refine Iterations.** This feature gathers radiosity energy from each face of an object and compares it with neighboring faces to smooth variations in lighting.

- **Filtering.** This radiosity post process, in which the effect is applied after the initial rendering, blurs lighting variations across surfaces.

- **Reflectance.** The percentage of light that bounces from a surface is the reflectance value of the material on the surface.

- **Color bleed.** The amount of color carried from one surface to another accompanied by the reflectance values.

Understanding Photometric Lights

The setup time for placing photometric lights is often faster than that for placing standard lights. However, this gain is usually counterbalanced by a longer radiosity calculation and rendering time, making radiosity rendering generally slower overall.

The quality of the bounced light and color bleed in radiosity rendering adds a dimension to the final rendering that viewers perceive even though they may not realize what it is that is different from a scanline rendering.

Modeling can be a very important factor in the productivity of radiosity rendering. Because the lighting information is stored in the vertices and distributed across the adjacent faces of the mesh, the radiosity solution will be significantly more successful when, as much as possible, the model has shared vertices at the intersections of faces. For example, if you have a room where the walls, floor, and ceiling are separate objects that pass through on another or abut one another without one object having vertices that correspond to vertices in the adjacent object, the radiosity solution will require very small meshing sizes and more processing to achieve acceptable results.

One the other hand, if a room is constructed so that the interior wall, floor, and ceiling are all part of the same mesh with a single vertex where two walls and the ceiling meet, the radiosity solution will be much more efficient and require lower meshing sizes and less processing. You can open a file from the CD-ROM called **Elevator_example.max** to see an extremely clean model created from a single box using some of the box modeling techniques presented in Chapter 7, *The Editable Poly: Box Modeling.*

tip

Despite the fact that using photometric lights achieves an effect much more like natural lighting, you still don't want to wear the hat of a lighting engineer or lighting designer when lighting a scene with photometric lights and radiosity rendering. You must approach the problem as a photographer would and add lights for accent or to draw the viewer's eye to important objects in the scene. You are still painting the scene with light, albeit with the extra benefit of the bounced light.

The model you'll use in this chapter has been optimized for radiosity rendering. It is the one-piece control tower from Chapter 4, *Modifiers: Stack Them High*, which has been assigned a thickness using the Shell modifier and has had the interior window panes edited so that they're inset into the frames. Using a model that has been optimized for radiosity lets you focus on the process of working with photometric lights and radiosity rendering without running into problems caused by the model.

As with everything in 3ds max 7, start small when using photometric lighting, and then work your way into bigger projects as you develop a feel for the process and optimizations that are available to you.

Placement and Adjustment

In the first exercise, you'll place photometric lights in the control tower scene and adjust some of the parameters to simulate the type of light you want. The light will be a Free Point light, similar to a standard Omni light.

You'll also learn to enable the Radiosity renderer and calculate the radiosity solution to correctly render the scene.

Finally, you'll learn to set the distribution pattern of the light to change it from a Free Point light with Isotropic distribution (in all directions) to Spot distribution (in a cone from the source).

Exercise 11.1: Creating and Positioning Photometric Lights

1. Open **Ch11_Interior01.max** from the CD-ROM and save it to your project folder with the name *Ch11_Interior02.max*. The scene is the interior of the control tower at night with some equipment and furniture added. Plain-colored materials have been assigned to the objects. Click the Quick Render button on the main toolbar to render the scene using the Scanline renderer (**Figure 11.1**). Quite boring, no? Right-click in the Top viewport to activate it.

FIGURE 11.1 *The interior of the control-tower room rendered using the default lights and the Scanline renderer.*

2. In the Lights category on the Create panel, click the arrow beside the Standard field drop-down menu and choose Photometric from the list. In the Object Type rollout, click the Free Point button and, in the Top viewport, pick in the center of the control tower. This places the Free Point light on the floor and changes the illumination in the Camera01 viewport (see **Figure 11.2** on the next page). Right-click in the Camera01 viewport and click the Quick Render button. The image is essentially black. This is because the Scanline renderer doesn't work predictably with photometric lights.

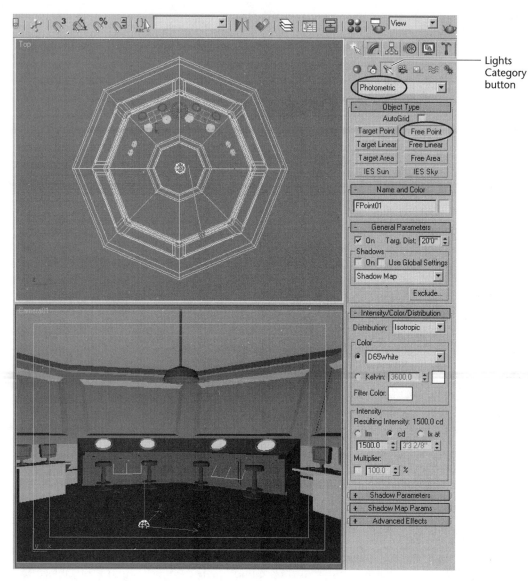

Figure 11.2 *Placing a Free Point photometric light in the Top viewport changes the lighting in the shaded viewport.*

3. From the main menu, choose Rendering > Advanced Lighting > Radiosity
    (**Figure 11.3**). This disables the Scanline renderer and enables the Radiosity
    renderer. If exposure control—the adjustment of the amount of light striking
    the "film"—hasn't already been assigned, a Radiosity dialog will display asking
    if you would like to use exposure control as recommended. Click the Yes button.
    Render the Camera01 viewport, and you'll see more light in the rendered image.

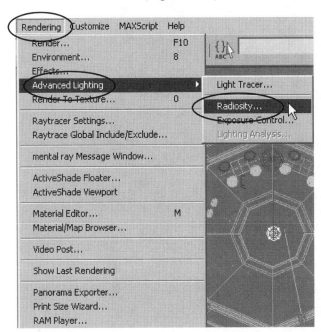

FIGURE 11.3 *Assign
the Radiosity renderer
from the Rendering
pull-down menu.*

4. To see the result of the photometric lights using the Radiosity renderer, you
    must first calculate the radiosity solution. In the Render Scene dialog, click the
    Advanced Lighting tab, and in the Radiosity Processing Parameters rollout,
    click the Start button (see **Figure 11.4** on the next page). After a few seconds
    of processing the solution, there is more apparent light in the rendering of the
    Camera01 viewport. The light is on the floor and not in a good position to
    create effective lighting for this scene. Close all dialogs and the Render Frame
    window if it's open.

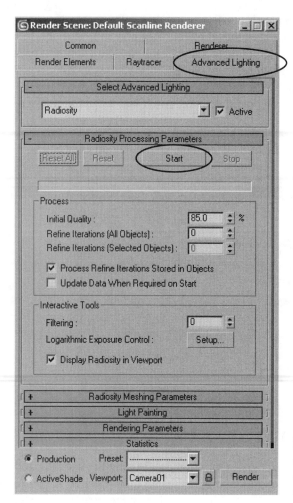

FIGURE 11.4 *The radiosity solution must be calculated, and the information stored in the mesh vertices.*

5. Now let's align FPoint01 with a fixture in the ceiling. In the Camera01 viewport, select FPoint01. On the main toolbar, click the Align button. In the Left viewport, pick the hanging light fixture at the left-center of the viewport (Lamp01 if you want to use the Select by Name command). In the Align Selection dialog, make sure X Position, Y Position, and Z Position checkboxes are selected and that the Center radio button is selected in both the Current Object and Target Object columns. This aligns the light to the geometric center of the lamp (**Figure 11.5**). In the Align Selection dialog, click the Apply button to set the current alignment. Click the Y Position checkbox and choose Minimum in both the Current Object and Target Object columns to place the bottom of the light at the bottom of the Lamp01 mesh. Click OK.

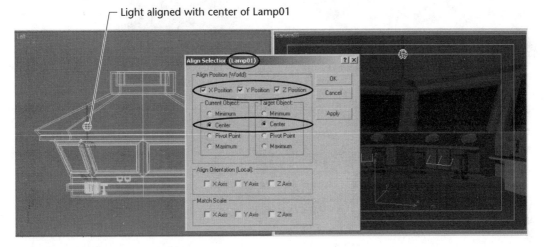

FIGURE 11.5 *You can use the Align tool to place the light in the fixture.*

6. Press the F10 function key and choose the Advanced Lighting tab. In the Radiosity Processing Parameters rollout, click the Reset All button. This discards the current radiosity solution. Click the Start button to recalculate the solution using the new light position. Render the Camera01 viewport, and you'll see the lighting has changed significantly, but doesn't yet appear very convincing. There are no shadows.

If you are constantly getting the Reset Radiosity Solution warning dialog, click the Do Not Ask Me this Again checkbox.

7. With FPoint01 still selected, in the General Parameters rollout on the Modify panel, click the On checkbox in the Shadows area (**Figure 11.6**). Render the Camera01 viewport. Notice that the shadows make a difference, especially from the Lamp01. All the light is focused downward from the fixture. This simulates a bare bulb in a light fixture.

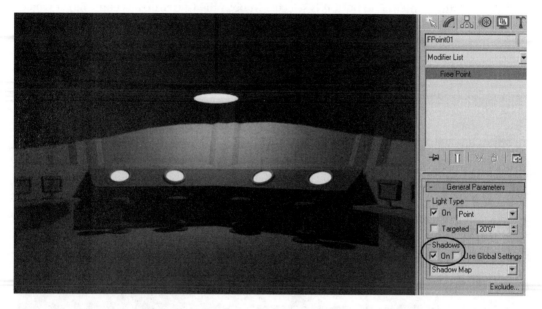

FIGURE 11.6 *Enabling shadows for the light is essential in creating authentic-looking light emanating from a light fixture.*

8. To change the distribution pattern of a Free Point light, in the Intensity/Color/Distribution rollout on the Modify panel, click the Isotropic field. Choose Spotlight from the drop-down list. The light changes form in the viewports to show two cones. The full intensity of the light shines in the inner light blue Hotspot/Beam cone, and it diminishes outward to the darker Falloff/Field cone. Outside these cones, no light or shadow emanates from this source. Expand the Spotlight Parameters rollout, and enter *120* in the Hotspot/Beam field and *150* in the Falloff/Field field to spread the light across more of the room (**Figure 11.7**).

It is not necessary to reset and recalculate the radiosity solution from a light in the scene for only a quick shadow and the direct illumination test.

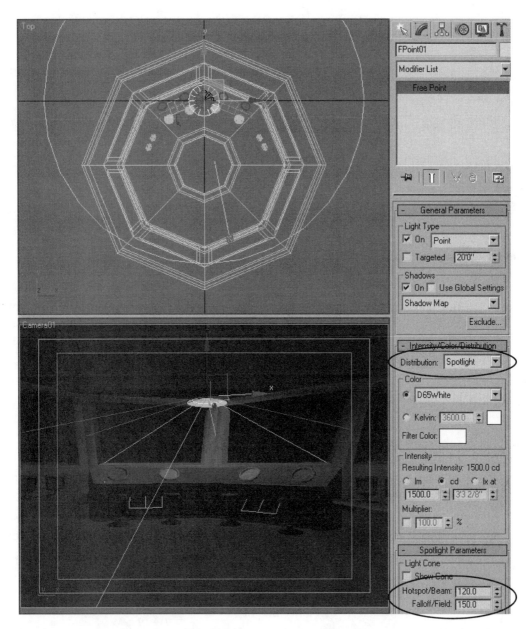

FIGURE 11.7 *Changing the Free Point light to Spotlight distribution beams the light downward and outward within cones from the light source.*

9. Open the Render Scene dialog (press F10) and click the Advanced Lighting tab. In the Radiosity Processing Parameters rollout, click the Reset All button to discard the current radiosity solution, and click Start to calculate a new solution with the new light distribution. Use Quick Render to render the Camera01 viewport.

10. Close all windows and dialogs and save the file; it should already be called *Ch11_Interior02.max*. The rendered image is still very dark for several reasons: It is a single weak bulb in a large room, the exposure control hasn't been adjusted, and the radiosity solution is using the default mesh to store lighting information. You'll correct these in upcoming exercises.

Controlling Lighting Using Exposure Control

As mentioned earlier, radiosity rendering is similar to photography in that if a scene is too bright or too dark to render a good image, you have to use exposure control to adjust the amount of light that reaches the "film" in the process.

When you enabled the Radiosity renderer earlier, you were asked if you wanted to use logarithmic exposure control. You clicked Yes to load it. Exposure control is a post process—that is, the effect is applied after the initial rendering—so you can make adjustments to it and render the scene without recalculating the radiosity solution.

The default Logarithmic Exposure Control option is usually the best choice for general use. It uses a logarithmic curve or S-curve to make the bright areas of a scene brighter and the dark areas darker more quickly than it changes the values in the mid-tone areas. This tends to increase the contrast of a scene for a more convincing appearance.

Applying Exposure Control

Exposure control lets you adjust several aspects of your rendered image that correspond to processes in photography.

The Brightness setting is much like the aperture of a camera lens: Open it to allow more light to strike the film in a dark scene, and close it when the scene is too bright.

Other options include contrast settings and the ability to raise or lower only the mid-tone levels while leaving the lights and darks as they are. Contrast and mid-tone control are more analogous to the control a photographer has in the darkroom while developing the film and processing the print.

While we could add more photometric lights or increase the intensity of the light in the scene, it is not the same as the control you get using exposure control.

In the next exercise, you'll practice using exposure control to adjust the look of the dark rendering inside the control tower so that some of the details in the shadow areas of the scene are visible, mainly in the ceiling and the shadows. Because it's a control-tower room, we don't want it too bright.

Exercise 11.2: Using Exposure Control to Brighten the Scene

1. Open **Ch11_Interior02.max** from your last exercise or from the CD-ROM and save it to your project folder with the name *Ch11_Interior03.max*. In the Rendering pull-down menu, choose Environment to open the Environment and Effects dialog.

2. In the Logarithmic Exposure Control Parameters rollout of the Environment and Effects dialog, enter *85* in the Brightness field (**Figure 11.8**). Render the Camera01 viewport. The scene becomes considerably brighter, showing some detail in the ceiling areas.

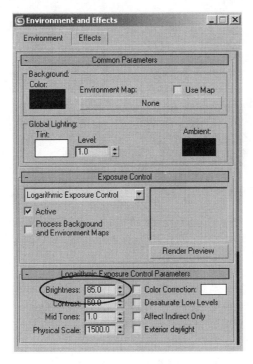

FIGURE 11.8 *To increase the overall brightness of the scene, adjust the exposure control settings by choosing Rendering > Environment.*

3. Enter *25* in the Contrast field and render the Camera01 viewport. This setting raises the levels of the shadows in the scene more than it affects the mid-tone areas. There is more detail showing in the ceiling area now.

4. Enter *1.5* in the Mid Tones field and render the Camera01 viewport. This raises the values in the directly lit areas more than in the darker or lighter areas, giving you more control over just those parts of your scene. As a result, you achieve a better balance in lighting without actually adjusting the lights themselves (**Figure 11.9**).

FIGURE 11.9 *Balancing the light in the scene can be accomplished without adjusting the lights by using exposure control. The result here is a brighter rendering with slightly higher values in the shadows than previously.*

5. Close all windows and dialogs and save the file. It should already be called *Ch11_Interior03.max*. All radiosity scenes will need to have exposure control values adjusted to fine-tune the rendered image.

While adjusting exposure control is an important function throughout the radiosity rendering process, it's not something you do only once to a scene and forget it. You'll continue to make ongoing adjustments to exposure control as you're making other changes to the variables that affect the lighting, such as adjusting the meshing and material.

Adjusting Meshing Parameters for Light Distribution

Once you've established a very basic lighting scheme and adjusted the rendered image using exposure control, you must begin refining the radiosity process to more accurately represent the lighting solution.

3ds max 7 creates a copy of the original model to use as the mesh for storing lighting information in the vertices. However, the vertices in that model are too widespread to accurately represent the light striking the surfaces. In the exercise that follows, you'll practice adjusting the meshing parameters to add vertices to the radiosity solution mesh that are closer than those in the copy max created. This makes the task of interpolating the lighting quality easier for the software because it's occurring over shorter distances.

Setting Radiosity Meshing at the Local Level

While it's possible to accomplish meshing globally, in which all objects are meshed using the same setting, it's seldom an efficient method. The objects that contribute most to the bounced lighting usually require the smallest mesh size, and objects that contribute little to the overall lighting can be meshed at a greater size or not at all.

At the beginning of the exercise, you'll set meshing parameters locally by object, and then you'll recalculate the radiosity solution and test-render the scene to see the results. It is wise to start with the default meshing sizes and decrease the amount until you get the result you are looking for.

As the radiosity solution is refined through meshing, you'll also have to adjust the parameters, the Refine Iterations, and the Filter values to approach an ideal lighting scenario.

Exercise 11.3: Fine-Tuning the Radiosity Solution

1. Open **Ch11_Interior03.max** from the CD-ROM and save it to your project folder with the name *Ch11_Interior04.max*. Press F10 to call the Rendering dialog and click the Advanced Lighting tab. In the Radiosity Processing Parameters rollout, click the Reset All button to discard the current radiosity solution. Then click the Start button to recalculate the scene. Make sure the Camera01 viewport is active and choose Quick Render from the main toolbar. From the Rendering pull-down menu, choose RAM Player. In the RAM Player dialog, click the Open Last Rendered Image in Channel A button and click OK in the RAM Player Configuration dialog to accept the default settings. Close the Rendered Frame window and minimize the RAM Player.

2. In the Camera01 viewport, select Tower_building01. This scene represents the walls, floor, ceiling, and windows objects and is a major contributor to the radiosity solution in this scene. Right-click on Tower_building01 and choose Properties from the Quad menu. In the Radiosity-only Properties area of the Object Properties dialog, clear the Use Global Subdivision Settings option (**Figure 11.10**). Click OK. The default meshing size is 3'3 2/8" or 1 meter. In the Render Scene dialog, click the Advanced Lighting tab, and then click Reset All. Click Start to recalculate using the new mesh size.

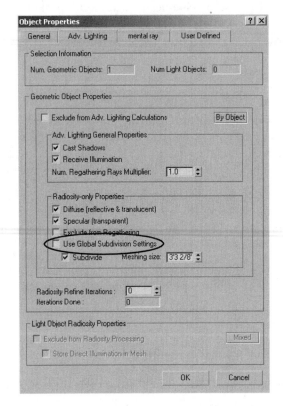

FIGURE 11.10 *In the Object Properties dialog, the meshing parameters can be set to local for each object in the scene.*

3. After the radiosity calculations are complete, render the Camera01 viewport. Maximize the RAM Player, click Open Last Rendered Image in Channel B, and click OK to load the image. Then click and drag in the RAM Player window to compare the rendering before meshing (left side) and after meshing (right side). Most of the change occurs in the ceiling and under the cabinets, with better definition of lighting and shadows. Also notice in the wire frame viewports that the new mesh contains vertices not more than 1 meter apart (**Figure 11.11**). Minimize the RAM Player and close the Rendered Frame window.

4. Right-click on Tower_building01. In the Object Properties dialog that appears, click on the Adv. Lighting tab and change the Meshing size to 1 foot. Click OK. In the Render Scene dialog, click Reset All to start the radiosity processing. The solution will take a little longer to calculate. Render the Camera01 viewport. Maximize the RAM Player and click Open Last Rendered Image in Channel B to compare it to the original mesh rendering. The quality of the radiosity solution is better, especially in the ceiling and cabinet area.

5. Using the Select by Name button on the main toolbar, select Control_panel01, Desk01, and Desk02. Right-click in the Camera01 viewport and choose Properties. On the Advanced Lighting tab, clear the Use Global Subdivision Settings checkbox and enter 2' in the Meshing Size field. Click OK. In the Render Scene dialog, click Reset All, and then click Start. Render the Camera01 viewport and compare this image to Channel A in the RAM Player. You'll notice the ceiling appears somewhat blotchy as the radiosity solution becomes more refined.

FIGURE 11.11 *The new radiosity solution shows meshing at 1 meter in the wireframe viewports and better definition of light and shadows in the shaded viewport and rendered image.*

6. In the Render Scene dialog, Radiosity Processing Parameters rollout, enter 5 in the Refine Iterations (All Objects) field. Click Reset All and then Start, and then render the Camera01 viewport. This time click Open Last Rendered Image in Channel A of the RAM Player. The Refine Iterations value makes five extra comparisons of the light on the faces and smoothes the results.

note

Because the original mesh was very well constructed using shared vertices, in which the surfaces of the mesh share edges and vertices, the Refine Iterations option will have less effect on the quality than models that aren't constructed as well.

You've probably noticed rough shadows and bright areas under the overhangs of the cabinet and desks in the scene. This is not a lighting issue so much as a shadow issue. Let's correct it.

7. Use the Select by Name button on the main toolbar to select FPoint01. In the Shadow Map Params rollout on the Modify panel, enter *2048* in the Size field (**Figure 11.12**). This is the resolution, in pixels, of the shadow map that is applied at render time. Render the Camera01 viewport, and you'll see more sharply defined shadows. Open this image in Channel B of the RAM Player window to compare the quality of the shadows with the last rendered image.

    The scene is looking quite good now—more light is being defined in the ceiling and under the cabinet and desks. However, we still need to minimize the blotchiness in the ceiling.

8. In the Radiosity Processing Parameters rollout of the Render Scene dialog, enter *1* in the Filtering field of the Interactive Tools section. Like exposure control, this is a post process, so you don't need to click Reset All and Start to redo the calculations again. Simply render the Camera01 viewport and open the rendered image in Channel A of the RAM Player. The ceiling is considerably smoother.

    (Filtering values above 3 or 4 can cause loss of detail in the rendered images, especially where you have small shadow details.)

FIGURE 11.12 *Not all lighting problems are directly caused by lighting and radiosity. The quality of shadows must often be adjusted to match the scene.*

9. In the Render Scene dialog, click Reset All to clear the radiosity solution. Saving files with the radiosity solution can create very large files on your hard drive. Close all windows and dialogs and save the file. It should already be called *Ch11_Interior04.max*.

Rendering radiosity scenes with photometric lighting is a balancing act among the model, the lighting, and the variables and adjustments of the radiosity solution and exposure control. With some practice, you'll soon develop a system that fits your workflow and typical projects, allowing you to more quickly choose an acceptable solution for your needs.

Controlling Radiosity Using Materials

The next level of control you have when rendering radiosity is with the materials in the scene. You'll learn more about materials in Chapters 12, 13, and 14, but in this and the next section you'll learn about some adjustments that influence the reflectance and color bleed in radiosity rendering, including color value and Advanced Lighting Override material.

The value or the brightness of the diffuse color (color in direct light) and ambient color (color in shaded areas) in a material affects the amount of light bounced from a surface. The hue (red, blue, and so on) of the material's color affects the tinting of the scene caused by color bleed. In the exercise that follows, you'll change the color of the floor material in the scene to affect the overall tint of the rendered image. Then you'll adjust the value (brightness) of the color to affect how much of the light striking the floor surface is bounced into the room.

Exercise 11.4: Adjusting the Hue and Value of Materials

1. Open **Ch11_Interior04.max** from the last exercise or from the CD-ROM and save it to your project folder as *Ch11_Interior05.max*. Press F10 to open the Render Scene dialog and click the Advanced Lighting tab. In the Radiosity Processing Parameters rollout, click the Start button to recalculate the current radiosity solution. Render the Camera01 viewport. Choose Rendering > RAM Player and in the RAM Player dialog, click the Open Last Rendered Image in Channel A button so that you can compare it to the new rendering in Channel B later.

2. On the main toolbar, click the Material Editor button. In the Material Editor dialog, click in the upper-left sample window, and then click on the Material/Map Navigator button. In the Material/Map Navigator dialog, highlight [3]floor: Material #2 [Standard] to go to that level (**Figure 11.13**).

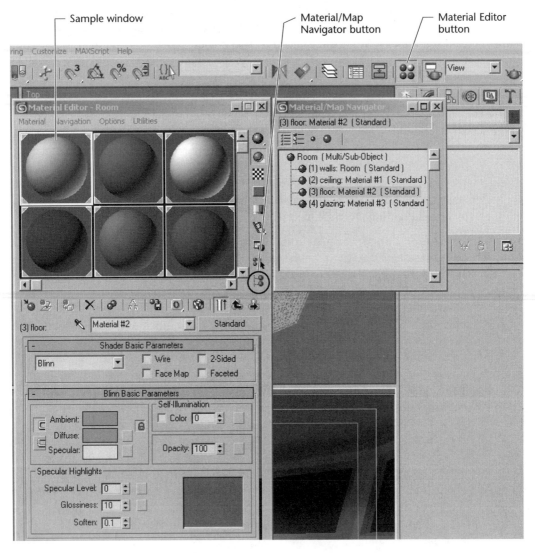

FIGURE 11.13 *In the Material Editor, click the Material/Map Navigator button to open the floor material.*

3. In the Blinn Basic Parameters rollout of the Material Editor, click the Ambient or Diffuse color swatch (they are locked together) to produce the Color Selector dialog. Enter *255* in the Hue field, *190* in the Saturation field, and *190* in the Value field for a red color (**Figure 11.14**). In the Render Scene dialog, click Reset All, and then click Start. Render the Camera01 viewport and open the rendered image in Channel B of the RAM Player. You'll see a much redder tint to all objects in the scene resulting from the floor's color bleed.

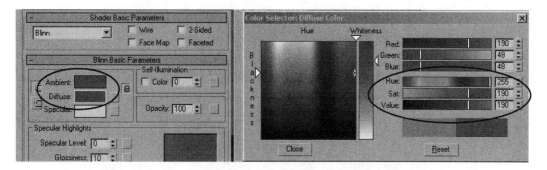

FIGURE 11.14 *Changing the material colors to red greatly affects the color of all objects in the scene because of the color bleed in the bounced light.*

4. In the Color Selector, enter *90* in the Value field and press Enter. Click Reset All, and start the radiosity process again, and render the Camera01 viewport. The color tint is still the same hue, but the overall brightness is lower because the material bounces less light. To view this in numeric values in the Material Editor, from the main menu choose Customize > Preferences, and then in the Prference Settings dialog click the Radiosity tab. Select the Display Reflectance & Transmittance Information option in the Material Editor section (see **Figure 11.15** on the next page). Click OK.

5. Close the Material Editor and open it again. Notice the Reflectance value is set at 35 percent for this material. Click the Diffuse color swatch and in the Color Selector dialog, enter *170* in the Value field. The Reflectance changes to 67 percent (see **Figure 11.16** on the next page). Reset and recalculate the radiosity solution and render the Camera01 viewport to see the change in the scene.

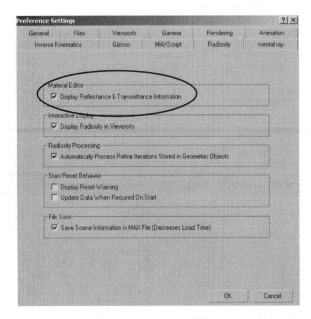

FIGURE 11.15 *You can enable the display of a material's reflectance from the Preference Settings dialog.*

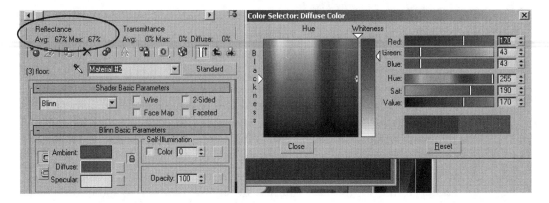

FIGURE 11.16 *A change in the color value displays in the Material Editor as the Reflectance value, expressed as a percentage, of the light striking the surface.*

6. In Render Scene dialog, click Reset All to clear the rendering solution and free your computer resources. Close all windows and dialogs and save the file. It should already be called *Ch11_Interior05.max*.

As you can see from this exercise, you gain lots of control over the brightness and the look of the scene by adjusting the materials in the scene—in this case, by changing only one material color.

Applying Advanced Lighting Override Material

There are times when you have worked long and hard to develop your materials used in both scanline-rendered and radiosity-rendered scenes, and it isn't practical to keep adjusting the values for each type of rendering.

By applying an Advanced Lighting Override material to your base material, you can control the reflectance value and the color bleed without adjusting the base material. The Advanced Lighting Override material type rides on top of your base material and lets you adjust multiplier values to override the existing reflectance, color bleed, and luminance values for that material.

Advanced Lighting Override material should be applied only when it is necessary because, as the name implies, the original material is first calculated then those values are overridden with the adjusted values, using valuable computer resources.

In the next exercise, you'll apply an Advanced Lighting Override material to control the amount of color bleed in the bounced light independent of the base material color. You'll also use a setting in Advanced Lighting Override that will make self-illuminated materials behave like any photometric light type.

Exercise 11.5: Controlling Material Lighting Effects

1. Open **Ch11_Interior05.max** from the last exercise or from the CD-ROM and save it to your project folder as *Ch11_Interior06.max*. Open the Render Scene dialog by pressing F10, and click the Start button in the Advanced Lighting tab to recalculate the radiosity solution. Render the Camera01 viewport and place the image in Channel A of the RAM Player. It should still be a very red rendition of the interior.

2. Open the Material Editor from the main toolbar. If you are not continuing from the previous lesson, you'll need to navigate to the [3]floor: Material #2 [Standard] material as before. In the Material Editor, click the Standard button on the right. This opens the Material/Map Browser dialog. In the Material/Map Browser list, double-click on Advanced Lighting Override (see **Figure 11.17** on the next page). In the Replace Material dialog, make sure the Keep Old Material as Sub-material radio button is selected and click OK.

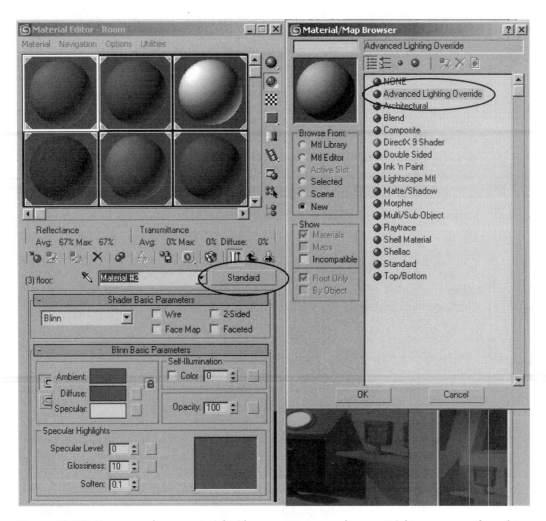

FIGURE 11.17 *You can replace a material with a new type or apply a material type on top of another using the Material Editor.*

3. In the Advanced Lighting Override Material rollout, enter *0.5* in the Color Bleed scale value (**Figure 11.18**). Click the Reset All button, recalculate the radiosity solution, render the Camera01 viewport, and open the new rendering in the RAM Player window in Channel B. Notice there's considerably less red bleed in the cabinet shadows and on the ceiling, but the brightness levels aren't affected.

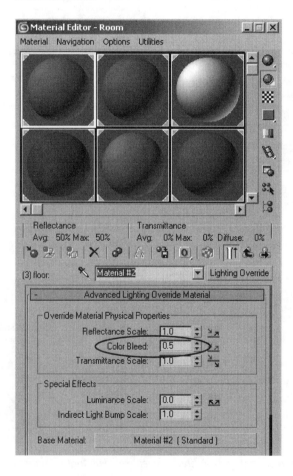

FIGURE 11.18 *The Advanced Lighting Override Material rollout has scale values for Color Bleed and Reflectance.*

4. In the Advanced Lighting Override Material rollout, enter *0.5* in the Reflectance Scale field. Reset and recalculate the radiosity solution, render the Camera01 viewport, and open the rendered image in Channel A of the RAM Player. This adjustment lowered the brightness of the reflectance from the floor without affecting the color bleed amount. You now have individual control over the values.

5. In the Material Editor, scroll the sample windows on the left to reveal the
    Radar material. Click the Material/Map Navigator button and choose the Radar
    screen material from the list (**Figure 11.19**).

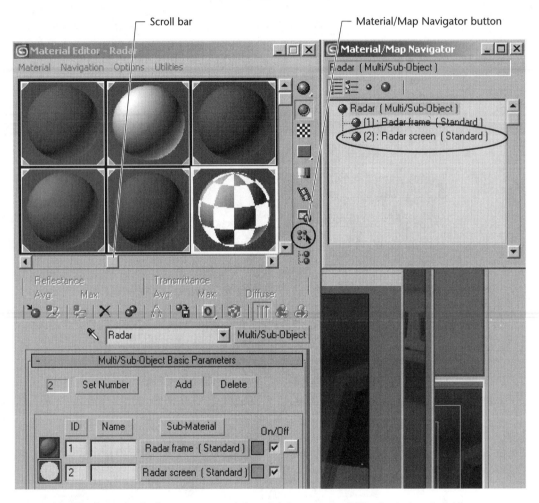

FIGURE 11.19 *Open the Radar screen material—a bright-green, self-illuminated material in a
Multi/Sub-Object material type.*

6. Click the Standard material button and double-click Advanced Lighting Override in the Material/Map Browser list. Choose Keep Old Material as Sub-material and click OK. In the Advanced Lighting Override Material rollout, enter *500* in the Luminance Scale field of the Special Effects section. Click Reset All, recalculate the radiosity, and render the Camera01 viewport. The ceiling will be washed with a soft green light emanating from the four radar screens on the console.

7. In the Render Scene dialog, click the Reset All button to discard the radiosity solution. Close all windows and dialogs. Save the file; it should already be called *Ch11_Interior06.max*.

You now have control over many aspects of radiosity rendering at the material level. While the lighting itself behaves according to the laws of physics, you still have plenty of artistic leeway to manipulate it to create convincing renderings.

Summary

In this chapter, you learned to place and adjust photometric lights in the scene. This type of light shares many of the same properties as real lights, such as the intensity and the attenuation values. You also learned to enable the Radiosity renderer, which calculates the effects of bounced light from photometric lights from surface to surface within the scene.

In addition, you learned that radiosity lighting requires the use of exposure control tools that regulate the amount of light striking the "film" of the renderer by adjusting the overall brightness levels or by adjusting contrast controls.

The ability to adjust material attributes, such as reflectance values and color bleeding, within the Advanced Lighting Override material is an important concept, as are the methods of using the Advanced Lighting Override material to make self-illuminated objects behave as photometric lights in the scene.

PART IV

Materials

CHAPTER 12

The Material Editor: Your Palette at a Glance

In This Chapter

It's usually the materials and lighting in your scene that make the final rendering successful or not. The model is somewhat important, but if you don't support the model with convincing materials that are well lighted, the end product will be a failure on most levels.

If you've read or listened to discussions about materials, you've probably encountered the term *realistic*. Realistic rendering, a rendering that the viewer mistakes for a photograph, is a common goal in computer visualization that depends heavily on the quality of materials and lighting in the scene.

However, realism is generally the last thing you should strive for when working with materials because there are too many elements in a realistic scene that you don't want, such as telephone wires, dents and scratches, or blowing trash. Instead, you should strive to create materials that convincingly convey the emotional impact you want to impress on the viewer. Traditional artists, for example, mix basic colors of paint on a wooden palette to achieve the exact color or shade they want to represent, depending on their intention, rather than an exact rendering of what they might be seeing before them. You must work in a similar manner in 3ds max 7.

There are several different areas in 3ds max 7 where color can be assigned. For example, the ambient, diffuse, and specular colors in the Material Editor all have color swatches you can change. You can also use specular highlights, which act as visual clues about the hardness of a material, to alter the material to make it convincing to your viewer.

In this chapter, you'll learn to use the Material Editor in 3ds max 7 to create materials that will be applied to objects in your scene to give them attributes such as color and shininess. The Material Editor is your *palette*, where you combine these components that make up materials. In addition, you'll learn how to apply more than one material to an object, to provide the added detail you need to render a more convincing scene.

This chapter covers the following topics:

- **Material colors.** You'll learn to adjust the color swatches for three of the most important components of a material: ambient, diffuse, and specular.

- **Specular highlights.** You'll learn to adjust the color, the brightness, the size, and the shape of this key material component, which simulates the light being scattered from a surface, indicating the surface's hardness.

- **Multi/Sub-Object Material type.** You'll learn to apply more than one material to a single object using the Multi/Sub-Object material type in conjunction with the Material ID numbers of faces.

> **note**
>
> It's not the intent of this chapter to review all the information on the Material Editor that you'll find in the 3ds max 7 manuals and online Help files. Once you've gleaned a basic knowledge of the Material Editor from these or other sources, you can use this chapter to learn about some intermediate-level fundamental applications that are not fully discussed in the documentation.

Key Terms

- **Diffuse color swatch.** The rectangle of color in the Material Editor that lets you adjust the color of a material in direct light.

- **Ambient color swatch.** The rectangle of color in the Material Editor that lets you adjust the color of a material in the shade.

- **Ambient lighting color.** This environment setting must be raised from the default 0 value to see any effects of the ambient color of a material in scanline rendering.

- **Color Selector.** This dialog lets you mix the primary hues and adjust the whiteness and blackness, as well as the brightness and gray levels of basic material colors.

- **Specular level.** This setting controls the brightness of specular highlights.

- **Glossiness.** Adjusting this setting changes the size of specular highlights.
- **Shader type.** A component of a material that adjusts the shape of specular highlights.
- **Standard material type.** The default material type in the Material Editor in 3ds max 7.
- **Multi/Sub-Object material type.** A special material type that lets you apply more than one material to a single object.
- **Material ID numbers.** Numbers that are applied to faces or polygons in a 3D object to control Multi/Sub-Object material assignments.

Adjusting Basic Colors

Many materials are composed of a solid color. For example, plastics, paint, and fluids often have no discernible color patterns but are a homogeneous single color. Used in the real world (and therefore in 3ds max 7 scenes), solid-colored surfaces take on a different appearance, depending on the lighting. They look brighter and more vibrant in direct light and rather dull in areas of shade.

New users of 3ds max 7 are apt to skip adjusting the color settings of materials and move on to other topics more interesting to them. However, thorough knowledge of the function of basic colors will give you more control over your final rendered images.

Ambient light (as opposed to ambient color) is a general level of illumination in a scene that comes from no apparent direction. Ambient light settings in 3ds max 7 are set by default to pure black or *off*, meaning that they have no effect on the ambient color. You'll learn to adjust the ambient light, as well as the ambient color.

tip

There are many ready-to-use sample materials that ship with 3ds max 7 that can be found in the material libraries folder. However, I recommend you use them only when you absolutely don't have time to create your own custom materials. Giving a presentation with materials that are exactly the same as your competition is not a way to impress the client.

Use the supplied sample materials as guides for creating your own variations until you have mastered the art of creating your own.

In this section, you'll learn about the significance of the Ambient and Diffuse color swatches of a Standard material type (**Figure 12.1**) and how to adjust them to control your basic material colors.

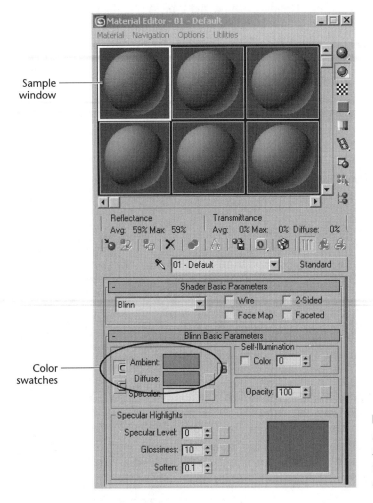

Sample window

Color swatches

FIGURE 12.1 *The default Material Editor in 3ds max 7, showing an active sample window and the ambient and diffuse color swatches.*

The ambient color of a material is the color in the shaded areas of the scene, while the diffuse color is the color in direct light.

The exercises in this section provide some practice in first adjusting the ambient and diffuse colors of a material and then adjusting the ambient lighting values, so that you can gain more control over solid-colored materials in your scenes.

Exercise 12.1: Adjusting Ambient and Diffuse Color

1. Open the file from the CD-ROM called **Ch12_color01.max**. Save it to your project folder with the name *Ch12_color02.max*. This scene contains the lofted wing from Chapter 5, *Lofting: Control Is Everything*.

2. On the main toolbar, click the Material Editor button or press *M* to open the Material Editor

> **caution**
>
> By default, the ambient and diffuse colors are locked together to be the same color. This is to avoid confusion in rendered images when photometric lighting and the radiosity renderer are used. The reflectance and color bleed (see Chapter 11, *Photometric Lights: Bouncing Basics*) are calculated from the diffuse color in 3ds max 7, and changes to the ambient color alone can alter the look of the object color and the bounced light color or reflectance differently.

dialog. Click and drag the sample window in the upper left onto the wing in the Perspective viewport. The wing will turn gray, and triangles will appear in the corners of the sample window to indicate the material is *hot*, or assigned to an object in the scene. In the Material Editor, change the material name from *01-Default* to *Paint Red* (**Figure 12.2**).

Triangles —

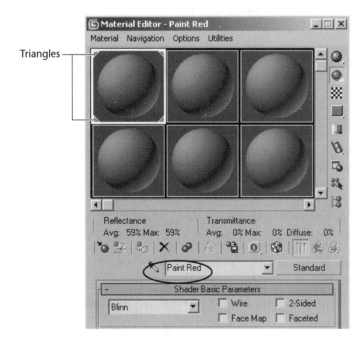

FIGURE 12.2 *Triangles in the corners of the sample window indicate a "hot" material named* Paint Red *is assigned to an object in the scene.*

3. In the Blinn Basic Parameters rollout, click the Diffuse color swatch (the large gray rectangle) to open the Color Selector dialog. There are three methods of changing color:

    • Pick and drag in the hue box and change the whiteness or blackness sliders.

    • Adjust the red, green, and blue gradients.

    • Adjust the hue, saturation, and value gradients.

    Adjusting any one affects the others, so it's mostly a matter of personal preference which method you use to set a color. Set the Diffuse color to bright red, for example, by clicking and dragging to the upper-left corner of the Hue box, and then sliding the whiteness slider to the top.

    You'll notice that the Diffuse and Ambient colors turned red because they are locked together by the button to the left of the swatches (**Figure 12.3**). The wing in the scene has also turned red because the material is hot.

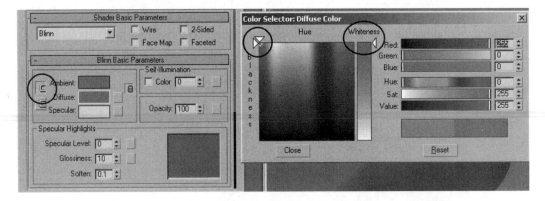

FIGURE 12.3 *Changing the Diffuse swatch to red also changes the Ambient swatch.*

4. At the far right of the main toolbar, click the Quick Render button to render the Perspective viewport. The lighting in the scene shows bright red along the left edge of the wing where direct light (diffuse color) is shining, and a very dark red shows in the shadows at the end of the wing (ambient color). From the Rendering pull-down menu, choose RAM Player. In the RAM Player, click the Open Last Rendered Image in Channel A, and click OK in the Configuration dialog to store the image for comparison later. Minimize the RAM Player.

5. In the Blinn Basic Parameters rollout of the Material Editor, click the yellow lock button to the left of the Ambient and Diffuse swatches to unlock the colors. Click in the Ambient color swatch and, in the Color Selector, pick at the top of the green gradient in the Hue box. This changes the color swatch to bright green. Render the Perspective viewport. Notice there's no change to the rendered image. This is because the ambient light in the scene is set to *0* or turned off.

6. To enable the ambient lighting, choose Rendering > Environment. In the Global Lighting area of the Common Parameters rollout, click the Ambient color swatch. In the Color Selector, enter *10* in the Value field and press Enter. This turns on the ambient lighting at a low level (**Figure 12.4**).

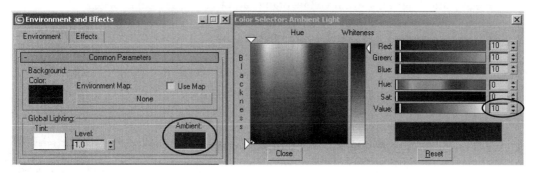

Figure 12.4 *The ambient light value must be increased before you can see the effects of ambient color changes.*

7. Render the Perspective viewport and maximize the RAM Player. In the RAM Player, click the Open Last Rendered Image in Channel B and click and drag in the RAM Player window to compare the images: without ambient light on the left and with green ambient color and low-level ambient light on the right.

The green is much more apparent in the darkest shadow areas but also influences the color along the top of the wing, which is slightly shaded. There is no change in the directly lit areas of the wing.

caution

Too much ambient light can wash out your scenes. Increasing the ambient light, even by small amounts, brightens the shadows, thus reducing overall contrast and robbing the scene of depth. Make sure you use ambient light values between 0 and 15 and use ambient colors that are somewhat darker than the diffuse colors in the material.

Typically, the ambient color is set to a complementary color, because artists of all types generally use complementary colors to attain a more pleasing psychological balance in the image. For example, a reddish/orange diffuse color would have a bluish/purple ambient color so that the image would be less "jarring" than if you used greenish tones.

Also, ambient light must be used at low levels and the colors used in ambient color are best when they are a somewhat darker complementary color of the diffuse color. For example, a night scene might be more convincing if the direct light is a warm yellow-orange and the shadows are a cooler blue or purple. This technique is used often in film lighting for night scenes.

For examples of illustrations in which this effect is used, see the work of Maxfield Parrish at http://parrish.artpassions.net/parrish.html

8. Experiment with different levels of ambient light and different ambient colors to develop a feel for how they affect the rendered scene. Close all dialogs and windows. Save the file. It should already be called *Ch12_color02.max*.

tip

The ambient light setting in the Environment dialog is a local setting. If you reset the current scene or open a new scene, the ambient light will be reset to *0*.

tip

If you need to reset the ambient and diffuse colors of your materials to be the same—for example, if you are using radiosity rendering and the effect is too pronounced—you can fix it on the Utilities panel by choosing More > Fix Ambient Utility. You can use this to adjust all materials or only selected materials.

Adjusting Specular Highlights in Materials

In my opinion, specular highlights, which are the scattered light bouncing from a surface and primarily a function of the molecular makeup of the material, do not receive enough attention in visualization. They really are the first visual clue for identifying most materials.

A hard surface has a tight molecular structure, so the light that strikes it is bounced almost directly back, causing a small, bright, hard-edged highlight. Soft materials, on the other hand, let the light penetrate the surface, absorbing some of it and scattering some of it widely, with only a small amount bouncing back to the viewer. This results in large, dull, and soft-edged specular highlight.

Also, specular highlights tend to add visual balance to the darker shaded areas of a scene to give a full range of contrast that gives a 2D image apparent "depth."

The Shader type used in the Material Editor controls the shape of the highlight in 3ds max 7. In the real world, the "grain" of the molecules and the surface conditions of the material are among some of the factors affecting the specular shape. For example, plastic tends to have round specular highlights for which the default Blinn shader works well. Rolled stainless steel, on the other hand, has elongated highlights caused by the molecules aligning themselves, much like wood grain. This effect can be simulated with the Anisotropic or Multi-Layer shader types.

The color of specular highlights is white or light gray for most materials; the exceptions are the "pure" metals like gold, copper, or lead, and materials like anodized aluminum where the color is baked into the molecules of the metal.

To effectively recreate specular highlights in 3ds max 7, you must first learn to see them in the real world. Often we take specular highlights for granted and fail to recognize their importance in the definition of 3D surfaces. Spend some time looking around your environment to train yourself to clearly identify the myriad of specular highlights and their effect on your perception of surfaces, and then use the tools in 3ds max 7 to create convincing materials.

In the next exercise you'll learn to adjust the following three components of specular highlights:

- **Specular level.** The brightness of the specular highlight
- **Glossiness.** The size of the specular highlight
- **Shader type.** Controls the shape of specular highlights

The Specular color swatch, located just below the Diffuse and Ambient color swatches in the Material Editor, adjusts the color of a specular highlight. The default very light gray is good for most situations.

Exercise 12.2: Adding Specular Highlights to the Wing

1. Open the file from the CD-ROM called **Ch12_specular01.max**. Save it to your project folder with the name *Ch12_specular02.max*. On the main toolbar, click the Quick Render button to render the Perspective viewport and, from the main menu, choose Rendering > RAM Player. In the RAM Player dialog, click the Open Last Rendered Image in Channel A button. In the RAM Player Configuration dialog, click OK to accept the default settings. Minimize the RAM Player.

2. On the main toolbar, click the Material Editor button. In the Blinn Basic
    Parameters rollout, Specular Highlights area, enter *100* in the Specular Level
    field and press Enter. Render the Perspective viewport. The sample window and
    the wing show a large, very bright specular highlight (**Figure 12.5**). This is not
    a convincing rendering. If most of the light is scattering back to the viewer, the
    specular highlight wouldn't be bright and soft-edged to represent a hard mater-
    ial. Maximize the RAM Player and click the Open Last Rendered Image in
    Channel B button. Then click OK to compare the image to the original.

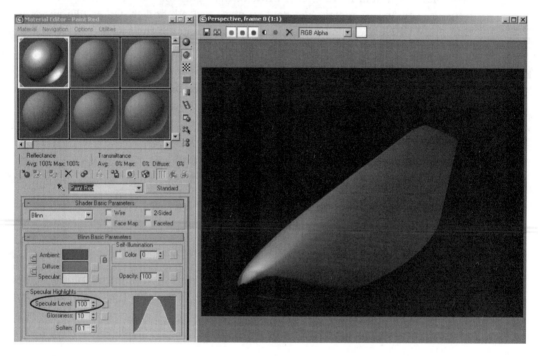

Figure 12.5 *A high specular level (brightness) with a low glossiness (size) is not a convincing specular
highlight.*

3. In the Blinn Basic Parameters rollout, enter *50* in the Glossiness field and
    press Enter. Render the Perspective viewport and open the rendered image in
    Channel B of the RAM Player. The material in the sample window and the
    wing now appear to be harder because the highlight is smaller and still bright
    (**Figure 12.6**). The closer molecules of the harder material don't scatter the
    light as much. Most light is bounced back. Hard plastic, paint, or ceramics
    would tend to have round, bright specular highlights.

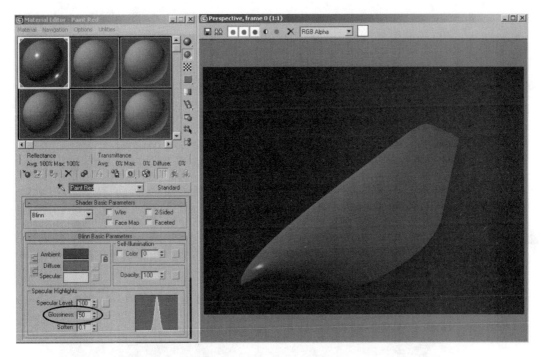

FIGURE 12.6 *The specular level and glossiness settings create specular highlights that make more sense visually when they are closer in value.*

4. In the Shader Basic Parameters rollout, click on the Blinn drop-down arrow and choose Anisotropic (different scale in different directions) from the list of shader types (**Figure 12.7**). Render the Perspective viewport and notice that the specular highlight is much longer and thinner along the length of the wing. This type of highlight might simulate something like wood grain or brush strokes in the paint, for example.

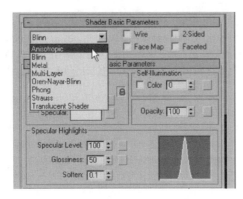

FIGURE 12.7 *You can choose a new shader type to affect the shape of the specular highlights.*

5. Choose the shader type called *Oren-Nayer-Blinn* from the Shader drop-down list and in the Specular Highlights section set Specular Level to *50* and Glossiness to *20*. Render the Perspective viewport. This could represent a very soft material like flat paint or cloth (**Figure 12.8**).

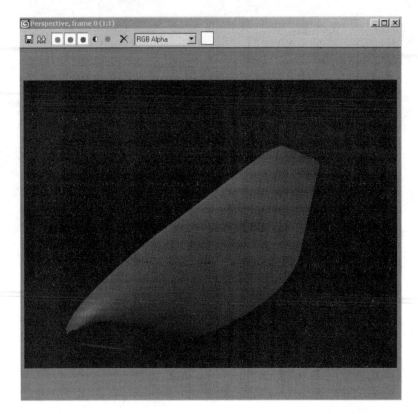

FIGURE 12.8 *The Oren-Nayer-Blinn shader usually works best with low specular level and glossiness settings.*

6. Experiment with different combinations of shader types and specular settings, rendering each change and comparing it to the original in the RAM Player. Close all windows and dialogs and save the file; it should already be named *Ch12_specular02.max*.

This brief overview of specular highlights hopefully will pique your interest to investigate them further, both in the real world and how you'll simulate them in 3ds max 7. Again, reality is not as important to visualization, in most cases, as your ability to convince the viewer that a material in your scene has certain properties.

Creating and Assigning a Multi/Sub-Object Material

Normally in 3ds max 7, if you apply a material to an object in a scene that already has a material on it, the original material will be replaced because you can only have one material per object.

There is a special material, however, called *Multi/Sub-Object*, that is comprised of one or more sub-materials. By default, the order of the sub-materials in the Material Editor corresponds to the Material ID numbers you've assigned or have been automatically assigned to faces of an object.

For example, a box primitive object is created using Material ID numbers 1 through 6, which are assigned to each side of the box. If you assign a Multi/Sub-Object material containing six materials to the box, each side will get one of the materials.

You can assign Material ID numbers to the face, polygon, or element sub-object level of mesh objects or polygon objects.

In the next exercise, you'll open a landscape similar to the one used in Chapter 10, *Standard Lights: Follow the Masters*. It contains hills in the background and a large flat area in the foreground, with a runway you cut into the mesh in Chapter 6, *3D Primitives: Building Blocks*, using the ShapeMerge compound object. If you remember, ShapeMerge projected a closed 2D shape onto the surface to cut new edges. You then converted to Editable Mesh and selected the new runway faces at the polygon sub-object level. You hopefully also had the foresight to name the polygon selection with the Named Selection option from the main toolbar. You'll use the named selection to reselect the faces, thus avoiding a complex manual selection process.

Exercise 12.3: Assigning More Than One Material to an Object

1. Open **Ch12_multi01.max** from the CD-ROM. Save it to your project folder with the name *Ch12_multi02.max*. It contains the mesh called Mountains01 and several lights from Chapter 10. Click the Display Panel button and, in the Hide by Category rollout, click the Lights checkbox (**Figure 12.9**). This hides all the lights (or any category you choose) to make your scenes easier to work with.

2. Select the Mountains01 landscape object in the Perspective viewport. In Stack view on the Modify panel, choose the Polygon sub-object mode. In the Top viewport, drag a selection window around the entire landscape to select all polygons. They will all turn red.

3. Open the Material Editor, and drag and drop the upper-left sample window (named Ground) onto the selection set of polygons. It is best to drag and drop the material onto areas of the object that have dense faces, since you have to actually drop the material on a visible edge of the mesh. This assigns the brown material to every polygon in the Mountains01 mesh.

Display Panel button

Figure 12.9 *You can hide whole categories from the Display panel of 3ds max 7 to make working and navigating the viewports easier.*

4. Scroll up on the Modify panel, if necessary, to find the Surface Properties rollout. In the Material section, you should find that all polygons have a Material ID set to *1* (**Figure 12.10**). If there's a different number in the Set ID field or if it's blank, then enter *1* and press Enter.

note

There is also a Select ID button and field in the Material area. This doesn't change the Material ID number of polygons. Instead, it let's you easily select a set of polygons that have had numbers assigned previously.

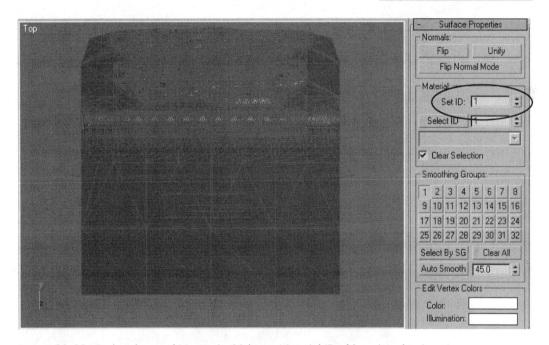

FIGURE 12.10 *Each polygon of Mountains01 has a Material ID of 1 assigned to it.*

5. You can also see the visible edges of the runway cut into the landscape in the Top and Perspective viewports. Even in this simple area of the mesh, it would take several mouse clicks to select all the faces that belong to the runway. On the main toolbar, click the drop-down arrow beside the Named Selection Set field and choose *runway* from the list (**Figure 12.11**). This will highlight just the runway polygons in red because you already created the named selection set in Chapter 6.

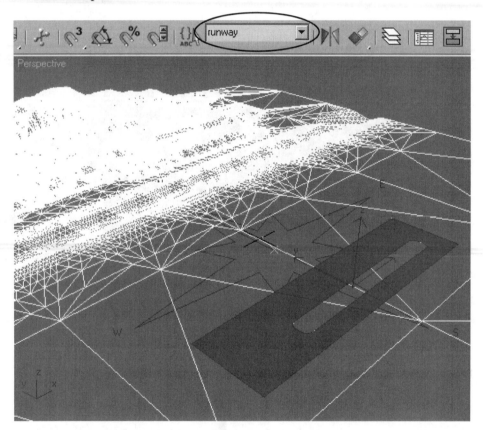

FIGURE 12.11 *You can access previously named selection sets from the main toolbar when you are at the appropriate sub-object level.*

6. In the Surface Properties rollout on the Modify panel, enter *2* in the Set ID field and press Enter. This assigns Material ID # 2 only to the selected polygons.

7. In the Material Editor, select the second sample window from the left in the top row to activate it, and then drag and drop it on the runway selection in the Perspective viewport. Rename the material *Runway*. This assigns the runway material only to the selected polygons. In Stack view on the Modify panel, highlight Editable Mesh at the top of the stack to exit sub-object mode. Render the Perspective viewport, and you should see the brown material on the ground and the gray material on the runway (**Figure 12.12**).

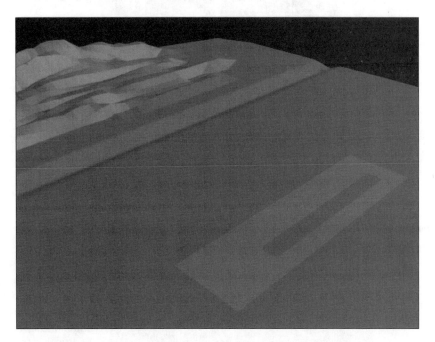

Figure 12.12 *You have dragged and dropped separate materials onto separate selection sets of polygons. The Mountains01 object now has two materials.*

You might be asking yourself at this point, "What about Multi/Sub-Object materials?" You have already created a Multi/Sub-Object material; you just haven't accessed it yet. Let's do that now.

8. In the Material Editor, select the right-most sample window in the top row. Click the Eyedropper button to the left of the Material Name field and click the landscape in the Perspective viewport. Name the new material *Mountains* (**Figure 12.13**). A Multi/Sub-Object material was automatically created from the two materials, Ground and Runway, corresponding to two Material IDs assigned to the mesh. This is evident by the checkerboard pattern on the sample sphere.

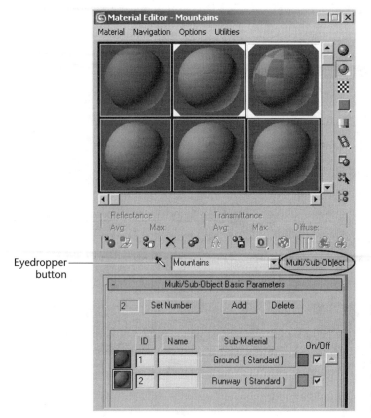

Eyedropper button

FIGURE 12.13 *Assigning materials to sub-object selection sets using different Material ID numbers lets you automatically create a Multi/Sub-Object material using the Eyedropper button.*

9. Close all windows and dialogs and save the file; it should already be called *Ch12_multi02.max*. Named selection sets, Material ID numbers, and Multi/Sub-Object materials are a powerful combination of tools to increase your production in 3ds max 7.

This shortcut for creating Multi/Sub-Object materials is convenient, but it's not the only method of creating them. You can always choose the Multi/Sub-Object material type to create a new material that has 10 other materials by default, including the Standard material in the sample window you are replacing. You can then pre-assign the Material IDs to the appropriate faces in the mesh so that when you drag and drop the Multi/Sub-Object material onto the mesh, the sub-materials will find the faces or polygons with the corresponding ID numbers. Either workflow produces the same results.

Learning this important technique lets you do things like assign different materials to different sides of a building, apply materials to the end caps of lofted objects, or apply horizontal bands of materials to a cylinder, to name a few standard scenarios.

The concept is very simple: Use one sub-material for every Material ID number, practice a little to get the process down, and you'll find Multi/Sub-Object materials help increase your productivity.

Summary

In this chapter, you have learned several production methods that are not especially easy for new users to 3ds max 7. The fundamentals of these workflows are covered here to give you a starting point on which to build your own.

If you learn the basics covered in this chapter and build upon that knowledge to add layers of depth and complexity to your materials—much like an artist adds layers of paint—you'll succeed in creating a much richer visual experience for your viewers.

CHAPTER 13

Maps: Patterns Before Your Eyes

In This Chapter

In the last chapter, you learned to change the basic color of the material in both the Diffuse and Ambient slots. In this chapter, you'll learn to apply maps, or patterns, to various material mapping slots. This is an important skill, as most of the materials you'll create in 3ds max 7 for production will contain patterns.

You can apply maps to determine the color of a material, or you can place maps in other slots, such as the Bump slot or the Opacity slot, to simulate geometry or transparency in materials.

While many types of maps are available in 3ds max 7, this chapter focuses on just two, procedural maps and bitmaps. Procedural maps are created mathematically at render time. They are very flexible because they contain so many parameters that can be adjusted to accomplish things like changing the size of the pattern or applying different colors to the maps themselves. However, procedural maps can take a bit longer to render because of the math involved. Bitmaps can be images of almost any kind and are readily available from Internet sources or by taking your own photographs. Unlike procedural maps, bitmaps have limited adjustments. Both map types are the most widely applied in 3ds max 7. These map patterns override the basic color of materials on the objects to which they are applied.

This chapter demonstrates how to use 3ds max 7 to create your own bitmaps, rather than use stock bitmaps from image libraries or those you create in paint software, and then apply them as colored text to the runway material you created in the last chapter. This method of creating bitmaps gives you added control and flexibility in editing. But before you can tackle such a task, you first need an introduction to Matte/Shadow material, which makes the landscape disappear in the rendered image, and Box Selected rendering, which renders only the selected objects in the scene.

You'll learn about the following topics in this chapter:

- **Procedural map.** You'll learn to apply this map type that is generated at render time, usually as a random pattern, but also as wood grain or marble patterns.

- **Bitmaps.** You'll learn to create your own custom bitmap images in 3ds max 7 and apply them to your materials. These images can be photographs, computer images, or animations in many of the common file formats, such as .tga, .png, .avi, or .mov.

- **Matte/Shadow material.** You'll learn to apply this special material, which makes the objects to which it is applied invisible in the rendered image but always allows the background image, if any, to show through. Matte/Shadow is used primarily to mask out portions of background photographs with 3D geometry, but you'll also learn how to use it in special cases.

- **Box Selected rendering.** You'll learn this method of rendering the scene, which displays an image only to the boundary of the selected objects in the scene. Box Selected is used to create images that can be reapplied as material maps that fit precisely with the extents of the object.

Key Terms

- **Self-Illumination maps.** This map slot makes the material look as if it's glowing from within by overriding the ambient (shaded) areas with full brightness. It could be used to simulate light bulbs or a glowing computer monitor, for example.

- **Bump maps.** Bump maps use the luminance value, or brightness of pixels, to give the illusion of added geometry when rendered. White pixels look as if they're raised, while black pixels do nothing. Gray pixels appear at intermediate levels.

- **Alpha channel.** Alpha channels contain embedded information used to make black areas of a bitmap fully transparent. Gray pixels will be semi-transparent. Only certain file types can contain alpha channels: .png, .tga, and .tif are the most commonly used files in 3ds max 7.

Procedural Maps

Many of the patterns found in materials in the natural world, such as grass, dirt, or cloudy skies, or in the world of the man-made, such as the surface of rusty metal, are random. These patterns might be the color variations of a material, the roughness of its surfaces, or perhaps the changes in the shininess of its surface. 3ds max 7 ships with maps, known as procedural maps, that generate different types of patterns. These include Noise, Smoke, or Dent, to name a few, which can be used to simulate those random occurrences in nature. Other procedural maps, like Falloff and Tiles, have more specific controls and are less random. For example, Falloff maps use the direction of face normals on surfaces to determine where the pattern gets applied, and Tiles maps form a controlled pattern of rectangular tiles.

In the first three exercises, you'll practice creating a new material for the sky in an outdoor scene using procedural maps in both the Color map slot and Self-Illumination map slot. Then in the two exercises that follow those, you'll edit the existing ground material to create random patterns that represent a southwestern U.S. landscape. These exercises illustrate how to apply procedural maps in the Color and Bump slots of a material and how to nest maps within other maps for increased randomness.

Creating a Sky Using a Gradient Ramp Map

In the first exercise, you'll create a new material to apply to the hemisphere that represents the sky. You'll use a Gradient Ramp map, which is a procedural map that lets you create bands of color. You'll also learn to adjust the size and position of the map and change the colors. Finally, you'll copy the color map into the Self-Illumination map slot, which will make the colors look like they glow from within, thus giving the sky more "depth."

Exercise 13.1: Creating and Applying the Sky Material

1. Open **Ch13_procedural01.max** from the CD-ROM and save it to your project folder with the name *Ch13_procedural02.max*. The scene contains Mountains01 and Skydome objects and several lights. From the main toolbar, click the Material Editor button or press *M* to open the Material Editor.

2. In the Material Editor, click the lower-left sample window to activate it. Change the name of the material to *Sky*. Drag and drop the sample window onto Skydome in the Camera02 viewport. The hemisphere will turn gray.

3. In the Blinn Basic Parameters rollout of the Material Editor, click the small gray Map Shortcut button to the right of the Diffuse color swatch and double-click the Gradient Ramp map type in the Material/Map Browser (**Figure 13.1**).

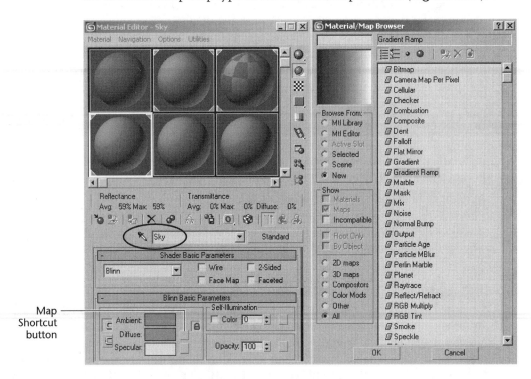

Map Shortcut button

FIGURE 13.1 *Place a Gradient Ramp in the Diffuse Color Map slot of the Sky material.*

4. In the Material Editor, click the Show Map in Viewport button (a blue and white box button), and notice the sky changes so that it's lighter on the left and darker on the right. The gradient is wrapping horizontally around the sample sphere and the skydome. To rotate the map so that it wraps vertically, enter *90* in the W: Angle field and press Enter (**Figure 13.2**).

Show Map in Viewport button

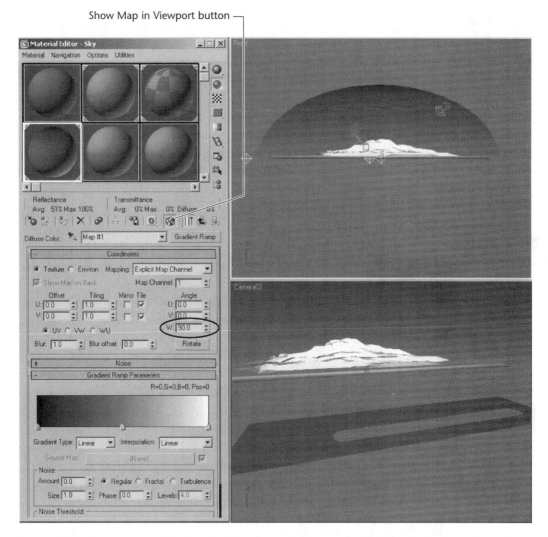

FIGURE 13.2 *You can rotate the Gradient Ramp map 90 degrees so that the gradient runs from "north pole" to "south pole" on the skydome in the scene.*

5. The gradient covers too much vertical area to be a convincing sky. To remedy this, enter *3* in the U Tiling field of the Coordinates rollout to compress the gradient so that it repeats three times vertically in the hemisphere. Now it doesn't cover the field of view in Camera02, so enter *0.15* in the V Offset field and press Enter. This moves the gradient up to fill the sky, which you can see in the Camera02 viewport (see **Figure 13.3** on the next page).

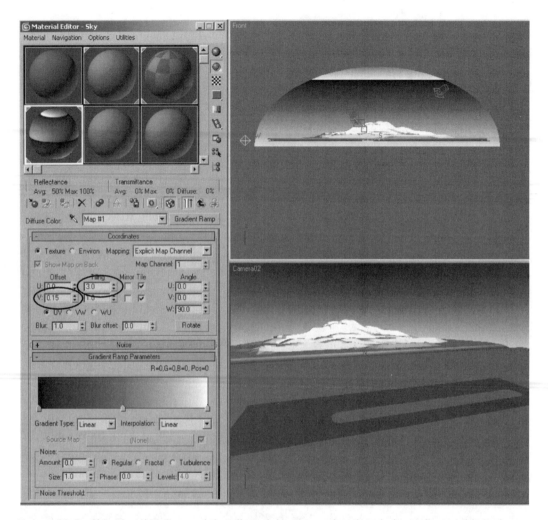

Figure 13.3 *Changing the tiling and the offset of the map makes the whole gradient visible in the Camera02 viewport. There is a little room above the viewport and a little below to allow for possible camera movement in the scene.*

note

In the Coordinates rollout, *U* stands for the horizontal or *X* axis, and *V* stands for the vertical or *Y* axis in map nomenclature. However, you must adjust the horizontal tiling of this Gradient Ramp map because it has been rotated 90 degrees in the *W* or *Z* axis.

tip

For the next few steps of the exercise, you may need to resize the Material Editor by picking and dragging at the bottom edge so that you can view the Gradient Ramp parameters.

6. You can change the color of the gradient by double-clicking one of the small flags at the bottom of the color gradient in the Gradient Ramp Parameters roll-out. Double-click the green (active) flag on the left side of the gradient. This opens the Color Selector where you can enter *0* in the Red field, *0* in the Green field, and *100* in the Blue field to create a rich blue at the top of the hemisphere (**Figure 13.4**).

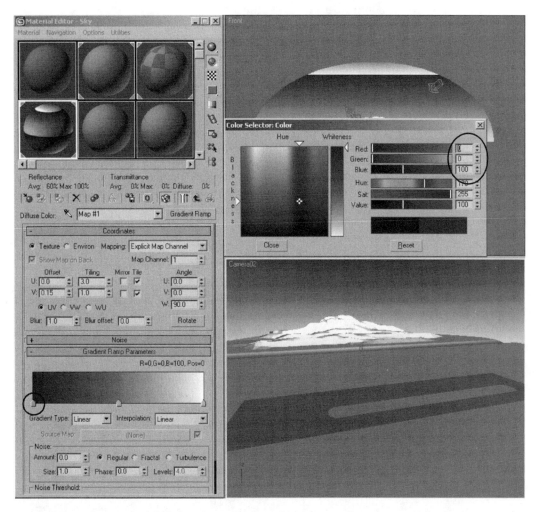

FIGURE 13.4 *Change the left flag in the gradient to dark blue to affect the top of the skydome.*

7. Click on the middle flag in the gradient to activate it. The Color Selector is already open, so you don't need to double-click. Change the Red and Green fields to *130* and set the Blue field to *240* for a light-blue middle to the gradient. The sky in the Camera02 viewport is now dark blue at the top, fading to white at the bottom.

8. Right now our sky is a bit too "perfect." In the Gradient Ramp Parameters rollout, enter *0.1* in the Noise Amount field, enter *2* in the Size field, and click the Fractal radio button. The noise parameters "disturb" the transition of the colors, and the fractal setting makes the new edges of the colors rougher so that they simulate clouds (**Figure 13.5**). Render the Camera02 viewport.

tip

The sky appears lighter at the horizon in the real world because you are looking through a denser atmosphere than when you look straight overhead.

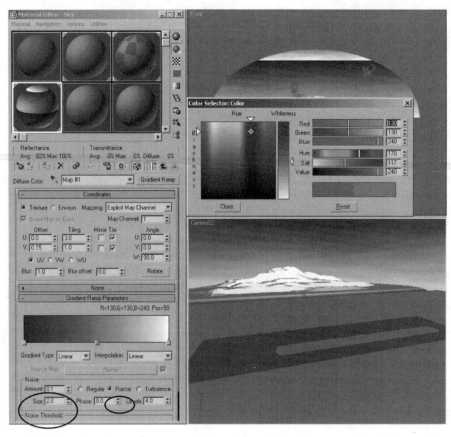

FIGURE 13.5 *Changing the Noise parameters of the Gradient Ramp map gives the appearance of thin clouds in the scene.*

To make the sky appear more vibrant, you'll copy the Diffuse color Gradient Ramp map into the Self-Illumination slot. Self-Illumination maps override any lighting in the scene, especially in the ambient areas, so that the material looks as if it glows.

9. Click on the Material/Map Navigator button at the bottom right of the sample windows and choose the top level of the Sky material. In the Blinn Basic Parameters rollout, click the Color checkbox in the Self-Illumination area. Drag and drop the *M* map shortcut from Diffuse onto the map shortcut for Self-Illumination. Make sure the Copy radio button is selected in the Copy (Instance) Map dialog (**Figure 13.6**). Click OK. The sample sphere appears to glow. If you render the Camera02 viewport, the sky will be much brighter.

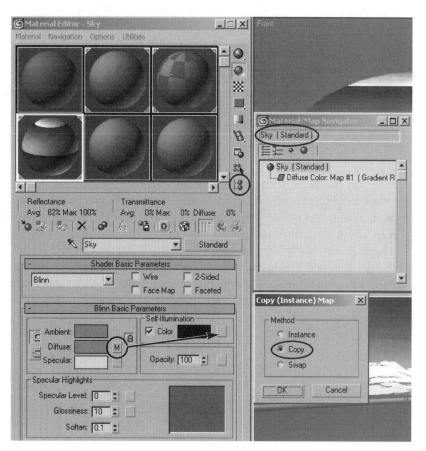

Figure 13.6 *Setting the Self-Illumination to Color and applying a map makes the colors of the map look as if they glow in the scene.*

The sky probably glows too much at this point. You can go to the Self-Illumination map level in the Material/Map Navigator and adjust the color flags to a darker value to reduce the effect. Or you can change the colors of the flags to make the sky look more like a dusk or dawn sky, for example. You can also change the position of the middle flag by dragging it in the gradient. Experiment to create your own skies.

10. Close all dialogs and windows and save the file. It should already be called *Ch13_procedural02.max*.

You now have an easily edited sky in your scene that can be viewed from most any horizontal camera angle.

Creating a material with the Gradient Ramp map offers a high level of flexibility in editing the colors and conditions of the sky in your scenes for a convincing look.

Adding Color to the Landscape

The sky is looking pretty good, but the flat brown landscape is just plain boring. In the next exercise, you'll learn to use a procedural map called *Falloff* to add variety to the landscape. The flatter areas of the landscape will be green and the sides of the steeper hills, where the grass won't grow, will be brown.

By default, the Falloff map has black-and-white colors. It functions by applying one color on the faces of the mesh that are perpendicular to the line of sight and the other color to the faces that are parallel. This won't work for this scene because the landscape colors would change as you moved through the scene, which wouldn't be very convincing. You'll adjust the map so that the faces that are perpendicular to the World Z-axis (the horizontal ground faces) are green and those parallel to the World Z-axis (the near vertical hillside faces) are brown. Faces that are 45 degrees to the World Z-axis will get a 50-50 mix of the two colors. You'll finally change the colors from black and white to green and brown and then make adjustments to the transition between the two colors.

Exercise 13.2: Adapting the Landscape Material

1. Open **Ch13_procedural02.max** from the last exercise or from the CD-ROM and save it to your project folder as *Ch13_procedural03.max*. Open the Material Editor and activate the Mountains material in the upper-right sample window. Click the Material/Map Navigator button to open it and highlight the [1] Ground [Standard] material level in the hierarchy list.

2. In the Blinn Basic Parameters rollout, click the Diffuse color map shortcut button just to the right of the color swatch, and double-click Falloff in the Material/Map Browser list. Render the Camera02 viewport and notice the faces of the landscape perpendicular to your line of sight are black, while those parallel are much lighter. Even the faces closest to you in the viewport are darker because of the viewing angle. The parallel faces won't appear white because of the lighting. The effect is very visible in the sample window (**Figure 13.7**).

FIGURE 13.7 *A Falloff map changes color on the mesh, based on the angle of faces to the viewer, which is set in the Falloff Parameters rollout.*

3. In the Falloff Parameters rollout, click the drop-down arrow corresponding to Falloff Direction and select World Z-axis from the list (**Figure 13.8**). Render the Camera02 viewport and notice the dark faces are the flat surfaces (perpendicular to the World Z-axis).

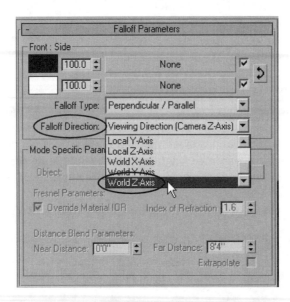

FIGURE 13.8 *Change the Falloff map to use the World Z-axis direction to define perpendicular and parallel faces.*

4. In the Falloff Parameters rollout, click the black color swatch and change it to a green. Any green will be fine for now. Edit the white color swatch so that it's a brown color. Render the Camera02 viewport and notice the ground is mostly green with just a slight amount of brown bleeding through on the sides of the hills.

5. Pan the Falloff Parameters rollout by clicking in an empty space and dragging upward to reveal the Mix Curve rollout, displaying the graph and gradient ramp. The Mix Curve determines the gradient between green and brown as the angle of faces change. In the Mix Curve rollout, click the Add Point button and click in two places along the black line in the graph. Click the Move button in the rollout, and move the two new points to resemble the graph in **Figure 13.9**. Render the Camera02 viewport. This new graph reveals more brown color with a sharper cutoff at the transition between brown and green in the distant hills.

Move button

Add Point button

FIGURE 13.9 *A steeper Mix Curve graph toward the left of the gradient increases the brown showing on the perpendicular.*

6.   Close all windows and dialogs and save the file. It should already be called *Ch13_procedural03.max.*

The landscape is less boring than it was at the beginning of this exercise, but we're not there yet.

Use this simple example of the Falloff procedural map to experiment on your own. You might want to create worn, curved objects in which the colors are faded more on the top than on the sides, or that type of car paint that changes color based on the direction in which you view it.

Increasing the Complexity of the Ground Material

In the next exercise, you'll increase the complexity of the colors in your ground material by using other procedural maps in place of the green and brown colors in the Falloff map you used in the last exercise. Each of these sub-maps will be a smaller pattern of two new colors to give much more variation across the landscape.

To add more apparent geometry to the scene, you'll apply the Noise procedural map to the Bump slot of the ground material. This gives the illusion of a bumpy, rather than smooth, landscape. The Bump map works on the principle that white pixels of the map appear to raise the geometry, while black pixels have no effect. Shades of gray affect the look based on their whiteness values. They make the scene appear much more complex, while adding no extra faces that would hamper productivity.

tip

Colored maps can be used in the Bump slot instead of grayscale maps, but it is very difficult to anticipate the luminance values of colored pixels.

Exercise 13.3: Adding Another Level of Complexity

1. Open **Ch13_procedural03.max** from the last exercise or from the CD-ROM. Save it to your project folder with the name *Ch13_procedural04.max*. Open the Material Editor and use the Material/Map Navigator to access the Diffuse Color: Map #3 [Falloff] level (the number of your map could be different).

2. In the Falloff Parameters rollout, click the None button to the right of the green color swatch and double-click Noise in the Material/Map Browser list (**Figure 13.10**). A Noise procedural map is a random pattern of two colors with parameters for size. Render the Camera02 viewport and notice the green has been replaced completely by a small black-and-white pattern.

3. In the Noise Parameters rollout, click the Fractal radio button for a rougher edge to the colors. Enter *200* in the Size field to make the pattern larger. Then click the Color #1 color swatch and, in the Color Selector, set red to *30*, green to *60*, and blue to *30* to obtain a grayish-green color. Click the color swatch for Color #2 and set its red to *200*, green to *200*, and blue to *40* for a dull yellow. Render the Camera02 viewport to see a soft-edged, equal balance of the two colors in a random pattern (**Figure 13.11**).

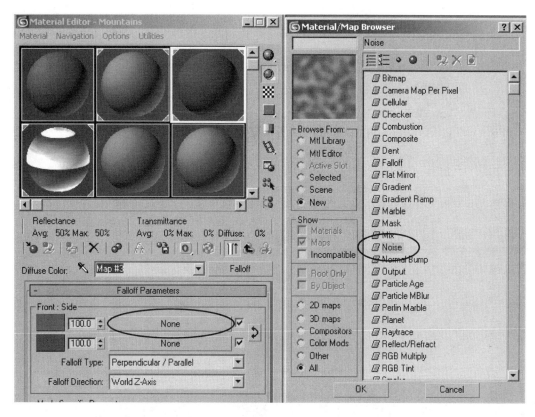

FIGURE 13.10 *The base colors of the Falloff map can be replaced with other maps for more complexity in the pattern.*

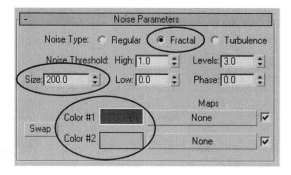

FIGURE 13.11 *The size of the pattern, the colors, and the roughness of color edges can be adjusted in the Noise Parameters rollout to change the appearance of the pattern in the scene.*

4. In the Material/Map Navigator, move up one level to the Diffuse Color Falloff map level. Click the None button to the right of the brown color swatch in the Falloff Parameters rollout and double-click Speckle in the Material/Map Browser list. You may need to scroll down in the list to find it. This procedural map is a white pattern with small black spots. In the Speckle Parameters rollout, change Color #2 from white to a light brown, in which red is set to *140*, green is *110*, and blue is *70*. Render the Camera02 viewport. The hillsides should look like speckled sand or rock.

5. Now the green areas appear too flat. In the Material/Map Navigator, return to the top level of [1]: Ground [Standard]. In the Maps rollout, click on the None button to the right of Bump and double-click Smoke in the Material/Map Browser list (**Figure 13.12**). In the Smoke Parameters rollout, enter *200* in the Size field to increase the size of the pattern. This is a random black-and-white pattern similar to the Noise map.

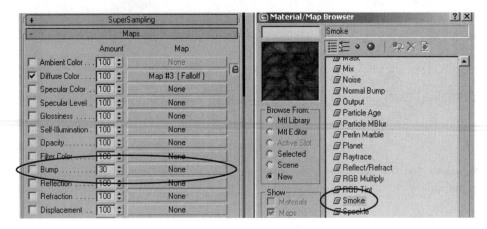

Figure 13.12 *Using the Smoke procedural map in the Bump slot of the material creates the illusion of extra geometry in the rendered image.*

6. Render the Camera02 viewport and notice how the land has changed from a flat surface to an apparently rough one (**Figure 13.13**). This is an effective illusion that reacts correctly to changes in the lighting or the viewing angle without adding geometry.

FIGURE 13.13 *The rendered image shows the bump pattern clearly on the landscape, especially in the foreground where the light strikes at an angle.*

7. Close all windows and dialogs and save the file. It should already be called *Ch13_procedural04.max*.

Using a few simple additions to the original material, your landscape is now looking more convincing.

Materials are very versatile for convincing the viewer of the colors in the scene and adding the illusion of complex geometry where none exists. You must use these techniques if you want to speed production while satisfying the visual requirements of the client at the same time.

Creating and Using a Bitmap with 3ds max 7

You can use Paint or other image creation software to create images for use as maps in 3ds max 7. However, if you need to make changes to the image you've used as a map, you have to open the other software and perhaps go through complex steps to edit the images, save the image and reload it into max's Material Editor.

A better alternative for many images used as maps is to create it right in 3ds max 7 so that you have all the powerful editing features at hand when you need to make changes.

In this section of the chapter, you'll learn how to use bitmaps as color information in your materials. You'll create a bitmap by rendering some hidden geometry in the scene to which you have applied a white, self-illuminated material. This material will render using a consistent white color, regardless of the lighting in the scene.

You'll also learn how to apply the Matte/Shadow material type, which makes an object invisible in the rendered image and allows only the background to show through, which in this case is black. Using Matte/Shadow material will allow you to render to the bounding box edges of the landscape for alignment purposes, without having the landscape be part of the bitmap. You'll also use 3ds max 7's Box Selected rendering type, which renders an image that matches the bounding box, or extents, of all selected objects. This, in turn, will allow you to use the image in the Diffuse color slot of a material and have the map fit the objects correctly when you apply a UVW Map modifier that fits the extents of the object. You'll learn more about mapping in Chapter 14, *Mapping Coordinates: Getting the Right Fit.*

Creating a Bitmap

In the first exercise, you'll create and apply the bitmap to the runway material to produce dashed runway lines and some text that might be painted on the runway surface. To help with the map placement, you'll also create a material that renders the landscape invisible.

Exercise 13.4: Creating and Applying Materials for the Bitmap

Display Panel button

1. Open the file **Ch13_bitmap01.max**.
   Save it to your project folder with the name *Ch13_bitmap02.max*. On the Hide rollout of the Display panel, click the Unhide All button (**Figure 13.14**). This will unhide an object with thick dashed lines and the text "Max Airport" positioned above the landscape.

   To keep the geometry from being obscured when it's rendered, it must be properly aligned with the runway in the Top viewport and above the landscape object.

   The objects appear to be misaligned in the Camera02 viewport because they're located a distance above the surface of the runway and are viewed from an angle.

   In the Properties dialog of the geometry, the Cast Shadows option has been cleared so that the object will not, under any lighting conditions, cast shadows onto the landscape. Any shadows would become part of the rendered image and make the image useless as a map for your purposes in this scene.

2. On the main toolbar, click the Material Editor button and highlight the bottom center sample window to activate it. Rename the material *pure white*. In the Blinn Basic Parameters rollout, click the Specular color swatch to open the Color Selector and change the color to pure white by dragging the Whiteness slider down. Drag and drop the color swatch onto the Diffuse color swatch and choose Copy in the Copy or Swap Colors dialog. This will change both the Diffuse and Ambient colors because they are locked together. The sample sphere appears light gray with a dark band in the ambient portion.

FIGURE 13.14 *Using Unhide All, you can display any hidden objects in the scene.*

3. In the Blinn Basic Parameters rollout, Self-Illumination area, click the Color checkbox. Drag and drop the specular color swatch onto the Self-Illumination color swatch that appears and choose Copy in the dialog. The sample sphere is now fully white and is not affected by the lighting in the sample window (**Figure 13.15**). Any object with this material assigned to it will also appear white in the shaded viewport.

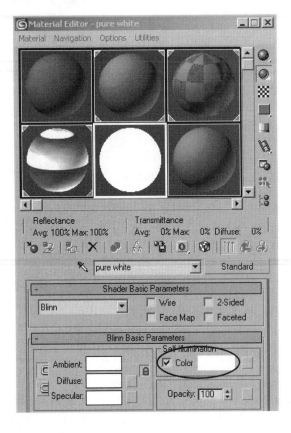

FIGURE 13.15 *A material with pure white color swatches will always render white under any lighting condition.*

4. Assign this material to the Runway_graphics01 object in the scene by dragging and dropping it onto the object in either the Top or Left viewport. Or you can first select the object in the scene and then click the Assign Material to Selection button below the sample windows in the Material Editor.

Dragging and dropping a sample window applies the material to only one object at a time. However, you can assign a material to many objects at once by selecting the objects and using the Assign Material to Selection button.

The next step is to create a Matte/Shadow material to apply to the landscape temporarily to make it invisible while allowing the black background to show through the object. The Box Selected rendering method will use the extremes of the mesh to determine the size of the rendered image to make mapping easier.

5. Activate the bottom-right sample window in the Material Editor. Rename it *Invisible.* Click the Standard button to the right of the name field and double click Matte/Shadow in the Material/Map Browser list (**Figure 13.16**). Drag and drop this material onto Mountains01 in the Camera02 viewport. The sample sphere will be invisible and the landscape will become gray in the shaded viewport.

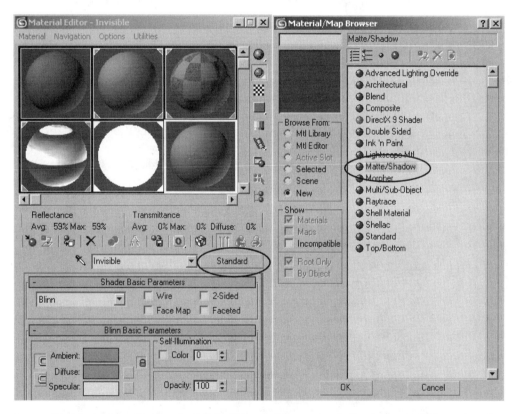

Figure 13.16 *A Matte/Shadow material will be used to render the landscape invisible so that the black background shows through the geometry.*

6. Close all windows and dialogs and save the file. It should already be called *Ch13_bitmap02.max.*

You've created and applied materials to produce an image that has white graphics on a black background.

Rendering the Bitmap to Fit the Geometry

You'll now render the white graphics against the black background. The image file format is a .png file with an alpha channel. The alpha channel is used to interpret black in the image as transparency in the material, letting the base color show through everywhere except in the white areas of the image when it is used as a map.

If this black-and-white image were created outside 3ds max 7, there would be no relationship between the size of the image and the geometry to which it was applied. So positioning the dashes and text would become a trial-and-error process. This exercise stresses the appropriate and easy placement of the map using Box Selected rendering.

Exercise 13.5: Using Box Selected Rendering

1. Open **Ch13_bitmap02.max** from the last exercise or from the CD-ROM and save it to your project folder with the name *Ch13_bitmap03.max*. Right-click in the Top viewport to activate it, and use the Select by Name button on the main toolbar to select the Mountains01 and Runway_graphics01 objects. At the far right of the main toolbar, click the Render Type drop-down menu and choose Box Selected from the list (**Figure 13.17**). This will render only the selected objects in the scene out to only the extents of the bounding box of the selection set.

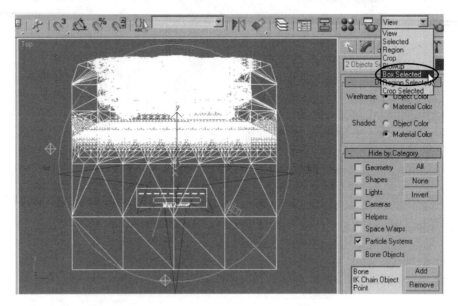

FIGURE 13.17 *From the drop down menu on the main toolbar, switch from the default View render type to Box Selected.*

2. Click the Render Scene button on the main toolbar to open the Render Scene dialog. Near the bottom of the Common tab, in the Render Output area, click the Files button. In the Render Output File dialog, navigate to your project folder in the Save In drop-down menu. Enter *runway_graphics.png* in the File Name field. Click the Save button and make sure the RGB 24-bit radio button is selected and that the Alpha Channel checkbox is selected in the PNG Configuration dialog (**Figure 13.18**). Click OK in the dialog.

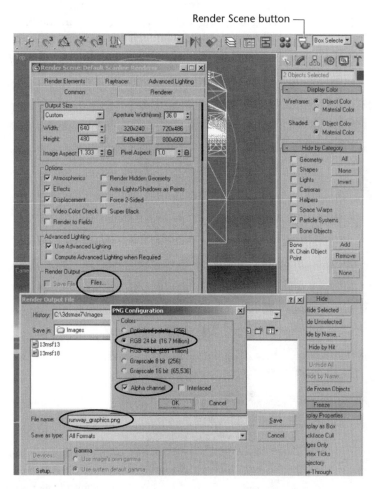

FIGURE 13.18 *You'll render a PNG file with an alpha channel to your project folder.*

3. In the Render Scene dialog, click the Render button at the lower right. Because you are using the Box Selected render type, the Render Bounding Box/Selected dialog appears with the width and height of the objects, expressed in pixels, selected in the scene. Enter *2000* in the Width field and press Enter. The Constrain Aspect Ratio option makes the Height 2020 pixels automatically (**Figure 13.19**). Click the Render button in this dialog to render the bitmap and save it to the project folder. The Render Frame window shows white graphics in the lower center of a black background (**Figure 13.20**). Close the Render Frame window. In the Render Scene dialog, select the Save File option in the Render Output section and close the dialog. In the Render Type drop-down list on the main toolbar, choose View render type. Click in an empty space in the Top viewport to deselect the objects.

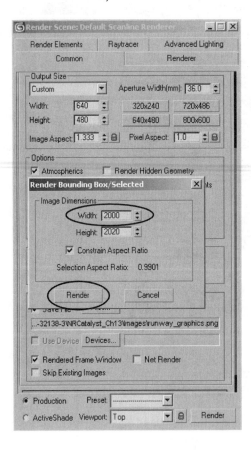

FIGURE 13.19 *Increase the size of the rendered image for a higher resolution bitmap.*

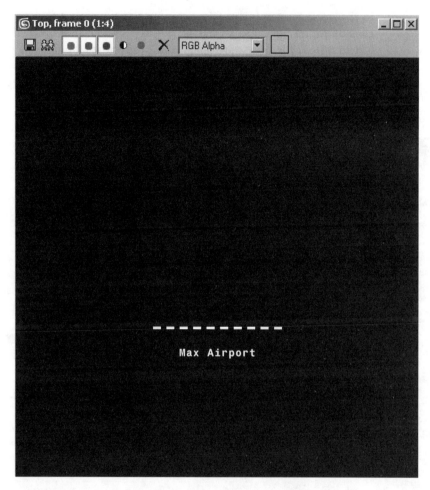

FIGURE 13.20 *The solid white graphics are rendered on a black background that will be interpreted as transparency in the Material Editor.*

4. You'll now edit the Runway material to add the bitmap you just created. On the main toolbar, click the Material Editor button to open it. Click in the upper right sample window to activate Mountains material. In the Material Editor, click the Material/Map Navigator and highlight the [2]: Runway [Standard] level in the list. In the Blinn Basic Parameters rollout, click the map shortcut button to the right of the Diffuse color swatch and double-click Bitmap in the Material/Map Browser list.

In the Select Bitmap Image File dialog, go to your project folder and double-click on runway_graphics in the list (**Figure 13.21**). Your image list will appear different from the one shown here. Click the Show Map in Viewport button below the sample windows, and the bitmap appears as black with white text on the runway in the shaded viewport when the material is reassigned.

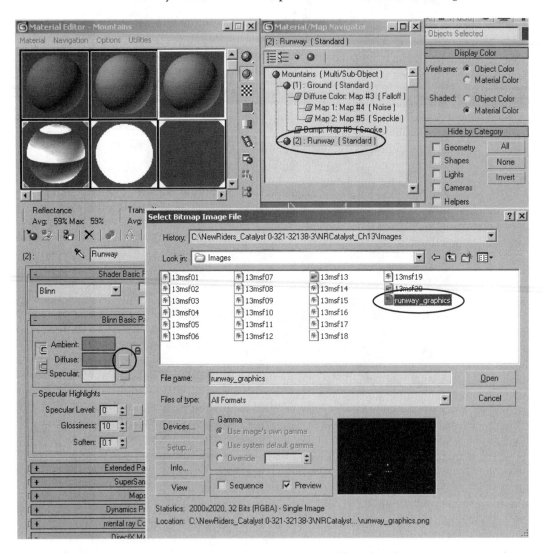

Figure 13.21 *Open the bitmap you rendered in Step 3 in the Diffuse slot of your runway material.*

5. In the Material/Map Navigator, highlight the top level of the Mountains [Multi/Sub-Object] material. Drag and drop this material onto the landscape to replace the Matte/Shadow material you assigned earlier. Select the Runway_graphics01 object in the scene and, in the Hide rollout of the Display panel, click the Hide Selected button. You don't need the object anymore in this scene.

6. Make sure the Camera02 viewport is active and click the Quick Render button on the main toolbar. The text and dashes will appear white on the runway. However, it doesn't quite fit correctly: the letter *p* is cut off at the bottom. Select the Mountains01 object and, in the Modifier List on the Modify panel, double-click the UVW Map modifier. Render the Camera02 viewport again, and notice the graphics shift to fit correctly on the runway (**Figure 13.22**).

You have adjusted the bitmaps mapping coordinates, something you'll learn more about in Chapter 14.

tip

The runway appears black in the shaded viewport when Show Map in Viewport is enabled because the viewports cannot display alpha channel information. The rendered image, however, respects the black alpha pixels and makes them transparent to show the base gray color of the material.

Figure 13.22 *By using the UVW Map modifier, the bitmap fits the object correctly with no adjustments when it has been rendered using the Box Selected render type.*

7. Close all windows and dialogs and save the file. It should already be called *Ch13_bitmap03.max*.

You have added to the complexity of assigned materials by taking advantage of an image using an alpha channel.

Even though you had previously applied materials to objects, you've learned that it's easy to edit those materials to add complexity for a more convincing look to the rendered images. Not only did you add color to the scene, but by using Bump maps in your material you also added the illusion of extra geometry.

Summary

In this chapter, you learned the following:

- Procedural maps provide flexibility in editing random patterns with controls for size, edge transitions between colors, and the ability to use maps within maps to give materials a more natural look.

- Bitmaps can be created directly in 3ds max 7 with the same modeling techniques and materials you use for the other objects in the scene, providing the advantage of not having to switch back and forth between various software packages.

- Matte/Shadow material, combined with Box Selected rendering, ensures precise mapping for the bitmaps you created in 3ds max 7.

With a little practice of all of the above, you can transform your featureless 3D objects into more dynamic and interesting scenes that look more real to your viewers.

CHAPTER 14

Mapping Coordinates: Getting the Right Fit

In This Chapter

So far in the book, you have learned to apply materials to objects with maps as patterns that don't have any specific size associated with them. Granted, you have changed the size parameters of some of the maps, but just to "eyeball" the pattern and until it looked right. For example, you changed the size of the Smoke map that you had applied as a Bump map on the landscape to make the pattern larger.

In the previous chapter, you also applied a UVW Map modifier to the landscape so that the graphics on the runway fit precisely. The UVW Map modifier adjusted itself to the extents of the landscape object so that the map fit exactly within those boundaries.

In this chapter, you'll practice editing the materials assigned to the interior of the control tower to make them more convincing in the scene. You'll apply tiles to the floor and make the floor reflective.

The radar console in the tower will get a checkered material that wraps around to conform to the curvature of the console to illustrate the special mapping properties of lofted objects. You'll create a radar screen material and apply an animation to the computer monitors.

This might seem like a lot to learn in one chapter, but the basic materials have been set up for you, and some of the steps are a repetition from the other materials-related chapters to help you develop a fluid workflow when creating and applying materials.

This chapter covers the following topics:

- **UVW mapping.** You'll learn to use the UVW Map modifier to accurately size maps based on real-world conditions. This will require you to analyze the map pattern and determine how much coverage one repetition of the map would represent in the real world.

- **Reflection mapping.** You'll learn to apply Reflection maps in the material and adjust the parameters of the reflections for maximum efficiency.

- **Mapping coordinates and lofted objects.** You'll learn to calculate the length of the loft path and the loft shape and adjust the repeats along the length and width of the lofted object to size the map pattern appropriately.

- **Map-masking techniques.** You'll also be introduced to the process of masking maps. This uses the luminance values of pixels in one map to mask out other maps.

- **Using image sequences as bitmaps.** You'll learn to assign and map a sequence of still images that will become an animated map that plays repeatedly on the computer monitor screens.

- **Compositing maps in layers.** You'll learn to use a Composite map type to layer two Gradient Ramp maps together.

Key Terms

- **Mapping coordinates.** Maps, or patterns, in your materials generally need to be the correct size to be convincing. Mapping coordinates are the numeric values that adjust the fit of patterns.

- **Masking.** Using the luminance, or brightness, values of a map's pixels to mask out or reveal an image or color below.

- **Compositing.** The process of applying in layers images that have transparency.

About the Exercises

For the exercises in this chapter, you'll apply UVW mapping coordinates to a floor-tile material so that the map pattern accurately reflects 6-inch-by-6-inch tiles.

You'll assign the Tiles map type to both the Color and the Bump slots of the floor material and make a determination of how much real-world area one repetition of the map covers. You'll then apply a UVW Map modifier to the polygons that make up the floor and adjust the gizmo of the Map modifier to represent that coverage.

In the case of the lofted radar console, you'll determine the length of the loft path and the loft shape and adjust the loft object parameters to make a Checker map conform to real-world sizes.

To get viewers to perceive what you want them to perceive, you must make sure your maps are the right size for your objects. For example, bricks or wood grain that are much too large or small are just not convincing.

Adjusting Map Sizes Using the UVW Map Modifier

When a UVW Map modifier is applied to an object, the gizmo automatically adjusts to fit the bounding box of the object with what is known as *Planar mapping coordinates*. Planar mapping projects the map in both directions perpendicular to the gizmo and sizes one repetition of the map to fit inside the gizmo. The map pattern then repeats, or tiles, over the entire surface of the object. You'll adjust the width and height of the gizmo to resize the map to your specifications.

In the first exercise, you'll create the map for the diffuse color of the material and then drag and drop a copy of the map into the Bump slot and adjust the colors of the new map to black and white for minimum and maximum bump amounts.

You'll also learn to apply a Raytrace Reflection map to the Reflection slot of the material. The Raytrace Reflection map accurately creates reflections on both curved and flat surfaces and is generally a convenient map to use for reflections. However, the math involved in calculating Raytrace reflections can be significant, and you'll learn methods of optimizing the process that will also result in better-looking reflections.

Exercise 14.1: Adding Convincing Tiles to the Floor

1. Open **Ch14_mapping01.max** from the CD-ROM. Save it to your project folder with the name *Ch14_mapping02.max*. This is the control room interior file with basic materials applied to objects in the scene. Many of the objects have more than one material, and therefore use the Multi/Sub-Object materials that correspond to Material ID numbers assigned to the faces or polygons.

2. On the main toolbar, click the Material Editor button or press *M* to open the Material Editor. Click in the upper-left sample window to activate the material called *Room*. It is a Multi/Sub-Object material consisting of four sub-materials. Click the Material/Map Navigator button in the Material Editor, and highlight the third sub-material called *Tile floor* in the list. In the Blinn Basic Parameters rollout, click the Map Shortcut button to the right of Diffuse color swatch and double-click Tiles in the Material/Map Browser.

3. Press Ctrl + L on the keyboard. This replaces the lighting in the scene with the default lighting setup so that you can see the maps in the shaded viewport more easily. In the Material Editor, click the Show Map in Viewport button (**Figure 14.1**). The floor in the shaded Camera01 viewport will turn gray, but you won't see the pattern because the object has no mapping coordinates assigned.

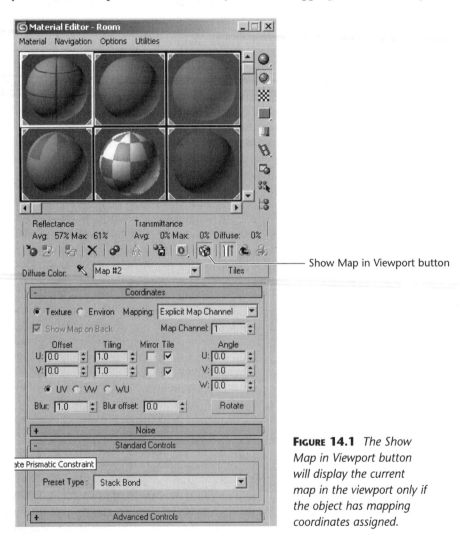

Show Map in Viewport button

FIGURE 14.1 *The Show Map in Viewport button will display the current map in the viewport only if the object has mapping coordinates assigned.*

4. In the camera viewports, select the Tower_
    building01 object. In Stack view on the Modify
    panel, highlight the Polygon sub-object mode.
    In the Camera01 viewport, pick anywhere on
    the floor to select the floor polygon; it will turn
    red. In the Modifier List on the Modify panel,
    click UVW Map. The Tiles map now shows on
    the floor in the Camera01 viewport, but the
    tiles are much too large to be convincing.

If the tile pattern looks especially distorted in the viewport, you can right-click on
the Camera01 label and choose
Texture Correction in the
menu. In any case, the map
will always render correctly.

5. To size the tiles correctly, you must first deter-
    mine what size tile you want. In this case, the tiles should each be 12 inches by
    12 inches. To better see the tile pattern in the Material Editor, toggle the Show
    End Result button off. Just the map pattern in the sample window will display,
    not the end result of the entire material. Notice there are four tiles across and
    four tiles down, so if each tile is 12 inches on a side, then the area covered by
    one repetition of this map is 4 feet by 4 feet (**Figure 14.2**).

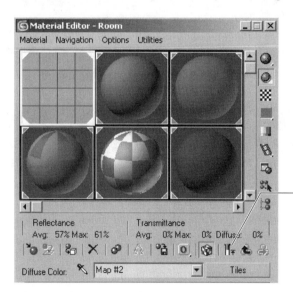

Show End Result button

FIGURE 14.2 *Toggling the Show End Result button lets you see one repetition of the map at the current level.*

6. Now you must adjust the size of the UVW Map gizmo to match the size you calculated in Step 5. In the Parameters rollout on the Modify panel, enter *4'* in both the Length and the Width fields and press Enter. In the Camera01 viewport, you'll see the orange gizmo is now 4 feet by 4 feet, and the tiles repeat outwardly in all directions (**Figure 14.3**).

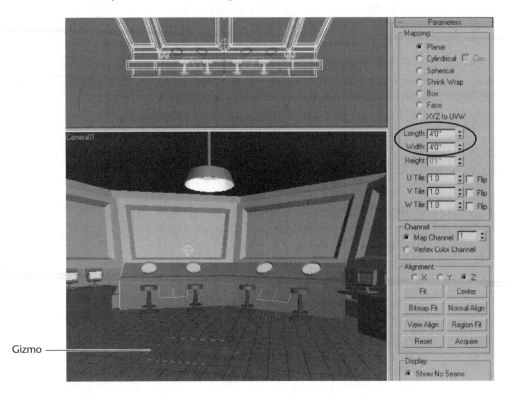

FIGURE 14.3 *Adjusting the size of the UVW Map gizmo changes the size of the tile pattern.*

7. In the Advanced Controls rollout of the Material Editor, click the Texture color swatch in the Tiles Setup area. In the Color Selector, set Red to *165*, Green to *75*, and Blue to *60*, for a terra-cotta color. In the Grout Setup area, click the Texture color swatch, and in the Color Selector, set Red to *200*, Green to *175*, and Blue to *115*, for a light-tan color. On the main toolbar, click the Quick Render button to render the Camera01 viewport (**Figure 14.4**).

Figure 14.4 *Change the colors of this Diffuse map to get a terra-cotta tile and tan grout.*

Next you'll clone the Tiles map from the Diffuse slot to the Bump slot in the Material Editor, and change the colors to white and black to get maximum effectiveness.

8. Click the Material/Map Navigator button and highlight the top level of Tile floor material. In the Maps rollout, click and drag the Diffuse Color Tiles map and drop it onto the Bump slot. In the Copy (Instance) Map dialog, click the Copy radio button and click OK. In the Material/Map Navigator, highlight the Bump map level. In the Advanced Controls rollout, Tiles Setup area, click the Texture color swatch and set it to pure white. In the Grout Setup area, click the Texture color swatch and set it to pure black. White pixels bump up; black pixels do nothing. Render the Camera01 viewport and notice the tiles appear slightly raised in the foreground and to the right.

9. Close all windows and dialogs and save the file. It should already be called *Ch14_mapping02.max*. You now have a dull terra-cotta tile floor with raised tiles.

note

Maps can be tileable, that is, their edges can be made to match so that there is no discernible repeating pattern, or they can be non-tileable, in which the four edges of the map are decidedly different and a distinct repeating pattern appears when applied to surfaces.

The process of adjusting maps to match real-world materials is relatively straightforward and will make your scenes much more convincing to the viewer. If the map you are using is a photograph of a section of something, such as a carpet or a stone wall, you would have to use your judgment as to how much area of the carpet or wall the photo actually covers. Regardless, the process is still the same.

Applying and Optimizing Reflections

Many materials in the real world reflect, and the reflections add depth and richness to the scene. However, in 3ds max 7 reflections can be expensive in terms of computer resources, so you must do all you can to optimize the math involved.

In the next exercise, you'll learn to apply a Reflection map called a *Raytrace* and optimize two settings in 3ds max 7 that will speed rendering and make the reflections look more convincing.

The first optimization involves adjusting the attenuation settings of the reflections. Reflected light and direct light both observe the physics of light based upon the inverse square law. You learned about light attenuation in Chapter 11, *Photometric Lights: Bouncing Basics*, so review that chapter if you need to.

The second optimization involves reducing the number of bounces in the reflections. Real-world reflections can reflect off other reflections to infinity. You might see this effect if you were in an elevator cab and the walls were mirrored. You could see yourself in the reflections until you were too small to recognize. By default, 3ds max 7 is set to reflect nine bounces deep, which is more than enough for most situations. You'll reduce this number to 3. This is a global setting in 3ds max 7 that affects all Raytrace reflections in the scene.

Exercise 14.2: Optimizing Reflections on the Tile Floor

1. Open **Ch14_mapping02.max** from the last exercise or from the CD-ROM. Save it to your project folder as *Ch14_mapping03.max*. On the main toolbar, click the Material Editor button to open the Material Editor and use the Material/Map Navigator to return to the top level of the Tile floor material. In the Maps rollout, click the None button to the right of Reflection. Double-click Raytrace in the Material/Map Browser. Render the Camera01 viewport, and you'll see extreme reflections over the entire floor (**Figure 14.5**).

caution

If you accidentally placed the Reflection map in the Refraction slot, the floor becomes invisible. To correct that, just drag and drop the Raytrace map from the Refraction slot to the Reflection slot and click the Swap radio button in the Copy (Instance) Map dialog.

Figure 14.5 *The default settings for a Raytrace Reflection map make the floor too reflective.*

2. In the Material/Map Navigator, highlight the Reflection level of the Tile floor material. In the Attenuation rollout of the Material Editor, click on the drop-down arrow for Falloff Type and choose Exponential from the list. On the main toolbar, click the Quick Render button and render the Camera01 viewport.

The reflections in the floor are now just barely visible at the bottom of the stools and the cabinets. Exponential attenuation uses a set of ranges to determine where the reflections start and where the reflections end (**Figure 14.6**). By default, the reflections begin at zero, or at the surface, and end 100 system units away from the surface. One system unit equals one inch by default in 3ds max 7. Beyond the end range, no more reflections have to be calculated, which can increase productivity considerably in typical scenes.

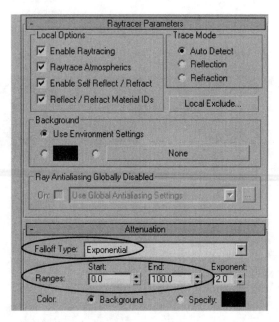

FIGURE 14.6 *The default Exponential attenuation settings reduce the reflections too much in this scene.*

3. In the Attenuation rollout, enter *200* in the End Range field and press Enter. Render the Camera01 viewport and notice the reflections now have a much more convincing look as they diminish from the surface and reflect nothing beyond 200 inches from the floor (**Figure 14.7**). The attenuation ranges are subjective, and you must choose values that work for your purposes. Close all windows and dialogs.

Increasing the start range will alter the reflections so that they are full strength out to that distance and then attenuate to the end range. The Exponent value determines how quickly the cutoff of the transition occurs between the two ranges.

FIGURE 14.7 *Setting the end range of the exponential attenuation to 200 works well for this scene.*

4. From the Rendering pull-down menu, choose Raytracer Settings. The Render Scene dialog appears. In the Raytracer Global Parameters rollout, Ray Depth Control area, enter 3 in the Maximum Depth field (**Figure 14.8**). A setting of 3 means that reflections within reflections can only go to a depth of 3.

When you have the attenuation for reflections set, they still may be too strong at the reflecting surface. In the Maps rollout of the Material Editor, you can adjust the Amount field to the left of the Map button to reduce the overall strength of the reflections.

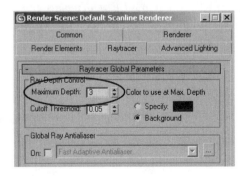

FIGURE 14.8 *Globally reducing the number of times reflections can reflect within reflections can speed renderings.*

The reduced reflections won't have any significance on the look of this particular scene and you probably won't notice any increased speed in the render time, because the scene is so small. However, in a scene with a typical number of reflections, reducing the caps on Maximum Depth can make a significant difference.

5. Close all windows and dialogs and save the file. It should already be called *Ch14_mapping03.max*. The adjustments you have made in this exercise not only make the scene look better, but more importantly, they can increase your productivity.

Reflections are very important for almost any scene because most materials in the real world have at least a little reflective quality. However, it is extremely important that you use the two techniques introduced here to reduce the overhead of the reflection calculations.

Using Masking for Better Map Control

Using one map alone usually won't give you the control you need to achieve the result you want. In this section, you'll learn to use a technique called *masking*, in which one map masks out the effects of another map. In this scene, the floor tiles and grout both have the same reflectivity, which is not usual in the real world. The more porous grout would tend to have less or almost no reflectivity.

In the mask, white pixels will allow the event, in this case reflection, to happen and black pixels will mask the effect out. You already have the appropriate map being used as the Bump map, so all you need to do is copy it to the Mask slot.

The masking exercise here will be very simple, but the concept is extremely important and should be something that you use constantly in your work.

Exercise 14.3: Applying a Mask Over the Reflection Map

1. Open **Ch14_mapping03.max** from the last exercise or from the CD-ROM. Save it to your project folder with the name *Ch14_mapping04.max*. On the main toolbar, click the Material Editor button to open the Material Editor, click the Materials/Map Navigator, and highlight the Reflection level of the Tile floor material.

2. Click the Raytrace button and double-click Mask in the Material/Map Browser list. Click the Keep Old Map As Sub Map radio button in the Replace Map dialog and click OK. This keeps the Raytrace map and applies a new, empty Mask level (**Figure 14.9**).

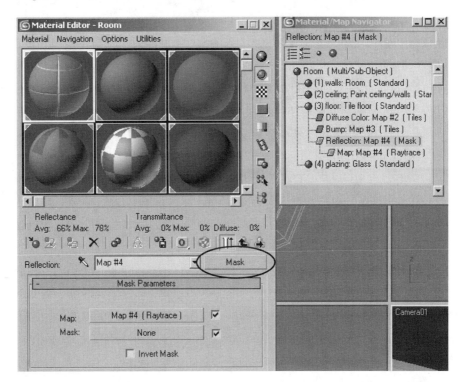

FIGURE 14.9. *By replacing one map with a new map and choosing Keep New Map As Sub Map, you can begin to layer maps.*

3. In the Material/Map Navigator, drag the Bump map from the Tile floor material and drop it onto the Mask None button in the Mask Parameters rollout in the Material Editor. In the Instance (Copy) Map dialog, click the Copy radio button and click OK (see **Figure 14.10** on the next page). The black pixels of the Tiles map are masking the reflections in the grout area. Render the Camera01 viewport to see the change. If you have difficulty seeing the difference the mask has made, you can clear the checkbox in the Mask Parameters rollout to the right of the Mask slot and render the viewport again. This checkbox toggles the map on or off. Remember to check the box again when you are finished comparing the images.

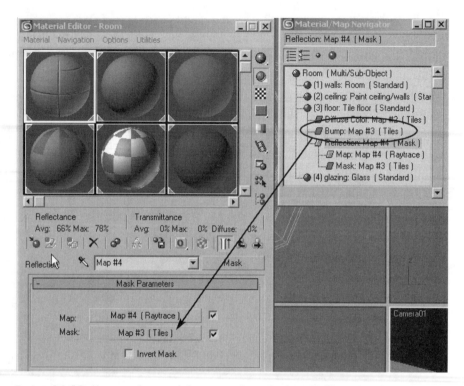

FIGURE 14.10 *You can drag and drop maps from the Material/Map Navigator into slots in the Material Editor rollouts.*

4. Close all dialogs and windows and save the file. It should already be called *Ch14_mapping04.max*.

Using this simple masking technique, you have added another layer of control to your maps and materials.

Again, the exercise was simple, but the concept you have learned about masking will be useful throughout to production workflow. The same technique could be used to create the illusion of puddles in a rainy street or, perhaps, graffiti on a brick wall.

Using Mapping Coordinates on Lofted Objects

Applying UVW Map modifiers to objects to control mapping coordinates is one method of resizing patterns on most objects. Lofted objects, however, generate their own mapping coordinates along the length of the loft path and around the loft shape. In the next exercise, you'll learn to calculate the length of the path and the shape and to apply those values to the length-and-width repeat of the pattern. Lofted mapping coordinates are especially powerful because they follow the curvature of the path. If you edit the path, the maps will change accordingly.

In the next exercise, you'll apply a checker pattern to the radar console and adjust the size of the individual checks to be 4 inches by 4 inches.

Exercise 14.4: Adjusting Patterns on Lofted Objects

1.   Open **Ch14_mapping04.max** from the last exercise or from the CD-ROM. Save it to your project folder with the name *Ch14_mapping05.max*. In the Camera01 viewport, select the console along the far wall called *Control_panel01*. Open the Material Editor from the main toolbar or by pressing *M*. In the Material Editor, click the blue sample sphere to activate the material called *Radar console*. In the Blinn Basic Parameters rollout, click the Map Shortcut button to the right of the Diffuse color swatch. In the Material/Map Browser, double-click Checker and, in the Material Editor, toggle on the Show Map in Viewport button. The console should turn to a black-and-white checker pattern, made up of two black and two white squares, which is repeated once along the length and once along the width (see **Figure 14.11** on the next page).

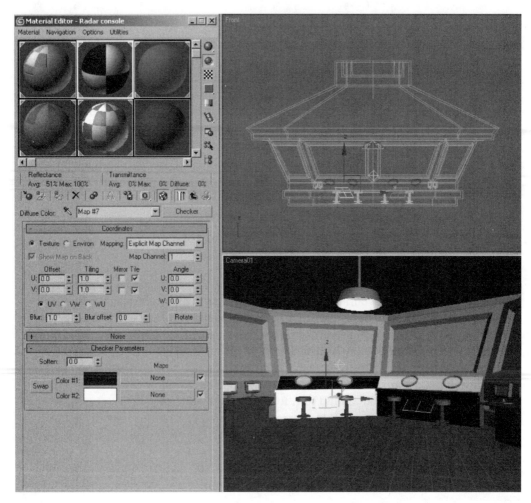

FIGURE 14.11 *The lofted object's native coordinates repeat the black-and-white checker pattern in the Diffuse Color slot along the length and the width one time.*

2. To determine how many times the checker pattern must repeat over the length and width so that each check is a certain size, you must first know the length of the path and the length of the shape that make up the loft object. On the main toolbar, click the Select by Name button. In the Select Objects dialog, List Types section, clear the checkbox for Geometry. This filters the names list to make it easier to choose 2D shapes. Double-click console_path in the list. On the Utilities panel, Utilities rollout, click the Measure button. In the Shapes area of the Measure rollout, you'll see that the length of the path is 26′6″. Jot this value down so that you'll remember it (**Figure 14.12**).

3. In the Camera01 viewport, select Control_panel01. In the Surface Parameters rollout on the Modify panel, highlight the Length Repeat field and press Ctrl + N to open the Numerical Expression Evaluator. On the Expression panel, enter the formula *(26.5*12)/8*. The numeral *8* is used in the formula because the tiles are supposed to be 4 inches by 4 inches, and the pattern is made up of two tiles in each direction. The result will display as 39.75 (**Figure 14.13**). Click the Paste button, and the result is automatically entered in the Length Repeat field. Four-inch-wide stripes appear on the lofted object.

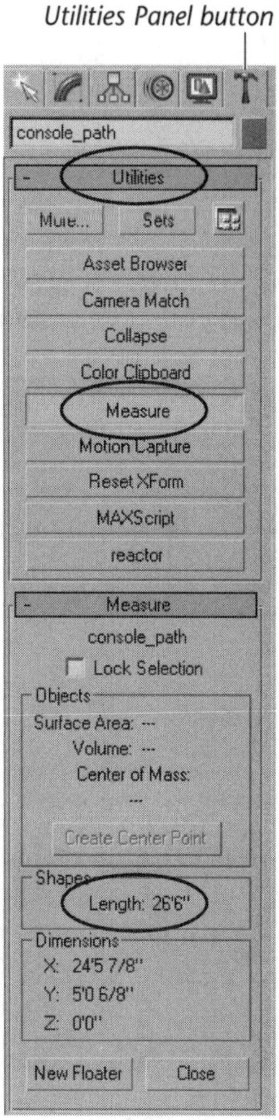

Utilities Panel button

Figure 14.12 *You can find a 2D shape's length in the Measure utility of the Utilities panel.*

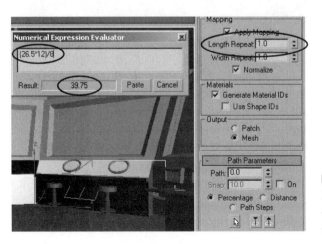

Figure 14.13 *The Numerical Expression Evaluator can be used to enter a mathematical formula for any highlighted numeric field.*

4. On the main toolbar, click the Select by Name button and double-click console_shape in the list. On the Utilities panel, Measure rollout, Shapes area, notice the length of the shape is 15′10 1/8″. We'll round that up to an even 16 feet for this exercise. Select Console_panel01, and in the Surface Parameters rollout of the Modify panel, highlight the Width Repeat field. Press Ctrl + N and, in the Numerical Expression Evaluator, change the formula to *16* for a result of 24, and click the Paste button. The checker pattern on the console will now be very near 4 inches by 4 inches (**Figure 14.14**). Render the Camera01 viewport for a better view of how the pattern actually looks.

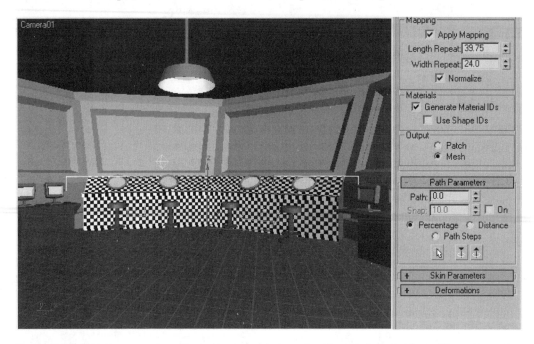

FIGURE 14.14 *Patterns can be adjusted to repeat in two directions on lofted objects. The pattern stays aligned with the object as it changes direction.*

5. Close all windows and dialogs and save the file. It should already be called *Ch14_mapping05.max*. While lofted objects can also have UVW Map modifiers applied, it usually makes sense to use the built-in mapping coordinates because they're the only mapping coordinates that conform to the curvature of the object.

Compositing Maps in Layers

While masking uses one map to hide or reveal another map based on the whiteness (or luminance value) of pixels, it can also be useful to combine two maps and see both of the maps in the material.

In this section of the chapter, you'll learn to use the Composite map type to combine two Gradient Ramp maps to form the concentric rings and sweeping indicator on the radar screen. The Composite map type relies on transparency information in the maps used.

In the last chapter, you learned to use the alpha channel inherent in some maps as transparency information to apply the graphics to the runway and still allow the base color to show through. In the next exercise, you won't have alpha channel information in the maps; instead, you'll use the RGB values of the map's pixels as transparency. Only certain map types such as, .png, .tif, and .tga, can have alpha channel information embedded in them. The Gradient Ramp map is a Procedural map that doesn't contain any alpha channel information.

Exercise 14.5: Compositing Two Maps with Transparency

1. Open **Ch14_mapping05.max** from the last exercise or from the CD-ROM. Save it to your project folder with the new name *Ch14_mapping06.max*. In the main toolbar, click the Material Editor button and activate the material sample window called *Radar*. Radar material (bright green and gray Multi/Sub-Object material) is hidden on the right side of the sample windows, so you must use the scroll button at the bottom of the sample windows, or pick between sample windows and drag left when you see the hand cursor.

2. In the Material Editor, click the Materials/Map Navigator button, and highlight the bottom material in the list called *Radar screen*. In the Self-Illumination section, the material has a bright-green color, which you'll override using two Gradient Ramp maps. The initial map type will be a Composite map. In the Blinn Basic Parameters rollout, Self-Illumination section, click the Map Shortcut button to the right of the color swatch. In the Material/Map Browser, double-click Composite in the list. In the Composite Parameters rollout, click the Map 1 None button and double-click Gradient Ramp in the list.

3. In the Gradient Ramp Parameters rollout, click and drag the middle flag at the bottom of the gradient off to one side. When you have dragged it as far as it will go, it turns red. When you release the mouse button, it is discarded. Right-click on the flag at the right end of the gradient and choose Edit Properties from the menu. In the Flag Properties dialog, click the color swatch on the

lower right. In the Color Selector dialog, change the color to a pure green by setting Red to *0*, Green to *255*, and Blue to *0*. In the Gradient Ramp Parameters rollout, Gradient Type drop-down list, choose Spiral (**Figure 14.15**).

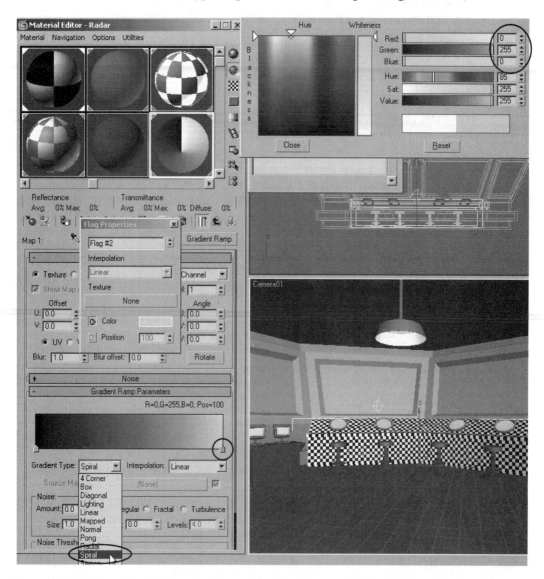

FIGURE 14.15 *One of the Self-Illumination maps will be a green-to-black spiral gradient that represents the sweep of the radar hand.*

4. In the Material/Map Navigator, move up one level to the Composite map in the Self-Illumination slot. In the Composite Parameters rollout, drag the Gradient Ramp map in slot 1 onto the None button for Map 2. In the Copy (Instance) Map dialog, click the Copy radio button and click OK. In the Material/Map Navigator dialog, highlight the bottom Gradient Ramp map level. In the Gradient Type drop-down list, choose Radial. In the Interpolation drop-down list choose Solid. This sequence of steps produces a solid black gradient—don't worry that the green flag is still there. Click anywhere in the black gradient field to create a new flag, and then click the right-most flag, which will turn green. Right-click and choose Copy from the menu. Click on the new flag in the black area to highlight it green, and then right-click and choose Paste. The flag is now green, and everything to the right in the gradient will turn green (**Figure 14.16**).

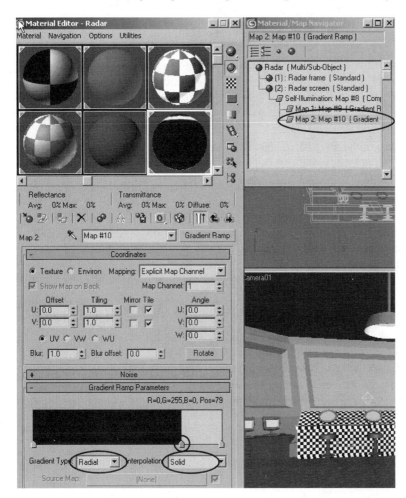

FIGURE 14.16 *This Gradient Ramp will be a radial gradient type with solid interpolation for a hard-edged transition between colors. This will be edited to represent rings on the radar screen.*

5. Click in the green area of the gradient and drag the new flag left to about the middle of the gradient. The gradient is now about half green and half black. Click somewhere in the black area and drag to the right past the existing key. You now have two green areas and two black areas in the gradient. Reposition the existing flags until you have a very thin green stripe in the middle of the gradient and a very thin green stripe at the far right of the gradient (**Figure 14.17**).

Your gradient doesn't have to look exactly like figure 14.17, and don't worry if it takes a few tries to get it looking approximately the same. Remember, if you make a mistake with the flags, you can drag them completely to one side to discard them and start again.

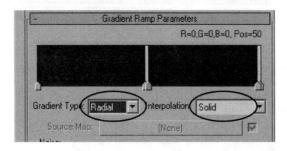

FIGURE 14.17 *To create concentric rings on the radar screen, you can use a Radial gradient type with two thin solid green stripes.*

6. On the main toolbar, click the Select by Name button. In the Select Objects dialog, List Types area, select the Geometry option and double-click Radar03 in the list. Press Alt + Q to isolate the selection to make it easier to visualize what will happen next. In the active Camera01 viewport, press *U* to switch to a User view. Click the Zoom Extents button at the lower right of the display to fill the viewport with the radar object. In the Material Editor, click the Show Map in Viewport button, and you'll see the two concentric rings on the black background (**Figure 14.18**).

7. Render the User viewport and notice that even though there are two maps on this material, only the Concentric Rings map renders. This is because the maps have no alpha information to determine transparency. In the Material Editor, expand the Output rollout. Check the Alpha from RGB Intensity checkbox. This tells the map to use a pseudotransparency based on the luminance value of the pixels; black pixels become transparent, whereas lighter pixels are opaque. Render the User viewport again, and notice you now have two maps composited for a more convincing radar screen (**Figure 14.19**).

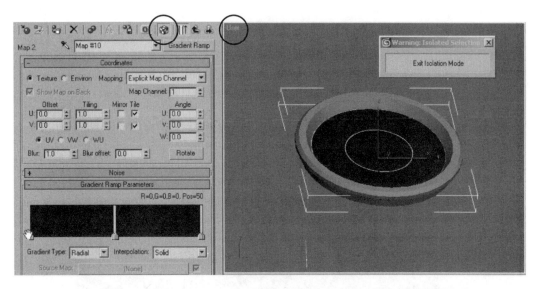

FIGURE 14.18 *It will be easier to work on the Composite maps if you isolate one of the radar objects and zoom in close on a User viewport so that you can see the result as you make changes.*

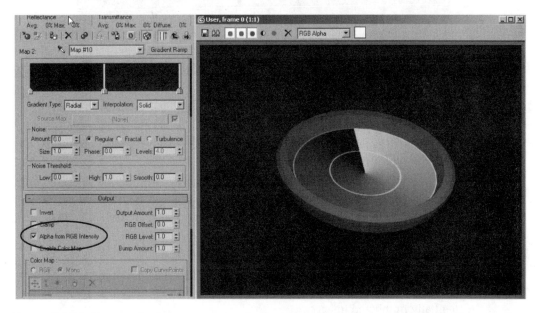

FIGURE 14.19 *You can simulate transparency in maps that don't have an alpha channel by using the Alpha from RGB Intensity option in the Output rollout of the maps.*

8. In the Warning: Isolated Selection dialog, click the yellow Exit Isolation Mode button to return all objects to the scene. With the User viewport active, press *C* to return to the Camera01 viewport and press Ctrl + L to return the scene to the initial lighting scheme. Render the Camera01 viewport and notice that all four of the radar screens have the new material (**Figure 14.20**).

FIGURE 14.20 *Returning to a scene with all objects and restoring the initial lighting layout results in an acceptable rendered image.*

9. Close all windows and dialogs, and save the file. It should already be called *Ch14_mapping06.max*.

Refining the materials in the scene has made a considerable difference in the look of the rendered image.

Using Image Sequences for Animated Maps

It's possible in 3ds max 7 to use animated maps in materials. The maps can be in the form of animated files, such as .avi files or .mov files, or they can be a series of sequentially numbered images.

In the next exercise, you'll map a short sequence of PNG files onto the computer monitors in the scene. A Multi/Sub-Object material has already been applied to the objects. You'll modify the material that has been applied to the monitor screens.

Exercise 14.6: Loading Sequential Images as Animated Maps

1. Open **Ch14_mapping06.max** from the previous exercise or from the CD-ROM. Save it to your project folder with the name *Ch14_mapping07.max*. Using the Select by Name button on the main toolbar, double-click Monitor01 to select it. Press Alt + Q to isolate the selection. In the Camera01 viewport, press *U* to switch to a User viewport. Click the Zoom Extents All button at the lower right of the display to fill the viewport with the monitor.

2. In Stack view on the Modify panel, notice there's a Poly Select modifier with a Material modifier above it. That combination of modifiers assigned Material ID #2 to the screen of the monitor. The screen faces will require a UVW Map modifier so that the map will fit correctly on the screen. In Stack view, highlight Material and click Hold/Yes in the Warning dialog. In the Modifier List, click UVW Map modifier. You will see the gizmo appear as an orange line across the center of the monitor because it is applied by default to the positive *Z*-axis of the object (**Figure 14.21**).

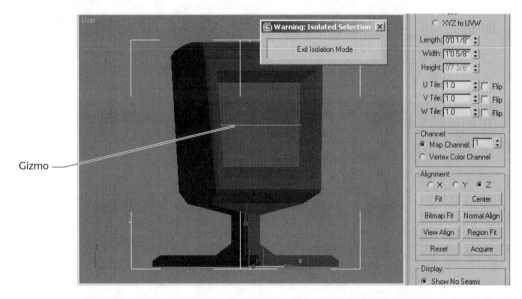

Gizmo

FIGURE 14.21 *The monitor-screen faces must have a UVW Map modifier for the material with the animated map to fit the screen.*

3. You may need to switch the User viewport to Wireframe mode or zoom in on the monitor in the Front viewport to see the gizmo. The gizmo must be perpendicular to the faces and sized to fit. On the Modify panel, Alignment area, click the Normal Align button. In the User viewport, click and hold on the monitor screen and move the cursor around slightly. You will see the gizmo flip to match the face normals. In the Alignment section, click the Fit button. This causes the gizmo to fit the selected faces (**Figure 14.22**). On the Modify panel, Stack view, highlight the top-level Poly Select modifier to exit sub-object mode.

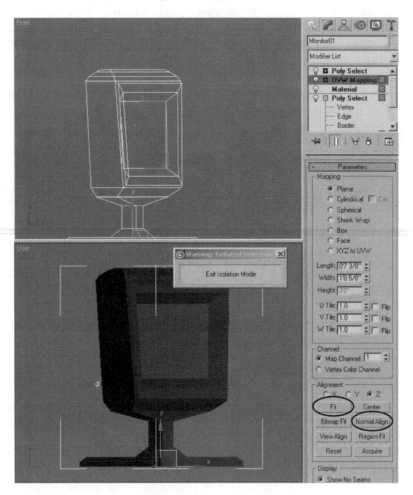

FIGURE 14.22 *You can align a UVW Map gizmo using the built-in tools in the Alignment section on the Modify panel.*

4. On the main toolbar, click the Material Editor button. Activate the sample window with a material called *Monitor*. In the Material/Map Navigator, highlight the second sub-material called *Screen*. In the Blinn Basic Parameters roll-out, click the gray shortcut button to the right of the Diffuse color swatch and double-click Bitmap in the Material/Map Browser list. In the Select Bitmap Image File dialog, navigate to the folder on the CD-ROM that contains the .max files for this chapter and highlight the first of a series of PNG files called *rocket0055*. At the bottom of the dialog, check the Sequence option (**Figure 14.23**). Click the Open button to load the files as a map. In the Image File List Control dialog, click OK.

tip

The image sequence is automatically converted to an IFL file format, which is actually what is applied in the material. It is simply an ASCII text file with all of the images in the sequence listed. You can edit the text file or create your own in any ASCII text editor, such as Notepad or WordPad.

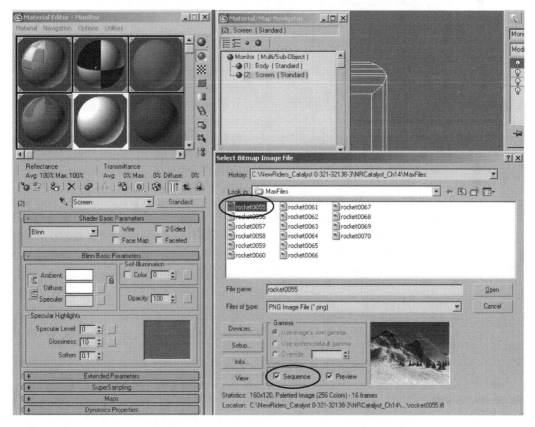

Figure 14.23 *You must select the first image in a sequence and then select the Sequence option to load the files as an animated map.*

5. In the Material Editor, click the Show Map in Viewport button. The dark image of the mountain landscape appears on the monitor. However, a monitor will glow in the dark room, so you need to clone this map into the Self-Illumination slot. In the Material/Map Navigator, move up one level to the Screen material. In the Blinn Basic Parameters rollout, drag and drop the *M* from the Diffuse Map Shortcut button to the Self-Illumination Map shortcut button. In the Copy (Instance) Map dialog, click the Instance radio button and click OK. In the Self-Illumination section, click the Color checkbox (**Figure 14.24**). The material sample sphere glows with the colors of the map. Scrub the Frame slider, located at the bottom of the display, back and forth. A missile is animated across the sample window. When the scene is rendered as an animation, each computer monitor will play this sequence of images repeatedly.

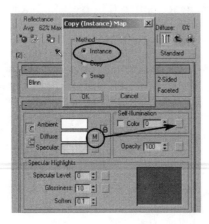

FIGURE 14.24
Using an Instance clone as a color map in Self-illumination causes the map to glow with the intensity of the colors in the map.

6. Close all windows and dialogs and click the Exit Isolation Mode button to return all objects to the scene. Right-click in the User viewport to activate it. Press *C* to return to the Camera01 viewport, and click the Quick Render button on the main toolbar. Save the file. It should already be called *Ch14_mapping07.max*.

Animated maps in materials are treated similarly to any other bitmap.

Summary

Learning the controls of the individual maps and how to combine maps in layers, especially Procedural map types, is paramount for creating complex yet easily edited materials.

Once you have the materials assigned and mapped to your objects and the lighting is set to create great-looking still images, it's time to start learning about animation to bring those scenes to life.

In the next chapter, you'll begin learning the fundamentals of moving objects over time.

PART V

Animation

CHAPTER 15

Keyframe Animation: One Step at a Time

In This Chapter

Modeling, lighting, and materials. So far you've learned techniques and methods to create static scenes. Now it's time to get things moving.

Animation in 3ds max 7 is fundamentally a simple and straightforward process called *keyframing*. This term derives from traditional hand-drawn cartoons, in which a master animator drew only the key positions of the character in the scenes. Then junior animators drew all of the positions in between, so that when the series of images was played back, it appeared as though the scene was moving.

In this chapter, you'll learn how to create a basic animation. The method involves setting 3ds max to a particular frame in an animation that represents a point in time, and assigning parameters, such as the position or rotation of an object, the color of an object, or the lighting in the scene. 3ds max 7 then records this information for that point in time, and then fills in all of the in-between steps from the previous position or color setting, thus creating an animation.

You'll also learn about dummy objects, which are helper objects that don't render but are used as animation aids. Animating with dummy objects requires that you take advantage of a process in 3ds max 7 called *hierarchical linking*. You'll also move a dummy object using a process called *Auto Key animation*, in which the dummy object is moved to a certain point in time or frame, and then keys are automatically created to record the original position and the new position of the dummy object.

In the exercises in this chapter, you'll animate a propeller rotating on its axis, but it involves only one rotation over a short period of time. You'll then learn to repeat that rotation continuously over the rest of the animation and to link the propeller, fuselage, and dummy so they all move together.

This chapter covers the following topics:

- **Fundamental keyframe animation.** You'll learn to set and adjust keyframes to animate the position and rotation of objects in the scene.
- **Repeating animation over time.** You'll learn to create a short segment of animation and then let the program continuously loop the motion over the full length of time.
- **Hierarchical linking.** You'll learn to set up parent and child relationships between animated objects as an extra level of control.

Key Terms

- **Keyframe.** A frame in time to record changes in the scene parameters.
- **Dummy objects.** Non-renderable objects in the scene used as aids to animation.
- **Parameters Out-of-Range.** Setting animation to repeat outside the range of keys you have set.

Keyframe Basics

Keyframe animation, using the Auto Key function, is quite straightforward and easy to use. You click the Auto Key button to turn the function on, move the Frame slider at the bottom of the display to any frame other than Frame 0, and change almost any parameter in the scene. A key will be created at Frame 0 and at the frame where you made the parameter change. The farther apart the keys are spaced, the slower the action because the amount of spacing represents more time.

By default, 3ds max 7 contains 100 frames of animation. The playback rate for animation in the USA is 30 frames per second, which equates to a length of 3.3 seconds of animation. You can adjust the animation length in the Time Configuration dialog, but for our purposes here, 100 frames is fine.

Setting Animation Keys

In the first exercise, you'll practice moving the dummy object in the scene a given distance over the default 100 frames of time. This will create two keys in the Frame slider, one at Frame 0 and one at Frame 100. Then we'll assume you've decided that the plane should remain motionless for a few frames before beginning to move and then sit motionless again for a bit at the end of the animation. You change the timing of the animation by moving keys in the Timeline (**Figure 15.1**).

caution

When the Auto Key button is toggled on, the button itself, the active viewport frame, and the Frame slider line turn bright red, indicating that any change you make to any parameter can become animated if you are not currently at Frame 0. Remember to toggle the Auto Key button off when you're not actually animating to avoid accidentally animating parameters you did not intend to animate.

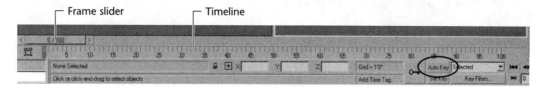

FIGURE 15.1 *Important tools in keyframe animation include the Timeline, the Auto Key button, and the Frame slider.*

Exercise 15.1: Animating the Position of an Object

1. Open **Ch15_plane01.max** from the CD-ROM. Save it to your project folder with the name *Ch15_plane02.max*. In the Perspective viewport, notice the airplane comprises one object, except for the propeller, which is its own separate object. You'll also see a bright green dummy object positioned between the wheels. These three objects are not connected in any way, so if you move any one of them, it moves independently of the others.

2. In the Perspective viewport, select Dummy_control, which is the green cube between the wheels of the airplane. On the main toolbar, click the Select and Move button. At the lower right of the display, toggle the Auto Key button on. The elements mentioned previously turn red in the display as a warning (see the Caution note).

3. Click and drag the Frame slider from Frame 0 to Frame 100. In the Perspective viewport, click on the *X*-axis restrict arrow of the Transform gizmo and move the dummy object straight forward to the edge of the Perspective viewport (**Figure 15.2**). Toggle the Auto Key button off.

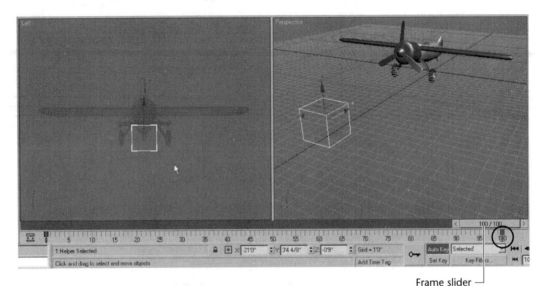

Frame slider

FIGURE 15.2 *By moving the dummy object forward at Frame 100 with the Auto Key toggled on, you create keys at Frame 0 and at Frame 100.*

4. Scrub the Frame slider back and forth along the timeline and notice the dummy object is animated from its original position to its new position over 100 frames. Drag the Frame slider back to Frame 0 when you have finished scrubbing it back and forth. You have now created an animation. Let's say you now decide, however, that the dummy object shouldn't actually start moving until Frame 20 and it should be in its final resting position at Frame 70. Click on the red rectangular key at Frame 0 and, when you see the black double-arrow cursor, drag the key to the right to Frame 20 (**Figure 15.3**). Scrub the Frame slider back and forth again and notice that the dummy sits still for the first 20 frames and then moves.

5. Click the key at Frame 100 and drag it left to Frame 70. Right-click in the Perspective viewport to activate it, and click the Play Animation button to the right of the Timeline to see the animation play back in the active viewport (**Figure 15.4**). The dummy object sits for 20 frames, moves 50 frames, and sits for 30 more frames before looping and starting again. The distance the dummy travels is the same as before, but the time between keys is less, which means it's moving faster.

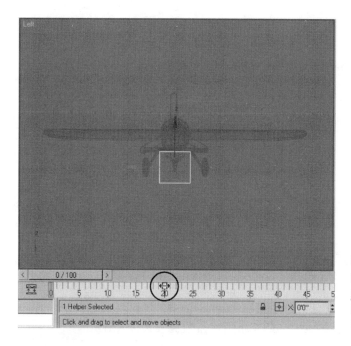

FIGURE 15.3 *Moving a key in the Timeline does not change the position of the animated object, but changes the time at which the event takes place.*

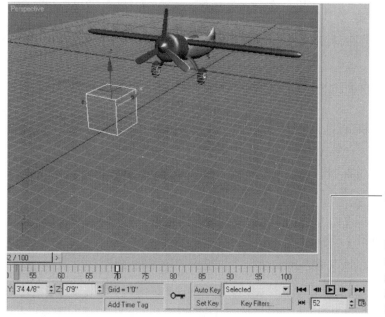

Play Animation button

FIGURE 15.4 *Keys that are closer together represent faster animation, because the same event takes less time.*

6. Position the Frame slider back to Frame 0 and save the file. It should already be called *Ch15_plane02.max*.

The animation in this simple exercise may not seem like much, but the concepts are the basis for most animation in 3ds max 7.

Animating the dummy object does not actually animate the plane, of course, but eventually the dummy object will act as the parent of the plane and pull it through the scene. This independent layer of animation is easier to edit without affecting any other animation the airplane may be required to have in the scene.

Animating the Rotation of the Dummy Object

Shortly after the dummy object comes to a stop at Frame 70, you'll want it to rotate 90 degrees counterclockwise, as seen from above. You'll use the Auto Key animation function again to generate the rotation keys. However, you do not want the rotation to start at Frame 0. Instead, it should begin at Frame 75 and end at Frame 90.

Exercise 15.2: Controlling the Start and End of an Object's Rotation

1. Open **Ch15_plane02.max** from the last exercise or from the CD-ROM. Save the file to your project folder with the name *Ch15_plane03.max*. Select the dummy_control object if it's not already selected.

2. You don't want the dummy object to start rotating until Frame 75. Drag the Frame slider to Frame 75 and right-click on the Frame Slider button. In the Create Key dialog, clear the Position and Scale checkboxes. You don't need to create keys for those two actions; you just need to create one for the rotation (**Figure 15.5**). Click OK. You do not need to have the Auto Key toggled on at this point.

3. Toggle the Auto Key button on and drag the Frame slider to Frame 90. On the main toolbar, click the Select and Rotate button and, at the bottom of the display, toggle the Absolute Mode Transform Type-In button to Offset Mode Transform Type-In. Enter *90* in the Z-axis Transform field (**Figure 15.6**) and press Enter. Toggle the Auto Key off and scrub the Frame slider back and forth to see the dummy object rotate in the Perspective viewport.

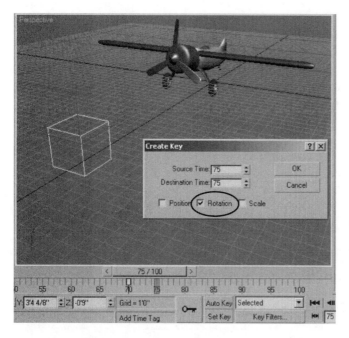

FIGURE 15.5 *You are recording the current rotation of 0 degrees for the dummy object at Frame 75 as a starting point for the rotation, which will end at Frame 90.*

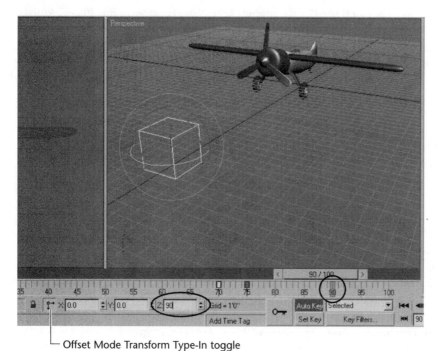

└─ Offset Mode Transform Type-In toggle

FIGURE 15.6
You can transform an object an exact amount by using the Offset Mode Transform Type-In toggle.

4. Click the Play Animation button to see the animation in the Perspective viewport. The dummy object moves forward between Frame 20 and Frame 70, pauses for five frames, and then slowly rotates for 90 degrees counterclockwise. Stop the animation and save the file; it should already be called *Ch15_plane03.max*.

tip

The keys in the timeline are color coded: Selected keys turn white, position keys are red, and rotation keys are green.

The process of creating rotation animations is the same as creating position animations when you use Auto Key mode. Each new key represents a change of a parameter in the scene at some specific point in time.

Creating a Continuously Looping Animation

You'll often want to set up an animation for an object over a few frames and then have it loop continuously throughout the entire animation. In the scene we're working on, for example, let's say you want to animate the airplane's propeller rotating about its Local *Z*-axis over 10 frames. This will simulate the propeller rotating at a slow idle speed, but you want the rotation to continue throughout the full 100 frames of animation.

To accomplish this, you'll use the Parameters Out-of-Range type in 3ds max 7, which can be accessed from Graph Editors on the main menu once you have the initial animation set.

Exercise 15.3: Applying a Parameters Out-of-Range Type

1. Open **Ch15_plane03.max** from the last exercise or from the CD-ROM. Save it to your project folder with the name *Ch15_plane04.max*. In the Perspective viewport, select the three-bladed propeller at the front of the airplane. Make sure the Frame slider is set to Frame 0.

2. On the main toolbar, make sure the Select and Rotate button is highlighted. It's apparent by looking at the Transform gizmo, especially in the Front viewport, that any rotation will be around the World axis and not the propeller's own axis. This is because the View reference coordinate system is active, and the Perspective viewport is active, which uses the World axis system. You can review Chapter 2, *Fundamental Concepts*, for more information on reference coordinate systems. In the drop-down list to the right of the Rotate button, switch from the View reference coordinate system to the Local reference coordinate system. You'll see the Rotate Transform gizmo align itself with the axis of the propeller (**Figure 15.7**).

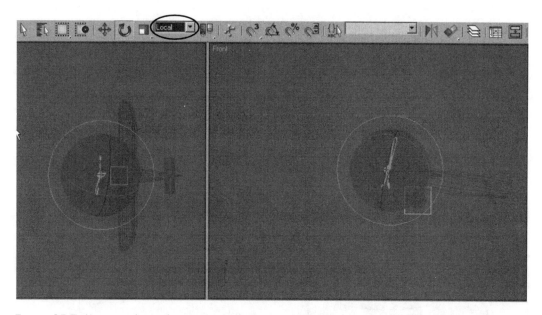

FIGURE 15.7 *You must be in the Local reference coordinate system to rotate the propeller in the correct axis.*

3. Toggle the Auto Key button on and drag the Frame slider to Frame 10. In the Perspective viewport, click on the Transform gizmo's *Z*-axis ring and drag to rotate the propeller clockwise about minus 325 degrees. As you drag, you can read the angle of rotation in the *Z*-axis Transform Type-In field near the bottom of the display. Toggle the Auto Key button off and drag the Frame slider back and forth to see the propeller rotate over 10 frames with no action in the remaining 90 frames. Return the Frame slider to Frame 0. You'll also see two green rotation keys, one at Frame 0 and one at Frame 10. On the main toolbar, set the reference coordinate system from Local back to View.

tip

You don't want to rotate the propeller 360 degrees because the position key would be the same at Frame 0 and at Frame 10, so a slight hesitation would result in the rotation.

tip

An attribute called the *Animation Controller* in 3ds max 7 has been changed to a Linear controller type on the propeller to make the rotation easier to apply in this example. You'll learn more about controllers in Chapter 16, *Controllers and Constraints: More Complexity, More Control.*

4. From the main menu, choose Graph Editors > Track View-Curve Editor (**Figure 15.8**). The left panel of the Curve Editor shows the selected object with the rotation transform highlighted. In the Track View-Curve Editor pull-down menu, choose Controller > Out-of-Range Types (**Figure 15.9**).

FIGURE 15.8 *The Out-of-Range Types options are accessible via the Track View-Curve Editor.*

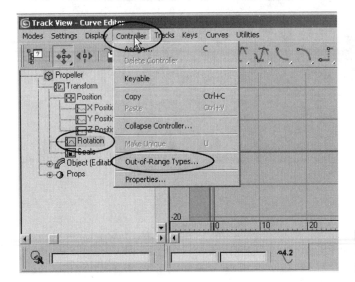

FIGURE 15.9 *Out-of-Range Types options let you generate repeating animations.*

5. In the Param Curve Out-of-Range Types dialog, click the small arrow box to the bottom right of the Cycle window (**Figure 15.10**). Click OK. Play the animation back in the Perspective viewport and notice the propeller turns smoothly and continuously over the entire range of frames.

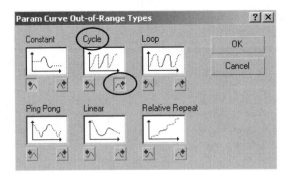

FIGURE 15.10 *The Cycle option allows the current 10 frames of animation to cycle continuously from Frame 11 to Frame 100, as indicated by the right arrow button. Clicking the left arrow button would mean that the animation is already in progress at Frame 0.*

6. Close any windows or dialogs and save the file. It should already be called *Ch15_plane04.max*.

Animating with the Out-of-Range types is much easier and more consistent than trying to set keys every 10 frames.

Keyframe animation is just a process of changing parameters at a certain point in time, while you're in Auto Key mode. To ensure that an animation begins at a certain point in time, you have learned to right-click on the Frame slider and use the Create Key dialog to record the current transform, move, rotate, or scale for the selected object. This is an important step to avoid having all of your animation start at Frame 0.

The Fundamentals of Hierarchical Linking

Two of the objects in your scene are animated, the dummy and the airplane's propeller. However, what you actually want to have happen is for all of the objects to move forward and rotate 90 degrees as if the airplane were taxiing for takeoff, all the while having the propeller rotate as if pulling the plane along.

The dummy object in the scene will handle all of the forward motion and rotation of the airplane and propeller, but at this point the three objects have no awareness of each other. You'll learn to use hierarchical linking to solve this problem. Again, hierarchical linking is a parent-child relationship between objects that is created by clicking the Select and Link button on the main toolbar, clicking on the child object, and dragging it to the parent object. As you drag, you'll see a rubber-band line stretching from the pivot point of the child object to your cursor. When the cursor is on the intended parent and you release the mouse button, the object will flash white briefly to indicate that the link has been successfully created.

Exercise 15.4: Establishing a Hierarchical Link Among Objects

1. Open **Ch15_plane04.max** from the last exercise or from the CD-ROM. Save the file to your project folder with the name *Ch15_plane05.max*. Scrub the Frames slider back and forth to make sure the animation is still intact.

2. Right-click in the Front viewport to activate it and click the Zoom Extents button on the lower right of the display to fill the viewport with the objects in the scene. On the main toolbar, click the Select and Link button (**Figure 15.11**).

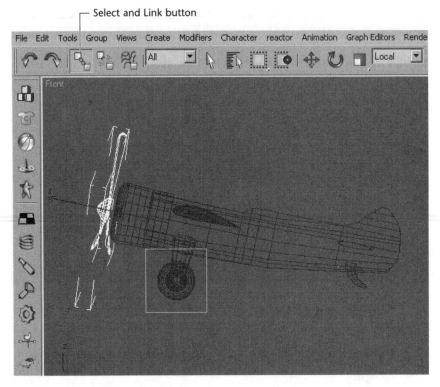

Figure 15.11 *The Select and Link button is used to establish a hierarchical link by clicking and dragging from the child to the parent object.*

3. In the Front viewport, click on the airplane and drag to the visible edge of the dummy object. You'll see the rubber band from the center of the wheel. When it is dragged over a valid object to link to, a white-and-gray box cursor appears (**Figure 15.12**). Release the mouse button; the dummy object briefly flashes white.

note

When the dummy object was created, its pivot point was aligned in the scene with the pivot point of the airplane. The airplane, on the other hand, has its pivot point aligned with the center of the pair of wheels. This ensures a natural-looking motion as the airplane turns following the action of its parent, the dummy.

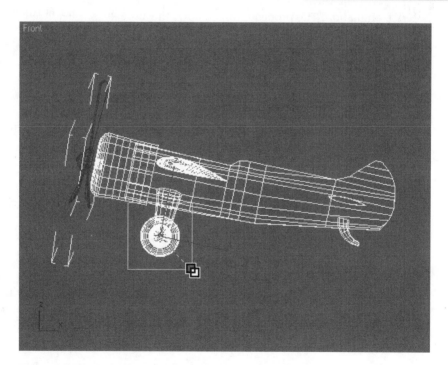

FIGURE 15.12 *Special cursors and rubber-band lines are indicators of valid objects that will accept hierarchical linking.*

4. Right-click in the Perspective viewport to activate it and click the Play Animation button. The dummy object pulls the plane forward, pauses momentarily, and then rotates 90 degrees. However, the propeller stays where it is and rotates easily, slicing through the airplane. Stop the animation and drag the Frame slider back to Frame 0. The Select and Link button should still be active. In the Front viewport, click on the propeller and drag to the airplane, and then release the mouse. The airplane flashes white. Activate the Perspective viewport and play the animation. The propeller now follows the airplane as the airplane follows the dummy. The animation should be convincing to most viewers. Stop the animation.

5. Save the file; it should already be called *Ch15_plane05.max*.

> **tip**
>
> You could have linked the propeller to the dummy object as well, and the animation would appear exactly the same as it does now. However, you may want the airplane to have other rotations not related to the dummy object. For example, the airplane may vibrate slightly or rotate forward under heavy braking, as it stops to make the turn. By linking child to parent and then parent to grandparent, the management of animation keys becomes more flexible and easier to keep track of.

By animating three objects independently and then hierarchically linking those objects, you have created a rather seamless animation.

Keep it simple! That should be your constant mantra while creating animations in 3ds max 7. Get into the habit of breaking complex animations up into independent manageable pieces and taking advantage of dummy objects and hierarchical linking to achieve the results you need.

Summary

Keyframe animation using the Auto Key function will be sufficient for most of your day-to-day production needs. The combination of the Timeline and Frame slider is conveniently located at the bottom of the display for both the initial animation and easy editing.

CHAPTER 16

Controllers and Constraints: More Complexity, More Control

In This Chapter

In the last chapter, you learned how to transform objects in the scene to make animations using the AutoCAD Key button. Manually generating the animation keys using the Auto Key function is a great way to create simple animations that require limited adjustments. But sometimes Auto Key doesn't give you the amount of control you need for more complex animations. In these cases, 3ds max 7 has animation controllers and constraints that use mathematical parameters, such as the Noise controller, which generates random animation to simulate vibrating objects, or the Path constraint, which uses 2D shapes to calculate trajectories like that of a roller coaster.

Controllers and constraints are the essence of complex animation in 3ds max 7. All objects have animation controllers assigned by default, which can be substituted for many other controllers or constraints that offer much more explicit control of how an object is animated.

In this chapter, you'll learn to replace the default controllers with other controllers and constraints that offer more power and flexibility in animating objects. Your primary concern in this chapter will be animating an airplane that taxis down the runway and adjusting its velocity along a path.

This chapter covers the following topics:

- **Animation controllers.** You'll learn to replace the default animation controllers with new constraints to animate the position of objects in the scene.
- **Track View Dope Sheet.** You'll learn to access the Dope Sheet graph editor so that you can adjust the range bar to change the length of an animation.
- **Ease curves.** You'll learn to adjust the velocity of an animated object visually by changing the curves of the graph.

Key Terms

- **Controllers.** Attributes assigned to objects or parameters for controlling animation.
- **Constraints.** Similar to controllers, except that they require other target objects in the scene to determine the animation.
- **Graph editors.** Display the animation as function curves in the Curve editor or as keys or range bars in the Dope Sheet dialog.
- **Ease curves.** Applied to the current animation of objects or parameters for a new level of adjustment while leaving the original animation intact.

Understanding Controllers and Constraints

All objects in 3ds max 7 have default animation controllers assigned to them at creation time. An animation controller, or constraint, acts as a "modifier" for the animated motion or parameters of an object. There are several types of animation controllers, which is the general term for all controllers and constraints. For example, 3D primitive objects are assigned a position controller, called *Position XYZ*, which lets you move an object freely through the scene, animated or not, with the potential of generating animation keys in any of the three axes. And the default rotation controller for the primitive objects is the Euler XYZ controller.

In the exercises in this chapter, you'll substitute a Path constraint for the default Position XYZ assigned to the dummy object. The dummy object acts as a parent to the airplane and propeller from the last chapter, and transforms them through the scene. The constraint relies on an outside object—a line in this case—to describe position changes for the dummy object. The result will be that the dummy object causes the airplane to taxi and turn onto the runway. You'll then learn to control the velocity of the animated dummy graphically as it moves along the path.

Transform animation controllers and constraints for Move, Rotate, and Scale transformations can be assigned to objects in either of two places: the Motion panel or the graph editors. All other parameters, such as the radius of a circle or the color of the material, must have the controllers and constraints assigned in the graph editors. You'll begin by learning to replace the default controllers with a new constraint on the Motion panel.

Assigning Constraints on the Motion Panel

In the scene you'll be working on, your task is to move the airplane down the taxiway, onto the runway, and into takeoff position. You'll actually be animating the position of the Dummy_control object; the hierarchically linked airplane and propeller child objects will follow along. To establish the animation path in the scene, you'll substitute a Path constraint for the default controller on the dummy object and choose a line.

You'll encounter a problem with the animation that makes the airplane turn in the wrong direction. You'll correct that by editing the line at the Vertex sub-object level and changing the first vertex to the opposite end to reverse the direction of the animation. You also need to enable the Follow option, which causes the dummy object to stay perpendicular to the path as it travels along it.

Exercise 16.1: Animating an Object with a Path Constraint

1. Open **Ch16_controller01.max** from the CD-ROM. Save it to your project folder with the name *Ch16_controller02.max*. This is a simplified landscape scene with the airplane you created in the previous chapter. There is no animation for the dummy object, but the propeller is still rotating continuously over the 100 frames. In the Camera02 viewport, select the dummy object called *Dummy_control* between the wheels of the airplane.

2. Click the Motion Panel button. On the Assign Controller rollout of the Motion panel, choose the Position: Position XYZ level from the list (**Figure 16.1**).

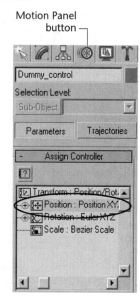

Motion Panel button

FIGURE 16.1 *Animation controllers and constraints can be assigned from the Motion panel.*

3. Click the Assign Controller button above and to the left of the list to open the Assign Position Controller dialog. Select Path Constraint from the list (**Figure 16.2**).

    You have assigned a constraint for the position of the dummy object, which requires outside information to function.

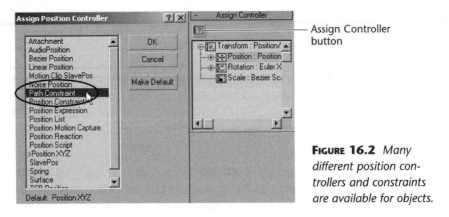

Assign Controller button

FIGURE 16.2 *Many different position controllers and constraints are available for objects.*

4. In the Path Parameters rollout, click the Add Path button and press *H*. In the Pick Object dialog, double-click *taxi_path* (**Figure 16.3**). The pivot point of the dummy object jumps to the first vertex of the path.

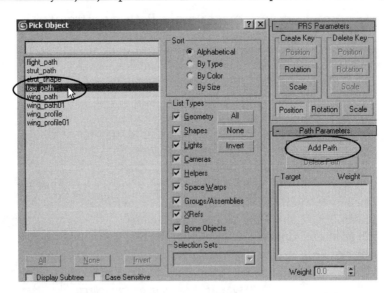

FIGURE 16.3 *You can pick a constraint path by pressing* H *and choosing a 2D shape from the list.*

The dummy object and its children are at the wrong end of the path. Animation keys were automatically created at Frame 0 and Frame 100, and if you scrub the Frame slider, you'll see the objects move to the other end of the path over the 100 frames. Let's correct this.

5. Return the Frame slider to Frame 0. On the main toolbar, click the Select Object button and, in the Top viewport, select *taxi_path*. On the Modify panel, Stack view, highlight the Vertex sub-object level. Select the vertex at the opposite end of the path from the dummy object. Right-click in the viewport and choose Make First from the quad menu (**Figure 16.4**). On the Modify panel, Stack view, click Editable Spline to exit sub-object mode.

Changing the first vertex position moves the dummy object and its children to the opposite end of the path at Frame 0.

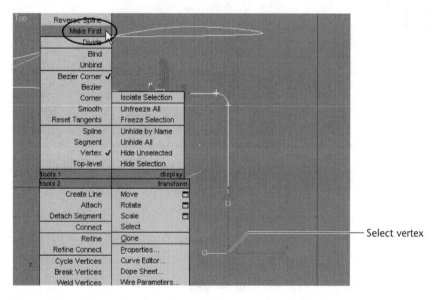

FIGURE 16.4 *The position of a shape's first vertex determines the starting point on an animation path.*

6. Scrub the Frame slider, and the airplane slides up the path and around the corner. In the Top viewport, select the dummy object and, on the Motion panel, Path Parameters rollout, select the Follow option in the Path Options section. This causes the tail of the airplane to point down the path. In the Axis section, select the Flip option (see **Figure 16.5** on the next page). Scrub the Frame slider, and the airplane moves down the path and around the corner into takeoff position.

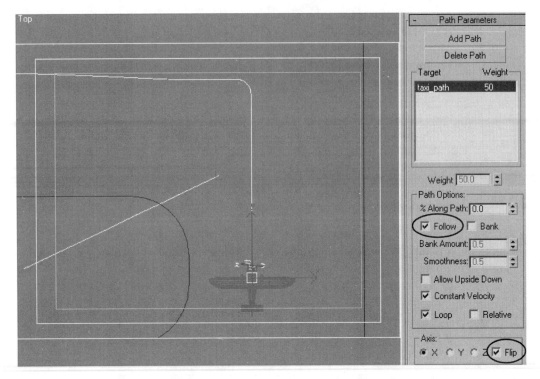

FIGURE 16.5 *Options are available to have animated objects follow or stay perpendicular to the path and to change the orientation of the object on the path.*

7. Save the file. It should already be called *Ch16_controller02.max*.

The Path constraint now has full control over the position of the dummy in the scene.

Adjusting the Length of an Animation

The Path constraint automatically animated the object over the entire length of the animation, in this case, 100 frames. Because the airplane will be taking off, you only want it to taxi in the early frames of the animation. In the next exercise, you'll learn to use the Track View Dope Sheet to adjust the animation of the dummy object using Range bars. You'll then use the Time Configuration dialog to change the overall length of the animation while keeping the current animation a constant percentage of the total.

Exercise 16.2: Using the Dope Sheet and Time Configuration

1. Open **Ch16_controller02.max** from the previous exercise or from the CD-ROM. Save it to your project folder with the name *Ch16_controller03.max*. In the Camera02 viewport, select the Dummy_control object if it's not already selected. From the main menu, choose Graphic Editors > Track View – Dope Sheet. By default, the Dope Sheet opens in Edit Keys mode, showing the animation keys for the selected object, which in this case is the dummy. On the Track View-Dope Sheet, click the Edit Ranges button to display a black line representing the length of the animation. The small white boxes at each end represent the start and the end of the animation (**Figure 16.6**).

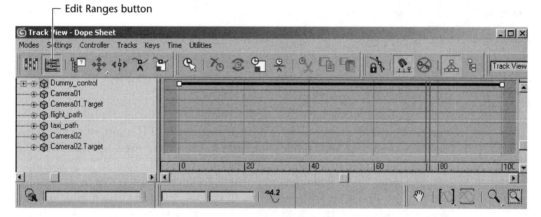

FIGURE 16.6 *Range bars, which are found in the Dope Sheet, can be used to adjust the length of an object's animation.*

2. In the Dope Sheet, move the cursor over the white box at the left end of the range bar. The cursor will change from an arrow to a small white box with a left-facing arrow. Click and drag the white box to the right until the yellow line is at Frame 20. Click the white box at the right end of the range bar and drag left until the yellow line is at Frame 40. Click on the Play Animation button at the lower right of the display. The airplane taxis only from Frame 20 to Frame 40. Stop the animation. Move the cursor over the middle of the black range bar; it turns to a small white box with arrows pointing in two directions. Click on the black range bar and slide left until the left yellow line is located at Frame 10 (see **Figure 16.7** on the next page). You have shifted the entire 20-frame animation to start at Frame 10 and end at Frame 30. Close the Dope Sheet.

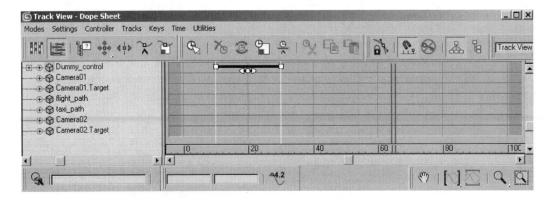

Figure 16.7 *You can move each end of the range bar independently to adjust the length of the object's animation or slide the entire range bar over time.*

Eventually you'll have the airplane take off and fly in a loop. Let's assume that you determined the entire animation needs to be longer and that the airplane taxis too fast.

3. At the bottom right of the display, click the Time Configuration button. In this dialog, you could change the end time or the length of the current animation, but this would only add additional frames to the end of the animation without adjusting the timing of the airplane animation, which you want to be proportionately longer to the total animation. In the Time Configuration dialog, Animation section, click the Re-scale Time button. In the Re-scale Time dialog, New section, enter *200* in the End Time field and click OK (**Figure 16.8**). Click OK again to close the Time Configuration dialog. This doubles the length of the entire animation, while also rescaling the airplane animation to be twice as long.

4. Play the animation. The airplane takes twice as long to taxi up to position and there are now 140 frames in which to animate the plane taking off. Stop the animation playback and drag the Frames slider back to Frame 0. Save the file; it should already be called *Ch16_controller03.max*.

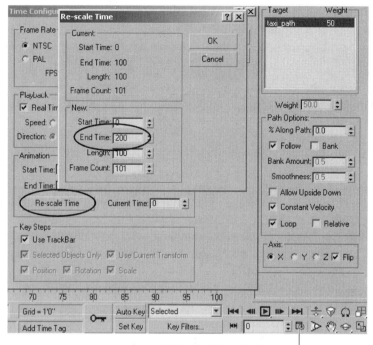

Time Configuration button ⌐

FIGURE 16.8 *Rescaling time increases the length of the animation and rescales any existing animation proportionately.*

Learning to Control the Velocity of Objects

In the last chapter, you learned you could control the speed of animated objects by adjusting the spacing of the animation keys in time and that position keys that are close together on the timeline represent faster motion.

However, in complex animations with many keys, adjusting the speed of an object becomes complicated, especially when it comes to changing the velocity of an object between keys. For example, if I want an object to start moving slowly, gradually build up speed, slow almost to a stop, and then quickly speed up again, working with the animation keys alone is not a practical solution.

One solution is to use Ease curves, which allow you to graphically adjust the velocity of animated objects. You'll learn more about them in the next exercise.

Applying an Ease Curve to Control Animation

Ease curves are superimposed over existing animation in the Track View Curve Editor to give you graphical control of velocity changes for the underlying animation.

In the next exercise, you'll use Ease curves to adjust the velocity of the taxiing airplane so that it gradually increases speed from its starting position, and then slows to make the turn. One advantage of using Ease curves is that if you make a mess of the animation, you can simply remove the curve and start again without affecting the original animation.

Exercise 16.3: Adjusting the Path Constraint Animation

1. Open **Ch16_controller03.max** from the last exercise or from the CD-ROM. Save it to your project folder with the name *Ch16_controller04.max*. On the main toolbar, click the Select by Name button and in the Select Objects list, double-click Dummy_control.

   The dummy object is animated with a Path constraint to move at a constant velocity along the 2D shape. You'll apply an Ease curve to visually adjust the velocity of the dummy object and its children.

2. From the main menu, choose Graphic Editors > Track View – Curve Editor. The graph shows a straight-line curve from Frame 20 to Frame 60, representing a constant velocity for the movement of the dummy object (**Figure 16.9**). While it's possible to modify this curve to change the velocity of the object, it's better not to change the original animation.

tip

The Track View Curve Editor has its own navigation tools, such as zoom and pan, located in the lower-right corner of the dialog.

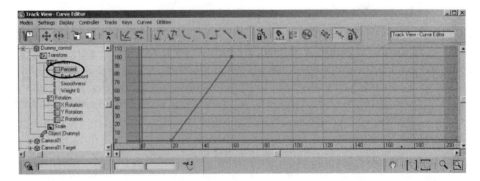

FIGURE 16.9 *The initial Curve Editor displays the position change, expressed as a percentage, of the dummy object along the path.*

3. In the Curve Editor's object-controller list on the left, click on the word *Percent* to ensure this is the only controller highlighted. In the Curve Editor dialog, click the Curves menu option and choose Apply – Ease Curve from the menu (**Figure 16.10**).

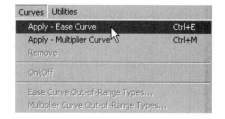

FIGURE 16.10 *Applying an Ease Curve leaves the underlying animation intact.*

4. You probably didn't notice anything change when you applied the Ease curve. However, a small plus sign (+) appeared in a circle to the left of Percent in the object list. Click on the plus sign to the left of Percent to expand it and gain access to the Ease curve. You now see two curves, Percent and Ease curve. Click Ease curve in the list to highlight it in yellow and to display a graph that represents the underlying constant velocity animation.

5. In the Curve Editor graph, click and drag the blue double-vertical bar to the right to scrub the animation and determine when the plane starts to round the corner, approximately at Frame 47. In the Curve Editor dialog, click the Add Keys button and pick the green curve line where it intersects the blue double-vertical bar to add a new key. Then, click the Move Keys button to exit Add Keys mode to avoid inadvertently adding any more keys (**Figure 16.11**).

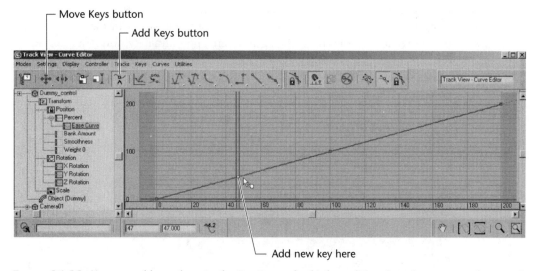

FIGURE **16.11** *You can add new keys to the Ease curve for further editing, but always remember to exit Add Keys mode when you are finished.*

6. Simply adding keys does not change the animation. You must also edit the curve. Click and drag the new key downward until the right-hand numeric field reads approximately 22.5. The curve is now flat at the left and, if you play the animation back in the Camera02 viewport, you'll see that the airplane hesitates for about 10 frames where the curve is flat, and then proceeds rapidly to the end. Stop the animation playback (**Figure 16.12**).

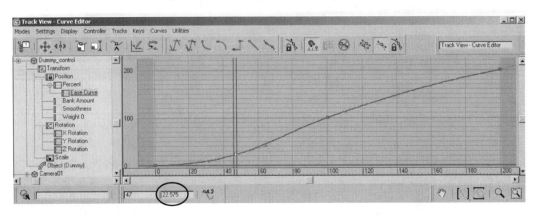

FIGURE 16.12 *Moving the new key at Frame 47 to about 22.5 percent along the path flattens the curve and slows the velocity.*

7. Highlight the number in the right numeric field, enter *50* and press Enter to move the key up to 50 percent of the way along the path. Click and move the blue tangency handles until the handles are approximately horizontal to flatten the curve near the key (**Figure 16.13**). Play the animation. The new curve causes the airplane to pause as it turns the corner and then accelerate to the end. Stop the animation.

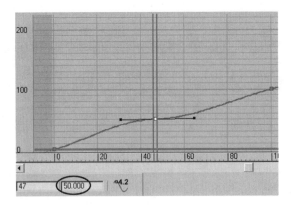

FIGURE 16.13 *Keys can be moved and tangency handles can be adjusted to modify the curve and change the velocity of the animation.*

8. Close the Track View Curve Editor and save the file. It should already be called *Ch16_controller04.max*.

The curve is your visual control of the velocity of the object. Where an Ease curve is flat, there is no forward velocity. Where the curve is steep on the right, the object is moving fast. Should the curve slope down to the right, the object would move backwards.

Summary

Animation controllers and constraints provide you options that go far beyond simple key framing by changing the fundamental parameters available for animation. They also let you use outside objects, such as paths in the case of a Path constraint, to set the initial animation.

In the next chapter, you'll learn more about velocity adjustment curves, more flexible options for hierarchical linking, and special animation tools called *solvers* for even more complex animations.

CHAPTER 17

Hierarchical Linking: Ease Meets Complexity

In This Chapter

In the last chapter, you learned how to apply Ease curves, which adjust the horizontal graph component, or time, of the Track View Curve Editor, thus giving you control over the velocity of animated objects. In this chapter, you'll practice another method of controlling velocity—applying Multiplier curves. This type of curve adjusts the vertical graph component, or value, of the Track View Curve Editor, thus providing graphical control of animated objects. Using Multiplier curves, you can increase the velocity of an object by adjusting a rotation-scaling value that is attached to the current velocity.

When you adjust an Ease curve to slow an animation down at a given point in time, it must speed up somewhere else, because the overall animation time remains the same. When you adjust a Multiplier curve to slow down or speed up an animation, it simply applies a scale factor to the current values and does not adjust the timing of the animation.

While Ease curves and Multiplier curves can often be used interchangeably, the fact that Ease curves adjust time and Multiplier curves adjust value offers added flexibility.

In this chapter, you'll also work with an animation controller called the *Attachment controller*. You have already learned the fundamentals of hierarchical linking; the Attachment controller enhances your ability to make full use of linking in more complex animations. In 3ds max 7, a hierarchically linked object can have only one parent at a time, but you'll learn to pass off the hierarchical link from one parent to another parent at any point in time during the animation. You'll use it to make the airplane take off and fly a loop over the runway; one hierarchical link will cause the airplane to taxi, the other will take over and fly the loop. This again allows you to keep your animations "modular" so that you can change one aspect of the animation without affecting the other aspects.

The scene you'll use in this chapter contains the hangar you used in Chapter 3, *2D Shapes: Starting with the Foundation*, placed alongside the runway with the addition of some hangar doors. You'll learn about a special attribute to hierarchical linking that will allow you to slide one door closed and have the others trail along in telescoping fashion to simulate the mechanism on real sliding-door systems.

This chapter covers the following topics:

- **Multiplier curves.** You'll learn to apply Multiplier curves to existing animations to scale the values of the underlying animation.

- **Link constraint.** You'll learn a method of passing the hierarchical link from one parent to another during an animation for more flexibility in managing simple animation segments that can be tied together in a continuous complex animation.

- **HD solver.** You'll learn to apply an Inverse Kinematics (IK) solver to hierarchically linked objects to change the relationship between the objects so that you can establish restrictions. For example, object A slides, and when it reaches a certain distance, object B slides along with it. Both objects can slide only a specific distance. A telescope is a good example of this type of mechanism.

Key Terms

- **Inverse kinematics.** Hierarchically linked objects can be set to operate from top-down (forward kinematics) or the bottom-up (inverse kinematics). Inverse kinematics enables the animated child object to drive the parent or parents. For example, you could animate a crate moving from a dock to a ship, then have the booms of a crane automatically follow the box's movement. This eliminates the need to keyframe all the objects independently.

- **Solver.** An animation solver controls the relationship of hierarchically linked objects to restrict or allow given transformations.

Applying Multiplier Curves

In this first exercise, you'll use the scene from the last chapter in which the airplane is taxiing down the runway, ready for takeoff. The animation of the propeller has been slowed significantly, so your first task will be to increase the speed of the rotation, at first only slightly as the plane is taxiing, and then considerably faster as it takes off. You'll apply a Multiplier curve to the existing animation much in the same way you applied an Ease curve to change the velocity of the dummy object that pulls the airplane down the path.

Exercise 17.1: Increasing the Speed of the Propeller

1. Open the file from the CD-ROM called **Ch17_attachment01.max.** Save it to your project folder with the name *Ch17_attachment02.max*. Click the Play Animation button to see the plane taxi forward in the Camera02 viewport. Notice the propeller is turning very slowly throughout the entire animation. Stop the animation and drag the Frame slider back to Frame 0.

2. In the Top viewport, select the propeller. Notice two keys are in the Timeline, representing a rotation of about 355 degrees over 200 frames. From the main menu, choose Graph Editors > Track View – Curve Editor. In the left column, the Y Rotation of the Euler XYZ controller should be highlighted. In the Curve Editor dialog, click Curves and choose Apply – Multiplier Curve from the menu (**Figure 17.1**).

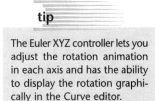

tip

The Euler XYZ controller lets you adjust the rotation animation in each axis and has the ability to display the rotation graphically in the Curve editor.

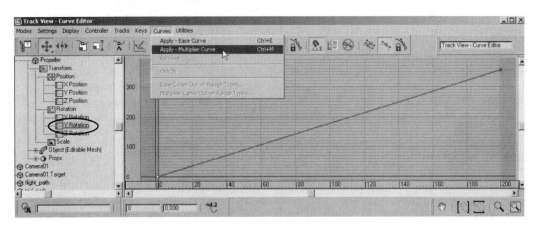

FIGURE 17.1 *Apply a Multiplier curve to the Y-rotation axis of the propeller.*

3. Click on the plus sign (+) to the left of Y Rotation on the list panel to expand Y Rotation. Highlight Multiplier Curve. A horizontal green line appears in the graph to the right, indicating a rotation multiplier of one throughout the entire animation. In the Curve Editor dialog, click the Add Keys button and click on the multiplier line near Frame 80 (**Figure 17.2**). Click the Move Keys button to exit Add Keys mode.

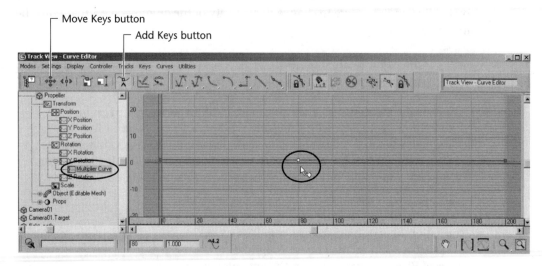

FIGURE 17.2 *Adding a new key to the multiplier line will act as an anchor at Frame 80.*

4. Select the key at the right end of the multiplier line. Notice in the numeric fields at the lower left of the graph that at Frame 200 the multiplier value is 1.000. Highlight the Multiplier Value field, enter *20*, and press Enter. The multiplier line now slopes upward in a curve from Frame 80 to Frame 200 (**Figure 17.3**). Play the animation and you will continue to see the propeller rotate slowly until Frame 80, and then the rotation speed will increase until it is 20 times its original speed. Stop the animation.

5. Close all dialogs and save the file. It should already be called *Ch17_attachment02.max*. The Multiplier curve does not mimic the underlying information like the Ease curve does; instead, it only scales current animation values.

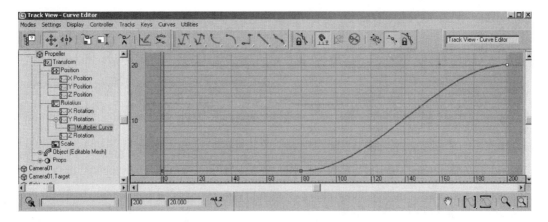

FIGURE 17.3 *The Multiplier curve has Bézier tangency information in the keys by default, so the effects are not abrupt.*

Switching Hierarchical Parents

As mentioned earlier, a hierarchically linked object can have one, and only one, parent throughout an animation. If a child object is linked to a parent object, and you link the child to another object, the new object becomes the parent, and any relationship of the child with the previous parent object is discarded, resulting in a completely different animation.

The only way to overcome this default hierarchical-linking limitation is to apply a Link constraint, which lets you pass hierarchical link control from one parent to another at any point in the animation.

Our current scene contains a dummy object with a Path controller that is animated along a looping path over the runway. This dummy starts at Frame 0 and ends at Frame 200, so in the following exercise you'll adjust the start time to be a few frames after the airplane has finished its taxiing. You'll then apply the Link constraint to the fuselage and pass the link at the appropriate frame so that the airplane flies a loop and lands again.

Exercise 17.2: Applying a Link Constraint to a Transform

1. Open **Ch17_attachment02.max** from the previous exercise or from the CD-ROM. Save it to your project folder with the name *Ch17_attachment03.max*. Right-click in the Camera02 viewport to activate it if it's not already, and press *C* to open the Select Camera dialog (**Figure 17.4**). Double-click on Camera01 in the list to switch to a camera looking down the runway. Play the animation. The dummy moves down the path, up in front of the camera, where it stalls and falls back slightly before continuing on. Stop the animation.

FIGURE 17.4 *Switch to a camera viewport looking down the runway at a dummy object traveling along a path.*

2. Drag the Frame slider back to Frame 0. In the Camera01 viewport, select the dummy object called *Dummy_fly*. From the main menu, choose Graph Editors > Track View – Dope Sheet. On the Dope Sheet, click the Edit Ranges button. Click and drag the white box on the left end of the range bar and drag it to the right to Frame 80 (**Figure 17.5**). Close the Track View Dope Sheet.

3. Play the animation. Dummy_fly sits at the beginning of the path for 80 frames and then takes off and flies the loop shortly after the airplane arrives at that position. Stop the animation and drag the Frame slider to Frame 0. In the Top viewport, select the airplane. On the Motion panel, Assign Controller rollout, highlight Transform at the top of the list. Click the

tip

As you adjust the position of the end of the range bar, you can see the corresponding key moving in the timeline to accurately place it on the correct frame.

Assign Controller button and double-click Link Constraint in the Assign Transform Controller dialog (**Figure 17.6**). The airplane will disappear from the viewports.

Edit Ranges button

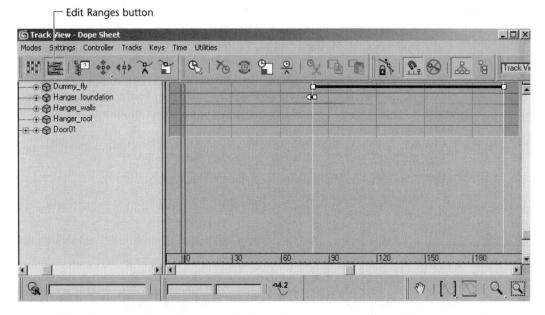

FIGURE 17.5 *Shortening the range bar in the Dope Sheet compresses the existing animation into a shorter time.*

Assign Controller button

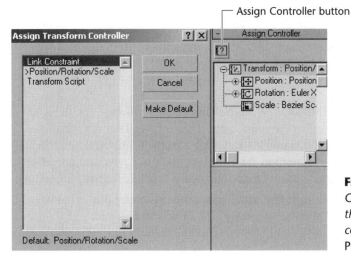

FIGURE 17.6 *A Link Constraint replaces the default Transform controller called Position/Rotation/Scale.*

4. In the Link Params rollout, click the Add Link button. In the Top viewport, pick the small dummy at the start of the taxi path called *Dummy_control*. On the main toolbar, click the Align button. In the Top viewport, pick Dummy_control again. In the Align Selection dialog, Align Orientation section, click the Y axis checkbox (**Figure 17.7**). Click OK. The Link constraint establishes a hierarchical link with the Fuselage as a child of Dummy_control at Frame 0. The Align tool realigns the pivot point of one object relative to the other and orients the airplane to face down the path.

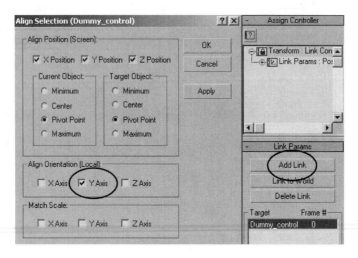

FIGURE 17.7 *Applying a Link constraint with no target object causes the selected object to go to the 0,0,0 World coordinate position, because an object with no specific parent is always linked to the world.*

5. Drag the Frame slider to Frame 70. In the Link Params rollout, click the Add Link button and, in the Top viewport, select Dummy_fly. Dummy_fly shows up as a target in the list at Frame 70. Right-click in the Camera01 viewport to activate it and play the animation. The airplane taxis to a stop, the propeller speeds up, and the airplane takes off and loops to a landing. Stop the animation.

6. Click the Add Link button in the Link Params rollout to exit that mode and save the file. It should already be called *Ch17_attachment03.max*.

Applying Inverse Kinematics and Animation Solvers

In inverse kinematics, the child object controls the chain of hierarchically linked objects. The best real-world example of this is probably the relationship between the hand, the forearm, and the upper arm. When you move your hand—the last in the family ancestry of the three "linked" objects—your forearm and upper arm both move accordingly in relation to one another.

In 3ds max 7, you can set up an Inverse Kinematics system using an animation solver, which will let you assign certain restrictions to the objects. For example, you wouldn't want your elbow to bend backwards if your hand tries to move too far, so you'd want to assign some restrictions to the elbow's movement.

Animation solvers restrict the motion of hierarchically linked joints in one of two ways: either in the rotational axes, like the arm-and-hand example, or in sliding joints. Sliding joints function in much the same way as a telescoping automobile antenna. You only want the top segment of the antenna to extend so far before it starts to pull the next segment along with it. Then when each segment is fully extended, you can't pull the entire object any farther.

In the next exercise, you'll practice controlling the sliding joints of hierarchically attached objects by applying an IK solver new to 3ds max 7 called the *History Dependent (HD) solver*. The HD solver is the only solver that allows you the control of sliding joints that you need for this example.

You'll work with three sliding doors for the airplane hangar. The HD solver lets you to manipulate the last door in the chain within a restricted range and have the other two doors respond accordingly.

Exercise 17.3: Creating a Sliding Door System

1. Open **Ch17_attachment03.max** from the last exercise or from the CD-ROM. Save it to your project folder with the name *Ch17_attachment04.max*. On the main toolbar, click on the drop-down arrow to the right of the Named Selection Sets field and choose Hanger from the list (**Figure 17.8**).

> **tip**
>
> The objects must be hierarchically linked before the HD solver will recognize the objects.

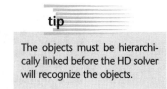

FIGURE 17.8 *A Named Selection Set has been created for all of the objects that belong to the airplane hangar.*

2. From the main menu, choose Tools > Isolate Selection, or press Alt + Q, to isolate all objects in the scene except the hangar. Click the Zoom Extents All Selected button to fill the orthographic viewports with the hangar objects. Right-click in the Top viewport to activate it, and use the Zoom Region tool to zoom in on the doors. The three doors have been linked hierarchically. The outermost door is a child of the middle door, and the middle door is a child of the inner door. Select the outer door called *Door03* (**Figure 17.9**).

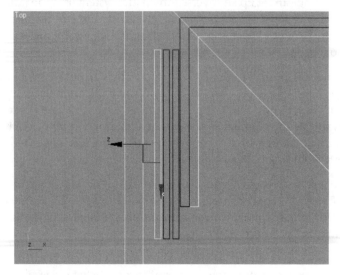

FIGURE 17.9 *You must be zoomed in close to the doors in the Top viewport to apply the HD solver.*

3. From the main menu, choose Animation > IK Solvers > HD Solver (**Figure 17.10**). As you move the cursor in the Top viewport, you'll see a rubber-band line attached to the pivot point of the door. Pick the edge of Door01, which is the inner door. Three diamond shaped "bones" have been created at the center of each door. These bones are the part of the HD solver that restricts the sliding joint.

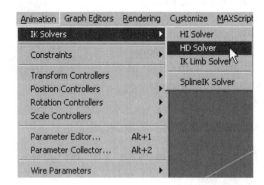

FIGURE 17.10 *The HD solver is one of four different solvers you can apply in 3ds max 7 to set up an Inverse Kinematics system.*

4. In the Top viewport, select Door01. On the Hierarchy panel, click the IK button and, in the Rotational Joints rollout, clear the Active checkbox for all three axes (**Figure 17.11**). Repeat this process for the other two doors to make certain all Rotation axes are turned off, or you may get unwanted and uncontrollable rotations.

Hierarchy Panel button

tip

IK solvers have the rotational joints set to active by default. You must deactivate the rotational joints for all objects in the hierarchical chain, or you risk uncontrolled rotations while setting up the restrictions.

5. In the Top viewport, select Door02, the middle door. On the Hierarchy panel, expand the Sliding Joints rollout. On the main toolbar, set the reference coordinate system to Parent. The solver's axes are determined by the object's hierarchical parent object. Click the Active checkbox for the *X*-axis and then click the Limited checkbox for the *X*-axis. In the To field, enter 9′4″ and press Enter (**Figure 17.12**).

FIGURE 17.11
Rotational joints are active by default; sliding joints are not.

FIGURE 17.12 *You are restricting the door to slide only in the positive X axis to a maximum of 9′4″.*

6. In the Object Parameters rollout, Sliding Joints section, click the Copy button to copy the sliding joint parameters to a buffer. In the Top viewport, select Door03 and, in the Object Parameters rollout, Sliding Joints section, click the Paste to button to paste the joint restrictions to the door.

7. Right-click in the Left viewport, click the Select and Move button on the main toolbar and slide the door in the left viewport along the *X*-axis. The door will only slide to a certain point and stop, but it will also automatically drag the middle door along with it as soon as it has reached the restricted distance. You cannot rotate or move the doors in any other axes.

8. Return the door to its original position. Click the Auto Key button to highlight it red and drag the Frame slider to Frame 50. In the Left viewport, move the door as far as it will go to the right and toggle the Auto Key button off. Play the animation. The doors slide closed over the first 50 frames of the animation. Stop the animation.

9. Save the file. It should already be called *Ch17_attachment04.max*.

Restricting the sliding joints of the hangar doors makes it much easier to create animations without manipulating and setting keys for all three doors.

Summary

By applying Multiplier curves, Link constraints, and HD solvers to objects in your scene, you have managed to create animations that are complex but easily edited.

By breaking animations into separate components—for example, one animation taxis the plane and the other animation lets the plane take off and fly around—you have simplified layers of control that you can adjust.

While many of the changes you made to this animation could have been executed in the Timeline, it's important that you learn to use the Track View Curve Editor and Track View Dope Sheet for a more global graphical view of the animation, and for access to controls like Ease curves and Multiplier curves that let you superimpose changes over existing animations.

PART VI

Special Effects

CHAPTER 18

Reactor Dynamics: Collision Detection

In This Chapter

There are many times when keyframing your animations is just not practical, because you would have to assign a key for almost every frame to get convincing motion. For example, if you want to create an animation that includes tumbling objects or a flag waving in the wind, it would require many attempts to keyframe the necessary randomness of the motion.

However, 3ds max 7 includes a component called *Reactor*, which calculates collisions between objects in an animated scene based on real-world physics. Using the Reactor dynamics and collision detection toolset, you can simply set the starting point and the object behavior and let the software do the work. A Reactor simulation automatically has gravity associated with it, and you can add other forms of forces, such as deflectors and wind.

Before you can use objects in a Reactor simulation, you must first assign them to collections that describe the basic characteristics of each object. For example, an object such as a flagpole, with a hard surface and defined shape, would be assigned as a rigid body object. An object that represents a soft shape, such as a flag, would be assigned as a cloth object, or perhaps a soft body object. Some objects, such as cloth and soft body objects, also require that special Reactor modifiers be added before they can be assigned to a specific collection.

Once objects are part of a collection, they must be assigned specific properties, such as mass and friction or elasticity for rigid body objects, and stiffness and air resistance for cloth objects.

There are also world variables that need to be assigned, such as the strength and direction of gravity forces or the collision tolerance, which is a mathematical field around each object that determines how close objects must be before the collisions are calculated.

This chapter covers the following topics:

- **Reactor collections.** You'll learn to assign objects in 3ds max 7 to specific Reactor collections that determine the general type of object used in the simulations.

- **Reactor modifiers.** You'll apply special Reactor modifiers that let you assign more detailed parameters that describe the characteristics of the object.

- **Reactor preview.** You'll learn to use the Preview window in Reactor, which lets you test your simulations without committing to a final animation.

Key Terms

- **World Scale**. This value sets a scale factor for 3ds max 7's force of gravity to that of the real world, roughly 32 feet per second squared in U.S. units.

- **Collision Tolerance**. This important setting in Reactor calculations is the distance around objects where the calculations are performed. It should be no less than 1/40th of the World Scale value for reliable calculations.

Using Reactor to Simulate Collision Detection

In this section, you'll work with a scene containing the airplane you created previously, which is circling a hangar, with, of all things, a pig suspended from its belly. Boxes are piled at the end of the runway. There is also a flagpole holding a flag made of what looks like a sheet of plywood with an imaginary country's emblem painted on it.

You'll learn to use the Reactor in 3ds max 7 to easily create animations that would be extremely difficult to accomplish manually. The pig will fall from the plane and topple the boxes, and the flag will flap lazily in the breeze.

Setting up Rigid Body Collections

The first type of Reactor collisions you'll learn about, rigid bodies, require you to add the object to a collection and change the properties of the objects. This first exercise makes the pig fall from the plane under the influence of gravity. The pig must belong to a Rigid Body collection before it will be recognized by Reactor calculations, and its weight properties must be adjusted to make it fall from the plane.

Exercise 18.1: Creating Object Collections and Adjusting Properties

1. Open **Ch18_reactor01.max** from the CD-ROM. Save it to your project folder with the name *Ch18_reactor02.max*. Play the animation. The airplane circles overhead with a small pink pig suspended from the airplane's belly. Stop the animation and return the Frame slider to Frame 0.

2. In the Front viewport, select the pig (between the wheels of the airplane), which has been hierarchically linked to the fuselage. In the Reactor toolbar on the left side of the display, click the Create Rigid Body Collection button. The Rigid Body Collection icon appears over the pig in all viewports. On the Modify panel, Pig has been added to the Rigid Bodies area, indicating it's a member of that collection (**Figure 18.1**).

Create Rigid Body Collection button   Rigid Body Collection icon

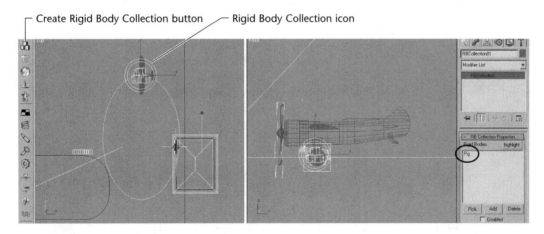

FIGURE 18.1 *An object must belong to a Reactor collection to be included in a simulation.*

3. In the Front viewport, select the pig. On the lower left of the Reactor toolbar, located at the left side of the display, click the Open Property Editor button. In the Rigid Body Properties dialog, enter *300* in the Mass field. In the Simulation Geometry rollout, click the Bounding Box radio button (**Figure 18.2**). Close the Rigid Body Properties dialog.

tip

Simulation Geometry lets you choose the type of surface used in collision simulations. For example, you have chosen Bounding Box for the pig, so the calculations are based on a box around the extremes of the pig for fast, efficient processing. A more accurate method that would use the actual pig geometry would be Concave Mesh. The concave areas under the pig's head and between the pig's feet would then be used to define the collisions and could take considerably longer to calculate.

Open Property Editor button

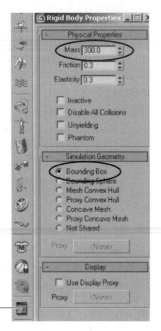

FIGURE 18.2 *Reactor objects must have properties assigned before they'll behave properly in a simulation.*

4. On the Utilities panel, Utilities rollout, click the Reactor button. In the Preview & Animation rollout, click the Preview in Window button. When the Reactor Real-Time Preview window appears, press *P*. A tiny pink pig falls straight down because of the pull of gravity (**Figure 18.3**). Press *P* again to toggle the preview off.

tip

You can change the display drivers if you need to. From the main menu, choose Customize > Preferences, and then click the Viewports tab and the Choose Driver button.

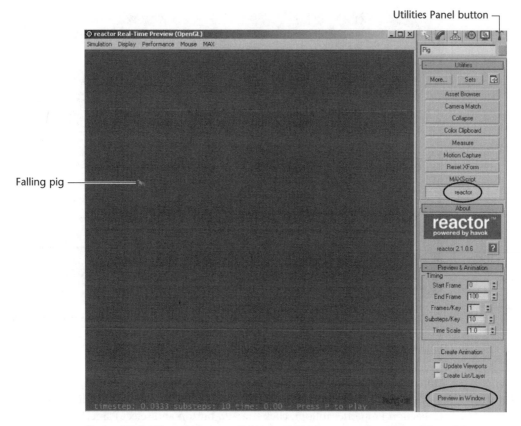

FIGURE 18.3 *If you have your 3ds max 7 display set to OpenGL or Direct 3D, you can preview the simulations in a separate window.*

Having a pig fall downward through the scene is not a particularly tricky animation, and is certainly not what you wanted. To remedy this, you'll place a Reactor plane in the scene that simulates a surface that is coplanar with the ground plane.

5. In the Reactor toolbar, click the Plane button (the checkered pattern button, sixth from the top of the bar). This opens the Helpers panel, and toggles on the Plane button in the Object Type rollout. In this rollout, click the AutoGrid checkbox. Then in the Camera02 viewport, click on the runway to place the Plane01 icon on the ground surface (see **Figure 18.4** on the next page). Clear the AutoGrid checkbox.

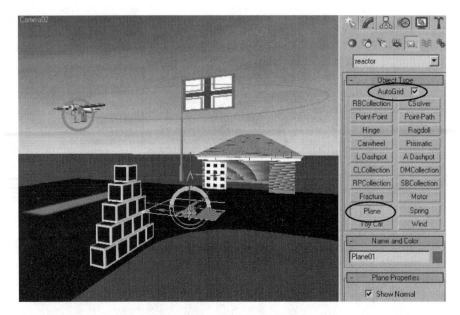

Figure 18.4 *The Plane button located on the Reactor toolbar opens the Helpers panel so that you can access the AutoGrid option, which lets you place objects on surfaces based on the direction of the face normals under the cursor.*

6. On the main toolbar, click the Select Object button. In the Camera02 viewport, pick the RBCollection01 icon that surrounds the pig. On the Modify panel, RB Collection Properties rollout, click the Add button and select Plane01 in the Select Rigid Bodies dialog to add the plane to the Rigid Body collection (**Figure 18.5**). On the Utilities panel, Reactor Preview & Animation rollout, click the Preview in Window button and then press *P*. The pig falls and bounces slightly as it strikes the Reactor plane.

    You can play the simulation again by clicking on the Simulation button in the Reactor Real-Time Preview window, choosing Reset, and then pressing *P* again. You can also zoom and pan in the window for a closer view of the falling pig. Close the Preview window.

7. Select the pig by clicking the Select by Name button on the main toolbar. Click the Open Property Editor button in the Reactor toolbar, enter *2.0* in the Elasticity field, and press Enter. Click the Preview & Window button. A World Analysis warning appears, stating that the Elasticity number is unrealistic (**Figure 18.6**). Click the Continue button and press *P* to see the pig bounce considerably higher when it hits the plane. Close the Preview window, and enter *1* in the Elasticity field of the Rigid Body Properties dialog, and press Enter. Close the dialog.

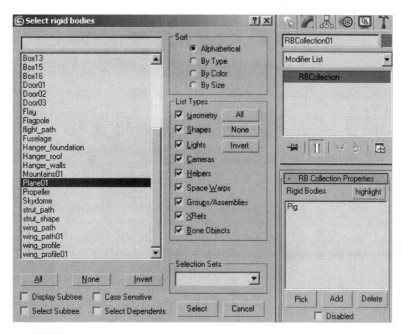

FIGURE 18.5 *Plane01 must be added to the Rigid Body collection to be included in the simulation along with the pig.*

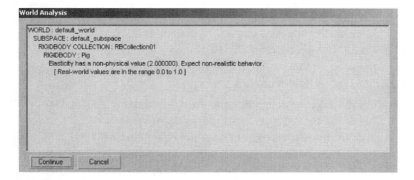

FIGURE 18.6 *If you enter unrealistic values in the simulation, the Reactor warns you that the values are unrealistic, but it still lets you try the simulation.*

8.   Save the file; it should already be called *Ch18_reactor02.max*.

Animating a pig falling is usually not difficult, but getting it to bounce convincingly could be time-consuming.

Performing Simulations Using Animated Objects

You've applied a Reactor simulation to a stationary object, the pig. What you'll learn to do next is have the pig fall from the circling airplane and tumble into the stack of boxes on the runway. This requires the pig to fall, not straight down, but on a trajectory based on the speed of the airplane. So the pig will have some forward velocity, provided by the motion of the airplane.

So far you've been calculating simulations from Frame 0 to Frame 100, the default settings for Reactor. In the next exercise, you'll start the simulation at Frame 22 and have it calculate to Frame 200, the last frame in the animation. The simulation will use the motion of the pig at Frame 21 and incorporate that velocity and direction in the calculations.

The boxes in the scene will also have to be added to the Rigid Body collection and will need to have their properties set to be included in the simulation.

Exercise 18.2: Adjusting the Simulation Timing

1. Open **Ch18_reactor02.max** from the previous exercise or from the CD-ROM. Save it to your project folder with the name *Ch18_reactor03.max*. In the Camera02 viewport, select the RBCollection01 icon. On the Modify panel, RB Collection Properties rollout, click the Add button. In the Select Rigid Bodies dialog, highlight Box01 through Box16 in the list and click the Select button to add the pile of boxes to the Rigid Body collection.

2. On the main toolbar, click the drop-down arrow beside Named Selection Sets and select Boxes from the list. On the Reactor toolbar, click the Open Property Editor button. In the Physical Properties rollout, enter *1.0* in the Mass field and press Enter. Enter *0.7* in the Elasticity field and press Enter. You can leave the Friction at the default setting of *0.3*. In the Simulation Geometry rollout, click the Bounding Box radio button (**Figure 18.7**). Close the dialog.

Next you'll change the timing of the simulation to create the pig's trajectory and include in the simulation all of the frames from your animation.

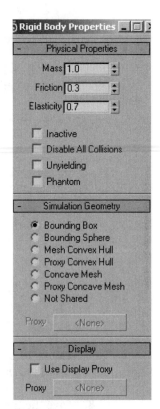

FIGURE 18.7 *Change the properties of the boxes to a mass of 1 kilogram with increased elasticity.*

3. On the Utilities panel, Preview & Animation rollout, Timing section, enter *22* in the Start Frame field and press Enter. Enter *200* in the End Frame field and press Enter (**Figure 18.8**). Click the Preview in Window button and press *P*. Notice that the boxes seem to explode long before the pig hits them.

The flying boxes are the result of the Collision Tolerance field in the World Scale section of the Utilities panel being set to almost 4 inches, which is the default setting. Collision Tolerance is the field around each object where the collision detection actually takes place. The boxes have been stacked so that there is a 1-inch space around each box, separating it from the next box. This confuses the simulation and they explode prematurely. Let's fix that.

4. Close the Preview window, and on the Utilities panel enter *1"* in the Col. Tolerance field. Press Enter. This value is approximately 1/40th of the World Scale value directly above it, the minimum acceptable value (**Figure 18.9**).

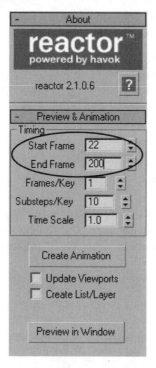

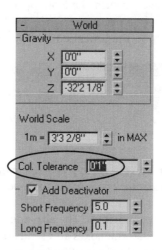

FIGURE 18.9 *The Collision Tolerance value should be no less than 1/40th of the World Scale value for reliable calculations.*

FIGURE 18.8 *You want the simulation to use the pig's motion in its calculations for the entire 200 frames of the animation.*

5. In the Preview & Animation rollout, click the Preview in Window button and press *P* to play the simulation. The pig flies through the air, strikes the boxes, and sends them scattering in all directions. Close the Preview window. Right-click in the Camera02 viewport to activate it. In the Preview & Animation rollout, click the Update Viewports checkbox.

You're going to actually create the simulation, which will write animation keys for all the objects in the scene that are part of the simulation. This step cannot be undone, so it's a good idea to use the Hold option to store the scene in a buffer so that you can use the Fetch command to recover the scene in its current state.

6. On the main menu, choose Edit > Hold. In the Preview & Animation rollout, click the Create Animation button. In the Reactor dialog, click the OK button. If something should go wrong with the final animation, you're safe because you have performed a Hold operation and can use Fetch to get back to that point if you need to (**Figure 18.10**). As the simulation is calculated, keys are written on the timeline for all the frames in the simulation.

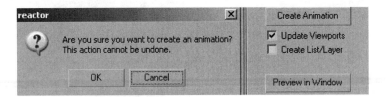

FIGURE 18.10 *Storing your scene in the Hold buffer is a wise idea before you create the animation of the simulation.*

7. Play the animation. The airplane circles overhead and drops the pig, which in turn strikes the boxes and sends them flying across the runway. Stop the animation and save the file. It should already be called *Ch18_reactor03.max*.

Setting Up a Cloth Simulation

In this section, you'll simulate the cloth flag draping convincingly in the scene and then blowing in the wind. Because the flag is hanging from a flagpole, you must first add the flagpole to a Rigid Body collection and fix its position in space; otherwise, the flagpole will fall because of gravity.

The flag itself must be assigned to a Cloth collection, but before that's possible, you must assign a Reactor Cloth modifier to the flag object. Also, the edge of the flag must be attached to the flagpole at the Vertex sub-object level to keep the flag from falling to the ground.

Finally, you will add and adjust a Reactor Wind simulation to the scene that will blow the flag. In 3ds max 7, you can animate the parameters of the Reactor Wind. Although you won't be animating the wind in this scene, it is an important feature to be aware of.

The Reactor Cloth simulation is completely separate from any previous simulations, which have been keyframed into your scene.

Exercise 18.3: Simulating a Flag

1. Open **Ch18_reactor03.max** from the previous exercise or from the CD-ROM. Save it to your project folder with the name *Ch18_reactor04.max*. You need to fix the flagpole so that it won't move because of the effects of gravity. In the Camera02 viewport, select the flagpole to the left of the hangar. On the Reactor toolbar, click the Create Rigid Body Collection button (this is the top icon on the toolbar) to create a new Rigid Body Collection icon with the flagpole added to the list on the Modify panel.

2. In the Camera02 viewport, select the flagpole again. On the Reactor toolbar, click the Open Property Editor button (Figure 18.2). In the Rigid Body Properties dialog, Physical Properties rollout, click the Unyielding checkbox. In the Simulation Geometry rollout, click the Bounding Box radio button (**Figure 18.11**).

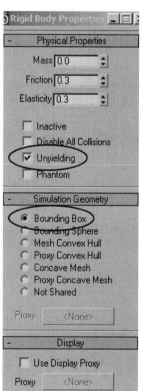

FIGURE 18.11
The unyielding rigid body object is not affected by other objects or forces in the scene, but is still included in the simulation. An unyielding object needs no Mass value.

3. In the Camera02 viewport, select the flag. On the Reactor toolbar, click the Apply Cloth Modifier button (the fourth icon from the bottom, a T-shirt with the letter *M*). On the Modify panel, Properties rollout, enter *0.1* in the Mass field, enter *0.5* in the Rel Density field, and press Enter. In the Force Model section, enter *0.05* in the Stiffness field and select the Avoid Self-Intersections option near the bottom of the panel (**Figure 18.12**). These settings make the flag somewhat lighter and keep it from passing through itself as it drapes.

The flag must now be fixed to the flagpole to keep it from falling to the ground.

4. Click the Zoom Extents All Selected button to fill the orthographic viewports with the flag. On the Modify panel, Stack view, click on the plus sign to the left of reactor Cloth to expand it. Highlight Vertex sub-object mode. In the Left viewport, drag a selection set around the vertical column of vertices next to the flagpole. On the Modify panel, Constraints rollout, click the Attach to Rigid Body button. Highlight the Attach To RigidBody entry in the list below the buttons. In the Attach to Rigid-Body rollout, click the None button and pick the flagpole in the Left viewport. The button will now read Flagpole (**Figure 18.13**). In the Stack view, choose Reactor Cloth to highlight it and exit Vertex sub-object mode.

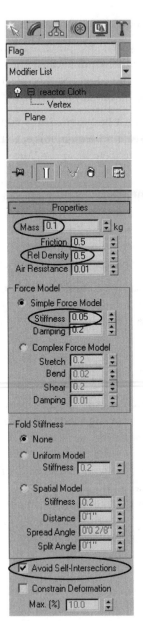

FIGURE 18.12 *The properties of the Reactor Cloth modifier are found on the Modify panel, not in the Properties dialog.*

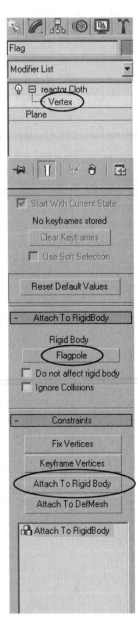

FIGURE 18.13 *Vertices of the flag must be attached to the rigid body flagpole to anchor one edge of the flag in place.*

5. The flag's modifier properties have been adjusted, but the flag doesn't yet belong to a collection. On the Reactor toolbar, click the Create Cloth Collection button (the second icon from the top, a T-shirt with the letter *C*). On the Utilities panel, Utilities rollout, click the Reactor button. In the Preview & Animation rollout, click the Preview in Window button. The World Analysis dialog appears, warning that "Bodies of Flag and Flagpole are interpenetrating." Cancel the World Analysis dialog and, in the Left viewport, move the flag slightly to the right, away from the flagpole. Remember the Collision Tolerance setting from the previous exercise was set to 1 inch? The flag and flagpole are closer than that tolerance. Click the Preview in Window button again and the Reactor Real-Time Preview window should open with no warnings. Press *P* to play the simulation and you will see the flag drop over time and swing around the flagpole (**Figure 18.14**).

6. Close the Preview window and save the file. It should already be called *Ch18_reactor04.max*.

The simulation has been set up and a preview has been made, but you are not quite ready to commit to animation keys.

FIGURE 18.14 *The simulation preview shows the flag falling and wrapping around the flagpole.*

Exercise 18.4: Adding a Wind Component

1. Open **Ch18_reactor04.max** from the previous exercise or from the CD-ROM. Save it to your project folder with the name *Ch18_reactor05.max*. Zoom out in the Left viewport so that you can see the hangar, the flag, and the airplane. On the Reactor toolbar, click the Create Wind button (looks like a rooster weather vane). Pick somewhere above the flag in the Left viewport to create the Wind icon (**Figure 18.15**).

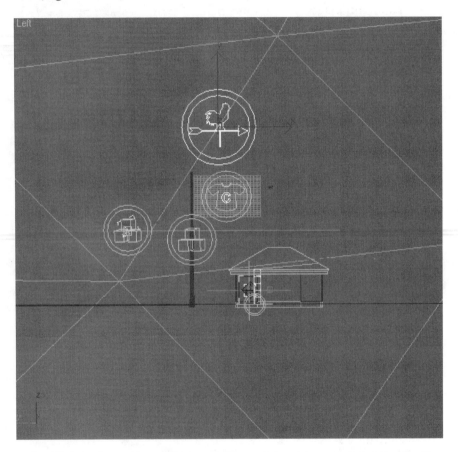

FIGURE 18.15 *The position of the icon in the scene is not important, but the direction of the weather vane's arrow is the same as the direction of the wind.*

2. To increase the strength of the wind, in the Properties rollout on the Modify panel, enter *50000* in the Wind Speed field and press Enter. In the Applies To section, deselect the Rigid Bodies checkbox. This causes the wind to act only on cloth objects in the scene and could save some calculation time (**Figure 18.16**).

> **tip**
>
> The wind-speed setting here seems highly unrealistic at 50,000 feet per second, but other factors, such as the weight of the flag, the density and stiffness of the flag, and its size come into play. Testing different variables until you get the look you want in the Preview window often works best.

3. On the Utilities panel, Preview & Animation rollout, select the Preview in Window button and press *P*. The flag falls more slowly now and blows about in the wind. Close the Preview window.

4. Right-click in the Camera02 viewport to activate it. From the main menu, choose Edit > Hold to save the scene to the Hold buffer. In the Utilities panel, Preview & Animation rollout, click the Create Animation button. Click the OK button in the Reactor dialog and the flight simulation will proceed through the 200 frames of animation. Right-click in the Camera02 viewport to activate it and click the Play Animation button. Stop the animation.

> **note**
>
> In the shaded viewport, the flag will appear to be invisible from the backside. However, it has a 2-sided material attribute applied to it and will render correctly.

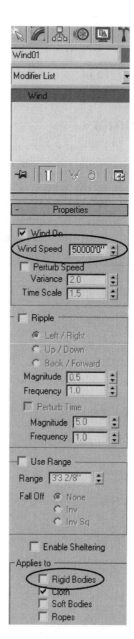

FIGURE 18.16 *The wind can be adjusted for speed and action and can be made to affect only certain categories of objects in the scene.*

5. Drag the Frame slider to Frame 0 and save the file. It should already be called *Ch18_reactor05.max*.

In just a few short exercises, you have created a very complex animation.

Summary

For many users new to 3ds max 7, the complexity of the animation you just created would have been much too difficult to animate by a hand with any convincing results.

By using Reactor, the burden of keeping track of all the deformations and interactions between bodies is handled efficiently by the tools. It's usually best to create small segments of animation using the Reactor and commit them to keyframes before moving on to the next segment. This reduces the overhead of the calculations and gives you more flexibility in editing should something go wrong.

CHAPTER 19

Particle Flow: A System for Organizing Chaos

In This Chapter

Let's liven up the scene a little bit with a component of 3ds max 7 called *particle systems*. Particles themselves can be used to simulate a wide range of seemingly random natural effects, such as smoke and fire, liquids, swarms of insects, and grass and hair growing on an object. They can be used to create thousands, if not millions, of objects in your scene. However, because they can be so dense and mathematically intensive, they can also overwhelm computer resources. Particle systems should be used sparingly to add visual interest and "punch" to your storyline, while keeping production efficiency in mind at all times.

This chapter focuses on Particle Flow, a particle system that lets you string together chains of events to control the behavior of particles in your scene. Particle Flow is the most flexible and manageable particle system in 3ds max 7, especially for new users. The Particle View dialog, used to edit Particle Flow systems, presents a good overview of all events that make up the particle system.

For the exercises, you'll use Particle Flow to create smoke trailing from the fuselage of the airplane you worked with in the last chapter. First you'll create an emitter that is the source of all the particles in the scene, and then you'll edit their behavior in the Particle View dialog, where you can visually manipulate the various operators that control such things as particle size and the speed of particles. You'll also practice using decision-branching operators, which direct particles based on a particle's age or the collision with other objects in the scene, and particle-material operators, which apply static or animated materials to particles.

This chapter covers the following topics:

- **Particle system.** You'll learn about an integrated system of particle emitters and operators that control the behavior of particles.
- **Decision-branching operations.** You'll learn how the flow of particles can be redirected to change their behavior based on information such as a particle's age, a percentage of the particles being emitted, or a particle's speed.
- **Particle materials.** You'll learn to apply materials to particle systems using material operators.

Key Terms

- **Particle Flow source.** A 3ds max interface icon that emits particles when placed in a scene.
- **Particle view.** A view where you can create particle events and adjust operators that determine particle behavior.
- **Operators.** Used to modify the particle system. You'll learn to adjust certain default operators and add new operators.
- **Particle event.** Functions like a container for operators to make it easier to manage groups of operators.

Setting up a Default Particle Flow System

The first step in creating a particle system is to place a Particle Flow source in the scene that will emit the initial particles and to open the Particle View dialog to see the structure and the wiring of the default system.

The Particle View dialog makes the creation of complex particle systems much more manageable by providing you with an overall view of the variables contained in individual events that can be wired together to produce the end result. Individual operators or whole events can be removed or simply disabled to allow easy experimentation while you are designing a particle system or to provide a method of "backward engineering" of existing particle systems.

To make smoke trail from the airplane as it circles overhead, you will need to hierarchically link the Particle Flow source to the airplane after it has been aligned to the center of the fuselage.

Exercise 19.1: Creating and Aligning a Particle Flow Source

1. Open **Ch19_pflow01.max** from the CD-ROM. Save it to your project folder with the name *Ch19_pflow02.max*. On the main toolbar, click the Select by Name button and highlight Camera02 and Fuselage in the Select Objects dialog list. Click the Select button. From the main menu, choose Tools > Isolate Selection, or press the Alt + Q keyboard shortcut, to hide all objects in the scene except Camera02 and Fuselage. In the Left viewport, select the airplane and click the Zoom Extents All Selected button to fill the orthographic viewports with the airplane. Click anywhere in the Left viewport to deselect the airplane.

2. On the Create panel, click the drop-down arrow beside Standard Primitives and choose Particle Systems from the list. On the Particle Systems panel, Object Type rollout, click the PF Source button. In the Left viewport, pick near the upper-left edge of the fuselage and drag to the lower-right edge to create a Particle Flow source (**Figure 19.1**).

Particle Flow Source

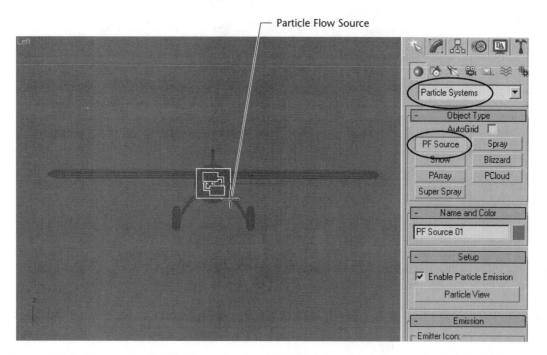

Figure 19.1 *You create a Particle Flow source by picking and dragging the icon to the desired initial size.*

3. The Particle Flow source looks correctly positioned in the Left viewport, but is actually out in space on the current working grid. On the main toolbar, click the Align button, and pick the Fuselage in the Left viewport. The initial alignment should be pivot-point-to-pivot-point in all three axes. In the Align Selection dialog, click the Center radio button in both the Current Object and Target Object columns to align the Particle Flow source to the geometric center of the fuselage (**Figure 19.2**). Click OK.

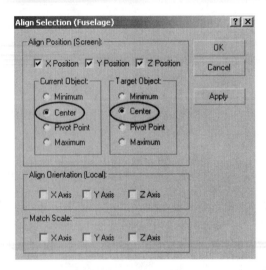

FIGURE 19.2 *The Align tool quickly centers the Particle Flow source on the airplane.*

4. Scrub the Frame slider. The plane begins to move and a small clump of particles is emitted from the Particle Flow source in the opposite direction that the airplane is headed. Drag the Frame slider to Frame 0 and zoom in on the PF Source icon in the Left viewport. On the main toolbar, click the Select and Link button. Pick on the edge of the icon and drag to the fuselage. A rubber band line runs from the icon's pivot point to the cursor. When you release the left mouse button over the airplane, it flashes white briefly to indicate the link has been made. Scrub the Frame slider; the particle system now curves along the path. This is because the Particle Flow source is a child of the airplane and moves with it (**Figure 19.3**). Move the Frame slider to Frame 0.

FIGURE 19.3 *Linking the icon to the airplane causes the particles to emit in a curve along the airplane's path.*

5. Make sure the PF Source icon is selected, and on the Modify panel, Setup roll-out, click the Particle View button to open the Particle View window (see **Figure 19.4** on the next page). On the upper-left panel of the Particle View dialog, you'll see the PF Source and Event 01 in the event display. On the lower-left panel, you'll see a list of operators in the operator display.

6. Drag the Frame slider to Frame 30 and render the Camera02 viewport. The default particles are solids formed by four-sided pyramids, or *tetrahedrons,* and do not yet resemble smoke. Move the Frame slider back to Frame 0. Close the Particle View dialog and click the Exit Isolation Mode button to unhide all the objects in the scene. Save the file. It should already be called *Ch19_pflow02.max.*

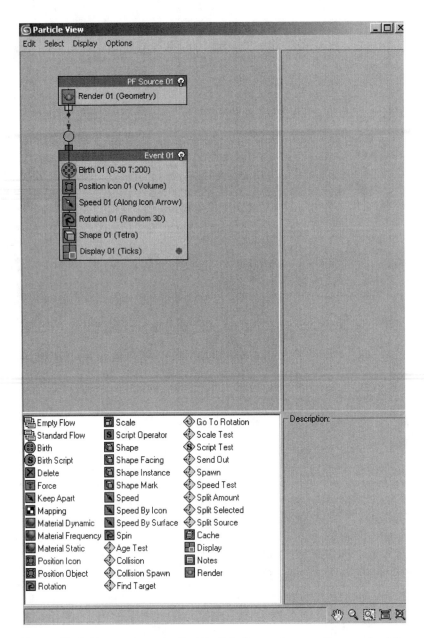

Figure 19.4 *You create and adjust Particle Flow systems on the panels of the Particle View dialog.*

Using Operators to Alter Particles

The default particles are not particularly useful for much of anything but to give you a basis to work from in designing your own particles. In the next exercise, you begin to modify some of the operators in Event 01 to change the frequency and the look of the particles trailing from the airplane. You'll focus on adjusting the number and timing of the particles being emitted and the speed at which they stream from the emitter icon.

Exercise 19.2: Adjusting Operators in the Default Event

1. Open **Ch19_pflow02.max** from the last exercise or from the CD-ROM. Save it to your project folder with the name *Ch19_pflow03.max*. Make sure the PF Source 01 icon is selected and, on the Modify panel, Setup rollout, click the Particle View button to open the Particle View window.

2. Highlight the Birth 01 operator at the top of Event 01. Once the operator is highlighted, you'll see the parameters rollout called *Birth 01* on the top-right panel (**Figure 19.5**). The Birth operator controls the start and stop time of the particles and the number of particles being emitted.

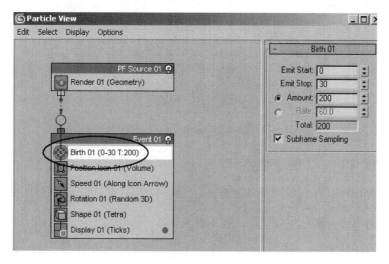

FIGURE 19.5 *Once you highlight an operator within an event, you'll gain access to the parameter values of that operator.*

You want the particles to be streaming from the airplane as if it has been constantly circling overhead. But as it is now, the particles start being born and only a few are visible at Frame 0. Let's fix this.

3. In the Birth 01 rollout, enter *-30* in the Emit Start field and press Enter. Now at Frame 0, all the particles defined by the Birth operator are already visible in the scene. Scrub the Frame slider. Notice that after Frame 30, no new particles are emitted, and the old ones just drift off to Frame 200. Enter *200* in the Emit Stop field, press Enter, and scrub the Frame slider to see that the particles are emitted continuously throughout the animation. The particles are less dense because the same number of particles are now being spread over 200 frames.

4. The default Birth01 event emits a total of 60 particles over the entire animation. To emit the 60 particles at a rate of 60 particles per second, click the Rate radio button. Type *75* in the Rate field and press Enter. Scrub the Frame slider to see the steadier flow of particles caused by this change

5. Highlight the Speed 01 operator in Event 01. In the Speed 01 rollout to the right, enter *1* in the Speed field and press Enter (**Figure 19.6**). This value is the speed at which each particle is traveling (1 foot per second) as it is emitted. Right-click in the Camera02 viewport to activate it and click the Play Animation button. The particles drift ever so slowly backward as they are emitted. Stop the animation.

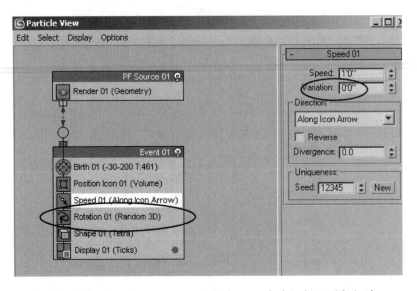

FIGURE 19.6 *The Speed operator controls the speed of each particle in the direction that the particles are emitted.*

6. Drag the Frame slider to Frame 200 and render the Camera02 viewport. A continuous ring of particles appears along the path of the airplane. The particles are emitted at a rate of 60 per second and live forever, so the particles created on Frame 1 still exist on Frame 200 (**Figure 19.7**). Close all windows and dialogs and save the file. It should already be called *Ch19_pflow03.max.*

Figure 19.7 *All the particles emitted in this animation still exist on the last frame.*

Preparing the Particles for Rendering

In the next exercise, you'll practice changing the particle type and applying materials to it. The type of smoke you want in this scene is a cartoon-style, white, puffy smoke, which would be difficult to convincingly apply to tetrahedron shapes. So you will replace each particle with a Shape Facing particle, which is a flat square that has special animation controllers that allow it to always be perpendicular to a chosen camera.

A material called Smoke is already in your Material Editor and consists of a radial Gradient Ramp map in the Diffuse color, the Self-Illumination, and the Opacity map slots. Because the Opacity map is white in the middle and black on the edges, the square shapes are invisible at the edges, so they appear round.

Exercise 19.3: Applying Materials in Particle Flow Systems

1. Open **Ch19_pflow03.max** from the last exercise or from the CD-ROM. Save it to your project folder with the name *Ch19_pflow04.max*. Select the PF Source 01 icon in the Left viewport and, on the Modify panel, Setup rollout, click the Particle View button. In the Particle View dialog, highlight the Shape 01 operator in Event 01. In the Shape 01 rollout, click Tetra from the Shape drop-down list. Notice that these default shapes can either be Vertex-, Tetra-, Cube-, or Sphere-shaped, none of which fits your needs for this exercise (**Figure 19.8**).

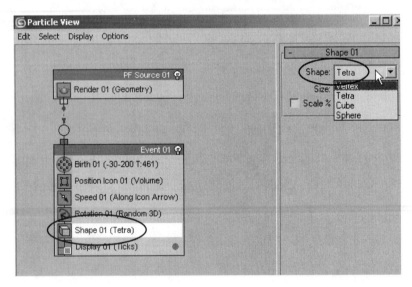

FIGURE 19.8 *The default Shape type is limited to four simple objects, none of which is ideal for the smoke in this scene.*

2. In Event 01, right-click on the Shape 01 operator, and choose Delete from the menu to remove the operator from the event. If you scrub the Frame slider, you'll still see particles in the scene, because the Display 01 operator in Event 01, which is set to display Ticks in the scene, controls the particles in the viewport. If you render the Camera02 viewport, there will be no particles in the rendered image.

3. In the operator list at the bottom of the Particle View dialog, click and drag the Shape Facing operator into Event 01. Release the left mouse button when you see the blue line appear below the Speed 01 operator (**Figure 19.9**). The blue line indicates you are inserting a new operator between two existing operators. A red line would indicate you are replacing the operator below the red line with the new one.

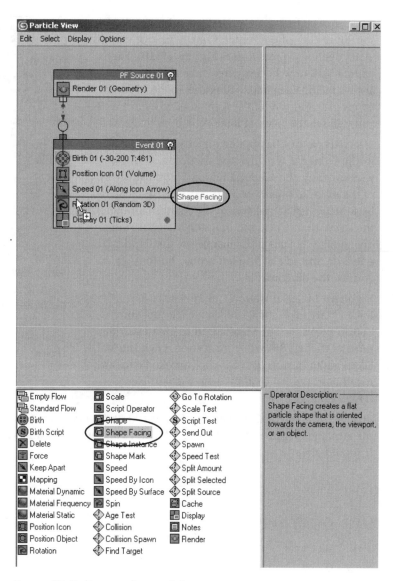

FIGURE 19.9 *You can drag and drop a new operator onto an event between two existing operators or replace an existing operator.*

4. Highlight the Shape Facing 01 operator in Events 01. In the Shape Facing 01 rollout, click the None button in the Look At Camera/Object section located at the top of the panel. Press *H* and, in the Pick Object dialog, double-click Camera02 from the list. This tells the new facing particles to always be perpendicular to

the line of sight from Camera02. In the Size/Width section of the rollout, enter *3* in the In World Space Units field, and press Enter (**Figure 19.10**). Each particle will now be a square, three feet on a side, always facing Camera02. Drag the Frame slider to Frame 100 and render the Camera02 viewport and you will see the mass of large square particles.

5. Materials cannot be applied directly to the particles in the scene by dragging and dropping a sample window from the Material Editor. You must use one of the material operators, in this case Material Static, because your material will never change throughout the animation. Click and drag the Material Static operator to PF Source 01, just below the Render 01 operator, and release the left mouse button when you see the blue line.

6. Highlight Material Static 01 in PF Source 01. In the Material Static 01 rollout, click the None button below Assign Material. In the Material/Map Browser dialog, Browse From section, click the Mtl Editor radio button. Double-click Smoke [Standard] material in the list to apply it to the particles (**Figure 19.11**).

7. Render the Camera02 viewport at Frame 100. Puffy balls of smoke trail behind the airplane (**Figure 19.12**). Close all dialogs and windows and save the file. It should already be called *Ch19_pflow04.max*.

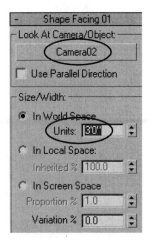

FIGURE 19.10 *Shape-Facing particles can be made to remain perpendicular to any object in the scene, but a camera is usually the logical choice.*

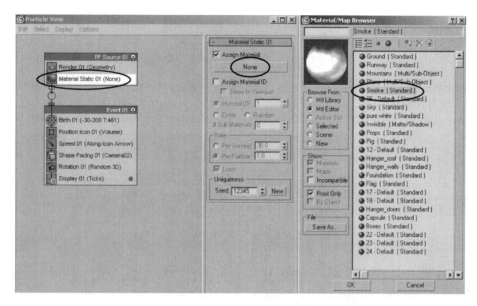

Figure 19.11 *A material operator placed in the Particle Flow source will affect all particles throughout the animation; whereas a material operator placed in an event will affect only the particles for the duration of the event.*

Figure 19.12 *Shape-facing particles with this particular smoke material render as puffs of smoke.*

Applying Decision-Branching Operators and Wiring

The ability to use decision-branching operators in Particle Flow systems to direct the process flow of particles out of one event and into another is certainly one of the most powerful features in 3ds max 7.

Decision branching can be based on the age of particles, the speed of particles, a percentage of the total number of particles, or the collision of particles with other objects in the scene, for example.

While decision branching can occur within an event to pass a subset of the particles on to the next operator in the event, the real power lies in the decision-branching operator's ability to direct particles out to other events.

In the next exercise, you'll use an Age Test operator to send particles that are older than a certain number of frames to a new event that contains a Delete operator. This enables you to control the length of the smoke trail behind the airplane.

Decision branching not only adds incredible functionality to Particle Flow systems, but makes the management of complex particle systems easier by isolating related groups of operators within events.

Exercise 19.4: Using an Age Test Operator to Delete Particles

1. Open **Ch19_pflow04.max** from the last exercise or from the CD-ROM. Save it to your project folder with the name *Ch19_pflow05.max*. In the Front viewport, select the PF Source 01 emitter at the center of the fuselage. (You might find it easier to use the Select by Name button on the main toolbar to select it.) On the Modify panel, Setup rollout, click the Particle View button to open the Particle View dialog.

2. Click and drag the Age Test decision-branching operator from the lower-left panel and drop it in Event 01, just below the Rotation 01 operator. To insert the new operator at that location, release the mouse button when you see the blue line below Rotation 01 (**Figure 19.13**). Decision-branching operators are indicated by a yellow diamond, and when you drop them onto an event, a blue wiring stub projects from the left side of the event window.

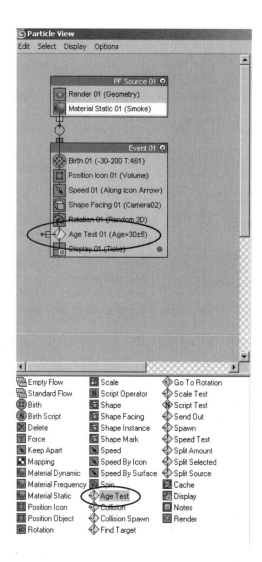

FIGURE 19.13
Decision-branching operators include a wiring stub when they are added to an event.

3. Highlight the Age Test 01 operator in Event 01. Notice on the right panel, Age Test 01 rollout, that Test Value is set to 30 frames with a 5-frame Variation setting. This means that any particles between 25-35 frames old will be randomly selected for branching to some other event, and all particles older than 35 frames will be redirected. Click and drag the Delete operator from the operator list to an area below the Event 01 window. This creates Event 02, which contains the Delete 01 operator and a new Display operator (see **Figure 19.14** on the next page). However, nothing has changed yet because the events are not wired together.

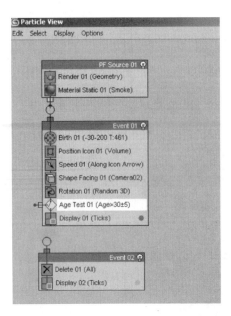

FIGURE 19.14 *A Delete operator becomes a new event, with a wiring receptor at the top, when dropped in empty space in the Particle View dialog.*

4. In the Particle View dialog, click the blue wiring stub on the Age Test 01 operator and drag to the circular wiring receptor at the top of Event 02. Release the left mouse button when you see the four-arrow cursor on the circular receptor (**Figure 19.15**). A blue wire will now connect the two events, with an arrow showing the direction of flow.

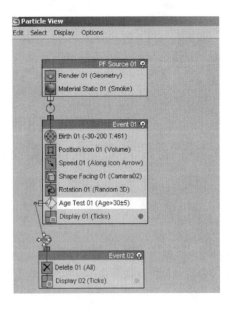

FIGURE 19.15 *Wiring a decision-branching operator to a new event is as simple as clicking and dragging.*

5. Make sure the Camera02 viewport is active, and drag the Frame slider to Frame 100. Render the Camera02 viewport. The trail of smoke isn't continuous around the path of the airplane anymore. Instead it dissipates a short distance behind the airplane (**Figure 19.16**). Event 02 has deleted all particles older than 35 frames.

FIGURE 19.16 *The Test Value number in the Age Test operator now determines the length of the smoke trail behind the airplane.*

6. Close all windows and dialogs. Play the animation back in the Camera02 viewport and you'll see that the smoke trail remains a constant length throughout the animation. Stop the animation, return the Frame slider to Frame 0, and save the file. It should already be called *Ch19_pflow05.max*.

Using Multiple Decision-Branching Operators in an Event

You have included a single decision-branching operator in Event 01, but it is also possible to use more than one decision-branching operator per event.

In the next exercise, you'll apply a Split Amount decision-branching operator to send half of the visible particles to a Scale operator in a new event that will cause the diverted particles to grow progressively smaller as they age.

Exercise 19.5: Using Split Amount Decision-Branching Operators

1. Open **Ch19_pflow05.max** from the previous exercise or from the CD-ROM. Save it to your project folder with the name *Ch19_pflow06.max*. Select the PF Source 01 emitter in the Front viewport. On the Modify panel, Setup rollout, click the Particle View button to open the Particle View dialog.

2. In the Particle View dialog, drag a Split Amount decision-branching operator from the decision list to just below the Age Test 01 operator in Event 01. Notice this Split Amount 01 operator is set to split 50 percent of the particles to a new event or operator. Highlight Split Amount 01 in Event 01. In the Split Amount 01 rollout, enter *75* in the Fraction of Particles Ratio field and press Enter. It also *appears* that the wiring runs from the Age Test 01 operator through the Split Amount 01 operator to Event 02, but it really doesn't. Click and drag on the gray bar at the top of Event 01 to move it to the right edge of the panel (**Figure 19.17**).

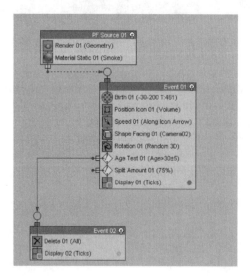

Figure 19.17 *Events can be reorganized in the Particle View so that you can see the wiring layout more easily.*

3. At the bottom right of the Particle View, click the Zoom button, and pick and drag the mouse downward on the Event panel to zoom out for more workspace. Click the Zoom button again to disable Zoom mode. Click the Scale operator in the operator list and drag it to the right of Event 02. A new Event 03 with a Scale 01 operator is added, as well as a new Display operator. Click the Split Amount 01 wiring stub and drag it to the wiring receptor of Event 03 (**Figure 19.18**).

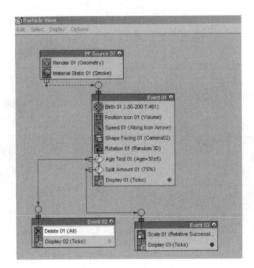

FIGURE 19.18 *75 percent of the particles older than 35 Frames will be sent to the Scale operator in Event 03.*

4. Highlight the Scale 01 operator in Event 03. In the Scale 01 rollout, click the drop-down arrow beside Type and choose Relative Successive from the list. Enter *98* in one of the Scale Factor fields and press Enter. All three fields will change to 98, because the Constrain Portions checkbox is active. Scrub the Frame slider to Frame 100 and render the Camera02 viewport. The smoke trail is now a mix of large particles and particles that become progressively smaller as they distance themselves from the airplane (see **Figure 19.19** on the next page).

Figure 19.19 *75 percent of the visible particles are being scaled smaller.*

5. In Event 02, click the blue icon to the left of the Delete 01 operator. The icon will turn gray and that operator is disabled. Render the Camera02 viewport, and you'll see a continuous stream of particles, with some of them being scaled. Click the gray Delete 01 icon to enable the operator again.

6. Close all open windows, drag the Frame slider to Frame 0, and save the file. It should already be called *Ch19_pflow06.max*.

Summary

Particle Flow systems are easy to set up and change because the Particle View dialog offers a visual method of organizing groups of operators in events. Also, using decision-branching operators that are wired to separate events provides a clean and easy-to-follow overview of the flow of particles.

The Particle Flow workflow encourages you to experiment with particles and develop alternate scenarios that can be rewired quickly. You also have the ability to disable individual operators, complete events to obtain different results, or troubleshoot problems in the system.

CHAPTER 20

Effects: Making It Special

In This Chapter

Special effects in 3ds max 7 could be considered almost any effect you might use in special situations to enhance the look of your rendered images. Some examples of special effects include Volume Light effects, which are similar to a shaft of sunlight in a dusty room or the glowing aura around a light fixture, and Motion Blur, in which fast-moving objects in a scene look like they have blurred trails behind them, which enhances the illusion of speed.

In this chapter, you'll use special effects to replace the smoke you created to trail behind the airplane in the last chapter with wispy steam or vapor. In another exercise, you'll create clouds that are 3D volumetric clouds rather than clouds that are applied as a map within a material.

You also learn about Normal mapping, which is perhaps not a special effect in the same sense as the others presented in this chapter, but a 3ds max 7 feature that lets you simulate geometry more convincingly than when using Bump maps.

This chapter covers the following topics:

- **Lens Effects Glow.** You'll learn to set the Material Effects channel (in the Material Editor), which cues a glow effect on all objects in the scene with that material.

- **Fire effect.** This environment effect is designed for creating flames and fire, but you'll learn to use it to create 3D clouds in the scene.

- **Normal maps.** You'll learn to create special Normal maps from complex 3D objects that can be used in materials to simulate the original geometry.

Key Terms

- **Material Effects channel.** This is a numeric value assigned in the Material Editor to indicate which material will have special effects applied.

- **Atmospheric Apparatus.** This Helper object functions as a container for 3D Fog and Fire effects.

- **Rendered to Texture.** This function lets you "bake" materials and lighting into the vertices of an object. You'll use it in this chapter to generate a Normal map for simulating geometry.

The When and Why of Special Effects

One important fact to keep in mind while you are learning the topics covered in this chapter is that special effects are just that—*special*. You should use these techniques only when they add content to the story you are trying to tell. Don't use them just because they're available in 3ds max 7 or because they look "cool."

The steam simulation and the 3D clouds you'll create in this chapter can use considerable computer resources if you are not careful with the parameters. For example, having the density set too high for both effects can slow your productivity, draw too much attention to the effect, and detract from the story you are trying to tell.

The Normal Bump mapping techniques, on the other hand, are designed as a way to enhance productivity. Normal mapping, used in conjunction with a Projection modifier, lets you simulate the detail from high-resolution models and project this simulated geometry onto much simpler models using these special Bump or Displacement maps.

Applying Rendering Effects

Rendering effects are a group of special effects that are applied at render time. They include effects such as Lens effects, Blurring, Depth of Field (to simulate camera-distance blurring), and Motion Blur (to give the animated objects the illusion of speed).

In this section, you'll learn to use a Lens effect called *Glow*. For 3ds max 7 to know where to apply it, you must either assign the object a special property called *G-Buffer Object channel*, or assign a Material Effects channel via the Material Editor if you don't want the whole object to glow, which is the case in the following exercise.

tip

The particle system used in the next exercise is emitting tetrahedron-shaped particles, to which the Glow effect will be applied. The appearance of the tetrahedrons in the rendered image would ruin the effect, so you'll apply a material to the particles that is completely transparent and has no specular highlights. The only function of this invisible material is to cue the Glow effect at render time using the Material Effects channel.

Exercise 20.1: Preparing the Particles and Material

1. Open **Ch20_steam01.max** from the CD-ROM. Save it to your project folder with the name *Ch20_steam02.max*. Drag the Frame slider to Frame 80. You'll see ticks representing tetrahedron particles trailing from the airplane. Render the Camera02 viewport. The tetrahedrons appear as junk falling from the plane—not exactly what you want in your scene (**Figure 20.1**). Close the Rendered Frame window.

Figure 20.1 *The particles in this scene are relatively large tetrahedrons, which you'll turn into steam.*

2.   Press *H* to open the Select Objects dialog, and select PF Source 01 from the list to assign the particle system. On the Modify panel, Setup rollout, click the Particle View button to open the Particle View dialog. This is the particle system from the previous chapter with a Shape operator in Event 01 instead of the Shape Facing operator. The material has also been removed from the PF Source 01 (**Figure 20.2**).

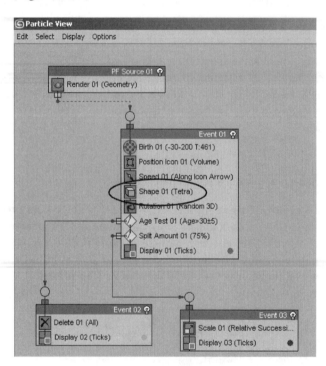

FIGURE 20.2 *The particles here are the same as the smoke you created in the last chapter, except the Shape operator has been changed and the material has been removed.*

3. On the main toolbar, click the Material Editor button or press *M*. Drag the horizontal scrollbar below the sample windows all the way to the right to access the last sample window in the top row called *Steam*. In the Blinn Basic Parameters rollout, enter *0* in the Opacity field and press Enter. In the Specular Highlights section, enter *0* in the Glossiness field and press Enter (**Figure 20.3**). The Specular Level setting should be left at the default 0. This makes the particles completely invisible, but if the Glossiness were left at something other than 0, you would see the specular highlights of the rotating particles.

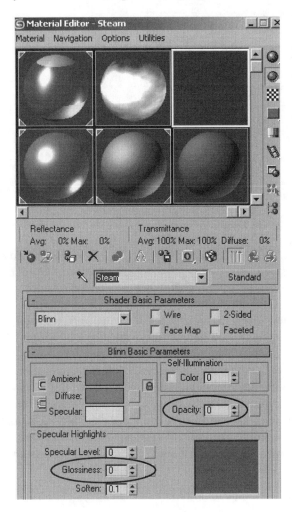

FIGURE 20.3 *The Opacity, Specular Level, and Glossiness values must be set to 0 for the material to be invisible under all conditions.*

4. In the Material Editor, click and hold the Material Effects Channel button to access the flyout buttons and choose Button 1 (**Figure 20.4**). Close the Material Editor. You could choose any number from 1 to 15 to cue an effect. The number itself has no meaning, with the exception of 0, which disables the function. Any object in the scene with this material assigned to it is capable of cueing any of the render effects in 3ds max 7.

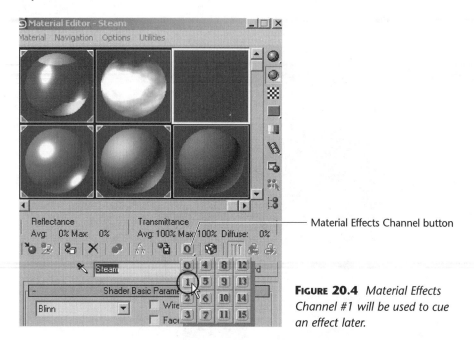

Material Effects Channel button

FIGURE 20.4 *Material Effects Channel #1 will be used to cue an effect later.*

5. In the Particle View dialog, drag the Material Static operator from the operator list in the bottom pane to just below Render 01 in the PF Source 01 window. Release the mouse button when you see the blue horizontal line. Remember, putting the Material Static operator in the PF Source assigns the material to the particles in all the events. Highlight Material Static 01 in the PF Source 01. In the Material Static 01 rollout, click the None button below Assign Material. In the Material/Map Browser, Browse From section, click the Mtl Editor radio button and select Steam material from the list (**Figure 20.5**). Render the Camera02 viewport. No particles appear in the scene because they have been assigned an invisible material.

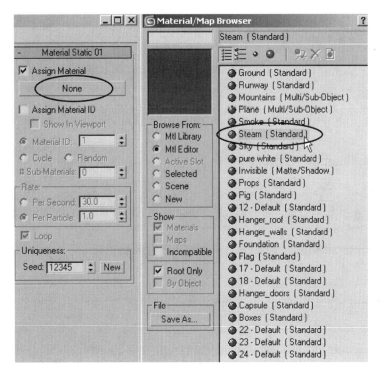

FIGURE 20.5 *Assigning the Steam material to a Material Static operator in the PF Source window ensures all particles will have that material.*

6. Close all dialogs and windows and save the file. It should already be called *Ch20_steam02.max*.

The invisible material on the particles is set to cue a Lens Effects Glow.

The Lens Effects Glow around each invisible particle is what you'll see in the rendered image. The spherical wispy glows will give the illusion of vapor or steam.

Exercise 20.2: Applying the Lens Effects Glow

1. Open **Ch20_steam02.max** from the last exercise or from the CD-ROM. Save it to your project folder with the name *Ch20_steam03.max*. Drag the Frame slider to Frame 80, if it is not already there. From the Rendering pull-down menu, choose Effects to open the Environment and Effects dialog. In the Effects rollout, click the Add button and choose Lens Effects from the list (see **Figure 20.6** on the next page).

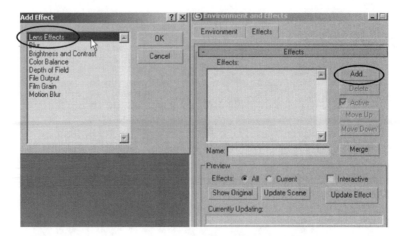

FIGURE 20.6 *You can access Lens effects by choosing Rendering > Effects.*

2. In the Environment and Effects dialog, Lens Effects Parameters rollout, high-light Glow in the left column and click the right-arrow button to push Glow into the right column. Right-click in the Camera02 viewport to make sure it is activated and, in the Environment and Effects dialog, Preview section, click the Interactive checkbox. This renders and opens a new window—not the Render Frame window, but the Effects Preview window (**Figure 20.7**).

FIGURE 20.7 *You can interactively monitor the progress of Effects changes in the Effects Preview window.*

3. Make sure Glow is highlighted in the right column. In the Glow Element rollout, Parameters tab, enter 5 in the Size field and 7 in the Intensity field and press Enter. In the Radial Color section, click the bright-red color swatch and, in the Color Selector, change the color to pure black (**Figure 20.8**). Close the dialog.

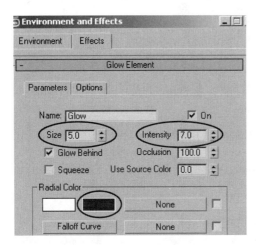

FIGURE 20.8 *The initial Glow settings are too large and too bright for this scene and may be slow to calculate.*

4. Click the Options tab, and in the Apply Element To section, deselect the Lights and Image checkboxes and select the Image Centers checkbox. In the Image Sources section, click the Effects ID checkbox (**Figure 20.9**). It is set by default to Material Effects Channel #1, the same channel that you assigned to your material. Here, it will cue the Glow effect.

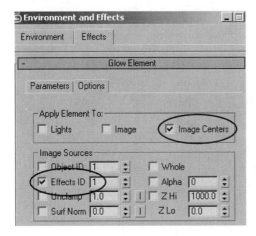

FIGURE 20.9 *The Glow effect must be set to recognize Material Effects Channel #1 to apply the glow correctly.*

5. Close all windows and dialogs and make sure the Camera02 viewport is active. Render the viewport and you will see it render normally, but there will be a pause at the end, and you can see in the progress bar of the Rendering dialog that the Current Task is calculating the Lens Effects. When it has finished calculating, the wispy trail appears behind the airplane in the Rendered Frame window.

tip

Be patient when working with effects in 3ds max 7. The calculation times for some effects can be rather lengthy, especially if you have a slower computer.

6. Close the Rendered Frame window and save the file; it should already be called *Ch20_steam03.max*.

You can experiment with the Lens Effects Glow parameters to create different illusions, but be careful to change only one parameter at a time to see the change before moving on to the next parameter. Otherwise, things can get confusing very quickly.

Creating Atmospheric Effects

Atmospheric effects in 3ds max 7 require that you first create a Helper object called *Atmospheric Apparatus*, which acts as a container to hold the 3D volume effect, in this case a Fire effect, which you'll adjust to look like clouds in the scene.

Exercise 20.3: Using the Fire Effect to Simulate Clouds

1. Open **Ch20_steam03.max** from the last exercise or from the CD-ROM. Save it to your project folder with the name *Ch20_steam04.max*. Right-click in the Top viewport to activate it and use the middle mouse wheel to zoom out until you can see the outline of the runway.

2. On the Create panel, Helpers category, click the drop-down arrow beside Standard and choose Atmospheric Apparatus from the list (**Figure 20.10**). In the Object Type rollout, click the BoxGizmo button. In the Top viewport, click near the lower-right corner of the runway and drag up and to the right to make a large square. Release the left mouse button and click to set the height (**Figure 20.11**). The exact size of the Box gizmo is not important; you will set the size in the next step.

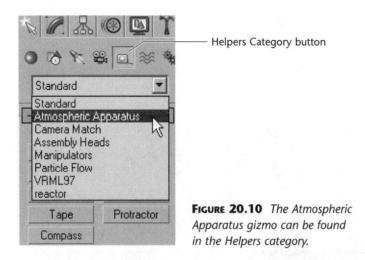

Helpers Category button

FIGURE 20.10 *The Atmospheric Apparatus gizmo can be found in the Helpers category.*

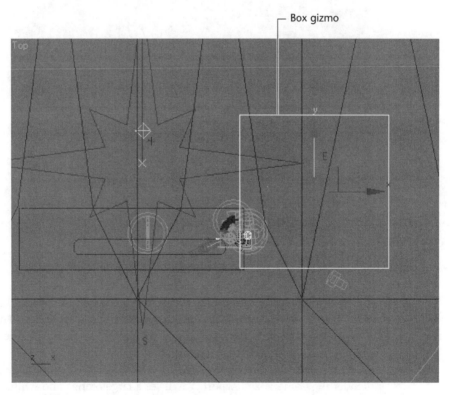

Box gizmo

FIGURE 20.11 *Create a Box gizmo in the Top viewport to act as a container for the clouds.*

3. On the Modify panel, Box Gizmo Parameters rollout, enter *500* in the Length and Width fields, *50* in the Height field, and press Enter. Click the Select and Move button on the main toolbar and zoom out in the Front viewport so that you can see the Move Transform gizmo, and move the atmospheric Box gizmo with the Y-axis restrict arrow until the bottom of the Box gizmo is just above the top of the flagpole (**Figure 20.12**).

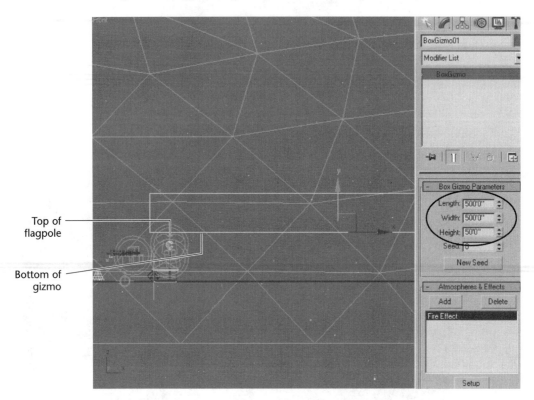

FIGURE 20.12 *The bottom of the clouds will be just above the top of the flagpole in the scene.*

4. On the Modify panel, Atmospheres & Effects rollout, click the Add button. Select Fire Effect from the list in the Add Atmosphere dialog. Highlight Fire Effect on the panel and click the Setup button at the bottom of the Atmospheres & Effects rollout to open the Environment and Effects dialog. In the Fire Effect Parameters rollout, notice that BoxGizmo01 is listed as the active gizmo (**Figure 20.13**). Render the Camera02 viewport. You'll see a large orange-and-white flame in the sky that needs to be adjusted to look like clouds.

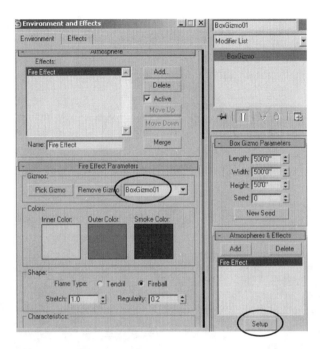

FIGURE 20.13 *You can add an effect directly to a gizmo from the Modify panel.*

5. In the Environment and Effects dialog, Fire Effect Parameters rollout, change the Inner Color swatch to pure white and the Outer Color swatch to a light bluish-gray—the exact color is up to you. In the Shape section, enter *0.2* in the Stretch field and *0.5* in the Regularity field and press Enter. In the Characteristics section, enter *750* in the Flame Size field and *2.0* in the Density field and press Enter (**Figure 20.14**).

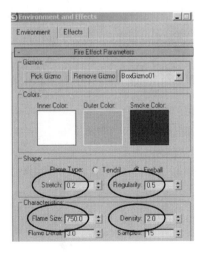

FIGURE 20.14 *The color and the size of the Fire effect must be adjusted to provide a billowing white cloud. The Stretch and Regularity settings adjust the type of cloud, while the Density makes it thinner.*

6. Render the Camera02 viewport, and you'll see a large white cloud spread out behind the flag and airplane (**Figure 20.15**). Experiment with some of the Fire Effect parameters for different cloud types. Close all windows and dialogs and save the file; it should already be called *Ch20_steam04.max*.

FIGURE 20.15 *The new 3D cloud is relatively convincing and can easily be changed to represent a variety of cloud types.*

By varying the parameters and using different Atmospheric Apparatus gizmos, you can use the Fire effect to simulate anything from soft candle flames to violent explosions, and even clouds, as is the case in this chapter. For example, try these alternate settings for a different cloud look: Increase the gizmo to 1000 x 1000 x 100. Use the following settings for the Flame effect: Set the Flame Type to Tendril, the Flame Size to 1000, the Density to 0.2, and the Flame Detail to 1.

Using a Projection Modifier and Normal Map

By now you surely have noticed that a common thread running throughout this book is the need for vigilance regarding the number of faces or polygons in your models so that you can make efficient use of your computer resources.

3ds max 7 has a feature called *Normal map*, which acts like an enhanced Bump map to simulate geometry. Whereas Bump maps use the luminance values of pixels to simulate height changes on the surface of objects, Normal maps use the direction of face normals in a high-resolution model to project the illusion of raised surface areas onto a low-resolution model. The result is a much higher-quality appearance while retaining a low face or polygon count.

You'll also learn in this section about a max 7 tool called *Render to Texture*, which can actually generate the Normal map from the details in the high-resolution model and then automatically apply the new map into the Bump slot of the material. However, this map is applied as a simple Bump map. You'll replace the old-style Bump map with the Normal Bump map type, using the Normal map as a sub map to greatly enhance the illusion of raised surfaces. The Normal Bump map processes the information stored in the Normal map more effectively.

In this first exercise, you'll practice using the Projection modifier, which projects mapping coordinates from a high-resolution model to a low-resolution model. In this scene, you'll take the model of a wooden crate that is made up of 57 faces and generate a Normal map to be projected onto a box with 12 faces—a significant savings in resources.

Exercise 20.4: Applying and Adjusting a Projection Modifier

1. Open **Ch20_normal01.max** from the CD-ROM. Save it to your project folder with the name *Ch20_normal02.max*. In the Perspective viewport, you'll see a brown polygon box and a green box with details modeled into it to represent a wooden crate. In the Perspective viewport, select the low poly Box01 on the left. On the Modify panel, Modifier List, choose the Projection modifier. A blue cage surrounds the box.

2. The low-resolution and high-resolution objects should overlap each other as closely as possible for the best results when using a Projection modifier. On the main toolbar, click the Align button and, in the Perspective viewport, pick the green box called *Box_detail*. In the Align Selection dialog, Align Position section, all three axes and the Pivot Point radio buttons should be selected (see **Figure 20.16** on the next page). Click OK. The two objects overlap very closely now.

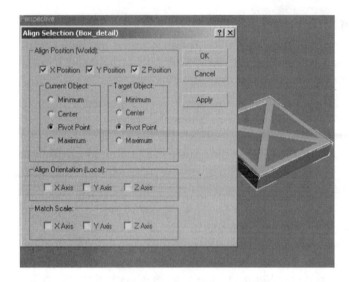

FIGURE 20.16 *For best results in using a Projection modifier, overlap the high-resolution and the low-resolution objects.*

3. On the Modify panel, Geometry Selection rollout, click the Pick List button and select Box_detail from the list. Use the Zoom Extents All Selected navigation tool to fill all viewports with the objects. Notice that the projected blue cage is slightly distorted at the corners (**Figure 20.17**).

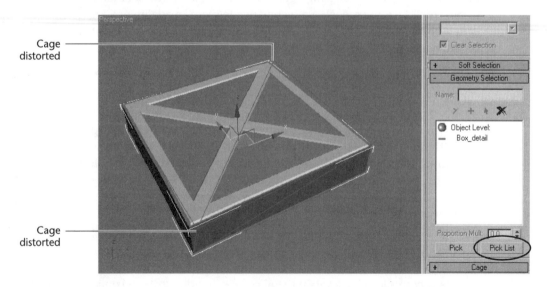

FIGURE 20.17 *The Projection cage becomes distorted as it is projected from the low-resolution object to the high-resolution object.*

4. The projection cage should be slightly larger than the high-resolution object. In Stack view, click the plus sign (+) to the left of Projection and highlight the Cage sub-object level. On the main toolbar, click the Select and Move button. Working in each viewport as necessary, move the vertices at the corners of the cage until the cage is just slightly larger than the green box all the way around (**Figure 20.18**). In Stack view, highlight Projection to exit sub-object mode.

5. Save the file; it should already be called *Ch20_normal02.max*.

   The Projection modifier is transferring mapping coordinates from the high-resolution box to the low-resolution box to ensure an accurately fitting Normal map.

tip

Zoom in on one corner in the Top viewport, select one vertex at the corner, and move it to superimpose it on top of the other at the same corner. Then use Window mode to select both vertices and move them to a new position slightly larger than the box. Repeat the procedure on the Front viewport until the cage is slightly larger than the box itself.

For more complex cages with more distortion, on the Modify panel, Cage rollout, click the Reset button to fit the cage to the object, and then use the Amount or Percent fields in the Push section to resize the cage.

FIGURE 20.18 *Adjust the cage, so that it is slightly larger than the high-resolution box.*

In the next exercise, you'll use the Render to Texture tool to generate a Normal map that is automatically applied to the Bump slot of the existing material as a bitmap on the low-resolution object. A feature of Render to Texture, called *Automatic Unwrap*, will also flatten the mapping coordinates of the high-resolution box, so that the Normal map fits correctly onto the low-resolution object.

Finally, you'll exchange the bitmap in the Bump slot for the new Normal Bump map type to take full advantage of the Normal map that you generated.

Exercise 20.5: Generating Normal Maps

1. Open **Ch20_normal02.max** from the previous exercise or from the CD-ROM. Save it to your project folder with the name *Ch20_normal03.max*. To open the Render to Texture dialog, on the main menu choose Rendering > Render to Texture.

2. In the Objects to Bake rollout, Projection Mapping section, deselect the Sub-Object Levels checkbox. Click the Options button. In the Projection Options dialog, Normal Map Space section, click the World radio button to project in the World reference coordinate system (**Figure 20.19**). Close the Projection Options dialog.

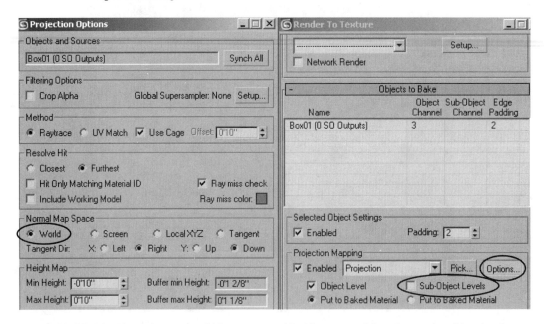

FIGURE 20.19 *The Normal map should be set to use World space and function at the object level.*

3. Notice in the Mapping Coordinates section that the Use Automatic Unwrap radio button is active. This will flatten the mapping coordinates so that all sides of the box are projected correctly. In the Output rollout, click the Add button and double-click the NormalsMap button to place it in the list above (**Figure 20.20**).

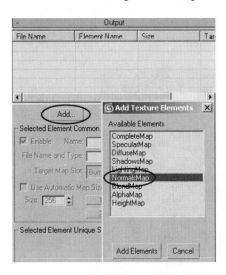

FIGURE 20.20 *You must indicate what type of map you want the Render to Texture tool to generate.*

4. In the Selected Element Common Settings section, make sure the Target Map Slot field is set to Bump, and click the 1024 button to create a map with that many pixels on each side. In the Baked Material rollout, Baked Material Settings section, click the Output into Source radio button. This will apply the map into the current material that is assigned to the low-resolution box (**Figure 20.21**).

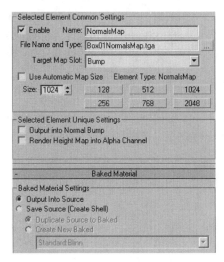

FIGURE 20.21 *A higher-resolution map will result in better apparent bump quality.*

5. At the bottom of the Render to Texture dialog, click the Render button. The rendered image represents the box unwrapped. You can clearly identify the top of the box in the upper-left corner of the Rendered Frame window and the well-lit side and chamfered edges at the lower right. The bottom of the box and the other sides have been rendered as pure black because they are not lit in the scene, which is not important for this exercise (**Figure 20.22**). Close the Rendered Frame window.

FIGURE 20.22 *The image rendered from the Render to Texture tool is automatically unwrapped and flattened.*

6. Close the Render to Texture dialog and open the Material Editor. In the Maps rollout, notice the Normals map has been applied to the Bump slot of this material and the sample window reveals a slight bump on the surface of the sample sphere. In the Material Editor, click the Material/Map Navigator button and highlight the Bump map in the list. In the Material Editor, click the Bitmap button and, in the Material/Map Browser dialog, double-click the Normal Bump map listing (**Figure 20.23**). In the Replace a Map dialog that appears, make sure that the Keep Old Map as Sub-map radio button is active, and click OK.

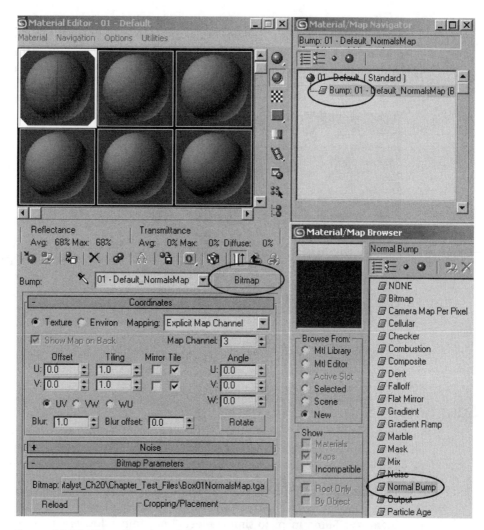

FIGURE 20.23 *You will replace the current Bitmap for the Normal Bump map while keeping the current Normal map as a sub-map.*

7. On the main toolbar, click the Select and Move button. In the Perspective viewport, move Box01 to the left of the detailed box and zoom in so that the objects fill the viewport. On the main toolbar, click the Quick Render button. In the Rendered Frame window, you'll see a convincing simulation of the high-resolution geometry on the low-resolution box (**Figure 20.24**).

Figure 20.24 *Even when viewed closely, the rendered objects appear similar and you save considerable resources using the mapped box.*

8. Close all windows and dialogs and save the file. It should already be called *Ch20_normal03.max*.

Summary

In this chapter, you practiced using several special effects techniques to generate steam and 3D clouds in your scene. As always, we've focused on hitting the right balance between enhancing your images and animations and conserving computer resources.

You also learned about a special effects technique that lets you transfer surface information from complex 3D geometry in the form of Normal maps, which can be applied in materials as Bump maps to simulate detail on simple, low-resolution objects for increased productivity.

Index

M

0735713677
Marc Saltzman
US$49.99

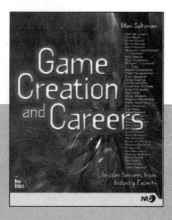

0735713634
Andrew Rollings, Dave Morris
US$49.99

1592730000
Jessica Mulligan,
Bridgette Patrovsky
US$49.99

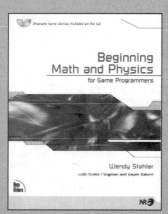

0735713901
Wendy Stahler with
Dustin Clingman and
Kaveh Kahrizi
US$45.00

0131020099
Daniel Sánchez-Crespo Dalmau
US$49.99

1592730019
Andrew Rollings,
Ernest Adams
US$49.99

Visit Peachpit on the Web at www.peachpit.com

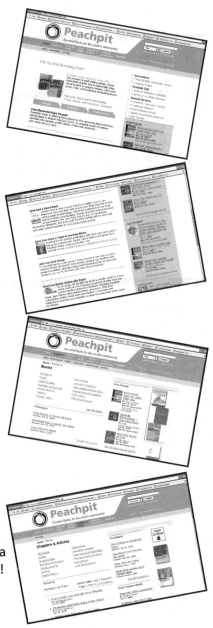

- Read the latest articles and download timesaving tipsheets from best-selling authors such as Scott Kelby, Robin Williams, Lynda Weinman, Ted Landau, and more!

- Join the Peachpit Club and save 25% off all your online purchases at peachpit.com every time you shop—plus enjoy free UPS ground shipping within the United States.

- Search through our entire collection of new and upcoming titles by author, ISBN, title, or topic. There's no easier way to find just the book you need.

- Sign up for newsletters offering special Peachpit savings and new book announcements so you're always the first to know about our newest books and killer deals.

- Did you know that Peachpit also publishes books by Apple, New Riders, Adobe Press, Macromedia Press, palmOne Press, and TechTV press? Swing by the Peachpit family section of the site and learn about all our partners and series.

- Got a great idea for a book? Check out our About section to find out how to submit a proposal. You could write our next best-seller!

You'll find all this and more at www.peachpit.com. Stop by and take a look today!